"He Doth Bestride the Narrow World Like a Colossus," a Herblock cartoon by Herbert Block, from the *Washington Post*, September 20, 1949. © *The Herb Block Foundation, Washington, DC.*

IN THE
SHADOW
OF FEAR

ALSO BY NICK BUNKER

Young Benjamin Franklin:
The Birth of Ingenuity

An Empire on the Edge:
How Britain Came to Fight America

Making Haste from Babylon:
The Mayflower Pilgrims and Their World

IN THE
SHADOW
OF FEAR

AMERICA AND
THE WORLD IN 1950

NICK BUNKER

BASIC BOOKS
New York

Basic Books
Hachette Book Group
1290 Avenue of the Americas, New York, NY 10104
www.basicbooks.com

Printed in the United States of America

First Edition: October 2023

Published by Basic Books, an imprint of Perseus Books, LLC, a subsidiary of
Hachette Book Group, Inc. The Basic Books name and logo is
a trademark of the Hachette Book Group.

The Hachette Speakers Bureau provides a wide range of authors for speaking events.
To find out more, go to hachettespeakersbureau.com or email
HachetteSpeakers@hbgusa.com.

Basic books may be purchased in bulk for business, educational, or promotional use.
For information, please contact your local bookseller or Hachette Book Group
Special Markets Department at special.markets@hbgusa.com.

The publisher is not responsible for websites (or their content)
that are not owned by the publisher.

Print book interior design by Jeff Williams.

Library of Congress Cataloging-in-Publication Data
Names: Bunker, Nick, author.
Title: In the shadow of fear: America and the world in 1950 / Nick Bunker.
Other titles: America and the world in 1950
Description: First edition. | New York: Basic Books, 2023. |
Includes bibliographical references and index.
Identifiers: LCCN 2023009228 | ISBN 9781541675544 (hardcover) |
ISBN 9781541675551 (ebook)
Subjects: LCSH: United States—Foreign relations—1945-1953. |
United States—Politics and government—1945-1953. |
Truman, Harry S., 1884-1972. | Anti-communist movements—
United States—History—20th century. | Communism—History—20th century. |
World politics—1945-1955.
Classification: LCC E813 .B86 2023 | DDC 327.73009/04—dc23/eng/20230519
LC record available at https://lccn.loc.gov/2023009228

ISBNs: 9781541675544 (hardcover), 9781541675551 (ebook)

LSC-C

Printing 1, 2023

In memory of
Herbert L. Margulis (1927–2021)
and
Morton L. Janklow (1930–2022)

At present, all except the most thoughtless
live under the shadow of fear.

—BERTRAND RUSSELL,
Values in the Atomic Age, 1949

CONTENTS

CONTENTS

*I*n history events have a rhythm of their own, but it cannot be measured like the beat of a pulse or the ticking of a metronome.

There are times like the summers of 1914 or 1939 when the approach of a climax is unmistakable; but these moments of obvious danger as a war draws near are the exception, not the rule. More often, the rhythm of events takes leaders by surprise. They fail to detect a turning point when the forces at work around them alter course. Even experts in the art of politics, used to the exercise of power, find themselves overwhelmed by a change in the tide of opinion, a switch in the tactics of an enemy, or a sudden convergence of factors long in the making but as yet only partly understood.

So it was with Harry Truman. In the fall of 1948, as he approached the end of his first term as president, Truman had judged the mood of his country correctly. A wary nation, a victor in war but still troubled by the memory of the Great Depression, the United States was not yet ready, he believed, to turn its back on Franklin D. Roosevelt and the New Deal and to vote the Democratic Party out of office.

Truman felt no complacency about his prospects of returning to the White House. He was too modest and too experienced for that. But his principles were firm, his program ambitious, and although he was sixty-four years old his enthusiasm remained. So did his energy. Truman believed that if he campaigned hard and let his opponent make mistakes, the election in November would be his.

Though skeptics from many sides expected his defeat, Truman achieved a famous victory, beating the Republican governor Thomas Dewey of New York; but his triumph was short-lived. The ballots had *not long been counted when, as Christmas 1948 approached, the economy sank into a recession.*

It was mild and brief, lasting only nine months. Even so, the 1949 recession derailed the president's plans for higher taxes to pay for roads, dams, irrigation, and federal spending on new schools and new teachers. Truman the lifelong Democrat urged Congress to pass what he called the Fair Deal—including health care for all, a new farm policy, and measures to strengthen the labor unions—only to see his program falter and succumb to its opponents. By the late summer of 1949, when this book begins, the recession had ended, but the forces at work in America and overseas were falling into a new pattern that the president had not anticipated.

In elections in New York that fall, the liberal wing of Truman's party retained its control of the city and won an extra seat in the Senate. The president rejoiced at what seemed to be a vote of confidence in his administration. For a while it seemed that perhaps in 1950 his Fair Deal might prevail in Washington; but once again his plans would be frustrated. In principle, Truman also remained committed to his program for Black civil rights. In practice, he quietly allowed it to drop down his list of laws to pass.

Amid new fears of Communism, the current of opinion turned against him. Sabotaged by feuds and divisions in his party, and caught off guard by the flailing punches of Senator Joseph McCarthy, Truman felt his authority slip away. By the time the Korean War broke out in June 1950 the Democrats were in retreat. The Republican Party scented blood as they wounded the president with relentless attacks on his foreign and domestic policies. Many Americans hoped that their country would pursue a middle way between the left and right. In the weeks before the war began, they saw only anger and division as the nation searched uneasily for a new direction.

And not only America. In Britain, France, and the defeated nations, painful recollections of the 1930s still cast their shadow, falling over the ruins left by World War II. In the western half of Germany, the occupying powers looked on with relief when the Germans picked as their chancellor a conservative centrist, Konrad Adenauer. Elsewhere the effort of rebuilding took its toll on statesmen who imposed austerity.

While Britain clung to much of its old empire under its new name as the Commonwealth, at home the British people, tired of rationing and high taxes, lost faith in their Labour government, which lurched toward electoral defeat. Meanwhile the French remained a nation as divided as they had been before the war. A calamity lay in wait for them in Indochina. The United States was gradually drawn toward the whirlpool.

All the while, the challenge of Asia grew more urgent. China had become a Communist state; India, having won its independence, refused to take sides in the Cold War; and when the Soviet Union signed a pact with Mao Zedong, the rhythm of events began to gather speed toward a destination yet unknown. All that was clear was this: Communist parties occupied the mansions of autocracy from Berlin and Prague to the frontier of Hong Kong. But what Communism meant by way of peace or war, how long it would endure, or what the future held for China were questions it would take another forty years to resolve.

For those who sought to read the signs of the times, including Americans puzzling over their country's new ascendancy, there were two points of reference that every debate had to encompass. The first was the centrality of Joseph Stalin. The Soviet dictator's inner thoughts could not be known, but they had to be guessed at nonetheless. The same was true of the strength and the weaponry of the state that he commanded, including the atom bomb that Stalin had just acquired.

The other point to grasp had to do with a defining feature of the United States. To a visitor from Europe, America's most striking quality was its industrial might. Those early years of the Cold War were a period simpler than our own, when economic strength could still be assessed by counting railroad miles or tons of coal and steel. It was also an age when America's industrial core, with its distinctive culture so different from those of other nations, was the principal theater of

American politics. In an arc that swept up from the Alleghenies to the Great Lakes, there lay the crucial zone that every president had to win and to hold.

We begin amid the multitudes on Labor Day, with Harry Truman on his way to Pittsburgh but soon to be overtaken by the unforeseen.

MONDAY,
SEPTEMBER 5, 1949

. . . the United States, this gigantic capitalist
organization, with its vast and superabundant
productive power—millions of people animated
by the profit motive.

—SIR WINSTON CHURCHILL[1]

I t was a Labor Day like any other in America. On Coney
Island where the subway ended at Surf Avenue, the crowds
surged onto the boardwalk eight hundred thousand strong.
With the epidemic of polio still at its height, the beach might
be a dangerous place that carried infection, but August had been
torrid, with many weeks without rain, and New York was one of
those postwar cities where the housing shortage was acute. And
so the people kept on coming in wave after human wave. They
came to escape the overcrowded walk-ups and the kitchen smells,
to stroll along the piers or around the Wonder Wheel, or to find
a bar with a radio to listen to the Brooklyn Dodgers playing at
Ebbets Field.

In the year after Pearl Harbor, FDR's vice-president had called the age in which he lived "the century of the common man." By now Henry Wallace had left the stage of politics, defeated in his bid for the White House in 1948; but as the century approached its halfway mark, Labor Day remained what it had always been. It was a holiday for the common man and woman, a last hurrah of summer before the autumn grind began.

You might think of Labor Day, 1949, as something resembling a vast and sprawling issue of *Life* magazine displaying every facet of the USA. In the day's events across the country you would see America's achievements, its foibles, its heroes and its villains, its conflicts and its traumas and the list of tasks it had yet to complete. You would also find the people. The federal census the following spring counted them at 150 million, forming a nation still in recovery from the cost and the effort of fighting World War II.

In Philadelphia on Labor Day you could see Joe DiMaggio making up time lost to military service by hitting the ball clear over the bleachers for his thirteenth home run of the season. Farther west over Cleveland, there were fighter planes racing in the sunshine, until a Mustang went down in a fiery crash. There were block parties, beauty pageants, rodeos, picnics, and parades, while Nebraska held what was said to be the largest hog show in its history. In Los Angeles, where the latest films opened first, you could watch James Cagney play a psychopath in his new movie, *White Heat*. The gossip columns said that Judy Garland had sung until the early hours at a birthday party for the young Leonard Bernstein. Meanwhile, Ginger Rogers was seeking her third divorce.

In the little town of Iron City, Georgia, the mayor made national news when he banned the Ku Klux Klan from wearing their hoods in public: that was the way things still were in parts of the South. And in Peekskill, to the north of New York City, the streets were strewn with bricks and broken glass. On Sunday afternoon, Paul Robeson, Black baritone and hero of the far left, had performed for an audience of fifteen thousand, more than half of whom were Communists, according to the *New York Times*. As the concert ended the violence had begun. Out to get Robeson if they could, a mob attacked the concertgoers, hurling rocks at their buses and overturning cars.

In every state, people lost their lives on roads left neglected while the nation was at war. Cars were old, drivers young, and the data showed that the number of drunks at the wheel had soared since 1945. During the long weekend the death toll in traffic accidents exceeded five hundred nationwide. In New Jersey a veteran descended into madness. Howard Unruh, who had fought at Bastogne, spent Labor Day brooding on his hatred of his neighbors. The following morning in the streets of Camden in the space of twenty minutes he shot thirteen people dead.

FOR HARRY TRUMAN Labor Day brought a welcome escape from the cares of office. For months the president had been at his desk, while beyond the executive suite the rest of the White House was emptied of its contents and about to be rebuilt. Here as well the August heat had been fiercer than usual, and Truman found himself surrounded by episodes of what he called "Potomac fever." It was the name he gave to the arrogance of Washington, its gossip, and the jostling for favors and for power. At the same time, the economy brought vexations of its own. Despite the end of the recession, there were still five million unemployed; and in the federal budget Truman had to cope with a deficit of $5 billion, or about 2 percent of the nation's economic output at the time.[2]

From overseas the previous week the wires had carried alarming news about the Russians. Soviet tanks were approaching Yugoslavia, or so it was reported. Like the other war scares of the era, this one had to be pondered and analyzed so that when Truman met the press, as he did every Thursday, he could strike the right note of calm confidence even when he felt nothing of the kind.

Truman never liked the phrase "Cold War." When he spoke to the reporters before the weekend, he preferred to describe his situation with the Kremlin as "a war of nerves." A president who studied history and maps, he believed that if there was to be a war with the Soviets it would begin in the Balkans, like the war that had taken Captain Truman with his field guns to the battlefields of France in 1918. The Balkans were a region mostly left to British intelligence to monitor, and they were as anxious as the president. Not until October would the British conclude that the Russian maneuvers were nothing but a show of strength, designed to undermine Marshal Tito but not to pave the way for an invasion.[3]

And so for Truman the morning of Labor Day came as all the more of a blessing. He could look forward to twenty-four hours away from the capital with the freedom to enjoy some of the things he loved the most: aviation, his family, speeches to Americans in the open air, and a visit to his hometown in Missouri. His schedule called for the president and the First Lady to fly first to Pittsburgh for the county fair, where Truman would appear in front of workers from the mills and from the mines. Then on he would go to Des Moines, Iowa, to address a gathering of veterans and farmers, before touching down at Kansas City in the dusk.

No one could miss the point that Truman wished to make. He saw farmers and labor as the heart of his coalition, and on Labor Day he would try to rally them around him once again. For those who knew their history as well as Truman did, his speeches would also evoke his heritage of ideas. While Truman respected the memory of Franklin Roosevelt, the modern president he most revered was a Democrat from an older generation.

In Pittsburgh and Des Moines Truman would revive the rhetoric of Woodrow Wilson. On another September day, in New Jersey in 1916, Wilson had begun his campaign for reelection with a speech that cast the Democrats as the party of social justice, standing up for labor and for farmers against the special interests of Wall Street and big business. Striving to keep things clear and simple, Truman still clung to a similar manifesto. His trip would accomplish something else as well, by reminding everyone of his midwestern roots.

Truman was proud of his origins and he believed that they had won him the affection of the people, giving him a common touch that Wilson the college professor had never quite displayed. At sundown when they arrived in their Missouri heartland, Mr. and Mrs. Truman would travel by car to Independence for one precious night together in the family home. It was a journey the president felt he had to make at a time when he was under fire from the press and his ratings from the public were declining.

In his first term Truman's popularity had swung wildly up and down, but the data from the polls had shown an underlying trend. His most persistent problem was inflation. It was always expected that prices would soar after the end of the fighting, as Americans hurried to spend the savings they had stored up during the wartime years of rationing and controls. But the transition from war to peace was hard to manage, and the president's officials quarreled with each other about how best to do the job. Policy fell into disarray. As demand began to surge for goods that were still in short supply, inflation took off, and voters chose to make Truman the culprit.[4]

When rents and prices leaped up in 1946, a year that also witnessed strikes in many industries, the president's ratings collapsed. The Republicans rejoiced and swept to victory in that year's elections, taking both houses of Congress. When prices leveled off,

Truman's popularity recovered. And then in the fall of 1948 he managed to transfer the blame for the high cost of living to the Grand Old Party. This feat of political engineering helped Truman recapture Congress and win his second term in office.

In the year that followed, the trends were harder to discern. Although prices fell in 1949, in the spring and summer support for the president began to dwindle too. Meanwhile, on Capitol Hill the Fair Deal lost what impetus it had once possessed. Overseas Truman could point to successes: the North Atlantic Treaty had been signed and ratified and the NATO alliance was gradually coming into being. With the Berlin airlift, he and the British had defeated Stalin's blockade of the city, and two years on from the launch of the Marshall Plan billions of dollars of economic aid were flowing into Europe. But the Communists had conquered almost all of China, and the end of the recession had failed to satisfy the press, some of which loathed the president with a passion. Truman saw Labor Day and the speeches he would give as an opportunity to renew his momentum.[5]

At a little after eleven o'clock the president's aircraft, sleek and very 1940s in its blue and silver livery, dipped through the clouds over Pittsburgh. Mrs. Truman was a nervous flier, worried about what it might do to her blood pressure, which was uncomfortably high; but the president adored his airplane. He was in fine form as they landed.

Impeccably trim in his light brown suit, and wearing a matching hat in light tan, he paused at the door of the aircraft to flash what the papers called "the famous Truman grin." There were photographs with mothers, children, and the mayor, an old Democrat ally, and then the motorcade headed for the fair. It was overcast and humid, but the rain held off. From the open top of his convertible Truman swept off his hat and waved to the crowd.

The local Republicans had sent along two elephants to steal some attention, but they had vanished from the scene by the time Truman's car swung into view along the racetrack. The president stood up and the people in the stands rose as well, "taking on the aspect," said the next day's *Pittsburgh Post-Gazette*, "of a tide washing up on the beach."

Truman looked relaxed and happy. He took his seat, the band played John Philip Sousa, and his fingers were seen tapping out the tune. The president was due to speak for only fifteen minutes. His message was to be as plain and direct as the city he was about to address.

President Truman meeting families at the airport in Pittsburgh before speaking at the Allegheny County Fair, Labor Day, 1949. *Associated Press / Shutterstock.*

The Arc of Prosperity

By 1949 Pittsburgh had become almost a cliché, the butt of stale jokes about its polluted air. Even so, it could still evoke prose poems from writers overwhelmed by the sense of power it conveyed. "A vast umbrella of soot," wrote one, "tells you that this is indeed steel's own citadel: civilization based on industrial aggrandizement reaches here its blackest and most brilliant flower."[6]

Pittsburgh was the home of U.S. Steel. Each year this company alone produced more steel than France and West Germany combined. America produced two-fifths of all the steel made in the world and more than twice as much as the annual output of Russia's latest Five-Year Plan. But for visitors from abroad, the sheer size of America's industrial base was not the only remarkable thing about it. Instead they came away fascinated, or perhaps alarmed, by its efficiency and by the business culture they encountered.

In 1947 the British had come close to disaster, stricken by a dreadful winter at a time when they were running out of dollars. In the hope of improving their economic performance, the following year the Labour government in London began to send teams of workers and managers across the Atlantic to study the techniques that made the United States so wealthy. In each industry they examined they found the same phenomenon: American output per worker was far higher than in Britain. At U.S. Steel, each employee produced twice as much metal in a working day as his counterpart on the other side of the Atlantic. As for American miners, each man dug out each year four times more coal than his distant cousins in Yorkshire or South Wales.[7]

As they searched for the secrets of American productivity, the British were struck by the atmosphere they found. Managers and workers alike were driven and competitive, refusing to tolerate the idle. Obsessed with output per man, the Americans laid off workers as soon as orders fell away. They also had incentives that the British could not match. With their higher wages and their lower taxes, American workers could buy cars, washing machines, and refrigerators, items either scarce or not to be found at all in the austerity Britain of the postwar years. The British noticed something else as well, a motivation they called "the compulsion of fear" in a nation without a safety net as ample as their welfare state at home.

Above all, the Americans automated their plants, filling them with machines driven by cheap electricity. To explain the origins of what they saw, the British would have to delve into the 1930s, because this was where the secret of Pittsburgh could be found. During the Great Depression, industrial America had no choice but to push on along the road of scientific management that Henry Ford and others had pioneered. The outcome was the mechanized, high-pressure economy that the British visitors observed.

With banks unable or unwilling to lend, the stock market broken, and profits collapsing, in the 1930s an American business that hoped to survive might try to make its workforce carry all the burdens of distress; but this was a strategy that could only go so far. Corporations also had to innovate. The decade before the crash of 1929 had already been fertile with invention, but during the slump the application of science became essential.

Conveyor belts and cranes to feed the assembly line, meters and gauges to control each process, roller bearings, welding machines, and high-speed cutting tools: all of these appeared on the American shopfloor. This era of hardship also proved to be an age of creativity, giving birth to a multitude of new products: nylon, rayon, and polyesters; automatic transmissions for automobiles; and a host of others, including stainless steel, television, and the new kitchen appliances whose sales would boom after the war. All of this required research. In 1920 America had fewer than 300 industrial laboratories. In 1931 there were 1,600, and by 1938, the year nylon was patented, there were more than 2,200.[8]

In 1935, when the second phase of Roosevelt's New Deal began, the pressure to innovate grew still more intense. At last there was a federal law, the Wagner Act for labor relations, that gave workers a secure and regulated route to join a union. There followed the tumult of 1936 and 1937, and the nationwide campaigns to unionize those industries that had fought to keep labor at bay. Some companies held out, but one giant after another—U.S. Steel, General Motors, and General Electric, to name only the largest—were compelled to recognize the unions. Hence the need for yet more innovation if corporations were to satisfy shareholders and employees at one and the same time. Out of all this, and then the vast expansion of output during World War II, there emerged the industrial system that would define the postwar years.

High wages and high productivity, and strong unions bargaining hard with corporate executives who had learned their trade in the conflicts of the 1930s: this was the American way. Nothing quite like it could be found anywhere else in the world. The aim of the Marshall Plan was to try to replicate it in Britain and in Western Europe: partly to hold the Soviets in check, partly to give the United States partners with whom to trade, but also because the creators of the plan truly believed that the American industrial system was the ideal modern way of life. The British would never quite master the system, and even in America it could not be seen everywhere. In Pittsburgh and its hinterland, it flourished in its most advanced form.[9]

The mightiest people in Pittsburgh at the time were two veterans of the battles of the age of FDR. If we had to name the twenty most powerful people in America in 1949, both of these forgotten men would have to appear on the list. One was Benjamin Franklin Fairless, aged fifty-nine, the president of U.S. Steel. The other was a sixty-three-year-old labor union leader named Philip Murray. Twelve years earlier, as president of the United Steelworkers, or USW, Murray had led the campaign for recognition to which

Fairless had to surrender. Phil Murray was also now the president of the Congress of Industrial Organizations, the CIO, a federation of unions whose six million members encompassed not only the steel and the auto industries but much of the rest of American manufacturing. Without Murray's approval, Truman could not have been Roosevelt's running mate in 1944.

In their different ways, both Murray and Fairless captured the essence of the system, including the social mobility it could promote. "I am an optimist," Fairless liked to tell reporters. A coal miner's son from Ohio, Fairless had earned his way through high school as a janitor and then, teaching school himself, he paid his way through college. He found a job building a steel mill, and with diligence and flair he rose to the top of his profession. Murray was a miner's son as well, born in Scotland, where he had first entered a mine at the age of ten. He and his father had left to dig coal for better wages in the United States, where Murray became a union man, the trusted aide of the most fearsome labor leader of the era, John L. Lewis of the United Mine Workers of America.[10]

In the fall of 1949, Phil Murray shared some of the faith in the future that Fairless always displayed. The contracts between the steelmakers and the union had expired in July, leaving the two men to wrangle over pay and benefits. A strike looked certain to occur; but disputes, strikes, and then new contracts were the way the system functioned, and Murray's case on behalf of his union also hinged on productivity and innovation.

Murray believed in what he had called in 1940 "constructive industrial statesmanship." "In this country," Murray had written, "we need to hold both employer and employee responsible . . . for the uninterrupted flow of production." It was this, and the application of machines and research, that would give his workers the standard of living Murray wanted them to have.[11]

As the halfway mark of the century drew near, the flow of production seemed unstoppable. Fairless's company sold more than a fifth of its steel to automakers, whose sales of cars had gone on rising throughout the 1949 recession. Come January, to mark the birth of a new decade, General Motors would launch its first automatic Chevrolet, destined to become an emblem of the 1950s. Meanwhile, south of Pittsburgh, Fairless was about to celebrate the opening of a new landmark, the Robena mine. It was to be the largest, most efficient coal mine in the world, complete with electric trains underground and automated washers to clean away the sulfur from the coal. Nothing like this existed in Europe. The Robena mine, like the new Chevrolet, symbolized the unique culture of America's industrial core.[12]

In those days Pittsburgh stood at the southwestern end of a great arc of prosperity that stretched from Milwaukee and Chicago through Indiana, Detroit, and Ohio as far as Buffalo to the east. Among the congressional districts in the region, nearly thirty were centered on a town or city that made steel. Scattered around them were many more districts where the voters earned high wages in the kind of factories the visitors from Britain had admired.

In 1949, nobody predicted that one day people would sneer at this part of the country and call it the "Rust Belt." The 1950 census would show that Washington, DC, with its lawyers and its lobbyists, had the highest median household income of any city in the nation. The second most affluent city was South Bend, Indiana, where Studebaker built automobiles, surrounded by other plants that made thermostats and gauges and brakes for cars and aircraft. Of the twelve cities with the highest average incomes, three were names we might see in a similar list today: not only Washington but also San Francisco and Stamford, Connecticut. The other nine all lay in the industrial arc of high wages and high pressure: South Bend and Chicago; Detroit, Cleveland, Toledo, and Milwaukee; Racine, Wisconsin; and Flint and Lansing, Michigan.[13]

If this was America's arc of prosperity, it also functioned as the cockpit of the nation's politics, the region the Republican Party had to win to end its long exile in the wilderness. Nearly twenty years had passed since one of their chosen men had last inhabited the White House. A party in a bitter, fractious mood, angry with themselves and with the president, by now the Republicans were desperate to recover control of Congress in 1950, and then to win back the presidency in 1952. To do so, they would have to defeat a political geography that seemed to be rigged against them. On Capitol Hill they held all but a few seats from California, an essential asset with its swiftly growing population, and they still occupied their old bastions in the Midwest and much of New England. But they had no hope of taking New York City, and Texas and the South remained solidly Democratic. If the Grand Old Party were to emerge from its era of humiliation, it had to capture the industrial heartland.

With so much at stake, Truman came to Pittsburgh on Labor Day to fortify his strongholds in the region. His fairground speech would be concise and combative, like Truman himself; but to many who read it next day in the papers, it would raise more questions than it answered.

Scare Words and Selfishness

Twenty minutes before noon, the sun broke through the clouds and the president rose to speak. He began, as he so often did, with a glimpse into a rural idyll from the past. When he was five, Harry Truman recalled, "my old grandfather took me in a cart with a strawberry roan horse, and drove me six miles to the county fair." And then he left nostalgia behind as he took on the enemies who were wrecking his Fair Deal.

His program was under attack, the president said in Pittsburgh, from what he called "an organized conspiracy of selfish interests" determined to roll back FDR's achievements. "There are a lot of paid agitators, promoters and so-called publicity experts,"

Truman told his audience, "who make a fat living by frightening the people." Their device of choice was what he called "the scare-word campaign."[14]

When Roosevelt's enemies wanted to destroy his program of reform, they had called it "socialism." After their defeat in 1948 they had retreated to a back room, where, said the president, "they decided that the old scare words had become a little mildewed." So they devised new labels with which to jeer at the Democratic Party and its platform. "Statism," "collectivism," and, worst of all, "the welfare state": these were the slogans the reactionaries coined to terrify the people. It wouldn't work, the president went on, because Americans knew that what the Fair Deal really meant was jobs and housing, health care, and a safe old age.

Truman meant it to be a rousing speech. There had been applause and cheers, he had ad-libbed a little, and his fifteen minutes had stretched out to twenty-two. Even so the president's plane took off on time and in Pittsburgh he had done what he intended. Tailored to fit across a column of newsprint, the phrase "scare words" would occupy the next day's headlines. Later in the trip one of the engines on his aircraft failed, causing a flutter of alarm, but in those days the press traveled on their own airplane and the incident remained a secret. There would be nothing to detract from Truman's message.

And yet perhaps his speech had not been what the occasion required. The president had avoided detail, choosing instead to paint his portrait of America in broad strokes and primary colors: progress versus conservatism, and the common good against the selfishness of his opponents. This was his usual style and it had a record of success: but could it rescue him from his predicament?

When a president arrives in office, he has only so much time on the mountaintop of high ideals before he must come down into the swamps of practicality. Ten months on from the election, scarcely a single item of Truman's Fair Deal had passed into law.

His boldest plan of all was universal health insurance. Although his allies on Capitol Hill had drafted a bill to bring it into being, it lay dormant in committee. In August the Senate had made it plain that the bill would never be enacted. Truman looked on as his liberal program floundered in the mud of Congress where every detail can be made an obstacle.[15]

All the changes the president wished to see would be difficult to pass, if they could pass at all. And while Congress dug in its heels, Truman was also struggling to convince some of the voters he saw as his best friends. In Iowa he hoped to make the case for his new farm policy, the Brannan Plan, named after his secretary of agriculture, Charles Brannan. The plan would have set production quotas, controlled the acreage that farmers could plant, and sent them checks to maintain their incomes. But the Corn Belt was thriving and few saw the need for change. In a region where the press mostly spoke for the GOP, the newspapers portrayed the Brannan Plan as something resembling a socialist plot.

While farmers began to turn their backs on Truman, so did the leaders of the labor unions. Failing to appear at the fairground, Phil Murray of the CIO kept his distance from a president who hoped to avert the steel strike that was drawing near. That afternoon Murray had taken to the radio to broadcast his own Labor Day message; and while in places it echoed what Truman had said, it carried a sharper edge of discontent and urgency.

Two years earlier, the Republicans had pushed a law through Congress that had horrified Murray and his colleagues. Passed with the help of many Democrats as well, the Taft-Hartley Act sought to undermine FDR's legacy by removing some of the rights that unions had won to recruit and to organize. Truman had tried to stop the new law with a veto but was overridden, and in 1949 he failed to muster the votes to repeal it. Murray lost faith in a president unable to deliver his own party, even when—as the Democrats did that year—they controlled both chambers of the Capitol.

Murray knew the reason for Truman's impotence. It lay, as it had lain since the late 1930s, in the blocking power in Congress of a conservative majority that cut across party lines. On the radio Murray called it "the coalition of northern Republicans and southern Dixiecrats," a phrase that would do as a rough description of the forces at work in Washington. In reality, the Democrats who voted as conservatives also included many from outside the South, but for the labor unions this was all the more frustrating. Like America's economic lead over other countries, the conservative coalition on Capitol Hill had come to seem as permanent a feature of the landscape as the smoke that drifted over Pittsburgh.[16]

Liberals yearned to break its grip on the nation and to rekindle the excitement of the New Deal years. Frustrated by the fate of the president's Fair Deal, they grumbled about Truman and his lack of progress. On the right, their Republican enemies grew still angrier, because, although they could block the president's program, they could not advance an agenda of their own.

This was not a moment of complacency when people wished only to hear the language of the past. On both sides of the political divide, observers called in 1949 for fresh ideas and new alignments. If there were flaws in Truman's way of doing things, one of them lay just here: he seemed to have too little to say that was original. Woodrow Wilson was a long time dead, and ideas that seemed radical in his day now carried a smell of the obsolete.

When Truman spoke about farmers and labor, he always had in mind the sufferings they had endured in the Great Depression. His duty, as he saw it, was to ensure that nothing of the kind could occur again. But he also conceived of his country as though America consisted of vast but sharply defined blocs of citizens, with labor and farmers as the largest, each of whose interests he hoped to satisfy. Seen in this light, Truman's task was to arbitrate between the different groups and devise a settlement that would do the best for them all. Truman wanted to be fair to everyone.

This was why he called his program the Fair Deal. It was a noble ambition; but by now America had evolved into a nation more fluid than the president imagined it to be.

Old allegiances were breaking down, and the solid blocs of voters that Truman counted on were changing shape and rearranging themselves in new combinations. Since the late 1930s there had been great shifts in the population, especially into the West. If Truman wished to renew his coalition, he should have traveled far beyond Pittsburgh and Iowa, to cities such as Phoenix, Oakland, or Los Angeles. He might also have toured the suburbs of the industrial core.

This was where the political battles of 1950 and the future would be fought: in the suburbs of Cleveland and Chicago and other cities like them, among a younger generation of voters with cars, mortgages, and televisions, whose view of the world had not been fixed by the Depression. Victory would go to those politicians who, whether they pored over the census or relied on intuition, could adjust to a new, less predictable electorate for whom the age of Woodrow Wilson and Franklin Roosevelt was fading out of sight.

COURTHOUSE MEDIOCRITY

Labor Day also placed on public display another weakness in Truman's modus operandi. In Pittsburgh it took the bulky form of his military aide, Major General Harry Vaughan.

The president's old army comrade loved his uniform, pressed to perfection with seven rows of medal ribbons fastened to his barrel of a chest. General Vaughan came off the aircraft right behind Truman, as though to tell everyone that he was still the boss's favorite. There were cheers but also catcalls, and somebody shouted, "Where's my deep freeze, Harry?" Vaughan, who liked his bourbon, had been known to lunge with his fist at a cameraman, but in Pittsburgh he smiled and waved amid the heckling. The jibes had to do with a scandal that was more than just Potomac Fever.

For years the press had been pursuing General Vaughan with stories about what they called "the Missouri Gang," Truman's collection of old friends whom he brought with him to the White House from Kansas City and St. Louis. These stories played their variations on a common theme: that out of too much loyalty to his cronies Truman promoted people who were second-rate. Most of this could be brushed aside; but in June 1949 a reporter had unearthed a tale of corruption in high places, with Vaughan implicated in the affair.

It concerned the so-called "five percenters," middlemen who offered to procure contracts from the government and the armed forces in return for a 5 percent commission. At the story's center was a wartime lieutenant colonel named Jim Hunt. Postwar Hunt had become a lobbyist, he threw parties on a yacht, and he did dirty work for bureaucrats in uniform as they squabbled for advancement at the Pentagon. The story ran and ran, and in July the army suspended its quartermaster general.[17]

Harry Vaughan could not deny that he knew Jim Hunt. It emerged that in 1945 one of Hunt's clients had made a gift of deep freezers to the president and his entourage. One found its way to the Truman home in Independence, one was shipped to Vaughan, and another went to John Snyder, the treasury secretary, another member of the Missouri Gang. Reporters cornered Vaughan and asked him what he thought about Jim Hunt. "Hell," replied the general, "there are 300 guys doing the same thing in Washington."[18]

Shortly before Labor Day the story reached its climax in Senate hearings. Nothing criminal came to light, and in the end Vaughan received only a rebuke, but the scandal injured Truman and served as a prelude to worse that lay ahead. Leading the hostile questions at the hearings were two Republicans who strove to widen the inquiry beyond some isolated graft inside the Beltway. One, whose name is little known today, was Senator Karl Mundt of South Dakota. In 1948, as chairman of the House Un-American Activities Committee, Mundt had begun the hue and cry against the lawyer and diplomat Alger Hiss, accused of being a Communist agent. The other was one of the youngest members of the Senate, Joseph R. McCarthy of Wisconsin.

As the five-percenter hearings unfolded in the August heat that made them all the more bad-tempered, Mundt and McCarthy tried to corner Harry Vaughan. The general made a poor impression as he lounged in his uniform, puffing on a long cigar while his fellow witnesses chain-smoked cigarettes. Outside the committee room, Senator McCarthy drew upon his contacts in the press, who gave him information they dared not print but could be aired in Congress.

Nagging away at Vaughan, McCarthy tried to forge connections between the general and the Mob. Into the picture came campaign finance, the owner of a racetrack in California, and the era's most notorious gangster, Frank Costello of New York. Although McCarthy was on to something—Costello and his crew had their claws in the flesh of Truman's party in the city— for the time being his questions struck a dead end. And while the senator went in search of more conspiracies to unmask, the press made the most of the five-percenter scandal.[19]

Of all the newspapers that hated the president, none did so with more venom than the *Chicago Tribune*. On Labor Day the *Tribune* led with a vicious piece that repeated old attacks on the Missouri Gang. "Probe Lifts Curtain on Boss Truman," ran the headline. For the most part, the story was merely ancient material about his party's infamous machine in Kansas City, but this kind of thing left its mark. At the same time, Truman came under fire from more sophisticated journalists whose sneering words were more subtle but perhaps more damaging.

This was the golden age of syndicated columnists, filing their copy in New York or Washington to be reprinted in every corner of the country. Among them Truman had a few allies, but they were outnumbered by his critics. As his Fair Deal failed to emerge from Congress, some of the most influential among them looked for new ways to cast him as an inferior duplicate of FDR. Another old accusation, this attack took hold, spreading around the president a miasma of disdain.

Among the syndicated writers of the era, two of the most brilliant were stars of the *New York Herald Tribune*, the Alsop brothers, Joseph and Stewart. Harvard and Yale men, and cousins of Eleanor Roosevelt, the Alsops looked down on Truman with an attitude of lofty condescension. In the case of Vaughan and the five percenters, they saw the hallmark of a flawed administration, tainted by what the Alsops called "its odor of courthouse politics and creeping mediocrity."[20]

Here was a noun—"mediocrity"—that could wound a president. His office has an aura; but once the aura has been pierced by attacks such as these, there are consequences soon to follow. The first might be this: in Congress the president's own party will begin to block his nominations for high office. This would happen to Truman in the fall of 1949. Another consequence might be strife in his cabinet, as discipline erodes and rivals conspire against each other. This would also be Truman's affliction before the year was out.

Truman was neither the first president nor the last who would lead a surly and divided party. All the while he retained one great advantage over his foreign counterparts: the peerless strength of America's economy. It was this—the productivity that Pittsburgh embodied—that gave the US dollar its intimidating power. And yet there lay ahead of Truman and his colleagues a sequence of events that would confound all their expectations. Mistakes would be made, and decisions would take themselves because no other option lay at hand. For better or for worse, the rhythm of events would close off alternatives and set new patterns for the future.

In the 2020s, when so many of us see a new Cold War in genesis, we might wish to recollect some features of the old one. In America decisions about foreign policy never take place in some hygienic laboratory cleansed from the mess and the complications of domestic politics. From time to time a great crisis occurs that seems to unite the two parties, but rarely can they set aside their differences for long. In Truman's era, the federal budget was a battleground where they could not be reconciled. In 1949 and 1950, the arguments about it did as much as wisdom or farsightedness to shape the way the United States pursued its goals abroad.

If this had been an ordinary period, the wrangling about the budget and so many other issues might have been merely routine. But the ten months that elapsed between Labor Day and the end of June 1950 were as critical as any in peacetime since the Civil War. After Hiroshima and victory in Europe, no one—not even those who had been isolationists before Pearl Harbor—could pretend that the United States might simply proceed along its way untroubled by what happened elsewhere. Choices had to be made about so many things: the hydrogen bomb, NATO, Korea and China and Taiwan, and Vietnam as well. These choices would turn out to be irrevocable, shaping the future for the next four decades.

At home another list of questions loomed before the nation, but the answers that were found proved to be inconclusive, leaving the next generation in search of fresh solutions. These ten months would finish with a crisis overseas, the outbreak of war in Korea, which set the conflict with the Soviets in stone, but they were also a time of deepening divisions inside America's domestic arena.

They witnessed not only the rise of Joe McCarthy, ushering in half a decade of embitterment, but also the end—or so it might be argued—of the era of Roosevelt's New Deal. As yet no new consensus had emerged to take its place.

This was a time of shock and surprise, when even the best informed found themselves in unfamiliar terrain where they had to draw new maps as they went along. On the Friday before Truman went to Pittsburgh, an aircraft took off from a runway in Japan. A B-29 bomber, modified for weather patrol and carrying Geiger counters, it flew toward Alaska and detected radiation in particles of dust drifting eastward in the sky. It would take a few weeks and many more missions for the science to be complete, but the conclusion could not be avoided. Three years earlier than America's experts had thought likely, the Russians had tested their first atom bomb.[21]

Among the first to hear the news was a member of Truman's cabinet whom no one could call mediocre. To manage America's expanding role overseas, the president relied on Dean Acheson, a secretary of state to whom he was bound by mutual loyalty and respect. Acheson also shared Truman's brand of liberalism; but in the months ahead it would be tested to its limits.

RUSSIA IN THE FALL

*F*or more than a year Stalin's Little Terror had been underway. In
February 1948 foreigners in Moscow had begun to feel the prewar mood of fear return. Their Russian contacts disappeared, and they
heard more frequent stories of arrests. The pressure fell most heavily on
the city's Jewish intellectuals and artists, who were told by the authorities that they were cosmopolitan and rootless. In 1949 the Soviet purge
extended to members of Stalin's upper echelon.[1]

   He demoted from the post of foreign minister his old protégé,
Vyacheslav Molotov, whose wife—an ethnic Jew—had been expelled
from the Communist Party. Molotov survived because his talents were
still useful, but not the party chiefs in Leningrad. One by one they
were eliminated, accused of some obscure regional conspiracy or of being
agents for the British. Purged as well was their contact in the Politburo, Nikolai Voznesenskii, the official who had drawn up the current
Five-Year Plan.

   By the autumn of 1949 the Soviet famine of the postwar years had
eased. Prices had been cut, and rationing had ended, but the benefits
flowed only to the city dwellers. While Muscovites could now eat meat
and buy bicycles and gramophones, hardships continued in the countryside. The peasants bore high taxes and were stripped of food despite the

shortages that still existed. The farms of Russia and Ukraine produced far less grain per head of population than the nation had grown on the eve of World War I. In response, in 1949 Stalin raised his planning targets still higher—for grain and steel and coal and making trucks and tractors and the rest.

Voznesenskii's crime, if crime it was, had been to blur some economic figures and mislead the Kremlin. On September 11, the Politburo voted to put him on trial, and he begged Stalin for mercy. He was arrested nonetheless, later to be shot like the victims of the purge of Leningrad.

No word of their disgrace reached the West. Unlike the show trials held during Stalin's Great Terror of the 1930s, the pursuit of Voznesenskii and his comrades took place in secrecy. Nor could observers from abroad trace the ebb and flow in Russia of the everyday apparatus of repression. What they mostly saw that year was another side of Stalinism, purges in the satellite republics behind the Iron Curtain. The Berlin blockade and airlift and Stalin's rift with Tito's Yugoslavia were followed by these episodes of persecution. In Albania, Bulgaria, and Hungary, party leaders were shot or sent to labor camps for being Trotskyites, or for being guilty, like the Yugoslavs, of "nationalist deviation" from the Moscow line. Catholic priests were arrested too.

In Budapest in September, the trial began of Lazlo Rajk, Hungary's former minister for foreign affairs, in full view of the Western press. Perhaps in the belief that his life would be spared, Rajk made a confession. He said he had plotted with Tito, America, and Sir Winston Churchill to mount a coup in Hungary and create a Balkan federation free from Soviet ties. Rajk was executed in October.

If a key existed to events in the Soviet bloc, perhaps it could be found in the textbook Stalin had issued in 1938. A history of the Soviet Communist Party, otherwise known as the Short Course, *the book remained in circulation in 1949 as his official wisdom. It spoke of the early Five-Year Plans and of Comrade Stakhanov, the hero of socialist labor hewing immense quantities of coal in the Donbas. The book gloried in the oppression of peasant farmers and the collectivization of the land. Stalin still believed in all of this. Written at the time of the Spanish Civil War, when the fascists claimed to have their fifth column behind enemy lines, the* Short Course *had also dealt in fear: Stalin's fear of assassins in his midst, spies and wreckers seeking to destroy the work the Bolsheviks had done.*

The elderly dictator seemed with his Little Terror of the late 1940s to be revisiting the obsessions of the previous decade. The Short Course *had described the Soviet Union's encirclement in the 1930s by imperialist powers bent on war. In the fall of 1949, the rhetoric from Moscow repeated the same line, with NATO and the Marshall Plan cited as the evidence of Western aggression.*

With Molotov sidelined, the role of Stalin's quasi-deputy now belonged to Georgy Malenkov. He led the campaign against Soviet Jews. On the anniversary of the October Revolution, Malenkov would speak in praise of that year's harvest and new triumphs of socialist workers, but also of encirclement again, this time by Truman and the British out to start a World War III. Malenkov rejoiced in America's recession. He saw it as the proof of capitalist decay.

Few observers followed the United States as closely as did the writers of Malenkov's speech or the journalists at Pravda *and* Izvestia. *The Soviet press wrote about Harry Vaughan and the five percenters, about Paul Robeson, the Peekskill riots, and the Klan, all part of what it called the oppression of progressives and Black Americans. Truman's announcement about the Russian atom bomb they dismissed as war talk meant to cause hysteria. Molotov, they said, had revealed in 1947 that the Soviets had the science. What the Americans detected was merely dust from Russian engineers blasting a hole to build a dam.*

In Stalin's hierarchy, the other man in favor in 1949 was Lavrentii Beria, the overseer of the Gulag. He also supervised the atomic program. Like his colleagues, Beria had risen and fallen over the years in Stalin's estimation. They were all kept in awe of the dictator, who shuffled them to and fro as a means to retain his full control. The bomb test in August, which showed what Soviet industry could achieve, restored to Beria some of his old prestige; but even he could feel the strains within the system. He was building with slave labor a canal between the Volga and the Don. His staff could tell how wasteful the Gulag was with human lives and how costly its achievements were. This was not a message Beria dared give to Stalin.

That fall another omen might also be perceived. If Westerners read Pravda, *they would find a heavy emphasis on Asia. In 1947 Moscow's experts on the region had begun to write about a struggle against imperialism that they saw occurring in Burma, Malaya, and Vietnam. By the fall of 1949 this had become a constant topic, reinforced by the victory of Mao Zedong in China. Frustrated in Berlin, was Stalin turning eastward in search of new successes? And if he was, when would the moment come when Stalin and America crossed swords?*

CHAPTER ONE

THE RELIEF PITCHER

Dean Acheson can get out of trouble with more style than any citizen of the republic, with the possible exception of Joe Page of the Yankees.

—JAMES RESTON *of the*
New York Times, *January 1950*[1]

I f all that mattered in government were hard work, integrity, and intellect, America could have asked for no finer public servant than Dean Acheson. At fifty-six, the secretary of state made a figure so imposing—six feet one, with a determined stride, and suits as finely cut as Cary Grant's—that often his physical presence eclipsed the inner qualities that made him what he was. Sometimes the press seemed more fascinated by Acheson's moustache than they were by his foreign policy.

As a student at Harvard he had roomed with Cole Porter. In retirement he wrote books in exquisite prose. He enjoyed parties, he was graceful, witty, but also sarcastic, and he did not suffer fools. And yet none of these details, colorful though they were, conveyed the essence of the talents Acheson brought to high office.

First and foremost Dean Acheson was a lawyer, and a lawyer of a very particular kind. Americans see nothing odd in the notion of entrusting a lawyer with their foreign policy, given how many lawyers have followed Thomas Jefferson in leading the State Department. But it is not the norm in other countries, and certainly not in Britain, where the foreign secretary must be a career politician and sit in Parliament. Nor do Americans always appreciate how their lawyers differ from those of other nations.

Dean Acheson was a case in point, a man who came armed with a legal training and philosophy with distinctive roots in time and circumstance. He took up the post of secretary of state early in 1949. In his first nine months in office his special blend of skill and experience served him and America exceedingly well. But the autumn would mark Acheson's high tide. After that he would find himself in perilous waters for which his career had not prepared him.

Hostile voices jeered at Acheson as an Anglophile, because his father was an English clergyman and his mother was Canadian. The secretary of state did sometimes show some nostalgia for the British Empire as it had been in the nineteenth century, with its navy, its financial might, and its commitment to free trade. Acheson also loved the countryside, not only the rural New England of his boyhood but also the Maryland farm where he spent each weekend. Even so, he was indelibly a product of industrial America. Its values and its confidence set the mental horizon within which Acheson thought about the world.

While his father was a bishop in Connecticut, his mother's family were liquor magnates so renowned that the press simply called them "the millionaire distillers of Toronto." In 1917 Acheson married the daughter of a wealthy attorney from Detroit whose principal client was Michigan's largest railroad. As for his closest friend in the Truman administration, apart from the president it was W. Averell Harriman, banker, investor, and diplomat, whom the Communists in France depicted as the hatchet man of Wall Street.[2]

The two men had known each other since they met as boys at Groton, a school for the elite, that Acheson loathed for its rigidity. There and at Yale he studied as little as he could. It was left to the law professors at Harvard, which he entered in 1915, to awaken the mind of Mr. Acheson. They did so at a time when some of the faculty at the Harvard Law School saw themselves as the conscience of America, intent on correcting the evils of free enterprise run wild. It was the heyday at Harvard of ideas that later came to be known as "legal realism." The gist of this could be found in the law review articles written by Acheson's mentor Felix Frankfurter. They give us clues to much of what Acheson tried to do at the State Department.

The task of the judge and the attorney, said Professor Frankfurter, was to settle controversies, replacing brute force by the rule of law. But in modern America the greatest of disputes had do with the rapacity of corporations, the squalor of the cities, and the rights of labor, women, and oppressed minorities. These disputes could not be resolved with old maxims culled from the cases on the library shelves. Instead, wrote Frankfurter, the lawyer had to study what he called "the forces of modern society"—that, and economics too—and "translate large words in terms of the realities of existence."[3]

Of this genre of the law the arch-exponent was Frankfurter's own teacher, Justice Louis D. Brandeis of the US Supreme Court. After Harvard, Acheson went to clerk for Brandeis and learned his famous method of immersion in social and economic data. This required long hours devoted to the facts of the cases Brandeis handled—mostly to do with strikes and labor law—and to the conditions of society from which each one arose. Acheson helped the justice sift through reams of detail to reach the underlying principles at stake so that Brandeis could produce a judgment of crystalline lucidity. "In drafting our opinion," Acheson would write in his memoirs, "the task was a novelist's—to make reality shine through the legal haze."[4]

The Brandeis method worked its alchemy on the young lawyer. He also absorbed the Brandeis philosophy of social justice and liberal reform. Brandeis had been Woodrow Wilson's ally and adviser—it was Wilson who had named him to the Supreme Court—and so in the early 1920s Acheson became a liberal himself, but a liberal of a Wilsonian kind. For him the liberal creed had to do with equity and fairness, and not with great programs of public spending or daring experiments with untested theories.

In America, Acheson believed, the task of the state was to intervene and regulate to defend the defenseless: to act, like a judge in the Old Testament, on behalf of what Acheson called "laboring people, poor and propertyless people—men, women, and children, pathetically weak in bargaining for their only asset, their labor." Principles such as these brought him into close alignment with his fellow Wilsonian, Harry Truman. As a junior senator, the future president had been another frequent guest at the Brandeis home.[5]

When it was time to make some money, Acheson joined a Washington firm, where again he was immersed in industry and finance. Besides labor law, which was Acheson's first love, Covington and Burling dealt in antitrust law, the regulation of utilities, and disputes arising from foreign debts left over from World War I. Here he could apply the Brandeis method in long negotiations while acquiring what he called "practical statesmanship." As Acheson put it, it fell to the lawyer in cases such as these "to understand at once the uniqueness of unprecedented situations and immediately to set about devising new and practical ways of dealing with them."[6]

All of this Acheson brought to his conduct of foreign policy. He never saw himself as a deep or original thinker about geopolitics, although sometimes he was. Chiefly he was a problem-solver and a pragmatist, but a pragmatist pledged to the liberal mission he had learned from Brandeis and Frankfurter. Acheson was also something else: he was a man shaped by the events of 1939.

Like a rainstorm that clears dust from the air, bringing the view sharply into focus, the outbreak of war in Europe permanently changed his vision of the future. Haunted by the nightmare of a broken world trampled by the armies of dictators, Acheson threw himself into the campaign for America to rearm. The views he formed at that moment would remain unchanged for the rest of his career.

"We must make ourselves so strong," Acheson said in a speech at Yale in November 1939, "that we shall not be caught defenseless or dangerously exposed in any even possible eventuality." America must have a navy and an air force adequate to strike across two oceans: not only to secure the homeland and the seas, but also to prevent what he called "the disintegration of the world order." And while the nation rebuilt its military strength, America must do other things as well.[7]

America must support the British and the French by supplying them with the arms they needed; contain Japan, not only with sanctions but also with a line of strong defenses, from the Philippines to Guam; and then, besides the military options, Acheson hoped to see creative action to eradicate the underlying causes of the global crisis. The roots of fascism lay, he believed, in the Great Depression and the misguided response from governments and central banks. All too many had opted to close their markets with tariffs and cartels, or had chosen to impoverish their neighbors with manipulations of their currency. Acheson called for a new farsightedness: free trade, the free flow of capital, and what he called "a stable international monetary system." It would be fair to weak and strong alike, but it would have the dollar at its heart.

Ten years from his oratory at Yale, Acheson remained the same man with the same views: a Brandeis liberal on a global scale. Serving at the State Department during World War II, he had helped to fashion the Bretton Woods agreement that sought to create the kind of monetary system he had advocated in his speech. Arriving back in the department in January 1949, he meant to build on what he had done. He also observed an early morning ritual with which he sustained his secular form of faith.

His Harvard mentor had risen to become Justice Frankfurter of the Supreme Court. Every morning Frankfurter would leave his home in Georgetown and head two blocks over to Acheson's house. Then the two men would walk side by side until they reached the State Department at Foggy Bottom. At 9:30 sharp Acheson would begin his morning meeting, running it like a Harvard seminar.

His first year in office attracted mostly favorable reviews. The wittiest and most acute assessment came from James Reston of the *New York Times*, who likened Acheson to a baseball star, Joe DiMaggio's teammate Joe Page. Page was the player who could always get the team out of trouble, coming in to pitch in the last two innings of a difficult game. When he clinched the World Series for the Yankees in October, the papers called Page "the greatest relief pitcher in baseball history." Something of the kind might be said about Dean Acheson. His predecessor at Foggy Bottom, General George C. Marshall, had unexpectedly retired on health grounds, passing the ball to Acheson who had to step swiftly up to the mound and begin to pitch in a hurry.

THE AREA OF DANGER

Acheson was the right person at the right time. During the war, the State Department had swollen in sheer numbers as well as in the breadth of its responsibilities. With five times as many staffers as in 1940, it had come to resemble a large, rambling law firm with a horde of demanding clients and a baffling docket of cases to pursue.

Acheson went to work to reshape the bureaucracy and address the caseload. By the time he arrived, the airlift had saved West Berlin from collapse, but somehow a deal still had to be struck with the Soviets to end the blockade and allow both sides to back away from a crisis neither wished to prolong. As for the fate of Germany as a whole, neither the Soviets nor the Western allies much liked the agreements they had reached at Potsdam in 1945 to determine its future. A new West Germany would have to be created, however much it might infuriate the Kremlin, but there were many puzzles to be solved about its role in Europe.

Meanwhile, the North Atlantic Treaty had to be negotiated and signed by the United States and its eleven allies, and then ratified by the Senate. But if NATO was going to be more than ink on paper, the British, the French, and the others would require military aid: trucks, tanks, field guns and shells, and, for Britain's Royal Air Force, a fleet of B-29 bombers. The package would cost at least $1 billion, and with Truman's budget already so constrained, the money would be difficult to find. The Marshall Plan would also need to be renewed by Congress, and this brought difficulties of its own.

The plan was supposed to build a vibrant economy in Europe. From Acheson's point of view, and from Averell Harriman's, it could only achieve its goal if the countries that received the aid—and this meant, above all, Great Britain and France—agreed to do away with tariffs, monopolies, and the other obstacles to free trade and free markets that he had decried so long ago at Yale. For the French and the British this might require something akin to a revolution in their economic way of life. They were wary and reluctant, unable to commit themselves to anything so radical.

In his memoirs Acheson complained about how long it took to work through his assignments. Later diplomats would count themselves lucky if they could accomplish a fraction of what he achieved in 1949. By the end of July, the NATO treaty had been signed and voted through, and the military aid was starting its journey through Congress. After a difficult conference with the Soviets in Paris, the Berlin blockade had also been lifted. The crowning moment came on August 15. The West Germans voted in their first elections, soon to be followed by the choice of Konrad Adenauer as chancellor.

A cynic might say that it was easy for American statesmen to corral their allies in an age when the dollar ruled supreme. Acheson's achievements had been remarkable all the same. With consummate skill he applied the "practical statesmanship" that he had mastered as a lawyer, based on the Brandeis technique of drawing out the essence of a multitude of details. An example was the Occupation Statute for West Germany, which had to be settled with the French and the British so that Adenauer's republic could come into existence. The statute began as a draft of fifty pages, with tacked on at the end two hundred caveats and quibbles. Acheson prodded the teams of officials to distill the issues into two brief memoranda, each one on just three sheets of paper. Within weeks the deal was done.[8]

If only every problem could be solved so neatly. Where these European matters were concerned, Acheson had been in his element, hacking a path through the detail but mostly dealing with British and French professionals, with whom he could make friends as well as do business. This had often been his style on Capitol Hill as well. "Acheson can both hold his whisky and tell funny anecdotes," wrote one observer, who remembered Acheson's earlier period at the State Department, when, over cocktails, he had charmed the leaders of the Senate. This had worked in wartime, but could Acheson still rely on their support?

By the late summer of 1949 the mood in politics had changed, giving way in Washington to a new atmosphere of tension. Acheson had no connection with the five-percenter scandal—he detested Harry Vaughan and told his staff not to take his calls—but he was not immune to attacks by the same Republicans who had gone after the general. Acheson's friends and enemies alike could see the weak points in his armor.[9]

China, a country of which he knew little, had become his problem to try to solve. "The area of crisis," the journalist Joseph Alsop had written in June, "is shifting to the Far East." This was a statement of the obvious, made soon after Shanghai fell to Mao, but the situation left Acheson exposed. No one could blame him for what was coming to be called "the loss of China," since Acheson had never been an Asia hand. But he could be criticized for failing to devise new policies to stem the Communist tide in the region. He also had to explain how it could be that since 1945 America had spent $2 billion to support the Nationalist regime in China only to see the triumph of Mao.[10]

Acheson's response had been clumsy. In early August the State Department released a huge report, the China White Paper, chronicling the downfall of the Nationalists, the Kuomintang (KMT), and blaming them and their leader, Chiang Kai-shek, for their defeat on the battlefield. In *Pravda* the Russians dismissed the White Paper as "1,054 pages of ignominy." In America there were many who agreed. Republican senators led the assault on Acheson, but they were joined by some Democrats as well.

It was not enough merely to analyze the past. Acheson now had to find an Asian program for the future. As he met the press to give them the White Paper, the secretary could only say that he had appointed a working party to review US policy for the region. It was to be conducted by his ambassador-at-large, Philip Jessup, an academic lawyer on leave from Columbia University;

and here, with the best of intentions, Acheson walked into a trap of his own making.

The author of influential books about international law, Jessup could certainly boast some fine credentials. A profile in *Collier's* magazine described him as "a lanky, long-nosed, rumple-suited college professor." He was a negotiator as adept as Acheson. At the United Nations in February, Jessup had discreetly opened talks with the Soviets to end the crisis in Berlin. *Collier's* chose to call him "the man who busted the blockade."[11]

Any official in America who attracts such glowing praise can expect to be vilified in equal measure, but in selecting Jessup as his Asian adviser Dean Acheson had chosen unwisely. The professor made an easy target for his critics. In July the first trial of Alger Hiss for perjury had ended with the jurors unable to reach a verdict; but during the proceedings Jessup had testified in favor of Hiss's character. The prosecution tried to undermine his evidence, linking Jessup to organizations said to be leftist and subversive. He also received a double-edged endorsement from the Soviets. *Collier's* quoted the Russian envoy to the UN describing Jessup as "a very good man, one of the most able, brilliant men in the United Nations." In time this, too, would be used against him.[12]

As the five-percenter scandal continued, eroding the prestige of the White House, the day drew closer when the Truman administration would face another onslaught, centered this time upon Communism rather than corruption. The warning signs were already visible. The Kuomintang had its allies in Washington and in the press, the so-called "China lobby." They were eager to chastise Jessup as a man of the left and as the principal author of the White Paper. He had been its editor in chief.[13]

And there matters rested on Labor Day. While Acheson went on searching for an Asia policy in the weeks that followed, the China lobby looked for ways to bring him down. Republicans were hoping to join up the dots—Hiss, Vaughan, Jessup, the State Department, the loss of China, Communism, and perhaps the Mob—to create a picture of an administration rotten at its heart. In placing his faith in Philip Jessup, the secretary of state had taken a political risk. It would only be worthwhile if Jessup could produce a strategy for Asia as persuasive as Acheson's policies for Europe.

While Acheson could never please the China lobby, he did have to convince another segment of opinion. Among the syndicated writers of the time, the most oracular was Walter Lippmann. In his columns in the *New York Herald Tribune* he plowed his distinctive furrow, but on the subject of Asia he spoke not only for himself but for the establishment Republicans of the East Coast. So far, Acheson had not persuaded them at all.

On the morning after Labor Day, Lippmann began a series of columns voicing doubts about the secretary of state. "The White Paper about China," Lippmann wrote, "deals with a diplomatic disaster—perhaps the greatest that this country has ever suffered. But after working his way through the pages, the reader is left to wonder what the State Department has learned." It was the question Acheson had to answer if he was to placate not only Lippmann but others still more influential. Some of Jessup's admirers had wanted him to stay at Columbia and become the university's president. Instead that accolade went to Dwight D. Eisenhower. And there the general sat in his office in Manhattan, biding his time and watching with mounting anxiety the unfolding of events in Washington and Asia.

September would bring another triumph for the secretary of state. The British—who had their own ideas about China and much else—were on their way to see Acheson with cap in hand. Two years on from their crisis of 1947, the British were sliding

Sir Stafford Cripps, Great Britain's chancellor of the exchequer, and Ernest Bevin, foreign secretary (at the microphone), meeting the New York press on board the *Mauretania* as they arrive for economic talks in Washington, September 6, 1949. *Keystone / Getty Images.*

into economic trouble once again, and they urgently needed Acheson's help. The outcome of their mission would display the relief pitcher at his most effective but leave more problems trailing in its wake.

Acheson could give Great Britain only a little of what it wanted; and the manner in which the British tried to solve their economic problem would antagonize the French. The episode would show just how difficult it was for the United States to shoulder all the new burdens the nation had acquired with victory in war. Both in Europe and in Asia, America's attempts at leadership produced a tangle of dilemmas, each one soluble only at the price of creating new quandaries elsewhere.

THE BRITISH OVERDRAFT

On the evening of September 6, the ocean liner *Mauretania* docked in the Hudson River carrying two English statesmen nearing the end of their careers. One was tall, lean, and frail, a vegetarian who never touched alcohol. The other was short and elephantine, often seen with a glass of brandy and a cigarette trailing from his lips.

The tall man was Sir Stafford Cripps, chancellor of the exchequer, the guardian of Britain's finances. The shorter of the two was Ernest Bevin, the foreign secretary and joint architect of NATO. Hated by some on the left of his own Labour Party, he was revered in his old domain, the British trade union movement, and even by some of his political opponents. When Bevin passed away, that organ of conservatism, the London *Times*, said "there was no questioning his greatness."[14]

After almost a decade in government, first in Churchill's wartime coalition and then in the Labour government elected in 1945, both Cripps and Bevin were exhausted. So severe was Bevin's heart disease that his doctor had come with him to the quayside in England. He would die in the spring of 1951 at the age of seventy. Cripps was in decline as well, obliged to spend a month that summer resting in a sanatorium in Switzerland. He was yet to be diagnosed with the cancer that would kill him in 1952, three days before his sixty-third birthday.

While Cripps and Bevin worked themselves to death in the service of their country, their poor health might also have been a metaphor for Britain's situation. Although not quite the bankrupt nation that its American critics liked to call it, Britain remained a country struggling to pay its way. Cripps had done what he could, leading a drive for exports, and, far from being a loose left-winger, he behaved as prudently as anyone might wish. Spending less than he received in taxes, Cripps used Marshall money and his budget surplus to pay down war debt, and with this species of austerity he kept inflation from bursting out of control. Britain was also meeting more than its share of the cost of the Cold War. While America pruned its military budget, the British began to rearm with a second generation of jet fighters; and no one was more eager than Ernest Bevin to have a British atom bomb, at whatever price.

Their problem was the same as it had been in 1947: the British were running out of foreign exchange. For much of their oil, and for cotton, wheat, timber, tobacco, and machine tools, Britain relied on North America; but the dollars with which to pay for them were disappearing. Despite the efforts the British had made to sell more goods abroad, their currency reserves were almost gone. For safety's sake, Cripps knew he ought to have gold and dollars worth £500 million. At the end of June his reserves were down to little more than £400 million, and when the number was announced, the markets took fright.[15]

After a run on sterling in 1939, the British had fixed their exchange rate at just above four dollars to the pound, where it still remained, defended by rigid controls. This rate of exchange could not be sustained. Unable to compete with Pittsburgh and Detroit, the British could earn dollars in America only with luxury products that carried a *cachet*. Scotch whisky was their biggest transatlantic export, followed by Scottish tweed, Yorkshire woolens, and the sort of bed and table linens you could buy at Macy's. But with sterling overvalued, and the United States in recession, their appeal had diminished. In practice, the British had to rely on dollars earned by their old colonies: principally, exports of rubber and tin from Malaya and cocoa beans and palm oil from West Africa. The American recession had cut into their sales.

Cripps strove to stem the hemorrhage of dollars with curbs on imports and cuts in food rations. This came at a high political cost: the Labour government faced a revolt of the middle classes, and especially London's suburbs, where it had lost municipal elections in the spring. The next set of figures would be published in October, and they would show that the dollar drain had gathered speed. If nothing was done, the British would exhaust their dollars and gold in the spring of 1950, a date all the more sensitive because it was also the deadline for their next general election.

Almost every European nation faced a problem similar to Britain's in this era of the "dollar gap." Until Europe rebuilt its economy and its exports to the rest of the globe, and while the United States remained unchallenged as the industrial leader of the world, the struggle to find dollars was bound to persist; but the special features of the British case aroused emotions in America that went far beyond the economics.

However much they admired Sir Winston Churchill, Americans also nursed anti-British feelings, woven out of resentments old and new. Irish Americans had their case to make against their former masters, and liberals disliked the British Empire for its racist ways and its protectionism. Many Republicans felt the same. For weeks before the *Mauretania* arrived, the press, including radio, ran fierce attacks on Britain and its leftists. After huge wartime loans, another at the end of 1945, and then Marshall aid, were the British going to ask America for more? In Congress it was said that Cripps would squander any money he was given on benefits for the idle or on the colonies. He and Bevin were "beggars yowling at the gate," wrote one New York columnist. The cartoons nearby were cruel and highly personal: Bevin and Cripps were a cartoonist's dream.[16]

The British found George Orwell used against them. His novel *1984* had just appeared, winning instant acclaim on both sides of the ocean. It was easy enough for Truman's critics on the right to point to the bleak, oppressive London depicted in the book as a warning of what forty years of socialism would do to a country. Keen to attack the president as well as the British, they linked them together, portraying Britain's welfare state as a form of tyranny that Truman's Fair Deal would foist on free Americans.

So extreme was the invective that the president had to intervene. A week before Labor Day, in front of the American Legion in Philadelphia, Truman spoke up for the nation's closest ally; but even he felt that the British had to change. Like many of Truman's most eloquent speeches, his address to the legion placed events in their global setting, ranging far beyond a sentimental appeal to 1940 and Churchill's finest hour. He praised Great Britain as a stalwart and essential friend, but dropped a diplomatic hint about its errors in years gone by. "The free nations are determined," the president said, "to avoid the mistakes of the past." In other words, the British must abandon those imperial habits that had shaped their conduct before and during World War II.[17]

Aware of the tirades against them in America, Bevin and Cripps came prepared. From an economic point of view they had their solution: they were going to devalue the British pound, so as to choke off imports and make their exports more competitive. This was still a secret of the utmost sensitivity, but they knew it was what Acheson wanted and that John Snyder at the US Treasury agreed that it had to be done. The decision had been hard to make, especially for Cripps, who feared the consequences for inflation and for Britain's standing abroad. In June he had quarreled in Brussels with Averell Harriman, who had bluntly insisted on devaluation: Harriman had a brusque way with diplomacy. Their verbal fracas had leaked into the press, adding to the pressure on the pound.

In early August, while Cripps was still in Switzerland, his colleagues overruled him and made their choice to devalue. The prime minister, Clement Attlee, wrote to Cripps to give him the news; and then in London there followed weeks of intense work, as British officials drew up a list of steps they wanted America to take in return.

Despite his ill health, Ernest Bevin would have to play a central role in what came next. Devaluation solved the short-term problem, but the British foreign secretary hoped for something far more ambitious than an economic package. For him, as for Harry Truman, the immediate crisis was merely one aspect of a worldwide panorama. It might also be an opportunity, to be grasped by Bevin, to forge a new kind of partnership with the United States, one rooted in the Cold War but with implications far beyond it.

Bevin hinted at this in New York on board the *Mauretania*. Smiling broadly to the press, he listed the things Britain and America had achieved together, headed by the NATO treaty and the West German republic. "All this," he said, "is progress toward one world outside the oligarchy of Soviet Russia." As he spoke, the ship's crew were unloading his baggage. The longshoremen refused to touch it and pickets had gathered by the pier, calling themselves the American-Irish Minutemen.[18]

Next morning Cripps and Bevin reached Foggy Bottom, where their meetings began with a session for the newsreels. "I never thought," said Bevin, "that a man with an overdraft would get such a wonderful welcome." Acheson roared with laughter and the cameras left.

The first session lasted sixty-two minutes. No notes were taken, and only nine people were present. The substance of the meeting had to be kept secret, even from Harriman, who was left in the dark. For the fourth time since the war with Napoleon, and despite the consternation it might cause in Europe, the British were going to debase their currency. To Snyder's relief, they would not request another dollar loan.

Cripps read a long statement that had taken three weeks to draft. Ahead of him there lay a battle with Churchill, who in Parliament still led the Conservative Party, and who long before in the 1920s had served as chancellor himself. On his feet in the House of Commons, and frail though he was, Cripps would have to defend the devaluation he had resisted for so long. His own left wingers would attack him too, because to prevent a surge of inflation he would have to be still more frugal, curtailing some of Labour's social programs.

All of this was now inevitable. The only alternative, if the pound remained at its old level, would have been to seal Britain and its Commonwealth into a siege economy still more tightly controlled. To keep the markets calm, sterling would have to be devalued on a Sunday and within two weeks. Cripps and Bevin would choose the new exchange rate at the last moment, and then Cripps would fly home to tell the nation the humiliating news.[19]

Seven months earlier, Secretary Snyder had caused a run on the pound with some ill-judged remarks to Congress. Now he could be more helpful. A leak would be disastrous, so he fibbed to the press when he briefed them about the talks. Bevin, whose teeth were causing him agony, went in search of an American dentist, while Cripps played up to his familiar image. Lunching at the National Press Club, he consumed a menu that spoke of his austere ways: an omelet, spinach, and a cup of tea.[20]

THE HEARTLAND AND THE RIM

For Acheson the British move was a personal victory. During the summer he had reined in Harriman, hoping to achieve the result they both wanted by more subtle means than his friend's. He had allayed the president's anxieties, and he had maintained firm but discreet pressure on the British. Acheson had also kept on a leash his mercurial aide, George Kennan, the State Department's head of policy and planning, for whom only the boldest of gestures would suffice to save the Western alliance.

In London that summer, Kennan had privately met British officials and proposed nothing less than an Anglo-American economic union that might include an exchange of citizenship. The

British listened carefully. They had a suggestion of their own: a plan for America to foot the bill for Britain's vast wartime debts to India. Acheson could not endorse either policy; but on the eve of the Washington talks, Kennan put his ideas into the public domain via the Alsops in the *Herald Tribune*.[21]

The first meeting in Washington had cleared the air and after that the talks unfolded calmly, but with grand schemes like Kennan's shunted aside. The British could not overcome an American reluctance to rise above the details and take a broader view. If Cripps returned to London empty-handed, with nothing but the news of devaluation, his mission would have failed; and therefore he proposed a list of fifteen steps he wanted America to take to help Britain earn more dollars. Teams of officials worked on every point but nothing fundamental changed, other than the value of the pound.

Snyder agreed to a few concessions: the United States would stockpile Malayan tin and rubber, do away with some red tape, and let the British use Marshall aid to buy more wheat from Canada. Even that was hard for Snyder to stomach, because of the opposition it might encounter from American farmers, whose loyalty was so vital to the president. He politely refused the rest of the British requests. While Cripps and Bevin wanted to draw far closer to their ally, the Americans—constrained by their fraught politics at home—had no flexibility to offer. Almost every item on the British list would antagonize some lobby with a voice in Congress that Snyder was anxious not to offend.[22]

Socialist though he was, Cripps openly admired American efficiency, and he wanted to see it copied in Britain. To make the most of the Marshall Plan, he had launched the initiative to send British fact-finding teams to industrial centers such as Pittsburgh. But in Washington, Cripps collided with another feature of US hegemony. With sterling devalued, the British could sell Americans more of their whisky, their textiles, and their Nigerian palm oil; but if this policy was to pave the way for lasting prosperity, Cripps would need something else as well. Like many a foreign finance minister in the years to come, he hoped to see the United States open its markets by reducing its own protective tariffs. Snyder could promise nothing of the kind. Cripps also wanted Truman to follow the British example and commit to full employment, to prevent recessions like the one just ended. Snyder did not like this idea at all. Congress, aghast at anything so liberal, had rejected just such a proposal during Truman's first administration.

Could Bevin do better in his talks with Acheson? He came bearing the fruits of a review by his officials of every element in Britain's foreign policy. Bevin and his staff knew, as they had known since the war, that Britain could not afford all its overseas commitments. This was why, during their economic crisis in 1947, the British had withdrawn their financial aid for the defense of Greece and Turkey, the step that had prompted the president to unveil the Truman Doctrine, pledging support for nations such as these against the Soviets, and then to enact the Marshall Plan. Two years on, British thinking had developed into a new concept that they hoped Acheson could share.

It was anti-communist, of course. Led by Bevin's most senior aide, the Russian-speaking diplomat Sir William Strang, the British Foreign Office drew up a series of papers that assessed the Soviet threat and then redefined their vision of Britain's role in the world. Completed in July 1949, the Strang review covered the ground that George Kennan had explored in his famous article, "The Sources of Soviet Conduct," published in the magazine *Foreign Affairs* in 1947. Like Kennan, the British drew upon Russian history to analyze the Kremlin's thinking and its strategy; and like Kennan they developed a theory of containment as the correct response. The Strang review was as fiercely anti-Soviet as anything Americans might have wished to see. If anything, the

British took a more aggressive line than Kennan's, and their perspective was broader than his.[23]

The Russians, said Strang, were "implacably hostile," and he
called for Britain and its allies "to resist, and if possible to curtail,"
the influence of Communism everywhere. Far from merely containing the Soviets, as Kennan wished to do, Strang hoped to roll
them back to their old frontiers of 1939. And while Kennan had
said little about the Middle East and Asia, Strang saw them as the
key to everything. He had recently made two long tours of both
regions, where he had embraced geopolitics on the grandest scale.

Strang had absorbed the ideas of two pioneers of that new
school of thought: the British geographer Sir Halford Mackinder
and the 1940s Yale scholar Nicholas J. Spykman. Like them, he
pondered on the strategic implications of geography, and above all
the phenomenon of Eurasia, the landmass that stretched from the
coast of France to the shores of the Pacific. Using a term coined by
Mackinder in the early 1900s, Strang called it "the Heartland." As
deep as it was wide, the Eurasian Heartland contained immense
resources impervious to attack, but it had mostly fallen under Stalin's and Mao's domination.[24]

To win the Cold War, Britain and its allies had to retain the
maritime regions that surrounded Eurasia. This Strang described
as "the sea-girt periphery, or what has been called the Rimland."
By this he meant the chain of British buttresses against the Soviets that extended from Gibraltar to the Suez Canal, and then
from Britain's bases in Iraq across the Indian Ocean to Singapore
and beyond. In his tour of the Rimland, Strang had met General
Douglas MacArthur in Tokyo, Prime Minister Jawaharlal Nehru
in India, the Shah of Iran, and the other friendly leaders of the
region, and he returned alarmed by what he found.

India could not feed itself and neither could Japan. In Malaya
the British were fighting a Communist insurgency while the

French were beleaguered in Vietnam. Strang would never use that 1970s phrase "the arc of crisis," but it was what he observed on his travels. He saw a Rimland in danger of collapse, with Communism poised to fill a vacuum of power. And if the Rimland fell, with it would go those economic assets on which Britain depended: not only the tin mines and plantations of Malaya, but also the British-run oil fields in the Persian Gulf that sent their tankers home by way of Suez.

How could the Rimland be secured? Not by British strength alone, depleted as it was. America would have to play its part. In late August, a week before Bevin sailed on the *Mauretania*, the Foreign Office finalized a long memorandum that set out its vision of joint defense with the United States of the periphery of Asia.[25]

In the weeks that followed the Washington talks, Bevin and Acheson met many times, went to see the musical *South Pacific* on Broadway, and talked all the time about their list of issues. Through the fog of words, Bevin tried to nudge the Americans ever more deeply into the Rimland. He wished to complete the transformation of Britain's empire into a voluntary league of free nations united against the Soviets. To secure the Rimland and address the food crisis of the region, he hoped for a Marshall Plan for Asia, with initial steps to be taken at a conference soon to be held at Colombo in Sri Lanka.

For this he wanted American money and Acheson's support. If they were forthcoming, Bevin would suggest the idea his officials had mentioned to Kennan, that Washington should take up the burden of gradually repaying Britain's debts to India. Bevin knew he could not ask for American troops and aircraft to fortify the Middle East, but he hoped one day to see them in the region.

None of this was feasible in 1949, and on one thing above all Bevin and Acheson were bound to disagree. Bevin intended to recognize the Communists in China as the lawful regime as soon as it could be shown that Mao controlled the country. The United States could not follow suit. Here Bevin touched upon an underlying flaw in Acheson's position. Although Acheson had America's wealth to draw upon, he was hemmed in by its partisan divisions. Neither he nor Truman could take a decision so radical. And if they could not recognize Red China, neither could they adopt an Asia policy as ambitious as the one the British wished to see them follow—or at any rate not yet.

Unlike Acheson and Truman, who had to cope with a turbulent Congress, Ernest Bevin could make foreign policy as he chose. "I'm not a dictator," Bevin once said, "but I know what I want and I know how to get it." Until the general election he had a majority in Parliament. Behind him he had the labor unions, who secured his position in his party. Bevin had also arranged with Churchill, with whom he had worked so closely in wartime, to take a common view of grand strategy overseas. Acheson could not make deals such as this with his opponents. For six years on Capitol Hill after 1943 there had mostly been a bipartisan approach to foreign policy. Amid the embitterment of Truman's second term, this agreement across the aisle was coming to an end.[26]

The difference between Britain and America was simply this. After ten years of rationing and scarcity, the British understood their limitations. It has often been said that after 1945 they clung to a deluded notion of their status as a great power, but this is a caricature of their position. The British knew their weaknesses; but they also knew exactly what they wanted to do in the world and that they needed American help to achieve it. The American plight was the opposite. The United States tended to underestimate its own resources. Nor did it know precisely where it wished to go. Acheson's lack of an Asian strategy was evidence of that; but this absence of direction also flowed from the collapse of consensus on Capitol Hill.

In their August memorandum, the British had been skeptical about America's grasp of global realities. "The United States," they wrote, "has been thrust into a position of world leadership before she has developed fully the experience and political and economic philosophy necessary for the role." Britain's ideas for Asia were too grandiose, still bearing the traces of an imperial past; but despite their patronizing tone, the British made a telling point. In the months that followed, Truman and his colleagues would be taken by surprise, at home and in Asia alike, and compelled to improvise at a hazardous time that called for clarity.[27]

CHINA

*S*hanghai, Xian, Wuhan, Changsha: by late summer all four of these *great cities of central China had fallen to the People's Liberation Army, or PLA. Each one brought its reminder of episodes from the war against Japan or of stages in Mao's career of revolution.*[1]

In Changsha, a thousand miles south of Beijing, as a young school-teacher Mao had written in 1919 the article that first made his name. He had called for a union of the masses—peasants, workers, students, women, and rickshaw drivers—so that China could arise and liberate itself. As yet he had barely read a word of Karl Marx. Even so, the young Mao had praised the Bolsheviks in Russia and above all their success on the battlefield.

"The army of the red flag surges forward," Mao had written then. Thirty years on, the taking of Changsha in August brought the PLA close to complete victory. On the map, the Kuomintang appeared to hold a quarter of the country. But although the KMT's capital remained at Chongqing, its leader Chiang Kai-shek was already moving his followers to Taiwan. Everywhere in 1949 his troops were in retreat.

It was a year of drought but also of floods, with the economy shattered and parts of China close to famine. Hyperinflation, for which the KMT bore much of the blame, had estranged Chiang and his party from almost every social group. For the PLA the way now lay open to Guangzhou in the south, so close to the British in Hong Kong. In September in the far northwest, the KMT gave up the province of Xinjiang without a fight.

The time had come for Mao to create a government and give China a constitution. He had also to define the "union of the masses" in new terms. The Marxist text he knew the best was Stalin's Short Course of the 1930s. Mao wished to emulate its program for collective farms and rapid industrialization by way of Five-Year Plans. Stalin restrained him, urging him to go slowly with land reform and to stick to the line of so-called New Democracy that Mao had adopted in 1940. This would mean forming a coalition government in Beijing, with a voice for other parties besides the Communists.

The China White Paper had deeply angered Mao. It drew from his pen a stream of articles denouncing Secretary Acheson as "the voice of the US bourgeoisie." In late June Mao had also written an essay, "On the People's Democratic Dictatorship," intended to sum up his ideology on the eve of triumph. A week later Pravda reprinted it to show that it had Stalin's approval.

The essay spoke of a world divided between imperialism and the socialist countries. China must "lean to one side," wrote Mao, which had to be toward the Soviets. But just what this might signify was still unclear. "Our present policy," Mao claimed, "is to regulate capitalism, not to destroy it." This appeared to imply a long period of transition, perhaps ten years or so, during which private property and free enterprise would continue side by side with state control.

Only then would China become truly socialist and begin to move toward what Mao called "the realm of Great Harmony," when classes would disappear and the state would wither away. But the signals Mao transmitted were mixed. In these writings he also spoke, like Stalin, of the need for unremitting struggle against counterrevolutionary forces at home. Mao praised the Soviet Communist Party as China's best teacher.

September brought the drafting of the constitution for the People's Republic. In Moscow that summer, Mao's lieutenant Liu Shaoqi had heard Stalin insist again on the need for coalition. On the face of things this appeared to be the outcome. Six hundred or so delegates assembled in Beijing, with nine political parties legally recognized; but the Chinese Communist Party had more than half the votes. The document they adopted, the Common Program, contained the ambiguities of all Mao's writings that summer, seeming to promise democracy and freedom while also speaking of the need to suppress reactionaries. But Article Two was as plain as could be: it called for the liberation of all of China's territory, which meant the conquest of Tibet and Taiwan.

Observers from abroad could choose their different ways to read the Common Program. Some might cling to the notion that Mao was chiefly an agrarian reformer, and not a true disciple of the Kremlin. Others spoke of Mao as an Asiatic Lenin. They could only speculate about his relationship with Stalin. This remained ambiguous as well.

Since perhaps as early as the spring of 1947, Mao had been trying to secure an invitation to go to Moscow, but Stalin had been wary and suspicious. Mao wanted help—loans to rebuild the Chinese economy, aircraft, and training for pilots to prepare for the invasion of Taiwan—but Stalin had his own priorities. The agreements he had signed with Roosevelt and Churchill at Yalta had awarded him a sphere of influence in northeastern China that he wished to preserve.

A few months after Yalta, Chiang Kai-shek and the KMT had been obliged to sign in August 1945 a treaty conceding this to Stalin. The Soviets had what amounted to control of two ports in the south of Manchuria: the naval base at Lushun and the cargo port at Dalian, across the Yellow Sea from North Korea. More important still were the Manchurian railroads. Also under Soviet domination, the Chinese Changchun Railroad linked these ports to Russia's route by rail across Siberia, shortening its path. From the point of view of geopolitics its value was clear: it protected the Soviet Far East.

For China, too, these assets were essential. In the post–Mao era, Manchuria would be eclipsed as China's economic surge took place more powerfully elsewhere. In 1949 it seemed to hold the key to the future, with its grain, its vast crop of soybeans, and its coal and iron ore.

If Mao wished to have the ports and the railroad returned to China, he would need a new treaty with the USSR. But when Liu Shaoqi raised the matter with Stalin that summer, the Soviet leader had chosen to evade the question. In September, Stalin agreed to give China some aircraft, but not to help Mao against Taiwan. He also withheld the invitation to Moscow that Mao was so eager to receive. Meanwhile, Dean Acheson looked on, expecting to see a rift develop between China and the Kremlin.

CHAPTER TWO

THE GRINDING MACHINE

I think we shall continue to win the cold war.

—SENATOR TOM CONNALLY, *September 1949*[1]

O n the evening of Sunday, September 18, the British devalued the pound. Since this was an age when public life in
London still required good manners, Sir Stafford Cripps
invited Churchill to Downing Street to be briefed before he told
the nation. The British had only three radio channels, but Cripps
broadcast on two of them, announcing not only the new rate for
sterling but also an increase in the price of bread. From Balmoral
Castle the king issued a proclamation closing the banks and the
stock exchange for a day to absorb the news.

The shock of the announcement lay in the scale of the devaluation. Cripps and Ernest Bevin had chosen to slash the value of
the pound against the dollar by some 31 percent. A far deeper cut
than even the shrewdest observers had thought likely, this move
would undermine the currencies of Britain's counterparts across
the English Channel. Radio Moscow offered a Marxist appraisal,
predicting what it called "financial panic throughout Marshal-
lized Europe." In Paris the news horrified the French government,
which met for four hours to decide what to do. In the words of
one official at the foreign ministry, the Quai d'Orsay, Cripps had

behaved "like a fraudulent banker," with the perfidy for which England was notorious. The new rate of $2.80 to the pound would force France into an emergency devaluation of the franc.[2]

Secretary Acheson had heard the news before both Churchill and the French, and for him it was a source of satisfaction. The British had done precisely as he wished. As for the widening rift between Paris and London, there was little he could do other than offer moral support. It was something Britain and France would have to mend between themselves. While Acheson was optimistic, his opponents in Congress took a different view. The news of Britain's devaluation came at a moment when Congress was eager to point out the frailties and disunity of Europe.

The Senate was about to debate Acheson's plan for military aid not only for America's NATO allies but also for Greece, Turkey, Iran, South Korea, and the Philippines. To fund the package, Truman was asking for more than $1.3 billion, and the senators were as restless about this as they were about Acheson's vagueness with regard to his policies for Asia. In his memoirs Acheson would dismiss the fraught debate about the NATO aid package as "a tempest in a teapot." In fact it more closely resembled the early tremors of an earthquake. During the verbal controversy in Congress the bipartisan approach to foreign affairs would come to the brink of collapse.[3]

It was said at the time that politics should stop at the water's edge. If there was one senator who epitomized this view of foreign policy, that man was Arthur Vandenberg, a Republican from Michigan, now sixty-five years old and a senator since 1928. In 1943 he had steered his party to the Mackinac Charter, named after the Michigan resort where it was drawn up, a statement committing the GOP to work in partnership with the Democrats to win the war and then to build a lasting peace. But proud though he was of that agreement, Vandenberg knew that it owed as much to cunning as it did to high ideals.

Determined to prevent FDR from winning a fourth term, the Republicans had wanted to take foreign policy, Roosevelt's strongest card, off the table in the 1944 presidential election. The Mackinac Charter gave them the means to do just this, and it was feasible because, in the autumn of 1943, victories were being won in every theater of the war and Stalin appeared to be a friend. Even the most stubborn of Republicans could sign up to the dream of a tranquil postwar world.[4]

Now all of this lay far in the past. The Soviets were allies no longer, and the GOP had failed not once but twice to retake the White House. In the fall of 1949 Vandenberg detected a new mood of discontent in the nation, expressed in the telegrams and letters that senators received from the public. "The whole country is in a state of nerves," he wrote to his wife in September. "Everybody is under tension. Nothing is right. . . . Everybody is mad about something." Vandenberg felt this mood spreading among his colleagues, who were growing less and less inclined to be bipartisan. In the spirit of Mackinac, he and most of his party in the Senate had voted to ratify the NATO treaty, but eleven Republicans had said no: a warning sign of more turmoil yet to come.[5]

In 1949 two sets of numbers defined Harry Truman's predicament. One was the arithmetic of Congress, meaning the likely balance of votes for and against his programs. Here the omens were unfavorable, as the Democrats in Congress remained unwilling to pass or even to consider bold legislation on the domestic front.

The other set of figures could be found in the federal budget, containing as it did the $5 billion deficit that Truman feared might widen still further in 1950. Time and again, the president had insisted that he would balance the books, and unlike many later politicians he meant to keep his word. Not only did he sincerely believe that budget deficits would pave the way to rampant inflation and the ruin of America, but he also had politics to consider.

As yet, he had not ruled out running again for the White House in 1952. He could not do so if he entered his campaign without keeping his budget promise.[6]

These two sets of numbers were connected, of course. If Congress was uneasy it was because the nation was uneasy too; and much of this could be traced back to a simple fact about the economy. Historians often refer to a postwar boom, but nothing of the kind had so far occurred. The average American was no better off than he or she had been at the hour of victory.

Wages had increased in dollars and cents per hour since the year of the Normandy landings, the peak of wartime production, but hours worked had fallen. Because of this, because of inflation, and because wartime bonuses had evaporated, in 1949 the average family's weekly earnings had shrunk in real terms by 10 percent since 1944. Allowing for taxes as well as inflation, then even in 1950, when the economy was growing fast, the spendable incomes of factory workers with children were 6 percent smaller than they had been at the time of D-Day. Others had fared still worse, especially those who did not have a labor union or who lived in one of the cities such as New York where, after wartime years when few homes were built, housing was scarce and rents had rocketed.[7]

Polls came and went; but the struggle to make ends meet almost always outranked the Soviet threat when Americans were asked to name the most urgent problem facing the nation. With the cost of living still so high, Congress would not vote for increased taxes that working families could not afford to pay. Truman's prospects of closing the gap in his budget receded over the horizon, to somewhere beyond the fall of 1952.

It was against this background that the president and Congress took all their decisions about the waging of the early phase of the Cold War. Truman was caught in a trap, between a Congress he could not rely upon and a budget deficit he could not close. The jaws of the trap had already closed around him in the early summer, when Congress began to dismember the Fair Deal into a few items that it might consider while ignoring the rest. They tightened still further during the Senate debate on military aid for NATO. It was a rambling affair that, like some long overture, contained all the themes to be played out in politics in the months to come.

Eight years earlier, in 1941, Congress had provided a far larger sum to supply arms and much else to Britain under the Lend-Lease Act. But that had been a complicated package of grants and loans, rather than an outright gift, and Congress had agreed to it at the height of the London Blitz, at a time when the British were also aligned with the United States against the growing threat from Japan. To write a huge check for arms to Europe in peacetime was a request of a kind no president had ever made.

Officially the package was known as the Foreign Military Assistance Bill of 1949; but in the House of Representatives it came to be described as "pouring money down a rat-hole." By a large majority, with seventy-one Democrats against the president, the House had voted in mid-August to slash the cost of the aid package for NATO to $800 million. Now it was the task of Truman's friends in the Senate to restore the original program with all its trucks and tanks and B-29s. His enemies found their leader in a Democrat by the name of Walter George.

Mr. George's Amendment

Congress is one of the poor relations of American history. If we think of the past as a spacious museum, then the portraits of presidents, painted in oils, hang in the grand salon at the top of the staircase. There are two obvious masterpieces, Abraham Lincoln and George Washington, about whose quality almost everyone will agree. Perhaps another ten or a dozen presidents recur so often in lists drawn up by connoisseurs of greatness that their reputations may be regarded as secure. Even so, the order in which they appear is mostly determined by each observer's partisan loyalties and by the politics of the passing moment.

Mere senators and members of Congress find themselves forgotten, unless they are plainly villains. Once they are dead, they might have a statue put up to them in the Capitol, or an office building nearby might bear their names. In the eyes of most visitors to the museum of the past, they have long since ceased to be more than curiosities. Their pictures might as well be faded watercolors in a basement.

And yet this is not the way the United States actually works. The nation cannot do without the endless grinding of the wheels of Congress. The Cold War produced a novel, *Advise and Consent* by Allen Drury, a bestseller in its time, which took this as its central theme. Today the book seems dated or even distasteful, complete with casual racism, an implausible plot, and a touch of homophobia. In 1960 both John F. Kennedy and Richard Nixon carried it with them during the presidential election campaign.

The novel made the impression it did because Drury, a Capitol Hill correspondent, put Congress, and not the White House, at the center of his picture. The historian of the Cold War should often do the same. Congress was the grinding machine through which decisions had to pass, and where presidents found their policies sliced down to something more humble by forgotten politicians who set the boundaries of what they could do. Friction was inherent in the system. The wheels of Congress carried dirt and rust and they snagged on obstacles left in their path by conflicts unresolved within the nation.

In the debate about arms for NATO the wheels struck a boulder in the form of Walter George. Now seventy-one years old, George had spoken as a Democrat for Georgia in the Senate since 1922. Since 1941 he had chaired the Senate's Finance Committee, with a break of two years after the Republicans took Congress in

1946. When the Democrats regained the Senate, George resumed his chairmanship.

Although the Democrats now had majorities in both chambers, Truman controlled neither them nor Walter George. Out of ninety-six seats in the Senate in 1949, the Democrats occupied fifty-three, but the president could count on barely half of them to support him come what may. In critical debates on contentious subjects, the rest would often waver to and fro, hedging their bets and flouting party discipline. Because the arms debate was not quite a crisis, in the end Truman and Acheson obtained what they desired, but they had reached the limit of what they could achieve.

In the previous Congress, the president had suffered two crushing defeats for which his fellow Democrats were largely to blame. The first had come when Truman vetoed the Taft-Hartley Act and Congress overrode the veto. Twenty Democrats in the Senate had voted with the Republican majority. A defeat still more cruel occurred in the spring of 1948, when the Republicans passed a tax-cutting bill, slashing income tax by nearly $5 billion, almost 15 percent of the federal budget. Truman vetoed the bill, but this time twenty-seven Democratic senators voted for the override. The tax cuts went through by seventy-seven votes to ten.[8]

If there had been no recession, the president might have regained some of the fiscal ground that he had lost, but the economic woes of 1949 ruined his chances of doing so. Taft-Hartley remained invincible, and most of Truman's Fair Deal had little hope of resurrection. Of the twenty-seven tax-cutting Democrats of 1948, twenty-one were still senators in 1949, and they included some of the most senior. The two most eminent of the twenty-one were Scott Lucas of Illinois, the majority leader, and Walter George.

It was never easy to manage a Democratic Party that tried to represent the Bronx and Savannah at one and the same time. The task had required all FDR's talents, and if it had not been for

World War II the effort would have defeated even him. In the debate about arms for NATO, the party's sectional divide could be seen in the gulf that separated Dean Acheson from Walter George. Although both were lawyers and both were Democrats, in almost every other way they were at odds.

Senator George feared the labor unions, he believed in the Senate, and he took his own view of social justice in Georgia and elsewhere. Born not to privilege but to poverty, he came from a family of cotton farmers close to the Alabama line. Here was another boy who had taught school to pay his way through college: not Yale or Harvard, but Mercer College near Macon. In his youth George was jeered at when he rode into town on a decrepit mule. As he grew older, and became a judge and an orator, he cultivated gravitas. He spoke slowly, and his cuffs and collar were always crisply starched. Even his wife called him "Mr. George."[9]

Of course he was firmly for segregation, quite as much as he was for propping up with subsidies the price of Georgia cotton. In the eyes of one detractor, George was "a cold and pompous shell of a man." To his admirers, comprising the entire contingent from the South in Congress, he figured as one of the world's great statesmen. FDR called him "a gentleman and a scholar," but added, "He and I do not speak the same language." In 1938 Roosevelt had tried to purge the senator from the Democratic Party, but the effort had failed. Eleven years on, Walter George could probably be counted as another of the twenty most powerful people in America.

In his home state George was unassailable, and this left him free to be as blunt as he chose. He shuddered at the thought of Truman's deficit. George believed, as many did, that military aid for NATO would become a recurring item, costing as much as $2 billion annually for many years to come. He offered an amendment to the bill cutting $500 million in the program for the current year—the reduction that the House had already made—with no commitment for anything in the years to follow. "Do not the poor, the people in the lower tax brackets, deserve a break in the matter of taxes?" the senator inquired.[10]

George had voted for NATO, but for him the core component of the Atlantic alliance lay not in money for military aid but in the fifth article of the treaty, the promise the allies had made to come to each other's defense. NATO must not be made, he told the Senate, "the excuse for engaging in an armaments race throughout the world," or a means for subsidizing leftists overseas. Looking across the ocean, George saw France, as he put it, "emaciated through socialist influences"; he saw Britain as weak and uncompetitive, its strength dissipated by high taxes; and he worried that America would go the same way. "The one hope for our world," he said, "is for America to remain strong and robust, able to make good under Article Five." And this required tax cuts and tight limits on the federal budget.

In all of this George had the support of what was coming to be known as "the economy bloc" in the Senate. Although the bloc cut across party lines, for Truman its most dangerous element lay in the Democrats within its ranks. The George amendment was defeated, but ten Democrats had voted with him. If they did the same thing where other issues were at stake, foreign or domestic, and if the Republicans could unite beside them, they could wreck any major bill Truman wished to promote.

Acheson, with his disdain for the messy realities of politics, chose to dismiss George and his allies as reactionaries; but their views were widely held and they had deep roots. In this opening phase of the Cold War, the people who cast decisive votes in Congress were often elderly men who had already been in early middle age when Lenin seized power in Petrograd. Did they think they were creating or defending a new world order, led by the United States, that would survive for fifty years or more?

They did to a degree, although few would have added the word "liberal" to describe it. Senator George had lost a son in the war, a navy flier killed while hunting for German submarines. After that, in the hope of preventing wars to come, he became an ardent supporter of the United Nations. But politicians of his generation were also still working over in their minds the memory of the Great Depression and its political effects. Truman could not expect George and his allies to forget the alarm they had felt in 1936 and 1937, when the labor unions were advancing and Roosevelt had moved to the left. All of this served to shape the views they took about the Fair Deal and the Soviet threat.

THE SENATE AND THE RAT-HOLE

The debate about arms for NATO spread over four days. It contained one moment of sadness. Shortly before the final vote was taken, Arthur Vandenberg rose to defend the bill against the case that Walter George had made. It was the last long speech he would give in the chamber. He was awaiting surgery for cancer in his left lung.

"Senators are a prolific source of advice," Acheson wrote many years later, "but most of it is bad." This was the jaundiced recollection of a man who had seen some senators at their worst. In reality, the debate about arms for NATO was far from the trivial matter that Acheson described in his memoirs. Instead the debate was arduous and sophisticated, leaving no stone unturned. With Vandenberg departing, the cause of bipartisan consensus found another Republican advocate in the shape of the Michigan senator's friend and colleague in the chamber, John Foster Dulles of New York. A lawyer tougher and more experienced even than Acheson, Senator Dulles made a formidable ally, helping to swing the debate in his favor; but his support would come at a price.

All the while in the background there lay the Asia question, so patently unresolved, on which Dulles sided with the hawks.[11]

As its most effective voice on the Senate floor, the China lobby had a Republican rising star, William Knowland of California, whose father owned the *Oakland Tribune*. To prevent him from raising a storm about China during the debate, a few days beforehand Vandenberg struck a deal with Knowland to inject $75 million into the bill, to be used, at Truman's discretion, for aid to anti-communists in "the general China area." It was a compromise, supported by Dulles, that was designed to allow arms to be sent to the Kuomintang on Taiwan, but only if Truman agreed.

In fact, the president did not mean to spend a single dollar to help the KMT and Chiang Kai-shek, but this vague formula did not oblige him to. A deliberate fudge, it was accepted by Tom Connally, Democrat from Texas, chairman of the Senate Foreign Relations Committee. Although passed into law as a political ploy, it proved to be the beginning of more than seven decades of US involvement, sometimes close, sometimes distant, but mostly ambiguous, with the affairs of this complicated island.

Although Connally felt some qualms about the NATO arms bill, he was at least one Democrat whom the president could trust. One year older than Walter George, he was another Wilsonian, who had campaigned long ago for America to join the League of Nations. Tall and theatrical with his bow tie and flowing white hair, Connally prided himself on his sense of humor and his generosity with quotes. "The work is so tedious, irksome and annoying," he once said after a peace conference with the Soviets. "You sit there all day going yah-yah-yah." He told anyone he met that the debate about aid for NATO was the toughest he had endured since the wrangling about arms for Britain in 1940 and 1941.[12]

As Connally spoke on the Senate floor, he could barely conceal the flaws in what Acheson proposed. On the face of it, the objective was easy to define. It was, said Connally, "to make effective fighting units out of the existing forces in Europe." At the time, the NATO allies had eighteen divisions in Europe, of which only one was American while the British had two stationed on the Rhine. But how many divisions did Stalin have? That fall, British and US intelligence toiled over an assessment of Russian strength and intentions, to be completed early in 1950. The Soviets, they estimated, had thirty-three divisions in East Germany, Poland, and the other satellite states, and another sixty in Ukraine and the western part of Russia.[13]

These estimates were secret, and so on the Senate floor Connally and his opponents had to juggle with cruder figures. The imbalance was stark nonetheless. Stalin's ground forces in or close to Europe outnumbered NATO's by more than five to one.

In support of the bill Connally cited General Omar Bradley, chairman of the Joint Chiefs of Staff, who had testified on its behalf. But Bradley had also let it be known to Congress that NATO would need between thirty-five and fifty divisions to deter a Soviet invasion. In the press the Alsop brothers, who had sources at the Pentagon, said the figure was at least forty-five. Numbers were tossed to and fro, but Connally could not refute an obvious objection. To get from eighteen divisions to forty-five would require the $1 billion of aid for Europe to become an annual payment for many years to come. How many years? Louis Johnson, the secretary of defense—an abrasive, cunning fellow who had his own agenda—had said four or five; but even this would take the program far beyond the next presidential election.

As the days went by, the debate ground forward in the way debates do in the Senate. It traveled back and forth over the same terrain, making occasional forays into the irrelevant, until the landscape had been viewed from every angle and every question had been asked. Like a chorus in Greek tragedy, the senators gloomily reflected on the risks that Acheson and Truman wished to run. Was it worth giving arms to allies who might lack the will to fight? One senator mentioned the fall of France in 1940; another defended the honor of the French by recalling their courage in 1916 at Verdun. What about the British? If the Russians crossed the Rhine, would the British retreat to a second Dunkirk? The French high command feared that they would. If they did, and France fell again, then the arms that Truman had sent would pass into Russian hands. The senators also wondered why the Europeans could not make their own weapons with the American machine tools they had bought with Marshall money.

In the wake of the British devaluation, questions of economics loomed large. Many senators shared the view most forcefully put by Averell Harriman: that if Western Europe were to prosper and defend itself, then it had to become a single market, free from tariffs and other restrictions to trade, with Britain an intrinsic part of the community. Until this occurred, or so it was argued, no amount however large of American aid would create a viable Europe united against Russia. There were many skeptics besides Walter George who doubted that such a thing would ever come into being, while Europe still relished its taste for socialism.

It also made no sense, according to some of the senators, to spend so much to arm the Europeans while the British were completing the job their bombers had begun. Under the Potsdam Agreement of 1945, the Allies were committed to dismantling much of Germany's heavy industry. This was still occurring in the Ruhr, part of Britain's zone of occupation. In London, Churchill and the Conservative Party wanted the dismantling to end, and Ernest Bevin privately agreed; but in Paris the issue aroused traumatic memories.

Never again would France allow the steel of the Ruhr to serve as the core of a German war machine. But in Chancellor Adenauer's West Germany both left and right resented the dismantling, and they were lobbying hard against it in America.

Through channels such as the *Chicago Tribune*, their complaints had reached the senators, including Walter George who wanted the German factories left intact.

So the debate unwound in its relentless way. It seems that Dean Acheson failed to notice a brief but ominous digression from a junior Democrat. Herbert O'Conor of Maryland, a freshman in the Senate, mostly followed the unwritten rule that newcomers should hold their tongues and defer to their elders, which for him meant Millard Tydings, the senior senator for his state. But while Tydings did his best for Tom Connally and the bill, O'Conor broke ranks with a sly little smear against the secretary of state.

A few days earlier, chairing a Senate subcommittee, O'Conor had taken evidence from Larry Kerley, a former agent with the Federal Bureau of Investigation. Kerley had repeated an old allegation that during World War II the State Department had vetoed the arrest of hundreds of Soviet agents. As O'Conor told the story on the Senate floor, he accused Acheson of failing even now to withhold visas from subversive aliens. "The cold fact," O'Conor went on, "is that agents of international Communism today move freely across our borders to engage in espionage."[14]

This had been said so many times before that it might have been ignored, except for O'Conor's timing—during a debate about a central element of Truman's foreign policy—and for the origins of Kerley's testimony. Kerley had left the FBI to become a reporter for a newspaper owned by William Randolph Hearst. From its California base, Hearst's empire of newsprint served, on a still grander scale than the *Oakland Tribune*, as an organ of the China lobby. And Hearst had hired Kerley to search for evidence that disloyal officials at the State Department had turned a blind eye to Soviet plots on American soil.[15]

Here was one more sign that Acheson's enemies, including some in his own party, were circling around him, probing his vulnerabilities. Perhaps the secretary noticed this: that no senator rose to offer a personal tribute to his good faith. Although Connally and Tydings would defend Acheson's bill, they would not risk their reputations on behalf of the man himself. Vote by vote, Congress was sliding away from him and from the president.

When the final roll call was taken, the Senate gave Truman more or less what he wanted; but the president's victory was not what it appeared. To anyone who studied the way the votes were cast, there and in the House, one thing should have been clear. Elections were approaching, and the balance of power in Congress was shifting in a new direction.

MONEY AND VOTES

Nobody will ever erect a statue of the federal budget. The subject defies the artist's hand. The novelist Allen Drury avoided the sordid details of taxes and finance. Although his successor Gore Vidal briefly ventured into the area in his Cold War novel *The Golden Age*, it lay beyond even his powers of irony. And yet it was always in matters of the budget that the forces at work in Congress and the country were most plainly visible.

In the House of Representatives, Walter George and the economy bloc had a staunch ally in the shape of Robert Doughton. Born a few months after Gettysburg, he was eighty-five years old and known to some as "Muley Bob." The nickname was a tribute to his stubbornness, displayed to the full in defense of the tobacco interests so influential in his state, North Carolina. He chaired the House Ways and Means Committee, which meant that Muley Bob and Senator George had the power to block any new tax and to reduce those that existed.[16]

Between them these two Democrats had Truman at their mercy. Both had voted with the Republicans in 1948 when they slashed the income tax, leaving a fiscal legacy that Truman could not escape. Combined with the recession and the cost of the

Marshall Plan, the tax cut accounted for his budget deficit, and there was nothing the president could do to reverse it. At the start of 1948 some fifty-four million people—fewer than half of all adult Americans—had been income-tax payers; and then, with bipartisan support, Republicans had taken more than seven million out of reach of the tax. It would be courting disaster at the ballot box for the Democrats to try to make them pay it once again.[17]

To close his budget gap and finance the Fair Deal, the president had asked Congress in January 1949 to give him $4 billion in extra taxes, mainly on business. Doughton dragged his feet until, in July, with the recession not quite over, Truman surrendered. No new taxes appeared. In search of alternatives, the White House and the Treasury mused for six months and assembled a list of tax loopholes that could be closed. On Capitol Hill most of this was stillborn as well. The widest loopholes were those that went to benefit drillers for oil and gas; and neither Tom Connally nor Sam Rayburn of Texas, the Democratic Speaker of the House, intended to allow oil companies to suffer. From political deadlock of the kind, no bold reforms could emerge.

In fact there were only three financial measures for which a majority in Congress would willingly vote. All of them had one thing in common: hard cash in the pockets of the poor or the underpaid, at a time when the high cost of living outweighed the Cold War in the scales of public opinion. Doughton and George most wanted to see a deep reduction in federal excise taxes, many of which remained at their high wartime level. The excise tax on transportation, above all: a cut in the price of a bus or train ticket would mean a great deal in the South. Besides that, Congress would vote for an increase in the federal minimum wage, provided it did not squeeze the profits of the farmer, or evolve into the socialism that George and Doughton abhorred. That fall, a bill was on its way through Congress to increase the minimum from forty cents an hour to seventy-five, and with the midterm elections approaching it seemed likely to pass. Congress was also minded to improve the lives of the elderly, something by now long overdue.

As the chairman of House Ways and Means in 1935, Doughton had reluctantly introduced FDR's original Social Security Act. A loose bundle of different benefits to assist the unemployed and the disabled as well as the aged, it was far from being a universal system. In 1949, out of a workforce of nearly sixty million, only thirty-five million were enrolled in the core program of old-age insurance funded by payroll taxes. Excluded were farmers and farm laborers, with among them the poorest workers in the nation, rural Blacks in the South. Left out as well were most of the self-employed and a multitude of working women, including millions of housekeepers, maids, and cooks, with Black women the most disadvantaged.

Despite the ravages of inflation, the benefit scales had not altered in fourteen years. While the program failed to satisfy the labor unions, neither did it give the poor what they required. The system included federal grants to help the states support the poor if they were aged more than sixty-five, but this only served to reveal the depth of America's divisions.[18]

It can be shown beyond doubt, with an array of statistics, that between the 1930s and the 1970s America became a more equal society—far more equal than it is today—with a narrowing gap between the incomes of the rich and the poor. This "great compression," as historians describe it, came about for many reasons, including the vast expansion of high school education, America's investment in college degrees, and the power of the labor unions. But trends such as these are plainly visible only in hindsight. An X-ray picture of the nation in 1950 would have revealed the distance yet to travel to fulfill Truman's dream of fairness.[19]

Although America had an arc of prosperity, it was balanced by an arc of deprivation. People spoke about a new industrial South, with its aircraft factories, shipyards, and the dams in the

Tennessee Valley, the legacy of the New Deal and the war. And yet eleven of the twelve poorest cities in the country could still be found in the old Confederacy. In Charleston, South Carolina, the average family had to get by on little more than half as much as an identical family in Chicago. This blunt fact about the United States—the relative poverty of the South—had been so visible for so long that it had become another cliché. Even when left unspoken it lingered in the background of every political debate, including those about the Soviet threat.

The burden of southern poverty fell most heavily on the aged. In New York State, fewer than one in ten of those over sixty-five qualified for welfare. In the South the figures ranged from 50 percent in Alabama, Texas, and Mississippi to 60 percent in Georgia and more than 80 percent in Louisiana. Politicians in the region had to reckon with this day-to-day reality and—if they were liberals—this meant that their liberalism had to be practical and direct. In Alabama, for example, Truman had a counterpart in Big Jim Folsom, the governor, who had assembled his own Fair Deal program focused on his state's fundamentals. Folsom wanted better roads—that other urgent need of the postwar years—and better pay for teachers, but most of all he wanted higher old-age pensions.[20]

Everyone knew that the elderly suffered most from inflation. Americans were demanding social security reform; and with only nine months to go until primary season would be at its peak, time was short. Truman and the Democrats, including Walter George and Muley Bob, knew they had to get something through Congress by midsummer 1950 at the latest. Hence some of the agitation about money spent on military aid for NATO, a program which—like the Marshall Plan—competed for dollars that might otherwise be spent improving lives in Little Rock or New Orleans.

All of this amounted to something far removed from the usual drama of a Cold War narrative: daring flights over the Baltic, the exchanges of spies at dawn, or famous words about containment or the Iron Curtain. Nevertheless, these tortuous debates in Congress were just as much a part of the story, forming the matrix within which foreign policy had to take shape. The problem was that Truman's budgets bore little resemblance to anything a Democrat would have endorsed in the decade before Lend-Lease and Pearl Harbor.

Budgets in the late 1940s were far simpler than they are today, and the math much harder to conceal or to manipulate. In his current fiscal year, set to end in June 1950, the president expected to spend about $43 billion, equivalent to about 16 percent of US gross national product at the time. Only a small fraction of the money went to fund domestic programs that would directly benefit his citizens. Despite all the sound and fury about the dangers of socialism and the welfare state, the federal cash spent on the elderly, the disabled, and the poor, and on health care, hospitals, or housing to replace the slums, came to a total of less than $5 billion, or just twelve cents in each budget dollar and less than 2 percent of the nation's economic output.[21]

This figure fell far short of the money allocated to "international affairs," the line in the budget that included the Marshall Plan. Overseas aid that year would come to about $6.5 billion, with the arms package for NATO adding yet another burden to be financed. Congress, so mindful of pressing needs at home, had reached the ceiling of the spending it would tolerate on rebuilding Europe or fighting the Cold War. By far the bulk of the federal budget was already eaten up by the cost of past wars or preparations for new wars to come: $13 billion for defense, $7 billion for benefits to veterans, and nearly $6 billion for interest on the national debt, mostly arising from World War II.

Harry Truman harbored no illusions about the fiscal challenges he faced. He had made the error of appointing Edwin Nourse, a traditional, orthodox economist, to chair his Council of Economic Advisers. Scandalized by Truman's Pittsburgh speech, which had sounded to him like a blank check for extravagance, Nourse warned that if deficits continued the nation was on course for bankruptcy. And although Nourse had fallen out of favor at the White House, John Snyder at the Treasury shared the same anxieties.[22]

In July, when Doughton made it clear that there would be no new taxes, the president had given both the Pentagon and the State Department tight limits on what they could spend in the fiscal year to end in June 1951. The Pentagon would have to stick to $13 billion once again. The State Department would receive just $4 billion to pay for all his international programs, which would mean a big reduction in the Marshall Plan. Throughout August and September 1949, Acheson fought to defend his overseas budget until a compromise was reached, but Truman left it on his desk unsigned. He did not have to decide until January, and so he let the matter lie.[23]

The deficit remained, looming ahead as an election issue. Meanwhile, the arithmetic of Congress looked more and more precarious, and it wrote the script for much of what would follow. In the House of Representatives, out of 434 districts the Democrats held 260, or 262 if one counted an independent liberal and a socialist in New York City. But only 187 of these could be described as bedrock for the party. This was the number the Democrats had held after their losses in 1946. If Truman had studied the data, and added all the other districts where a Democratic member of Congress had won 55 percent or more of the votes, he would have come to a figure of 204 relatively safe seats for his side. This left 58 swing districts that the Democrats might lose in November 1950.[24]

On a map the pattern was unmistakable. Nearly two-thirds of the party's safe districts lay in the old Confederacy and the border states of 1861. Between them they sent 132 Democrats to Capitol Hill. The mountain states and Oklahoma, with its oil and gas, were good for 14. Another 42 of the reliable Democratic seats in the House came from those northern cities where the labor unions were strong, and so too the Black and the Jewish vote. Los Angeles and Oakland gave the party 6 more.

Although the Democratic swing seats were widely scattered, there was a pattern here as well, to be seen in the districts that had flipped Republican in 1946 and then back to Truman's party in 1948. They could be found in places such as Philadelphia, Queens in New York, and the outer regions of Chicago. Swing districts could be found in industrial Ohio, Indiana, and Wisconsin as well as in Seattle and Newark, New Jersey. Most were high-wage cities that had boomed in wartime but had expanding suburbs, a housing shortage, and a sharpening ethnic divide.

Such was the geography of politics. The occasional Republican foresaw the day when he or she would reach out to conservatives in the South and detach them from the Democratic Party. As yet this remained barely even a concept. For a Republican strategist in touch with reality, the path to victory in 1950 or in 1952 would have to run through cities such as Akron and Milwaukee and the Chicago suburbs. If they could, as many Republicans hoped, secure Dwight D. Eisenhower as their candidate for president, then they might sweep much of the country, but so far the general was keeping his own counsel. One other thing they had to do in 1950. They had to fight an aggressive campaign in California, win another of its seats in the Senate, and capture the congressional districts in Los Angeles held by Truman's side.

In the fall of 1949, what passed for expert opinion continued to sneer at Republican chances of revival. While the polls showed the president losing ground, it could not be said that his opponents were strong. The Republicans needed to find new causes to fight for and new stories to tell; or, failing that, an old cause or old story they could revitalize. This was what Senators Mundt and McCarthy were seeking as they went after Harry Vaughan with their talk of corruption in the corridors of power. And if the GOP could find such a story, and inflict with it more damage than they had achieved with the Vaughan affair, then their prospects might be better than the experts believed.

Already the Republicans had a likely candidate in Illinois, where the stakes were high. It was Everett Dirksen, a veteran of the House, eloquent, popular, and running for the Senate. His opponent in this finely balanced state would be Senator Scott Lucas, the Democratic majority leader, who had voted for the tax cuts of 1948 and dare not antagonize the voters by trying to reverse them. The same logic applied elsewhere, pushing Democrats toward the economy bloc and tying Truman's fiscal hands more tightly.

In the August debate in the House of Representatives about arms for NATO, the revolt against Acheson and Truman had extended far beyond the South. The Democrats who voted to halve the military aid for Europe had included four from New York City, of whom only one could be called a campaigner for peace. Adam Clayton Powell Jr., sitting for Harlem, one of the two Black members of Congress, the victim of slurs and endless rebuffs to the civil rights bills that he introduced: How could he vote to send weapons to Britain and France while they still occupied their colonies in Africa? The other three rebels from New York were perhaps more typical. They came from across the river in Queens, where there were Irish American voters dismayed by the shipping of arms to the British.[25]

The doubts about NATO voiced in the House had been identical to those in the Senate, and the same questions had been asked. The House had shown the same reluctance to praise the secretary of state. When the votes were cast, there were rebel Democrats in seven industrial states in the North and the Midwest where the party's grip was weakening. And all the while there hung over these debates the specter of the Bomb.

ANTICIPATING WAR

Senator Brien McMahon, a Democrat from Connecticut, had lived nearly forty-six years in the world and acquired the assets a politician needed for success in Washington. His wife, who was tall and blond, was reputed to be the greatest beauty in the capital. Together they hosted soirées at the city's most exclusive venue, the F Street Club, of which it was said that "to belong to it is the mark of having arrived."

Handsome, stocky, and Irish, McMahon had served in the 1930s as an assistant attorney general in the Department of Justice, leading jointly with the FBI the hunt for John Dillinger, the gangster. An early disciple of Roosevelt and the New Deal, after the war McMahon distanced himself from the left. Seen by himself and others as perhaps a future president, he clung to the middle of the road, and this had served him well.[26]

McMahon aspired to be Connally's successor as chairman of the Foreign Relations Committee; but in the meantime, he already counted among those twenty-odd people at the summit of America's structures of power. Despite his relative youth, he chaired the joint panel in Congress that oversaw atomic energy. On the afternoon of September 22, McMahon went to see the president and was privately told about the Russian bomb, the day before Truman was due to tell the world.

It seems that McMahon had been tipped off in advance. Since July he had been calling, like the Joint Chiefs, for a rapid increase in the US nuclear arsenal. In constant touch with the Atomic Energy Commission and the Pentagon, he also had his scientific sources. Just before he went to meet the president, McMahon rose in the Senate with a speech that was evidently well prepared. Although he revealed no secrets, he mapped out the ground on which Truman would have to operate after the announcement. On the face of it, McMahon was merely defending Truman's request for aid for NATO against the cuts that Walter George demanded. By the time he sat down, McMahon had come close to committing his country not only to expanding its atomic inventory but also to building something still more lethal.[27]

"The day will come," McMahon said, "when the Soviet Union shall achieve atomic weapons. When that day will be, no man knows, but that it will come is as certain as that I stand on the floor of the Senate." Since McMahon was about to see Truman to be told this very thing, his visionary powers were clearly less than supernatural.

Politely disagreeing with Senator George, he made another prediction: "We must anticipate war with the Soviet Union as soon as they have the wherewithal." To those who doubted that Russian planes could reach America, McMahon outlined a terrifying prospect: that the Soviets might place atom bombs in the holds of tramp steamers and send them up the Hudson or the Potomac. "Thirty-five million of our people would be blown into kingdom come," said the senator, who was no stranger to appalling forecasts.

As his senior aide on the Atomic Energy Committee, he had hired a young air force veteran, William Borden, who in 1944 had seen a German V-2 rocket streak past his Liberator bomber. Two years later, Borden wrote *There Will Be No Time*, a pioneering book on military strategy for an age of nuclear warheads and transatlantic missiles. A writer in the *Boston Globe* turned the book into an imaginary World War III in which the Russians launch a sneak attack with upgraded, atomically armed V-2s, only to be defeated when America retaliates. The story ends when the Kremlin surrenders and US Marines land in Russia. Later McMahon sought out Borden and recruited him.[28]

By the fall of 1949, both Borden and McMahon knew that scientists possessed at least the outline concept of a weapon far more destructive than those used against Japan. It would be a thermonuclear device, a "Super Bomb." First publicly discussed by an Austrian physicist in a book published in 1946, the idea had been examined in wartime by the American experts at Los Alamos. In the week when news broke of the Soviet atomic test, it was still too soon for McMahon and Borden to press for an American Super Bomb; but the concept already featured in their thinking.

If you agreed with McMahon that a Russia with atomic weapons would go to war with the United States, how could you refuse to build a Super Bomb if such a thing were feasible? A program of the kind would be complex and fraught with controversy, but in Congress the politics were simple. The alignment of forces made the Super Bomb program all but inevitable.

Again it came down to money and votes, but behind the votes there lay powerful interests that split the nation. Of the ten Democrats in the Senate who voted for George's amendment to slash the funds for NATO, two sat alongside Senator McMahon on the Atomic Energy Committee. One was the junior senator for Georgia, Richard Russell Jr., while the other—Edwin Johnson—spoke for Colorado. Both men had voted for the Republican tax cuts of 1948; both belonged to the economy bloc; and they had every reason to support the Super Bomb.

Coming from a state that mined uranium and lay deep in the country, Edwin Johnson had seen no urgent need to ship arms to Europe: the air force and the nuclear shield would suffice to protect America. Russell agreed, calling for the money bound for NATO to be spent instead on tax cuts as well as on bomber planes, fighters, and more atom bombs. He and Senator Johnson would make effective allies for McMahon if the latter called for a new, still more apocalyptic kind of weapon. So effective, in fact, especially if they enlisted the press to help them, that the lobby for the air force and the Super Bomb could sweep away all opposition. At any time they pleased, McMahon and his colleagues could reach across the aisle to Republican members of the economy bloc.[29]

On September 23 Truman informed the American people that the Soviets had tested their first atomic device. Startling though it was, the announcement failed to send a wave of panic through the nation, perhaps because by now, after Orwell's *1984* and many other prophecies of doom, Americans were used to being told to be alarmed. Besides, the president had other worries to contend with, and the country faced a different kind of crisis.

THE FRENCH COALITION

*I*n Paris the economic shock caused by the British could have only one result. Since the Fourth Republic came into being in 1946, France had been led by a coalition that struggled to govern from the center. One of its members, the socialist Guy Mollet, called it a Third Force, defending the nation against the extremes of left and right. Others saw it as "government by tremors." Crises came and went, some minor and some grave, shaking confidence at home and abroad. Ministers came and went as well. Two weeks after the British devalued the pound, the French premier resigned, unable to cope with the consequences.[1]

Outside the government stood the Communists, speaking for a quarter of the voters, with the largest bloc of seats in the National Assembly. On the right and also excluded from power was General Charles de Gaulle with his own party, the RPF, which pledged to restore France to its former grandeur. The Third Force in the middle was in fact a fractious crowd of socialists, Christian Democrats—known as the MRP—and elderly survivors from the centrist radicals of the 1930s.

If these veterans had a leader, it was Édouard Herriot, now seventy-seven. He had first entered politics long before World War I on the side of Colonel Dreyfus, the Jewish victim of persecution by the *right. Herriot was still the Speaker of the Assembly, his presence another reminder of how long French memories were. Germany remained a source of fear. Would the West Germans swing to the left, and make a deal with Stalin to reunify their country? Or would they reassert their nationalism, and rearm with the strength of the Ruhr behind them? Chancellor Adenauer could not yet be relied upon, because in the Bundestag in Bonn his majority was small.*

Three other problems afflicted the French: poverty, inflation, and Indochina. Until the British devalued sterling, 1949 had been a year of hope and progress. Industry recovered, prices fell, and Marshall aid continued. Even so, in real terms the manual workers of Paris and its region were earning far less than in 1938. Compelled to cut the value of the franc, the government feared the rekindling of inflation that seemed certain to be the result. A ministerial crisis could not be averted.

Although wages were being kept under strict control, some socialists within the Third Force government wanted this to end so that the labor unions could bargain freely for a raise. When their colleagues said no, two ministers resigned. Unable to reconcile the different voices in his cabinet, the premier followed suit on October 5. It took three weeks to find his successor, the wartime resistance hero Georges Bidault, one of the founders of the MRP. He solved the problem for a while by keeping the wage controls in place while awarding extra money to the lowest paid.

In foreign policy Bidault, like General de Gaulle, dreamed of rebuilding French prestige. Bidault detested Stalin, and he backed NATO strongly, but he also wished to retain French assets overseas. France's empire was now known as the Union Française, *a title meant to convey the government's long-term aim of granting most of the colonies a measure of self-rule. But Bidault clung to French North Africa, which he would never willingly abandon. Nor could he solve the problem of Indochina; and that fall it produced a scandal that shook this government of tremors once again.*

France could no more give up Indochina than the British could relinquish Malaya or Nigeria. The rice and rubber exports it produced earned dollars and sterling and sent dividends to investors in Paris, where all this supported the franc. But neither could the French keep Indochina peaceful and secure. Three years of fighting against Ho Chi Minh and his nationalist movement, the Viet Minh, had drained their resources and brought no victories.

As Mao Zedong's army approached Vietnam's frontier, making contact with Ho and feeding him supplies, the situation worsened. Ho's commander General Vo Nguyen Giap was leading offensives in the north; in the south, guerrilla war threatened the rice fields of the Mekong Delta. Partly to placate American opinion, the French proposed to give Vietnam some independence. The last emperor of Annam, Bao Dai, came back from exile in France to lead a government of national unity as an alternative to Ho Chi Minh. Unconvinced, Dean Acheson withheld US support until he could see a genuine transfer of power.

The scandal that came to light in September had to do with a leak of military secrets. Late one night in Paris, a scuffle broke out on a bus between an army veteran and two Vietnamese supporters of the Viet Minh. The police arrived and searched them all. On one of the Vietnamese men they found pages from a classified report written by General Georges Revers, chief of the French army's general staff.

The Rapport Revers *gave a bleak assessment of the war in Indochina. Keen to concentrate on NATO and defend the Rhine, Revers wished to retreat from his outposts near the Chinese border. He proposed to pull French forces back to a redoubt around Hanoi and the port of Haiphong. Revers insisted that to hold this enclave and the south of the country France must have American aid.*

The French Secret Service hunted for the source of the leak of the report; and as they did so, they also uncovered a tale of corruption and intrigue involving Revers and a fellow general. The latter was in

Tunisia but wanted to be moved to Saigon. At the time, French officials posted to Vietnam could enrich themselves through currency swindles and kickbacks. The "Affair of the Generals," as it was known, dragged on until the following spring, bringing attacks from left and right that threatened to undermine Bidault's cabinet.

The Americans watched all this with dismay. Their ambassador in Paris, David Bruce, admired only one of France's leaders: the foreign minister, Robert Schuman of the MRP. Catholic, pious, and a life-long celibate, Schuman had endured jail by the Nazis and then exile in Germany, escaped, and spent much of the war sheltered in monasteries and convents. Bilingual in French and German, and born in 1886 not in France but in Luxembourg, he was also seen as the only person who could do business with Chancellor Adenauer.

In Washington in September, in the presence of Ernest Bevin, Acheson told Schuman that he must find a way to bring France and West Germany together. Schuman accepted the challenge. This would be his principal task in 1950. As for Indochina, Ambassador Bruce—a close friend of Acheson's—tried to persuade the State Department to accept the Bao Dai solution.

Meanwhile, the French in Vietnam strove to make the case for American military help. With General Revers now in disgrace, they preferred, for the time being, to keep their chain of strongpoints along the Chinese frontier, defended by the Foreign Legion and linked by a road called Route Coloniale 4. Seventy miles inland along RC4 was their fortified base at Lang Son. If Lang Son fell, the French officials warned, the Communists would swallow the whole of Southeast Asia.

CHAPTER THREE

AN AUTUMN
OF DISCONTENT

In this day and time a few men, because they
cannot agree about particular items, can almost
paralyze the economy of this country.

—DWIGHT D. EISENHOWER, *October 1949*[1]

N
o one expected Harry Truman to win the Cold War at a
stroke. Against the Soviets any game the president played
would have to be a long one, whether he opted for diplomacy, containment, or confrontation. His dilemmas on the home
front were more acute and more immediate. If the lights went out
in American cities or the heating failed in wintertime, the blow
to his standing would be instant. It might also be impossible to
repair.

During the wave of strikes in 1946, Truman had acted with
determination, ending a railroad dispute by threatening to draft
the strikers into the army. He also seized the coal mines, when
another long stoppage came close to bringing the nation to a
halt. But these were temporary measures, politically risky, and
some might say they merely stored up problems for the future. In
America in peacetime, industries such as coal or steel had their
own dynamics that no politician could dictate.

In the fall of 1949, the end of the recession brought the return of unrest. At one minute after midnight on October 1, there began a strike of the kind that Truman feared and strove to prevent. It was a national strike in steel, led by Phil Murray of the CIO, the second in the industry since the end of World War II. October 1 was a Saturday, but weekends made no difference in a business where the mills were meant to run without a break. The blast furnaces and ovens were gradually cooled down. As the smoke cleared over Pittsburgh, the pickets assembled by the gates, setting up makeshift kitchens for sandwiches and soup.

Across America the steelworkers on strike numbered more than half a million, but that autumn the strife in industry reached out to encompass many more. Twelve days earlier, the coal mines had gone on strike as well. During the summer, the United Mine Workers had staged a long series of partial stoppages designed to run down the nation's stocks of coal before cold weather set in, but now they shut the mines entirely.

The following year, with the dispute nearing its climax, Truman would tell one of his advisers that the coal strike of 1950 was the worst crisis of his presidency. "We desperately need coal," the president said, "and I cannot mine coal with the army, bayonets, and all that sort of thing." More than a third of Americans still heated their homes with solid fuel. Although the utilities were switching their boilers to oil and gas, the nation burned more than a million tons of coal each day. And of course America needed steel as well, to make the cars and home appliances whose sales had helped to lift the nation out of its temporary slump.[2]

That fall, according to the Federal Reserve, nearly five million American families planned to buy an automobile. Another seven million intended to purchase a washing machine, a refrigerator, a vacuum cleaner, or—the most popular choice—a television set. This was the year when, even with a screen of only seven inches, television became a product for the multitude. At the start of

In the left foreground wearing a hat, Philip Murray, president of the United Steelworkers and the Congress for Industrial Organizations, climbing to the platform to address a rally of striking steelworkers in Youngstown, Ohio, October 11, 1949. *Julian C. Wilson, for Associated Press / Shutterstock.*

1949 a television could be found in a million homes in the United States. By the spring of 1950 when the census was taken, the number had grown to five million, giving one in ten families the means to watch Milton Berle. And yet even the entertainer relied on the products made by Murray's men. To make cathode-ray tubes you needed aluminum, but the steelworkers shut down the smelters as well as the mills.

In one way or another in these postwar years, everything depended on coal and steel. Every statesman of the period knew that this was so, not only in the United States but also in the Soviet bloc, in Western Europe, and in Japan. The politics of steel and coal could make or break a government, especially in Great Britain, where this remained the case for nearly another forty years. One consequence was this: an abiding sense of vulnerability that beset the occupants of the seats of power, even in America with its vast resources.

Viewed in long retrospect, the consumer boom of the 1950s and the 1960s might look like something predestined, part of a great wave of economic expansion that would not peak until Richard Nixon occupied the White House. This was not how it appeared in its early phase. As yet it remained impossible to say with confidence that America had broken through into sustained prosperity. There were economists, some of them the finest of the age, who looked back to the 1930s and feared a relapse into a second Great Depression. They had found a term—"secular stagnation"—to describe what had occurred after 1929 and what might happen again.[3]

This fear that everything would go wrong haunted the Truman administration. Inflation remained one obvious enemy, but at a deeper level the president and his advisers worried that human beings with their passions and self-interest would wreck any chance of lasting affluence. From the point of view of both Eisenhower and Truman, the threat to prosperity lay in people's heads, in rigid attitudes and failures of vision. If capital and labor could not live in harmony, then in a new era of industrial discord prosperity would slip away. And by "capital" and "labor" they meant not abstractions in a textbook, but individuals of flesh and blood: shrewd, experienced people, such as Murray or Benjamin Fairless or their counterparts in other industries, men more powerful than all but a handful of politicians. Most alarming of all, from Truman's standpoint, was John L. Lewis, who had led the United Mine Workers (UMW) for nearly thirty years.

"The trouble with me," Katharine Hepburn had said in a film in 1938, "is that I never could decide whether I wanted to be Joan of Arc, Florence Nightingale, or John L. Lewis." By then Lewis had become a household name, an unmistakable presence on the American scene with his vast eyebrows, his booming voice, and his command of Shakespeare and the King James Bible. First the ally of Franklin Roosevelt and then his bitter foe, Lewis was a master of strategy as well as of the English language. He likened himself not to Joan of Arc but to Napoleon.

Both during and after World War II, Lewis had inspired the enmity of politicians and the public alike. In 1946, when the government seized control of the mines to force Lewis to negotiate with the mine owners, Truman had said that he would not appoint the miners' leader as the nation's dogcatcher in chief. Lewis replied by calling the president "a malignant, scheming sort of individual, dangerous to the United States." By the fall of 1949, Lewis had become an ogre to the press, to most of Congress, and to the voters.

He and Murray had not planned their strikes together. The two old comrades had fallen out during World War II, when Murray had thrown his weight fully behind FDR. By now Murray and Lewis were barely on speaking terms and the miners had long since left the CIO. Nevertheless, the combined effect of the stoppages might push the economy back into recession.

Of the two strikes, steel posed the lesser threat. The logistics meant that a battle over steel could only last five weeks or so before both sides had to negotiate. Automakers, the largest customers, kept stocks of steel that would last about that long. General Electric would have to stop making refrigerators on Day 31. At that point, the captains of industry who sat on each other's boards would begin to pressure U.S. Steel and the other companies to reach a settlement.[4]

Five weeks was also the longest the steelworkers could hold out before the hardship started to become intolerable. If it dragged on, Truman might use the Taft-Hartley Act to force the men back to work for eighty days while the two sides looked for a settlement, or, as a last resort, he might seize the steel mills in the national interest. Truman, who still wished to repeal Taft-Hartley, was reluctant to take either step. Meanwhile, neither the unions nor the steel companies wished to have Washington meddling in their affairs.

In the coalfields the situation seemed far more worrying, because the stakes appeared too high to permit a compromise. As oil and gas took market share, and Britain and the German Ruhr stepped up their output of coal, the mine owners refused to sign any contract that would cost them money they could not recover in their prices. For Lewis and the UMW, the strike was also one they had to win. Knowing that the miners would soon see their bargaining power diminish, Lewis was striving to achieve lasting gains before the union felt the full impact of gas and oil and competition from abroad. More wily and aggressive than Murray, and accustomed to operating at the limits of the law, Lewis planned to make the dispute last as long as necessary. He was after victory, even if he had to bring the railroads to a halt or force the Broadway theaters to switch off their lights.

This was American reality: a tough, unsentimental affair, a matter of hard bargaining backed up with muscle, with the nation looking on either with sympathy or, more likely—when Lewis was involved—with weary suspicion. Both sides were grappling with issues that went far beyond the personal clashes between Lewis, Truman, and the owners of the mines. Behind both the coal and the steel disputes lay fundamental problems that Truman and his Democrats had so far proved powerless to resolve.

Neither the coal stoppage nor the steel strike arose from a simple quarrel about hourly rates of pay. Of course both unions were seeking higher wages, but the core of the disputes lay elsewhere, in their quest for the kind of benefits Truman's Fair Deal would have supplied, but that Congress refused to provide. The steelworkers wanted not only pensions but also lifetime health insurance, both to be funded by the companies, while the miners demanded an extra royalty on every ton of coal they mined. It would be paid into a welfare fund that had been set up in 1947 and was managed by the union.

If on their tours of American industry the British visitors had paused to study the miners' welfare fund, they would have noticed that it looked familiar. The fund paid for pensions, for hospital treatment, and for dental care, for eye tests and glasses, and for midwives and other benefits for miners and their families. In other words, American miners had their own version of the British welfare state, financed not with taxes but with the royalties per ton.

There were labor leaders at the time who hoped to see the United States embrace the British model. Not John L. Lewis, too cynical or too wise to trust a government of any party; but they did include Phil Murray, and above all Walter Reuther, president of the United Auto Workers (UAW), who knew Britain well and campaigned for the creation in America of a British form of welfare state. But this was precisely the kind of idea that enraged Truman's opponents. With his Fair Deal all but dead in Congress, nothing of the sort could come to pass, and the labor unions had to fend for themselves. They had to squeeze what benefits they could from U.S. Steel, GE, and the rest, even if it meant the sort of strife in industry that Truman dreaded.

The least naïve of people, the labor leaders knew that they must not push their luck too far, lest they deliver Congress to the Republicans in 1950. Even now, at the apex of their strength, unions represented only one in four American workers. Their pace of recruitment had slowed to a crawl. Unable to penetrate much of the South and parts of the West, where, with the help of the Taft-Hartley Act, states were passing anti-union laws, they could not claim to speak for the nation as a whole. Nor could they say that they were truly disadvantaged.

Hourly wages in coal, steel, and the auto industry were already far higher than those earned by the vast army of the unorganized: store clerks, typists, nurses, cooks and waitresses, bank tellers, and workers in a host of other occupations. These were the people—especially women, who made up nearly a third of the workforce—whom Truman had neglected to address on Labor Day. If the Fair Deal had come to fruition, including Truman's doomed farm policy, which was intended to keep down the price of food at the store, they would have reaped the benefits. Instead, they were left at the mercy of inflation, with every reason to resent the unions if trains could not run for lack of coal or if strikes closed the subway.

Aware of all this, Phil Murray was determined not to allow his members to be portrayed as bullies from the left. That fall he began a purge of what remained of Communist Party influence in unions belonging to the CIO. Like Walter Reuther in Detroit, Murray hoped to define a new middle ground in American politics with the unions as its advocates. The trouble with the middle of the road is that mostly it resembles a cratered no-man's-land over which rival forces vie for power.

THE MIDDLE WAY

That autumn many people were looking for the center ground. Among them in Congress were senators who, like Brien Mc-Mahon, aspired to run for the White House, while state capitals had governors with the same ambition. To the relief of most Republicans Tom Dewey of New York was close to giving up at last, after losing first to FDR and then to Truman. This left their party with a centrist option in the form of Harold Stassen, ex-governor of Minnesota and frequent presidential candidate, a Republican who often sounded like a Democrat. Known as the Minnesota Moose because of his height, his physique, and his love for his rifle and the woods, Stassen seemed to be everywhere that fall. He even spoke in the South, where his party colleagues dared not venture.

From time to time, people would speculate about a candidate for president from the business world. He would be an equivalent in real life of the fictional aviation tycoon with political ambitions played by Spencer Tracy in the 1948 film *State of the Union*, a favorite of Truman's. If such a candidate came to the fore, he might bridge party divisions and plant himself in the middle of the road. One possibility might be Paul Hoffman, the administrator of the Marshall Plan, whom a journalist described as a "vigorous moderate with an attractive smile." The affluent town of South Bend, Indiana, owed at least some of its success to Hoffman, because he had rescued Studebaker after it collapsed in 1933, and then led the company for fifteen years without a strike. While he urged Europeans to forge a single market and copy America's industrial model, at home Hoffman beat the drum for partnership between the government, the unions, and business.[5]

Democrats spoke about another presidential hopeful, the new governor of Illinois, Adlai Stevenson. In Springfield, Stevenson was trying with mixed success to enact his own modest equivalent of Truman's Fair Deal. His private life counted against him, because he was nearing the end of a marriage even more calamitous than Tracy's with Miss Hepburn in *State of the Union*. Stevenson was headed for divorce in an era when this might still disqualify him from the highest office in the land. But if he could jump this hurdle, Stevenson might run for the White House from the middle ground.[6]

To support him in the race, Stevenson could call upon intellectuals who required a standard-bearer. As if in reply to Truman's speech in Pittsburgh, the week of Labor Day had seen the publication of a book, *The Vital Center*, by the Harvard historian Arthur M. Schlesinger Jr., who would come to be close to Stevenson. His book served in the next decade as a manifesto for liberals, firmly anti-communist but leaning to the left.

Quietly dismissive of Truman, whom Schlesinger mentioned rarely and with little warmth, the book dealt more with concepts than with practicalities. Since 1946, when he had written a famous article for *Life* magazine dissecting the American Communist Party, Schlesinger had been fighting a verbal war against the Marxists. Two years later he had seen them at close quarters in Paris, where he spent the summer as an aide to his friend Averell Harriman. *The Vital Center* began as a French treatise might do, with an essay in existential philosophy.

"Western man in the middle of the twentieth century," Schlesinger wrote, "is tense, uncertain, adrift. We look upon our epoch as a time of troubles, an age of anxiety." In a time of total war waged by vast industrial machines, when for many the comforts of religious faith had disappeared, people felt lost and dehumanized. "Our modern industrial economy," Schlesinger went on, "based on impersonality, interchangeability and speed, has worn away the old protective securities without creating new ones." The appeal of totalitarian ideas, he argued, whether of the right or of the left, lay in the false promise they offered of certainty that would do away with angst. As he put it pithily, "Communism fills empty lives."[7]

Despite the faithless anguish that he saw around him, Schlesinger remained, as he always would, an optimist about America. Protected by two oceans and endowed with natural resources, the United States had spiritual assets as well—above all "national ingenuity" and "a stubborn tradition of hope"—which offered the world an alternative to tyranny. Schlesinger had seen the best of these qualities displayed in Roosevelt's New Deal. To keep the flame of FDR alive, he and like-minded friends had created a new organization, Americans for Democratic Action (ADA), with Eleanor Roosevelt as its guardian angel, and among its members

Walter Reuther of the autoworkers. Schlesinger meant *The Vital Center* to be the ADA's manifesto. He gave it a grand subtitle: *The Politics of Freedom*.

A book so thoughtful and well written was bound to attract attention. Even Walter Lippmann, a sage who was hard to please, praised it in his column. But *The Vital Center* was much better at saying what it was against than what it was for. Schlesinger detested Stalin, John L. Lewis, and leftist screenwriters in Hollywood, but he also hated red-baiters such as Senator Karl Mundt. He described them as "Neanderthals." Nor did he think highly of business and its lobbyists. Schlesinger called them "the characteristic expression of the capitalist libido."[8]

Not until Chapter 18 did the reader arrive at a program of practical measures. Overseas, Schlesinger approved of the Marshall Plan, containment of the Soviets, and American help for moderate reformers in Asia; at home he was for civil rights and civil liberties, provided genuine Communists were purged. He liked Phil Murray and he admired Walter Reuther. In language like Paul Hoffman's, he urged the unions to set aside self-interest and enter a new partnership with government and industry. Other than that, Schlesinger was vague. To remove what he called "the social sources of anxiety," he hoped for some kind of welfare state; but he was silent about the details. When it came to the tangible matters the Fair Deal was supposed to address—housing, health insurance, farm policy, and the rest—his analysis petered out after a paragraph or two.

"The center is vital," Schlesinger wrote, "the center must hold." But by this he meant the center ground between competing ideologies and theories, and not the center ground of what Americans actually thought or felt or what they wanted. This Schlesinger preferred not to investigate. His book made the impact it did because, as the 1950s drew near, so many people felt troubled by what seemed to be the new embitterment of politics.

It was the same mood of bitterness Senator Arthur Vandenberg had felt when he sensed a rising tide of anger in the nation. To address it, you would need not only a new consensus of ideas but also a plan of action, pragmatic and achievable; but Congress had blocked the only plan that Truman had devised. So far, liberals of Schlesinger's variety had failed to offer practical alternatives.

In late October, an event took place in Manhattan devoted to the yearning for the middle ground. A festival for centrists, it was the annual speakers' forum held by the *New York Herald Tribune* at the Waldorf Astoria Hotel and networked by radio across the nation. Cosmopolitan and stylish, high-minded but lively, until its sad demise in the 1960s, the *Herald Tribune* spoke for liberal Republicans, a species even then endangered. The forum had all the qualities for which the paper was known.[9]

Besides *South Pacific*, the hottest ticket in New York that fall was the French chanteuse Edith Piaf, singing in cabaret. Somehow the *Herald Tribune* coaxed her along to the forum to perform for the delegates. On the final day they heard from India's prime minister, Jawaharlal Nehru, who spoke about world peace. But by common consent the speakers who left the deepest mark were two men who, in their different ways, both claimed to occupy the center ground.

One was Governor Adlai Stevenson, there to explain to America "the kind of Democrat I am." He believed in free markets and free enterprise, but he wanted social justice too. Government, he said, should be small and local, inspired by pragmatism and not by ideology. Three years earlier, meeting Stevenson for the first time, Schlesinger had found him witty and utterly charming, but later he would also compare Stevenson to an acrobat performing tricky feats on the high wire. It was a perceptive comment that summed up the dilemmas of the centrist. "I have no fixed principles," Stevenson told the *Herald Tribune* forum, "by which every issue is to be automatically resolved."[10]

This was Stevenson's strength but also his weakness. In the battle for the middle ground, if you did not have fixed principles you did at least require a record of achievement; and so far Stevenson, despite his charm, had done little of substance to make him look like a president-in-waiting. He could be overshadowed by rivals who had made their names in wartime. And no one possessed a finer résumé than his fellow speaker on the *Herald Tribune*'s platform, the hero of Operation Overlord.

It seemed to many Americans in 1949 that all roads led to Dwight D. Eisenhower. In his office at Columbia, where he had taken up his post as university president, the general received a stream of Republican eminences imploring him to take a political stand. Governor Dewey visited him in July to urge him to prepare to run for the White House in 1952; and then in September, Clare Boothe Luce arrived hoping to cast her spell upon the general. The enlightened conservative incarnate, spouse of the publisher of *Time* and *Life*, Luce had represented a Connecticut district in the previous Congress. Renowned for her powers of persuasion, she had drawn from Nehru the remark after their first meeting that "charming and lovely women are nature's autocrats." Luce tried the same tactics on Eisenhower, carefully avoiding a direct mention of the White House but trying to tempt him toward it. She went away disappointed.[11]

The general continued to hold his fire, discreetly sidestepping each appeal for his support. Even so, Eisenhower was inching toward the hustings, prodded along by the sentiment shared by so many: that Americans needed to converge around the center. "How I wish," he wrote in his diary that summer, "that both parties had the courage to go out for militant advocacy to the middle of the road." That year Eisenhower gave three major speeches—at

Columbia in June, in St. Louis on Labor Day, and then at the *Herald Tribune* forum—and each time he said exactly this.

The least metaphysical of people, Eisenhower did not see the middle ground as a concept. For Ike it was the home of practical achievers. He was close not only to Paul Hoffman but also to Senator Vandenberg and to Harriman the ubiquitous. Influenced by them, but even more so by his memories of D-Day—that triumph of planning and focused industrial might—the general declared himself for "progress down the center . . . the truly creative area for constructive social action."

All three of Ike's speeches were eloquent and forceful; but they acquired a still sharper edge from their context, the coal and steel disputes. "Two great American industries," Eisenhower told his audience in New York in October, "are today shut down because a few men cannot see eye to eye." Since the early 1930s, when he had risen in the army as a young staff officer drawing up plans for wartime mobilization, he had been fascinated by industry and its potential. And so the general called for management and labor to cooperate with a single purpose. What would it be? "Productivity," said Eisenhower, "the increased productivity that alone can better the position of labor, of management, of all America."[12]

Remove the word "America" and replace it with the name of any Western European country, and you could find here the mantra of almost every leading politician of the age. Sir Stafford Cripps and Prime Minister Clement Attlee said the same thing in London. You would hear it in Brussels and Rome as well. Eisenhower's difficult old ally General de Gaulle gave all but identical speeches as he prowled in the wings of French national life. In Bordeaux in September, de Gaulle had spoken of the need to bring workers, managers, and the owners of industry together "to transform our productivity" and to do away with the poverty that disfigured much of France.[13]

Everywhere statesmen, journalists, academics, and the clergy were issuing calls for national unity, coupled with the warning that the Soviets stood ready to exploit the effects of discord in the West. The sources of this yearning for consensus could be found in the recollections of the 1930s that still troubled so many minds. On both sides of the Atlantic, among opinion formers there existed a kind of political unconscious, filled with memories of the Great Depression, the rise of fascism, and strife between the left and right. These shadows from the past gave birth to a dream of a middle way, a new path to a new future that would avoid a recurrence of the traumas of the decade before World War II. At the same time the legacy of old conflicts still at work—whether they had arisen between capital and labor, from the legacy in America of slavery and the Jim Crow laws, or from the colonial heritage of Europe—could only provoke new symptoms of anxiety.

In the United States that autumn and winter the center proved impossible to find. Politics grew more irate, the rhetoric more shrill, and divisions ever deeper. The tragedy of 1950 would be this: that while the center might be vital, the center did not hold.

THE NAVAL MUTINY OF 1949

October brought with it some resolution in industry, but drift and indecision in the government. On Halloween, Bethlehem Steel cracked first in the steel strike, offering Murray and his union about two-thirds of the wages and benefits they had been seeking. The other steel companies did the same, deals were agreed, and plant by plant the men went back to work. Meanwhile the coal dispute dragged on, developing into a series of intermittent stoppages of work but still with no hint of reconciliation. Already damaged by the five-percenter affair, Truman's prestige suffered another blow that same month when Congress rejected one of his nominees.

The axe fell upon Leland Olds, a New Deal liberal, whom the president had chosen to serve a third term as a regulator on the board of the Federal Power Commission. "I want to state simply and categorically," Olds had been obliged to declare, "that I am not a Communist." Even so, the allegation that he belonged to the far left cost him his career. His nomination failed in the Senate by an overwhelming majority, with the oil and gas industry rejoicing at the outcome. Besides Lyndon Johnson of Texas, the leader of the pack against Leland Olds was the same Senator Edwin Johnson, Democrat of Colorado, who in the NATO arms debate had voted with Walter George and the economy bloc and would soon be pressing for a Super Bomb.[14]

Time and again questions arising from defense kept pushing almost everything else to one side. This could hardly be otherwise. With the Fair Deal mostly blocked, taxes were set neither to rise nor to fall, and unless and until the president invoked the Taft-Hartley Act he and the nation were merely bystanders to the coal strike. Given its scale within the budget and the news of Stalin's bomb, defense was bound to dominate the Washington agenda. The Asia question ran a close second.

For Truman all this might be very dangerous. Forced upon him by Congress and by his own budget philosophy, his July decision to keep the Pentagon's spending down to $13 billion had swiftly leaked into the public domain. It had left him no room to maneuver. In the face of an unpredictable Soviet opponent, the president needed flexibility, a margin of additional resources to meet any military threats that might appear, but this he did not have. Nor did he and his generals yet possess a long-range view of national security.

At this early stage of the Cold War, the strategic plans that could be made were all emergency plans, put together in a hurry and based on assumptions about Soviet intentions and capabilities that often could not be verified. While the Joint Chiefs of

Staff and the civilian officials debated policy behind closed doors, in public Truman had no choice but to sound serene. This only led his critics to accuse him of complacency.

The worst of it was that Truman could not trust the man he had sent in to run the Pentagon. Louis Johnson, the secretary of defense, aged fifty-eight, was only the second holder of that office, created two years earlier to unify the management of the armed forces. A Washington lawyer, Johnson had a history before Pearl Harbor as a loyal supporter of FDR, serving as assistant secretary of war. In that post he had done something for which the nation owed him a debt of gratitude, when he had pushed for maximum output of the B-17 Flying Fortress. He was an inch taller than Dean Acheson and soon to become his bitter rival.

Louis Johnson prided himself on accomplishing tasks that others could not perform. Born the son of a Virginia storekeeper, in college he had boxed as a heavyweight. The young Johnson would show off—or so the story went—by lifting up the rear of a Model T Ford. In politics he had done almost the equivalent. In the fall of 1948, as Truman's chief fundraiser, he rescued campaign finances that had seemed hopeless. Still at a fighting weight of two hundred pounds, Johnson took over at the Pentagon at the end of March 1949. There again he took steps that other politicians would not have the courage to attempt.[15]

It was conventional wisdom at the time that the defense establishment was bloated with waste. Asked how he meant to tackle each task he had to accomplish, Johnson replied, "Get them done quickly. Get them done economically. Get them done efficiently." In April the navy had laid down the keel of a new aircraft carrier, the *United States*, the world's largest and most advanced. Louis Johnson canceled it five days later. In late August he announced something most would see as politically lethal: base closures and cuts that would remove eighty thousand civilians from the payroll. While that autumn Acheson struggled to protect his budget for foreign aid, Johnson did the opposite, placidly accepting the money he was given.[16]

This is not the usual behavior of a secretary of defense. In the eyes of his friends Louis Johnson was acting as the loyal servant of his president, slicing away unnecessary spending. His critics saw him as an egotist intent on a play for the White House even if he harmed America's security. Johnson had remained close to his southern roots, and in particular to Senator Harry Byrd, leader of Virginia's Democratic machine, a member of Walter George's economy bloc. With their support, but also with his record as a New Dealer, Johnson could plausibly seek his party's nomination as another candidate from the center.

Johnson's entourage at the Pentagon made no secret of the fact that the White House was his goal. As his principal deputy he had chosen an old friend, Steve Early, who had been FDR's press secretary, and they cultivated journalists. Favorable stories and interviews appeared accompanied by pictures of Johnson looking stern and statesmanlike. "He is as prominent as Milton Berle," said one writer, "and probably has a larger following. . . . [H]e brings to his new job a fixed habit of success." The following year, the newspapers that had flattered Johnson would turn upon him as a pariah.[17]

Always a divisive figure, Johnson thrived on public confrontation and the high profile it gave him. Far from embarrassing the secretary, the five-percenter stories served his purposes, building his case for an efficiency drive. Look closely at the testimony given on Capitol Hill, and you might even suspect that via his friends in the press Johnson had fed Joe McCarthy with his line of questioning. That episode was followed by a sequel in October, when the Pentagon descended into civil war. At a moment of the utmost sensitivity, with the implications of the Soviet bomb still being assessed, the navy broke ranks from its fellow services in an affair that came to be known as "the revolt of the admirals." It concerned a bomber—the B-36—which, like so many military aircraft down the years, aroused a fierce controversy about its cost and its strategic value.

The B-36 was expensive, slow, and cumbersome. In the words of one of Johnson's aides, it was "pretty much of a lemon." But the B-36 featured as the principal weapon in the only war plan that the Joint Chiefs could draw up. Both the plan and the bomber had Johnson's full support. Code-named "Off Tackle," the war plan envisaged a scenario in which Stalin had captured most of Europe and Britain's airfields were under attack. If this came to pass, the task of waging war would chiefly fall to the long-distance bombers of the US Strategic Air Command.

With its range of up to ten thousand miles, in theory the B-36 could strike at Moscow or any other Russian target from bases beyond the reach of Soviet reprisal. In practice, without escorts to defend it the bomber might merely be shot down by interceptors that could surpass its speed and altitude. That autumn, allied observers saw flying over Berlin a new swept-wing jet fighter, deployed in exercises by the Russians. It might be that the B-36 was already obsolete.[18]

Aghast at Johnson's veto of the aircraft carrier, the US Navy had fought back with a campaign of leaks and lobbying to denigrate the B-36. A group of navy fliers concocted a corruption story about irregularities in the procurement of the aircraft. Although this flimsy tale soon collapsed, the navy could still assemble a powerful case against the bomber from evidence about its obvious flaws. It seemed to Congress that it must resolve the issues with the help of testimony from the very top. For two weeks in October the House Armed Services Committee heard from the service chiefs as well as from their chairman, Omar Bradley; from Eisenhower; and from Louis Johnson. The hearings were remarkable in three respects: the depth of the expertise displayed; the zeal with which the navy rebelled against the Pentagon; and the fact that all of this occurred in public.

The witnesses delved into the heart of the strategic thinking of the time. Leading for the navy, Admiral Arthur Radford made a case not only against the B-36 but also against the very concept of strategic bombing. Could an unescorted bomber reach its target? The answer would depend upon Soviet defenses and radar. Both of these were matters for conjecture, but Radford fielded experts who argued that the Russians had the means to repel an atomic blitz.

Suppose the bombers did get through, what then? Area bombing of the British kind had failed to defeat Hitler, the admiral pointed out; and even with atomic weapons, the problem remained of hitting the target from a high altitude. According to Radford, an atomic blitz would be ineffective and unethical. "In planning to wage a war," Radford said, "we must look to the peace to follow . . . a war of annihilation would be politically and economically senseless."[19]

Here was a serving officer, an Okinawa veteran, in open mutiny against the Pentagon's core doctrine. Worse was to follow. Radford's superior was Admiral Louis Denfeld, chief of naval operations. When his turn came to testify, Denfeld meant to put the case for the navy and its carriers as the best means to project American air power. But in doing so he mentioned two secret Pentagon studies that had questioned the feasibility of an atomic strike at Russia.

So far Truman had seen neither report; but from Denfeld's evidence and from material that surfaced in the press, their tenor seemed to be clear. In response, Bradley and Eisenhower defended strategic bombing, turning the tide against the navy. But it had been a Pyrrhic victory, won at the expense of embarrassing the

"The Ramparts We Watch," a Herblock cartoon by Herbert Block, from the *Washington Post*, October 21, 1949. © *The Herb Block Foundation, Washington, DC.*

president, exposing weak points in US strategy, and supplying the Soviets with indiscreet details. A week later, on Louis Johnson's advice, Truman fired Admiral Denfeld from his post.[20]

Just as the British devaluation marked the peak of Dean Acheson's career, so Johnson's victory over the admirals signaled the end of his rise to power and the start of his decline. His operating style and the testimony in the hearings had sown doubts about his wisdom, his integrity, and the nation's military readiness. "All of our services," Johnson had to admit to Congress, "army, navy, and air, are far weaker than ideal appraisals might call for." Probed about how he would meet his targets for reducing costs, Johnson said he would save money by cutting pilots' flying hours. It was a curious option to propose at a time when the air force lay at the center of the Pentagon's vision of a future war.[21]

The revolt of the admirals left Eisenhower weary and exasperated. Capitol Hill was discontented too. The hearings had come at the close of a session—Congress adjourned in the third week of October, not to return until January—that had begun with the president's call for a Fair Deal and ended with this troubling episode. And then, in a television show in Manhattan on November 1, Senator Edwin Johnson chose to divulge a detail still more sensitive than those the navy had revealed.

The nemesis of Leland Olds appeared in a live debate about the question, "Is there too much secrecy in our atomic program?" Senator Johnson told the viewers that at Los Alamos work was underway to build a Super Bomb, "a thousand times the effect of that terrible bomb that was dropped at Nagasaki." Later he would perversely claim that he was merely trying to illustrate the need to stop up leaks.[22]

It seems that few people saw the show, because it took eighteen days for Edwin Johnson's words to be reported in the *Washington Post*. Another month had yet to pass before the new weapon came to be publicly known as the hydrogen bomb. The president had barely begun to consider its development. Those who knew Washington would draw their own conclusion: that Senator Johnson meant to force Truman's hand. Before the story appeared, the president had won another victory, but it would be among his last. It would take place in New York.

NORTHEAST ASIA

*I*n the words that autumn of Syngman Rhee, the president of South Korea, his nation was "a body cut in half." Since the summer of 1945, the 38th parallel, that arbitrary boundary contrived by America and Russia, had divided the peninsula. A border that ignored natural frontiers, it left many anomalies. None proved more awkward than the territory of Ongjin.[1]

Fifty miles northwest of Seoul, Ongjin was an enclave of South Korea but isolated by the parallel and accessible only by sea. If border clashes were to take place anywhere, they would most likely happen here. Along the parallel in 1949, sporadic fighting had occurred, becoming more intense in May and causing some alarm in both Washington and Moscow. In June, South Korean forces occupied the dominating feature of Ongjin, the mountain of Unpa-San, which straddled the border; and Kim Il-sung, the North Korean dictator, was determined to recapture it that autumn.

On both sides of the parallel, war hawks yearned to see Korea reunified by force. While visiting Moscow in March, Kim had asked for help to invade the South only to be rebuffed by Stalin. In late September Rhee was telling anyone prepared to listen that it was time, as he put it, to "clean up the North." Since he was notoriously volatile it was hard to tell how serious he was; but he said the same thing many times.

In the fall of 1949, neither America nor the USSR wanted war in Korea, but their motivations were entirely different. Both nations had withdrawn their troops: the US army had departed at the end of June, leaving behind only six hundred military advisers and an air force unit to oversee Seoul's airport. But America's position was ambiguous. The Joint Chiefs took the view that in a World War III Korea would not be strategically vital. The State Department, on the other hand, believed that abandoning the South to Communism would jeopardize America's role in the rest of Asia. According to a compromise adopted earlier that year, the United States would give South Korea economic and military aid to help it survive and defend itself. Washington would make no firm commitment beyond that.

For Stalin, insofar as anyone could read his mind, Korea mattered far more. It formed part of the great mosaic of northeastern Asia, fashioned for almost fifty years by the rivalry between Russia and Japan. In 1910 Korea had become an intrinsic part of the Japanese Empire. Rice to feed Japan came from Korea's agrarian south. Its northern regions had evolved in the 1930s into an extension of Japan's interests in Manchuria, with coal mines, steelworks, and electric power from dams the Japanese erected. From all parts of Korea they took migrant labor to be exploited in Japan.

Stalin knew the value of North Korea, its resources, and the factories and power plants the Japanese had left behind in 1945. Whatever the outcome of the Kremlin's dealings with Mao Zedong, Kim's republic had to be kept Communist. Its seaport of Wonsan might serve as a substitute for Dalian and Lushun. Like them, North Korea helped to form a protective shield around Siberia. When Stalin surveyed the region, he also saw possibilities in Korea's offshore neighbor to the east.

The spring and summer of 1949 were a troubled period for Japan. Still under occupation by America, with General Douglas MacArthur in command in Tokyo, Japan had yet to begin its postwar economic *miracle. Inflation ran rampant here as well. In response, America had sent a banker, Joseph Dodge, to apply shock therapy. Japan was "walking on stilts," said Dodge, with its economy propped up by subsidies that had to be ended. Since the "Dodge Line" that he recommended called for a balanced budget and deep spending cuts by the government, some in Japan preferred to call his policy the "Dodge Whirlwind." It was bound to lead to huge layoffs of workers, especially on the railroads.*

As Japanese prime minister Yoshida Shigeru passed the Dodge Line into law, the Japanese Communist Party called for strikes and protests. In a general election that year it had taken only 10 percent of the votes, but its leader, Tokuda Kyuichi, saw the government's new policy as an opportunity. Until now, with Soviet approval, Tokuda had clung to peaceful tactics, an approach advocated by his deputy, Nosaka Sanzo. Now this seemed to change. In June Tokuda spoke of a "September revolution." A long strike began at Toshiba and then July and August saw incidents of violence.

In Tokyo the president of Japan's national railroad went missing, and his mutilated corpse was found on a railroad track. Six weeks later near the city of Fukushima, a passenger train was derailed and three people died. The police arrested twenty suspects, ten of whom were Communists, and their trial for sabotage became a national sensation. In Moscow, Stalin asked for an appraisal of the situation in Japan, with a view perhaps to ending Nosaka's peaceful line and instead insisting on a revolutionary struggle.

All of this occurred as Mao's new republic was taking shape in China. Meanwhile, Ho Chi Minh was gaining ground in Vietnam. In Malaya, the British had eight thousand troops trying to subdue an uprising by Communist guerrillas. It was against this background that Stalin paid close personal attention to the case made by Kim Il-sung for an invasion of South Korea, for which Kim would need Soviet weapons and supplies.

In September, the Soviet embassy in Pyongyang sent its analysis to Stalin. The diplomats described Rhee's regime as weak and unpopular, beset by soaring prices, shortages of food, and a lack of electricity, because of North Korea's control of the coal and the dams. The Russian envoys also saw signs of local resistance against the coercive character of Rhee's republic. Rhee's forces had just completed the brutal suppression of an insurgency on the island of Cheju, with perhaps as many as thirty thousand people killed; but it was thought that dissident bands of partisans were still at large on the mainland.

Kim's arguments were simple: invade now, to take advantage of all this, before South Korea's army was strong enough to threaten the North. The people of both republics wanted reunification, Kim claimed, and war was the only means to achieve it. On September 24, Stalin said no again; but only after a careful review by the Soviet Politburo, led in this case by Comrade Molotov.

They did not object in principle to Kim's talk of an armed struggle. The Politburo's case against invasion was pragmatic. Kim's army was too weak for a decisive victory, the evidence about the partisans was too flimsy, America would probably intervene, and the world would blame the war on the USSR.

Stalin's emissary in Pyongyang, Terentii Shtykov, backed an alternative suggestion: a limited campaign to take Ongjin alone. Stalin rejected this as well. Shtykov gave these messages to Kim, who appeared to accept them. And then in October Kim sent his troops to retake Unpa-san. This caused outrage in Moscow. Stalin reprimanded Shtykov for failing to prevent the attack and told him there must be no further aggression along the 38th parallel. The time was not yet right; but in January Stalin's view would change.

CHAPTER FOUR

ASPHALT JUNGLES

To be a successful politician you have to be on intimate terms with sin.

—WILLIAM J. O'DWYER, *mayor of New York*[1]

New York City on a Tuesday in November: warm and sunny, perfect weather for election day. A breeze blew over the Hudson from the Jersey shore as if to waft the voters to the polling booths. Some voting machines failed to function, while in Brooklyn a Democratic precinct captain took a swing with his fist at a Republican, knocking out a few of his teeth. Otherwise, November 8 passed off without incident. In politics at least, it was a day of calm good humor suddenly descending on the city after weeks of rallies, smears, and rhetoric, with some bigotry but also with principled debate, between candidates whose profiles were as sharp and clear as the skyline seen from Staten Island.

As always in New York, the list of offices to fill covered many pages, but everyone knew where the excitement could be found. Mayor William O'Dwyer was up for reelection. Irish and a Democrat, he was fifty-nine years old, sleek and handsome in the newsreels, a widower engaged to a fashion model. He loved to quote the poetry of W. B. Yeats. On the same day, the voters of New York State would also have to pick a senator to send to Washington.

The incumbent was the Republican John Foster Dulles, Governor Dewey's appointee after his predecessor had left the Senate through ill health. At the age of sixty-one, Senator Dulles was fighting his first election and discovering a zest for combat.

"I am not in New York politics," Truman had told reporters that summer, but this was a fib. Of course he cared deeply about the outcome of these two elections. The Empire State was so rich, so big, and so influential that its politics were always more than local.[2]

Between them the mayor of New York and the governor in Albany employed more teachers, policemen, and civil servants than the army had GIs. Among America's elected officials the governor and the mayor ranked next to Truman in power and prestige. And when the next time came to choose a president, New York would have forty-five seats in the electoral college. Any trend visible here might be taken as an omen for the country as a whole.

While Mayor O'Dwyer was almost certain to win his race, his margin of victory would be scrutinized across the nation. On the Republican side, the stakes were equally high. Dulles and Dewey were closely aligned, so closely in fact that if Dulles failed to be elected, then Dewey's era as the party's dominant figure would also come to an end. With most Republicans already impatient for a new direction, this would lead to a contest nationwide for the party's leadership.

With so much at stake, the election campaigns in New York were bound to be fierce. There was also another reason why these elections had their implications so far beyond the confines of the city and the state. They might serve as a referendum not only on the president and his program but also on the way his party functioned.

It has often been said that politics in postwar America took place in FDR's shadow. In New York City another ghost haunted the campaign. O'Dwyer could not escape the memory of his predecessor, Fiorello La Guardia, who had died in 1947 but would always remain the benchmark by which a mayor would be appraised. Wise, ruthless, and determined, an ally of FDR, but one who retained his independence, La Guardia belonged to a species of politician that in the twenty-first century is long since extinct.[3]

He was a "Fusion" mayor, elected to office three times as a Republican but also as the candidate for socialists, restless Democrats, and independent voters who later organized the city's own creation, the New York Liberal Party. In 1949 there were Fusion mayors in New Orleans and Los Angeles. Their raison d'être was the same as La Guardia's had been. Fusion mayors spoke for cross-party good government, but their defining feature was what they stood against. They were the enemies of political machines, which, for the most part, meant the old urban machines of the Democratic Party.

The big-city machines were the Achilles' heel of Harry Truman. When his enemies called him Boss Truman, this was what they had in mind: his party's reliance on the machines with their taint of graft, their padded city payrolls, and their manipulation of the voting register. And while the accusation might have been unjust when applied to the president, who could claim to have won in 1948 without depending on their votes, it carried more weight when made against a mayor like Bill O'Dwyer.

Some observers argued that the machines were in decline. In Boston two years earlier, the corrupt James J. Curley had broken off his final term as mayor to serve time in a federal prison; and in Chicago, Mayor Edward Kelly, another machine politician, had been ousted by his fellow Democrats. Even so, the Chicago machine continued to flourish, and likewise the Democratic machines in all five boroughs of New York City.

They found a vocal defender in FDR's old comrade Edward J. Flynn, the elegant master of maneuver who led the Democratic Party in the Bronx. To explain the value of machines, in 1947 Flynn had published a remarkable book, *You're the Boss*, exploring the realities of politics. On its dust jacket it carried glowing words of praise from Eleanor Roosevelt. Readers would look in vain in its pages for pieties about the Constitution or the Founders. Instead, Boss Flynn wrote about the basics: how to win elections and to stay in power.

The tactics Flynn described and used himself—handing out city jobs and favors—might be irregular, but for him the end result justified the means. "Political machines," Flynn wrote, "far from being anachronisms, are as modern as the combustion engine, and as indispensable." He believed in the New Deal, and he did not see how it could have come to pass without the kind of politics he practiced. America owed the New Deal, wrote Flynn, to FDR's creation of what Flynn called "the greatest vote-getting machine, both state and federal, that has ever been known." Eager to fire the machine back into life, Flynn and his allies created in New York in 1949 what they saw as the perfect slate of candidates, with O'Dwyer at the head of the ticket.[4]

The trouble was the timing. In the wake of the five-percenter affair and all the innuendoes in Congress and the press about the Missouri Gang, the fall of 1949 saw big-city corruption reemerge as a national talking point. And this was another source of danger for the White House. For the president, Boss Flynn and his counterparts in other cities were threatening to become an acute embarrassment.

As Hollywood knew, Americans found grim excitement in stories that depicted the big city as a dark and threatening place where conspirators lurked in the gloom. After James Cagney's intense performance in *White Heat*, there followed another masterpiece of film noir, this time from the director John Huston. That autumn he began to shoot *The Asphalt Jungle*. It was set in a blighted industrial town where illegal gambling flourished and the cops and lawyers were corrupt. "Just politics—good old dirty politics," says a crooked attorney, describing the way he spends his evenings. The movie ends with the police chief warning of the need for endless vigilance. Without it, he says, "the predatory beasts take over—the jungle wins."

Entertainment though they were, films such as this helped foster notions that would come to shape the politics of 1950. They carried the message that evil stalked the streets and America had enemies within. Books, radio shows, and newspaper exposés told a similar story. And, as so often in this era, reminders of the 1930s added another layer of anxiety. Huston's film followed hard upon the heels of another movie about political corruption, one that evoked more images from that painful time.

Voters who cast their ballots in New York could spend the evening watching *All the King's Men*, because the distributors chose to release it in the city on election day. Although the film was set postwar, few could fail to recognize its central figure as a veiled portrait of Senator Huey Long of Louisiana, gunned down in Baton Rouge in 1935. The machine the Kingfish had created still endured in the state under his brother Earl, Louisiana's governor. Everywhere corruption kept recurring as a theme, feeding what one election campaigner in New York called "a reservoir of distrust" that might overflow and undermine the Truman administration.[5]

However much Truman and Acheson might wish to keep the public focused on the great affairs of state—the Fair Deal, NATO, and the Soviet threat—the American public had ideas of its own. Different forms of worry might merge with each other to create a general mood of fretful discontent. While phobias about corruption and crime eroded the ground on which Truman stood, they came mingled with other anxieties that he could not allay. Foremost among them was the fear of Communism.

Months before Senator McCarthy emerged in 1950 as the nation's loudest anti-communist, the riots at Peekskill in the late summer of 1949 had shown the depths of the anger upon which he could draw. Because the singer and activist Paul Robeson was the target, and because Robeson was Black, the emotions unleashed at Peekskill had been all the more extreme. With his magnificent voice, his outspoken demands for civil rights, and his praise of the Soviet Union, Robeson cut across the landscape of the time. Perhaps the most challenging American of his day, he was loved by some but reviled by many more.[6]

And yet even if Robeson had never sung at Peekskill, the hatred he attracted would have found some other outlet. The riot's origins lay in another story unfolding in New York. That fall, the city witnessed the climax of the longest criminal trial in the nation's history. For nine months in 1949 a jury heard the federal case against twelve leaders of the Communist Party of the United States (CPUSA), accused of conspiracy to overthrow the government. Robeson spoke in their defense, and the Peekskill concert was intended to raise money for their legal costs. On October 14 the jury convicted eleven of the men—two of whom were Black—and the judge jailed six of their lawyers for contempt.

In popular memory, the trial of the Communist Party leaders has been overshadowed by the almost simultaneous trials of Alger Hiss in another chamber of the same courthouse. That autumn, the conspiracy trial drew larger crowds, it caused more agitation, and its consequences were profound. By making every party meeting a felony, the verdict struck the CPUSA a blow from which it could not recover, and the trial paved the way for the intense anti-communism of the following year. In this heated climate of opinion New York prepared to go to the polls.

BROOKLYN VERSUS YALE

The 1949 candidates for mayor had a host of issues on which they might campaign. And since most of them were issues that New York had in common with other cities, the elections here were a proxy for other contests yet to come in the rest of the nation.

The August drought in the region had stretched into the fall, until, as the election approached, the reservoirs in the Catskills were running dry. Water was chronically scarce in postwar New York as the overcrowded city competed for supplies with the suburbs so swiftly expanding around it. Besides new pipes and reservoirs, the city's eight million people also required another six hundred thousand dwellings, or so it was reckoned at the time. They needed new schools as well, to cope with a birth rate now 50 percent above the prewar average. And all too many of the families lived in deprivation. Manhattan, the poorest borough of the five, had the statistics of a city in the South, with a median income per household much the same as those of New Orleans and Memphis.[7]

Everyone knew that these were the urgent problems facing the city of New York—poverty, housing, education, and the water shortage—these and the traffic that crammed the avenues, after many years when the war effort took precedence over roads and bridges. Mayor O'Dwyer tried to keep all this at the center of attention, because here he had a record on which he could run.

Born in County Mayo, O'Dwyer had arrived in 1910 through Ellis Island and risen like a character conceived by Warner Brothers. He had carried bricks and plastered walls, heaved coal on cargo ships, tended the bar at the Plaza Hotel, and served six years as a policeman on the beat. Qualifying as a lawyer, O'Dwyer made his name as the Brooklyn district attorney, sending the gangsters of Murder, Inc. to Sing Sing and the electric chair.

In his first term as mayor, he had doubled the subway fare from five cents to a dime. Many had thought this politically impossible, but it proved his credentials as a trustee of the city's money. O'Dwyer had also built hospitals, schools, and housing projects with the help of his ally Robert Moses, the city's head of construction. Between them they brought the United Nations to New York. With Mayor O'Dwyer's blessing, Moses began to build the bridges and roads that would reshape the city. In the fall of 1949, Moses was carving a path for an expressway that would slice the Bronx in two.

In old age, O'Dwyer would proudly recall these achievements when, for days on end, he recorded an oral history of his life and times. Those interviews would also show him to be a lonely man filled with melancholy and regret. Bitter at the memory of his downfall from high office, he wished most of all that he had never run for his second term as mayor.[8]

Persuading him to do so had not been easy. O'Dwyer had told the world in May that one term was enough. The episode was murky, like so much else in New York, with competing rumors about the mayor's motives and speculation that it was some cunning form of election tactic. But Boss Flynn had gone to work to twist his arm, so had Truman and the labor unions, and so, it was said, had the pope in Rome. For Pius XII, the Catholic schools of the Archdiocese of New York were mighty weapons in the arsenal of faith. At last, in July, O'Dwyer had accepted the inevitable. After a meeting with the president in Washington, he confirmed that he would be a candidate.

In the mayoral race, O'Dwyer had two opponents each of whom represented different facets of the city and the era. On the left was the only true socialist on Capitol Hill, Vito Marcantonio, from the American Labor Party (ALP), a remnant of the 1930s. Sitting for East Harlem, the district next to Adam Clayton Powell Jr.'s, he aroused still more controversy than Powell. An O'Dwyer aide called Marcantonio "the greatest demagogue the country has ever seen"; but one person's demagogue is another's hero, and the congressman spoke for constituents who needed to be heard.

For Marcantonio the issues in the race were civil rights, housing, taxes, and the subway. Like many people then and now, he saw New York as a city in thrall to the owners of real estate and their lobbyists. Rents should be frozen, said Marcantonio, and landlords reassessed for higher taxes that would fund new homes for the poor and the restoration of the five-cent subway fare. Although he was vilified by many—because the ALP had Communist connections, and because he worked for Black and Puerto Rican interests—Marcantonio was strong in Manhattan. He had few supporters elsewhere.[9]

With the labor unions mostly backing O'Dwyer, the principal challenge had to come from a centrist by the name of Newbold Morris. Although his prospects of success were remote, Morris intended to tap the reservoir of distrust that one of his aides had described. Portraying himself as La Guardia come again, Morris hoped to cast over Mayor O'Dwyer a thick pall of sleaze. It was the only strategy that might do the trick, and it would leave its mark in the months ahead.

Six feet three, rich and athletic, Newbold Morris had been an oarsman at Yale. Under La Guardia, to whom he was devoted, he had led New York's city council, a feeble body that mayors either dominated or ignored. The O'Dwyer camp called Morris a Boy Scout, but he was a Boy Scout with means and with some powerful backers. Morris stood in 1949 as the Fusion candidate, selected by the Republicans and the Liberal Party of New York at a time when the Liberals seemed to be on a roll.

At the peak of its fortunes in 1950, the Liberal Party spoke for fewer than one in ten voters in the city, but it mattered far more than its size would suggest. Here was a party that already foreshadowed the urban politics of the 1960s. Positioned in the "vital center" that was talked about so much, and committed to civil rights and Truman's Fair Deal, its membership overlapped in New York City with the Americans for Democratic Action that Schlesinger had helped to create. And at this moment when there were many calls for realignment, the Liberal Party was doing rather well.[10]

Earlier in 1949, the Liberals had won a spectacular triumph in the city. In an election on Manhattan's Upper West Side, they had fielded as their winning candidate none other than Franklin D. Roosevelt Jr. In a district where half the voters were Jewish and conservatives were sparse, the son of FDR had run for Congress against an opponent from Tammany Hall, the name people gave to Manhattan's Democratic machine. While his victory owed something to his mother's support, FDR Jr. also had the backing of two names that would resonate in the years to come. One was a stalwart of the ADA, Senator Hubert Humphrey; the other was Schlesinger's future hero, the young congressman John F. Kennedy from Boston.

With money to spend and the wind in his sails, Newbold Morris prepared for the fray. But to do so he had to decide precisely where he stood. Mrs. Roosevelt could not come out for Morris because in the mayoral race she was pledged to Ed Flynn and Bill O'Dwyer. And while he had his liberal views, Morris could not embrace the Fair Deal entirely, for fear of losing the Republican vote. Facing the usual dilemma of the centrist, obliged to satisfy two kinds of voters and offend neither one, Morris chose to run a highly personal campaign.

Soon after Labor Day he took to the airwaves, prefacing his first radio address with the "Star-Spangled Banner," sung by an operatic soprano from the Met. There followed a diatribe against O'Dwyer, in which Morris branded the mayor "a phoney," a "flip-flopper," and a friend of gangsters. Mayor O'Dwyer presided, Morris alleged, over a city hall riddled with graft. Into the speech he dropped another name with resonance. It was the same name that Senator McCarthy had thrown at Harry Vaughan: the name of the mobster Frank Costello.

When O'Dwyer died in 1964, the *New York Times* would describe the former mayor as "warm, gregarious, and fallible." It was the paper's genteel way of referring to the scandals with which he would come to be identified. Above all, O'Dwyer would be remembered for his alleged dealings with Costello, the theme that would dominate the Morris campaign.[11]

Of all the predators that stalked the jungles of America, Frank Costello was by now the most notorious. Described as a big shot, a hoodlum, and a gambling czar—the epithets were many—he was, according to *Collier's* magazine, "the number one mystery man of the American underworld and the political scene." Born in Italy in 1891 as Francesco Castiglia, or so it was said, he had risen through the ranks of crime during Prohibition. In the late 1940s, any reader of the press knew where to find him. Costello's daily routine, detailed in print, took him from his apartment on Central Park West to the Waldorf Astoria, where in his dark blue suit he would lunch on a whiskey sour, espresso, and baked scrod.

In January 1949 the papers had run stories about a party he hosted at the Copacabana nightclub. Old bootlegger though he was, Costello had seen fit to stage the event to raise funds for the Salvation Army. Among the guests were not only the leaders of Tammany Hall but also a squad of the New York judges they had helped to elect. It was this, the party at the nightclub and Costello's connections with Tammany, that Morris alluded to on the radio.

When the campaigning began in earnest in October, Morris went still further. With each week that went by, he grew more explicit with his charges that Costello was the power behind O'Dwyer's throne. There was a racket, said Morris, with Costello as its mastermind, paying off the New York Police Department in return for allowing the dice and numbers games to prosper. Under O'Dwyer, the Morris camp alleged, New York had become a wide-open town plagued by illegal gambling, narcotics, and prostitution, all of them controlled by Costello and his crew.[12]

How did O'Dwyer reply? His campaign team had somehow obtained a copy of Morris's itinerary. With the help of the police, who issued permits for this sort of thing, they sent their sound trucks to occupy the street corners where the Ivy League Boy Scout was due to appear. Other than that, O'Dwyer tried to ignore the rhetoric of sleaze, talking about housing, hospitals, and schools, along with his letter of support from Robert Moses. To fend off charges that he was labor's captive, O'Dwyer declared that the Communist Party had infiltrated the transit unions and the city's welfare agency. Only he could root them out again.

And yet corruption, graft, and gangsters were stories that refused to die. As Morris was launching his campaign, so deLesseps Morrison, the Fusion mayor of New Orleans, spoke out against Frank Costello. That year Morrison presided over the American Municipal Association, speaking for ten thousand towns and cities, and he demanded a federal probe into the mobster's influence. "A national and international syndicate," said Mayor Morrison in September, "which is reportedly headed by Costello is attempting to seize political power in key cities of the nation." He named Chicago, Los Angeles, and his own city, and he linked Costello to the Baton Rouge machine of Governor Earl Long.[13]

In New York the attacks on Bill O'Dwyer reached their peak when Newbold Morris placed his advertising in the tabloids. *Don't Gamble with O'Dwyer—Tammany Machine Government*, the copy ran, with a cartoon of a slot machine spewing out tokens labeled "Graft," "Bookies," "Slums," "Padded Payrolls," and "Costello." A book had recently appeared, titled *Our Sovereign State*, compiling nationwide stories of corruption. Four days before the election, one of the book's most sensational lines became another Morris campaign ad. It alleged that O'Dwyer had been a frequent guest at Costello's apartment, where "the boys would feast on caviar, thick steaks, and vintage wines."[14]

This detail strayed beyond the facts; but while the caviar was fictional, O'Dwyer could not deny that he knew Costello. Four years earlier, when O'Dwyer first ran for mayor, it had been revealed that he had visited the mobster's home at least once. A grand jury had also found some discrepancies in the mayor's investigation long ago of Murder, Inc. They hinted at collusion to convict the hit men from the rank and file while leaving the crime overlords untouched.

All of this O'Dwyer would try to explain away; but behind the scenes his position was precarious. If he had refused to run again, then the Democratic nomination would have gone to Frank Hogan, the district attorney for Manhattan. Upright and scandal-free, but also close to both Dewey and Eisenhower, Hogan was investigating the mayor, whom he found devious and unreliable. He kept a private diary that shows that his inquiries were part of his efforts to ensnare Costello.[15]

Working with Miles McDonald, the Brooklyn DA, Hogan was also gathering evidence about police corruption. This was not a figment of anyone's imagination. From Brooklyn a picture was emerging of systematic payoffs by bookmakers to the police, running into hundreds of thousands of dollars. The mayor was as close as could be to the police department. He was one of their own. And when the story broke, as break it would after the election, neither O'Dwyer nor the Democratic Party in New York could evade responsibility. Meanwhile the race to choose a senator was reaching its own climax, in a different atmosphere but one equally intense.

In Brooklyn in the closing days of Democratic Party campaigning before the New York elections of November 1949, left to right: Congressman Franklin D. Roosevelt Jr.; Mayor William J. O'Dwyer; former governor Herbert Lehman; John Cashmore, Brooklyn borough president; and Brooklyn's district attorney Miles McDonald, who was investigating the borough's gambling rackets. *Brooklyn Daily Eagle photographs, Center for Brooklyn History, Brooklyn Public Library.*

FAIR DEALER AGAINST COLD WARRIOR

There existed in the late 1940s a group of women and men who proudly wore the label FRBC. Death had thinned their ranks, but those who remained could say that they had been "For Roosevelt Before Chicago." In 1932 they belonged to the small band of the committed who had been FDR's supporters long before the convention in that city picked him as the Democratic nominee for president.[16]

While the most august of them were Eleanor Roosevelt and Frances Perkins, who had been FDR's labor secretary, the group also included Ed Flynn of the Bronx. Determined to defend Truman and the Fair Deal, Boss Flynn sought out in 1949 the most distinguished male survivor of the FRBCs to run for the Senate in the Empire State. This was Herbert Lehman, aged seventy-one, a Democratic candidate who seemed to have it all. He had integrity, ideas, a record of achievement, and two qualities essential for a politician to survive in New York: a thick skin and a sense of humor.

For a decade until 1942, Lehman had served as governor of the state, rolling out in parallel with Roosevelt's New Deal a similar program of his own. Hugely industrious, always with a desk full of papers, he was high of mind and short of stature, hurrying to and fro with an unlit pipe clenched between his teeth. Like FDR, he understood the political value of a pet. In his Albany years, Governor Lehman kept a dog called Budget; and when she produced two pups he called them Deficit and Surplus.[17]

A former partner in his family's banking firm, Lehman had money, but his wealth made neither for arrogance nor for ostentation. In the 1930s he had been a friend of the labor unions and he retained their full support, with Phil Murray of the CIO strongly behind him. From his residence on Park Avenue, Lehman also reached out to his Black and Latino neighbors forty blocks to the north. Few white candidates in America could show a finer record on behalf of civil rights. Lehman would make this a theme of his election campaign.

And yet there were those who found something in him to dislike: the fact that Herbert Lehman was a Jew. Anonymous letters reached the Democratic Party leaders and the press warning that Catholic voters would shun Lehman in November. Antisemites abounded at the time; but in this case they sought to attach their nastiness to a genuine problem that beset Truman's Fair Deal and threatened to divide the voters.[18]

With America's birth rate reaching new peaks, the president wanted federal aid for education. Hardly controversial, one might think; but in the grinding machine on Capitol Hill his proposals had been mangled to produce a piece of draft legislation, known as the Barden Bill, that would exclude church schools from receiving government money. And this feature of the bill had gravely offended Cardinal Francis Spellman, the Catholic archbishop of New York. While the cardinal liked Mayor O'Dwyer, with his school-building program, the cardinal could not abide Lehman's friend and ally, the widow of FDR. In July, Spellman branded Eleanor Roosevelt anti-Catholic and accused her of "discrimination unworthy of an American mother." Her crime had been to support the Barden Bill.[19]

Over the years her opponents had called Mrs. Roosevelt many things, but Spellman's choice of words went too far. Outraged, Lehman sprang publicly to her defense. The Barden Bill had little hope of passage in Congress, and so in late August the cardinal mended his rift with the former first lady over afternoon tea at the FDR estate at Hyde Park. But as the campaign began the issue still loomed over Lehman. Every vote was precious in New York, and a feud with the Catholic Church might be fatal.

To clinch his election to the Senate, Lehman needed a winning margin of at least half a million votes in the metropolis to overcome the Republican vote upstate. And the worry was that the old Roosevelt coalition was beginning to erode. As Queens grew rapidly and spilled out into Long Island, O'Dwyer and his team saw their Irish and Italian voters becoming suburbanites and leaving the Democratic fold. Added to that were anxieties about the Catholic vote in Buffalo, about the polarization displayed at Peekskill, and about the coal and steel strikes.[20]

Similar worries plagued the Democrats in many other states and cities. Would the suburbs abandon the president? Were the unions becoming a liability, as some workers prospered while others were left behind? Would the Communist threat, real or exaggerated, split the nation and erode support for Truman's party? In Chicago especially, another factor was also at work: white fear that the city's new public housing would bring Black residents to white neighborhoods. Mayor Edward Kelly had owed his downfall only partly to his habit of turning a blind eye to graft. He had also paid the price for advocating for integrated housing.[21]

In the race for the Senate in New York, all these issues had their role to play, but so did geopolitics, which could not be ignored. The election could not be isolated from the Cold War, and neither party wished it to be. Both Republicans and Democrats selected candidates who had chiefly spent the postwar years immersed in foreign policy. It was as though both sides saw the campaign as a battle of the titans where the outcome would show which party was best fitted not only to speak for New York on Capitol Hill but also to stand up to the Russians.

As director general of the United Nations Relief and Rehabilitation Administration, Herbert Lehman had helped to lead the first phase of the rebuilding of Europe. His Republican opponent could claim to have been present at a still earlier creation. Although twelve years younger than Lehman, John Foster Dulles had served in the US delegation at the Versailles peace conference in 1919, and later he knew everything there was to know about German war debts and reparations. In 1948, in the absence of Dean Acheson, he had been George Marshall's trusted counselor in Europe. If Dewey had won the presidency, Dulles would have become his secretary of state.

A spiteful British diplomat once described Dulles as "the woolliest type of useless pontificating American." This had to do with Dulles's custom of voicing his Presbyterian beliefs at every opportunity. Mixing religion and politics is something the British always find embarrassing; but few British officials at the time could have correctly appraised Mr. Dulles. As a Wall Street lawyer he had spent most of his career in a world they barely knew and that most Americans would find equally remote and rarefied.[22]

Acting for railroad companies and banks in the 1930s, Dulles had represented the "economic royalists" that FDR had denounced during his second campaign for the White House. Although he spoke out about foreign affairs and religion, during the New Deal years Dulles had remained a bystander to domestic politics. Only in the 1940s did he emerge as a truly public figure, with two aspects of his character bringing him success. One was his undoubted intellect. Far from being woolly, Dulles had been trained as a philosopher and dealt in rigorous logic. Entering Princeton poorly prepared, a youth of slender means, he had failed with his first essays, badly written and littered with mistakes. He set to work, graduated second in his class, and won a scholarship to Paris.

In any negotiation Dulles made a formidable opponent. His other attribute was this: cast-iron anti-communism, grounded not only in Christian faith but also in his study of the works of Lenin. "Soviet Communism starts with an atheistic premise," Dulles wrote in his book *War or Peace*, published in the spring of 1950. "Everything else flows from that premise. If there is no God, there is no moral or natural law." In Dulles's eyes, the Soviets knew no reality but force. "They recognize and respect power in others," he wrote, "but they have only contempt for pleading that stems from weakness or fear. This is the nature of our self-styled enemy."[23]

Since Dulles believed in NATO and the Marshall Plan, he did not wish to launch a frontal assault on Truman's foreign policy. That fall, he was doing his best to defend it in Congress; but, believing as he did that the Cold War was a spiritual contest against a godless foe, he could build another kind of case against the White House and Herbert Lehman. He took as his target Truman's speeches on Labor Day. If the Fair Deal came to pass, said Dulles, it would undermine the nation's finest assets in the global struggle: its moral virtue and its love of freedom. The state, said Dulles, "is assuming an almost total responsibility for public welfare. . . . [T]he trend to statism needs to be stopped now and here." He likened Truman's program and the British welfare state to Marx's dictatorship of the proletariat. "It is because my opponent stands for things like that," Dulles said, "that the Soviet Communists are in his corner."[24]

Although Lehman the former banker made an unlikely Bolshevik, here Dulles seized on a weakness in his opponent's demographics. In the Senate race, Marcantonio and the American Labor Party ran no candidate of their own but instead endorsed Lehman, which implied, said Dulles, that he had the support of the Reds. In 1948, Dulles pointed out, five hundred thousand New Yorkers had opted for the ultra-liberal Henry Wallace for president, and this—according to the Dulles logic—meant that if Lehman won the race with their votes, he would owe his majority to fellow travelers of Moscow.

Stripped of emotive language, this would be a fair comment: the five boroughs *were* exceptional, with an array of attitudes unlikely to prevail in more than a handful of other cities. But Dulles also dabbled in prejudice. Upstate in October in a small town, he declared, "If you could see the kind of people in New York City making up this bloc that is voting for my opponent, if you could see it with your own eyes, I know that you would be out, every last man and woman of you, on election day." This sounded like a catchall slur, aimed at Jews, Blacks, Latinos, and anyone else who looked "un-American." Lehman called it bigotry. He used the same word when Governor Dewey spoke of "a holy crusade" for Dulles, in what looked like a play for the Catholic electorate.[25]

As each week went by the language grew more strident. The election became what both parties wished it to be: a plebiscite on Truman's Fair Deal. Lehman had nailed his colors to the Fair Deal mast, borrowing phrases from the president's Pittsburgh address. His campaign reached its climax at rallies where Lehman and O'Dwyer appeared alongside not only Eleanor Roosevelt and Phil Murray but also—to give the blessing of the White House—Truman's vice-president Alben Barkley. The mayor, who proudly termed New York "the Welfare City," called the two races "a strategic election." O'Dwyer portrayed them as a battle between the Fair Deal and the forces of reaction, pointing the way to the ballots due in 1950 and in 1952.[26]

TRUMAN'S LAST TRIUMPH

On election night the president stationed himself in Washington before his perfect audience, the Women's National Democratic Club. As the voting returns came in, he read them aloud to a chorus of cheers. Fair Deal liberals had won by a landslide not only in New York but also in Cleveland and Pittsburgh, those essential pivots of the arc of prosperity, where Democratic mayors returned to office.

While Bill O'Dwyer swept home to victory, Lehman's win was still more impressive. In the city he took two-thirds of the vote, while upstate and on Long Island the pattern was everywhere the same: a big swing to the Democrats, especially in the suburbs of New York. If it was a dismal night for Dulles, it was still worse for Governor Dewey. The following day, most observers prophesied his political demise.

Late in the campaign some items of news had given Truman's party a tailwind. The steel strike had ended just in time. Rumors had also spread that John L. Lewis was about to call the miners back to work. Best of all for the Democrats, they had made a modest breakthrough in Congress shortly before it adjourned.

In October, Harry Truman had signed into law the increase in the federal minimum wage. To raise it to seventy-five cents an hour had required four years of arduous work in the face of resistance from the farming states, but at last the wage went up. Hedged around by exemptions, especially of workers in retail, who were some of the worst paid, the measure would benefit fewer than one in thirty members of the labor force. It also served to underline the point that the only Fair Deal policies that could pass through Congress were those that cost not a penny in new taxes. Even so, it was a win. After the angst of the past few months, the five-percenter affair, the Pentagon feuds, and the China White Paper, 1950 seemed to beckon the president forward with new hopes of progress.

In New York, however, the mayoral election had left behind unfinished business. Word reached O'Dwyer that the district attorneys—Frank Hogan in Manhattan and Miles McDonald in Brooklyn—were continuing their investigation. The mayor became alarmed, telling visitors that Hogan was out to get him. And while the evidence piled up about the Brooklyn gambling rackets, the Frank Costello story grew and grew.

In that autumn of 1949 a cult of Costello developed in America, an obsession with the man, his money, and the power he might possess. And while the fascination with Costello partly arose from the usual spurious glamor of gangsters with or without guns, its origins also lay in something more profound. It drew upon that widespread, even pervasive feeling that the nation contained troubling forces that might poison the body politic.

Costello encouraged the cult around his name by sometimes granting interviews to journalists. Among them was one of Truman's favorite reporters, Ed Folliard of the *Washington Post*. After lunch with Costello at the Waldorf, Folliard wrote a seven-part series to be carried in papers across the nation. Claiming to show "what has been happening in this era of American life," the reporter described "a shadowland" inhabited by what he called "tygoons," led by Costello: men with one foot in the underworld and another in legitimate commerce. He could not say how big their empires were, but of one thing Folliard was sure: that the gambling czars could only survive thanks to conniving politicians.[27]

Folliard's series began to run in late November. In the same week, *Time* magazine appeared with Costello's frowning face on the cover, and ten days later the Brooklyn corruption story broke. "Lucrative Gambling Rackets Feed Vast Crime Syndicate," ran the headline in the *Brooklyn Eagle*. As yet the police were not the focus of the story—their turn would come in the new year—and therefore the scandal did not yet touch Mayor O'Dwyer directly. However, the momentum was swiftly gathering behind calls for a congressional investigation of organized crime nationwide.[28]

The pressure for such an inquiry could be resisted for a while. Since illegal gambling was a matter for the states, neither the Justice Department nor the FBI could move against it. At first the US attorney general chose to prevaricate, throwing the matter back to governors and mayors. But this stance was hard to maintain. What if the rackets spilled over, as surely they must, into tax evasion or narcotics, or if bookmakers used wire services that crossed state lines? If Democrats blocked a national probe of racketeering, their enemies would say they were scared of what it might reveal about their party machines. Here was another story that would eat away at Truman when Congress reassembled.

For the time being, the Republicans remained preoccupied by a postmortem on their debacle in New York. They had the backing of only a third of Americans, said a new Gallup poll that rammed home the message from the election. Whether they tacked to left, right, or center, the outcome was the same: defeat. The party's liberal wing, chiefly sent to Congress from the Northeast or parts of the Pacific Northwest, wanted them to accept much of the New Deal's legacy; but this was what Governor Dewey had done in 1948. Dulles had chosen the opposite path, veering to the right. This had failed as well. If only Eisenhower would enter the fray on the Republican side: but Ike still kept them at arm's length, spending his days raising money for Columbia University and worrying about the damage the Pentagon's feuds were doing to military morale.[29]

Some Republicans hoped that Clare Boothe Luce would run for the Senate. Others saw the party's savior in the centrist governor Earl Warren of California. Personalities aside, a critical problem remained. While they could combine with southern Democrats in Congress to frustrate the Fair Deal, the Republicans had no rousing battle cry of policies to call the American people to their side.

And yet their position was less hopeless than the pundits said. The same Gallup poll had also found that 20 percent of Americans backed neither party. Later polls during the Korean War showed that between a quarter and a third of voters were convinced that it made no difference which one held office. There existed a reservoir not only of distrust but also of apathy, which meant a pool of undecideds open to be persuaded. If events surprised the nation or if emotions could be aroused, the initiative in politics was there to be grasped.

What if, instead of devising new policies, the Republican Party changed its tactics and its style? The Truman camp was displaying fault lines and flaws that a combative opponent might crack open. Because Dean Acheson and Louis Johnson were by now estranged by rivalry, the chances were that one or the other or both would make some error that could be exploited. The Taiwan question looked promising for Republicans. So did the corruption stories and the coal dispute, and above all the Communist menace. One lesson to be drawn from the New York defeat was this: Dulles had achieved nothing by clinging to bipartisan foreign policy. After the election he retreated to a log cabin on an island in Lake Ontario and began to write *War or Peace*. In the book he would call for a harder line against the Soviets.

To make the most of all this, the GOP would have to decide just where it stood on every issue. It would also require an alliance between different generations of the party: between an Old Guard still fighting the fights of the 1930s and younger activists who had served in World War II. Fresh faces of just such a kind were appearing.

In Arizona in November, a wartime army pilot won his first election, taking a seat on the Phoenix City Council. Barry Goldwater was forty years old and belonged to a local Republican Party pledged to rid Phoenix of gambling and prostitution. Five days earlier in Los Angeles, Congressman Richard Nixon, aged thirty-six, had announced that he would be running for the Senate. While Goldwater made no headlines outside Arizona, Nixon had already become mildly famous nationwide. This he owed to his work in the House alongside Karl Mundt in the pursuit of Alger Hiss. The Republican National Committee (RNC) soon adopted him as one of its most trustworthy speakers. Because Nixon was eloquent, a Quaker, and a family man who had served in the Pacific, the party could safely send him to any venue to talk about the Hiss case and much else.

In August the RNC had fired its chairman, a Dewey loyalist, and replaced him with Guy Gabrielson, a lawyer from New Jersey. A defeat for the party's liberal contingent, his anointing as the GOP's chief organizer would help shift the Republican platform to the right. But for Gabrielson, a young man such as Nixon offered not so much new ideas as an attractive style and manner, a smooth appeal to the silent and the uncommitted. California had a wide middle ground of independent voters for whom Nixon might be an ideal candidate.[30]

As Truman rejoiced and the press scoffed at the chances of a Republican rebirth, in fact the party was starting to rebuild. A shift in its tactics could also be seen that fall in the language of another of its younger members, a Republican senator whom no one could describe as safe or smooth. Joe McCarthy of Wisconsin was volatile, intemperate, and unpopular with some colleagues in a Senate chamber where he broke the rules of deference. But McCarthy had also supported a notable centrist, the Minnesota Moose, Harold Stassen, backing him for the White House in 1948. In the Senate he had mostly voted as a moderate. Nor had McCarthy been one of those Republicans most vocal about the risk of Red subversion.

Only in October 1949, during a feud with the editor of the *Madison Capital Times*, did he begin a war of words against a Soviet fifth column in America. On November 11, a few days before he turned forty-one, McCarthy gave a speech warning that this and other newspapers were the tools of Communism. The following week the second trial of Alger Hiss began. By the time it ended, the Republican revival was at hand.[31]

MAO IN MOSCOW—1

A t last, on November 5, 1949, the invitation arrived: Mao was to go to Moscow. With Stalin due to celebrate his seventieth birthday in December, the timing was opportune. On November 30, Chongqing fell, and Chiang Kai-shek departed to Taiwan. A few days later Mao boarded the train for Russia, leaving behind him a country in urgent need of whatever help the Soviets could provide.[1]

The fall of the Kuomintang had not brought an end to hyperinflation. Prices had soared again in China in October, as speculators hoarded the commodities that were still in short supply. Mao's economic commissars applied a policy they had pioneered in wartime in provinces recaptured from Japan, gathering grain, cotton, and salt into the hands of the state, then selling them back to the people at guaranteed prices fixed in their new currency, the renminbi. Not until the spring of 1950 would this begin to bring some stability.

With Mao on the train came Stalin's personal envoy, Ivan Kovalev. He occupied his time writing a report on China that portrayed a government in chaos. To Kovalev, Mao seemed nervous, even frightened, at the prospect of meeting the Soviet leader. His health was poor. Russian doctors would find that Mao, a heavy smoker, had arterial disease and an early stage of emphysema. On the journey he caught a cold, and in Moscow he would suffer from dizzy spells and frequent headaches.

Mao's stay in Moscow began badly. At the railroad station on December 16, Molotov was waiting to greet him with other members of the Politburo; but Mao found them stiff, unfriendly, even rude. This did not bode well. Mao's primary aim was to obtain a new treaty to replace the one the Kuomintang had signed with the Soviets in 1945. Since October observers in the West had been saying that this was Mao's objective; and if a new treaty failed to emerge, they would see it as a sign of what Secretary Acheson believed would come to pass, a split between China and the USSR. The cold reception Mao was given at the station left him disappointed and uneasy, worried perhaps that such a split might occur.

That evening at the Kremlin, Mao met Stalin for two hours. First Mao spoke about China's economic plight; but when he turned to the subject of a new treaty, Stalin replied with a clear refusal. He could not give up Russia's naval base at Lushun or the Chinese Changchun Railroad without endangering the other agreements reached at Yalta. This Stalin would not do. Mao left the meeting without a timetable for further discussions. Consigned to a dacha in a Moscow suburb, he grew agitated.

By now the Kremlin halls were filled with gifts for Stalin, some of them appropriate and some bizarre. Freight cars arrived from Warsaw bearing presents. Communists in Paris sent nylon stockings, while from Romania a radio arrived that lit up with Stalin's picture when it was tuned in to broadcasts from Moscow. On December 21, Stalin's birthday, Pravda devoted its entire issue to flattery from the Politburo. Malenkov wrote of Stalin's policy of "peaceful coexistence" with the capitalist powers. Beria declared that thanks to Comrade Stalin, Soviet industry now ranked second only to America's.

That evening at the Bolshoi Theater, Mao gave a birthday speech in Stalin's honor, but spent the rest of the occasion seated in silence. The following day at the Kremlin he endured a five-hour banquet, *which, according to one eyewitness, left Mao sullen and exhausted. The greatest ballerina of the day, Maya Plisetskaya, nervously danced a sequence from a Russian classic. Scared that she might slip and fall, she also dared not let her eyes meet Stalin's: her father had been shot in a purge in 1938. Plisetskaya saw Stalin murmur something to Mao. What, she asked herself, "were the ones who control fates talking about?"*

Secluded at the dacha once again, with still no schedule for negotiations, Mao grew restless. In an atmosphere of mutual suspicion the time dragged by. Kovalev gave Stalin his report, warning him that in Beijing there were pro-Americans and saboteurs. Later that day, the twenty-fourth, Mao and Stalin met again. During four hours of inconclusive talks, there was still no mention of a treaty; Stalin chiefly wished to discuss the prospects for the Communists in Japan and Indochina. Again Mao came away from the meeting without a promise of another conversation.

Mao felt he must bring things to a head. In the dacha he raged in front of Kovalev, pounding a table. Describing the scene in later years, Mao recalled the words he had used as he complained about the lack of progress: "I said that I have three tasks here: first to eat, second to sleep, and third to shit." Whether Mao's fury was genuine or feigned, it had its effect. The dacha was bugged, and in due course Molotov arrived. He had been sent to assess the Chinese leader. Foreign diplomats had often found Molotov impossible, with his habit of long silences broken only by the repetition of a rigid Moscow line. It is said that he merely listened impassively to Mao.

In treating Mao in such a way, keeping him at bay in the dacha, what was Stalin seeking to achieve? Did he fear that Mao might be another Marshal Tito, pursuing Chinese interests alien from Moscow's? Or did Stalin merely mean to demonstrate that the Soviets were still the senior partner, despite the scale of Mao's military success? This was scarcely necessary. Or was Stalin responding to developments abroad?

From Washington reports arrived of debates underway within the Pentagon and the State Department about America's future role in Asia. Since the middle of November, it had also been an open secret in London that the British would give diplomatic recognition to Mao's new republic. India seemed poised to do the same. Was Stalin waiting to see what moves they made? Then or later, no one could be certain why Stalin behaved as he did; but his tactics of delay could not be sustained for long.

The outside world knew that Mao had been at Stalin's side at the Bolshoi. They had heard nothing since. If the silence were prolonged into 1950, speculation would begin to mount about perhaps a terminal rift between the two leaders. At the Kremlin meanwhile, Molotov reported back, advising Stalin to see Mao again. On December 30 India recognized Red China. Two days later, as January began the diplomatic logjam broke in Moscow.

CHAPTER FIVE

FROM CINCINNATI TO TAIWAN

We had for some reason this pro-Communist attitude in the State Department.

—SENATOR ROBERT A. TAFT, *December 30, 1949*[1]

I t was once said of Franklin Roosevelt that while other leaders won renown for their defiant gestures—Churchill's V for Victory, or Hitler's *Sieg Heil*—FDR simply licked a finger and held it in the air to see which way the wind was blowing. The observation came from Clare Boothe Luce. She had in mind Roosevelt's tireless maneuvers to keep abreast of shifts in public opinion. At the end of 1949 this was precisely the talent that American politics required.[2]

Three years later Dwight Eisenhower would win a presidential election, an outcome that many at the time and since have seen as a great turning point in the life of the nation. Up to a point it was, since Eisenhower's victory ended the long years of Democratic Party dominance and brought a transition in foreign policy from Dean Acheson to John Foster Dulles. But that election was really lost and won long before the fall of 1952.

"Korea, Communism, and Corruption"—these, it was said at the time, were the issues that gave Ike his triumph over Adlai

Stevenson. They first began to flow together in the closing days of 1949 and early in 1950. There took place a very American sequence of events: a foreign policy crisis and a national security scare coming in a season when the coal strike, the tales of corruption, and the disarray at the Pentagon had already created a mood of unrest and damaged the president's reputation. The result was a turning of the tide of political opinion of just the kind that FDR's antennae would have registered, but which the Democratic Party of Harry Truman did not recognize until it was too late.

The crisis in foreign policy had to do with Asia. It arose, as such crises mostly do, from the impossibility of finding permanent answers to enduring questions that recurred to trouble each new administration. In almost every decade since the 1890s, when the great powers sought to disassemble China into rival spheres of influence, Americans had been obliged to think hard about their Asian strategy. Four great events had taken place: Japan's defeat of Russia in 1904–1905, its war against China that began in 1937, Pearl Harbor and the Pacific conflict that followed, and then the triumph of Mao Zedong. Each one was a chapter in a long narrative about imperial rivalry in the region, about Japan's rebirth as a great power, and about China's arduous struggle to free itself from external domination.

If Japan was emerging as an industrial and naval force in the world, how should America respond? The answers that came from Washington had varied from one presidency to another; but the question never vanished. When the atom bombs fell on Hiroshima and Nagasaki and Japan surrendered in 1945, the nature of the question changed, but the United States now found itself all the more deeply involved in the affairs of its former enemy. Likewise with China. Here the questions were harder to frame, because China was still so poor, so agrarian, and so divided; but when the Western imperialists and Russia scrambled for influence there in the years around 1900, they did so because they saw China's vast potential. The United States could not permit either China as a whole or its most essential regions to fall into the hands of its rivals or enemies. And yet this was precisely what had threatened to occur so many times in the first half of the century.

In practice, the great questions about Asia tended to be broken down in Washington into smaller puzzles that different parts of the government were supposed to try to solve. At the end of 1949, in the aftermath of Communist victory in China, the State Department and the Joint Chiefs of Staff were struggling with them yet again. On the one hand, they had to find a new grand strategy for Asia as a whole, including Japan; on the other, they had to assess in detail what the new Red China meant for their defenses in the Pacific.

Where should the American perimeter be drawn? Here was a question that had persisted ever since the United States first occupied the Philippines in 1898. The trauma of Pearl Harbor and then the Battle of Midway in 1942 had shown how high the stakes might be. Never again would America's armed forces allow themselves to be pushed back to Hawaii, or to be deprived, as they were in 1941, of their freedom of navigation to Australia, Singapore, and the Chinese mainland. But with the onset of the Cold War the question of just where to draw the line of defense had reached a much higher level of complexity. There were new elements in play: the need to ensure the safety of Japan, the threat from Soviet submarines and aircraft, the risk of more Communist uprisings in Southeast Asia, and the question of how to share the burden of regional defense with the French and British.[3]

None of this could be resolved on a map table in the Pentagon. After the budget cuts pushed through by Secretary of Defense Louis Johnson, resources would be thinly stretched. The decision about what to defend and where to put the ships, troops, and airplanes would be less strategic than political; and, in the atmosphere of Christmas 1949, any solutions the Truman administration offered would produce a fierce contest on the terrain of public opinion. As the end of the year approached, the strongest, most distinctive personalities in American politics and the military would collide around the subject of Asia. Among them was the man his admirers called "Mister Republican."

An Enemy of the People

If there was a member of the GOP who felt most deeply the need for the party to sharpen its edge, that man was Senator Robert A. Taft, its de facto leader in Congress. "The only way to handle Truman," Taft had written earlier that year, "was to hit him every time he opened his mouth." In November 1950, Taft would be up for reelection in Ohio. Already he was organizing hard. As he did so, he became all the more aggressive.[4]

Ohio belonged to the arc of prosperity, and on that battlefield Bob Taft's greatest enemies—the labor unions—were strong, and their banners plainly visible. Knowing that he had them and their money against him, Taft had begun his campaign in the fall. While Congress was in recess, other senators boarded PanAm Clippers to tour the world. Taft stuck to the highways and the country roads. He drove his own car from his home in Cincinnati to every corner of the state, pausing only for brief trips back to Washington, where his staff were assembling ammunition for the next session of the Senate.

Taft called the tour his "report to the people." During his journeys around Ohio, he tried not only to gauge the mood of the Midwest but also to nudge it along the path he wished it to follow. As he freely admitted, Taft intended to arouse the apathetic and to provoke them to share his sense of crisis. In the spring he had begun a weekly radio show. By December—with the blunt turn of phrase for which he was famous—he was telling his listeners that too many of them simply did not care. Truman's deficit, high taxes, the loss of China, universal health insurance, and the Brannan Plan for farmers: between them they might spell the death of liberty. So might those Americans too lazy or too smug to venture an opinion or to vote. "That attitude of mind," said Taft, "is likely to bring an end altogether to the theory of a free people running their government."

To jolt the voters out of their complacency, the senator would have to mount constant attacks against Truman and those around him. In the circumstances of the day, this enterprise was almost certain to involve anti-communism of the fiercest kind. What we have come to remember as McCarthyism might also be described as merely the wild side of Taftism.[5]

Coming from a Republican as exalted as Bob Taft, the case against the Truman administration would carry all the more weight. During his journeys around Ohio, the senator passed his sixtieth birthday. As the son of a president, William Howard Taft, he had started ahead of the field in the race for name recognition; but Bob Taft also had an image that could not be mistaken. His bald head, his eyeglasses, and his habit, like a college dean's, of wagging his finger up and down to emphasize each point he made: Taft was a gift to front page and newsreel alike.

The Democrat Sam Rayburn, Speaker of the House of Representatives, dismissed Bob Taft as "a small man with an excellent press." This was more a tribute to the trouble Taft caused for the Democratic Party than a balanced view. It was also said at the time that Taft ranked second only to former Supreme Court justice Louis Brandeis among the most brilliant graduates of Harvard Law School. In the opinion of many, Taft was the finest debater and maker of new laws that America possessed. He studied hard, he fought hard, and he did not surrender.

Some saw him as a gifted man whose ambition led him to strike attitudes that went to extremes, so that he displayed what the journalist John Gunther called "an almost pathological setness of vision and stubbornness." Taft's admirers pointed to his record of achievement in the Senate. Conservative though he was, in favor of small budgets and always a critic of the New Deal, Taft had also promoted measures that some might call liberal. The miners' leader John L. Lewis described him as "an enemy of the people," because of the Taft-Hartley Act that bore his name. Others believed that Taft's conservatism was compassionate.[6]

"For all the deceptive coloration of his rhetoric," Arthur M. Schlesinger Jr. had written in 1947, "Taft can no longer be regarded as the arch-reactionary." What Schlesinger had in mind was the Housing Act ultimately passed by Congress in the summer of 1949 to provide federal money for slum clearance and public housing. This was the law that would help New York and other cities build their housing projects in the years to come. Democrats liked to claim it as a victory for Truman's Fair Deal measure. In reality the Housing Act was largely Taft's handiwork, the fruit of three years of attention to detail and of many tussles with his own party.

With his housing bill enacted, Taft could turn his mind to the issue where he was weakest. Before Pearl Harbor, his watchword in foreign policy had been "America First." Taft's enemies still threw at him the many foolish things he had said in 1941, when he poured scorn on the notion that Japan might attack the United States. The charge that Taft had been a blinkered isolationist was all the easier to revive when he voted against the NATO treaty and the shipments of arms to Europe.

If he were to run for president in 1952, Taft could not afford to be portrayed as merely a narrow-minded naysayer in foreign affairs. He had to engage more closely with the subject and advance his own view of what America should do abroad. Like Dulles, who was now immersed in the writing of his book, the senator also harbored doubts about the Truman cabinet's posture toward the Soviets. Nor did he trust the secretary of state. The antipathy was mutual. In an angry exchange on Capitol Hill in 1944, Dean Acheson had called Taft "unscrupulous" after Taft opposed his pride and joy, the Bretton Woods system for managing the dollar and other currencies worldwide.[7]

As Yale men who both sat on the board of their alma mater, Taft and Acheson had to try to keep their differences within the bounds of decorum. But in December 1949, with Congress due to reassemble soon, Taft had to define a new, more positive doctrine of his own. This he would do with a long statement of principles that he gave at the end of that month in an interview with a newspaper in Dayton. He also had to couple his policy ideas with the aggression he thought necessary to galvanize the voters. All of this would lead with a logic of its own to the notion that would become so potent in 1950: the charge that the State Department was pro-communist.

To bring the issues to a head, Senator Taft required an urgent question he could raise when Congress reconvened. He would find it on an island at the entrance to the South China Sea.

THE TAIWAN QUESTION

All year the issue of Taiwan (or Formosa, as Americans still called it) had been drawing nearer to America's horizon. At last it could no longer be ignored or pushed aside. Nor could Truman or Acheson delay much longer the publication of their new policy for Asia. For this the deadline was the first week of January, when Congress would meet again and the president would have to be ready with his State of the Union address.

At the end of October, Acheson believed that he had settled the matter of Taiwan when, at the National Security Council, Truman approved his recommended policy: a firm refusal to give even the most basic of military aid to the Kuomintang in their efforts to hold the island. Acheson believed that Taiwan would fall to Mao

"Senator Taft's Foreign Policy," by Daniel Fitzpatrick, from the *St. Louis Post-Dispatch*, January 15, 1950. *St. Louis Post-Dispatch Editorial Cartoon Collection, State Historical Society of Missouri, Columbia Research Center.*

by the end of 1950; that any arms America sent would be taken by the Communists; and that US military support would merely jeopardize the wider Asian strategy that his adviser Philip Jessup was striving to develop in his professorial style. On November 3 the news was given to a smiling and courteous Chiang Kai-shek in the Taiwanese capital of Taipei. At the time, the generalissimo had one foot there and another still in his mainland China base at Chongqing.[8]

Only one feature of the meeting appeared to have troubled Chiang's serenity. Chiang took offense at Acheson's warning that America would suspend any more economic aid until the KMT could prove that its regime on Taiwan would be free from the kind of misrule that the China White Paper had narrated at such length. On November 9, as the Communist army closed in on Chongqing, Chiang formally replied to Acheson's message. He promised that the KMT on Taiwan would pursue land reform, democracy, and good government. Then he asked again for money and for military aid in the form of American advisers.

A week later, Acheson refused this request as well. And with that, as far as the State Department was concerned, the Taiwan question ended. But the generalissimo did not yield so easily. On the island he would soon have three hundred thousand soldiers and a million refugees who had fled from the mainland. In America he could call upon the China lobby and his ambassador Wellington Koo in Washington. Above all, he had perhaps his most effective weapon, his spouse Madam Chiang, in splendid residence in a mock Tudor mansion in the New York suburb of Riverdale. As clearly as any Republican in Congress, she and Ambassador Koo could see the schisms in the Truman camp.[9]

Within days of quelling the revolt of the admirals, the defense secretary took up the KMT's cause. Louis Johnson's aides had been privately meeting with Ambassador Koo; and then on October 22, Johnson went to Riverdale for dinner. Since midsummer he had been letting it be known that he did not think much of Acheson's Asian strategy, or rather his lack of one. Although the two men were supposed to be working together to report to Truman about the Super Bomb, Secretary Johnson had no qualms about undermining his colleague.

Soon after his tête-à-tête with Madam Chiang, Johnson asked the army chief of staff for a new report about Taiwan's defensibility. The general in question was Joseph Lawton Collins—"Lightning Joe"—famed for his exploits after D-Day, when around the French town of Saint-Lô he had led the armored breakout from Normandy. He could not tell a lie; and besides, the Pentagon had thick files about Taiwan, dating from 1943 and 1944 when the decision had to be made between this island and Luzon as a target for assault.[10]

At that time, the US high command had opted against a landing on Taiwan for reasons that included its difficult shoreline and its mountainous interior. Lightning Joe and his staff also knew that the Japanese had left the island with a robust infrastructure of railroads, highways, and airfields. Collins would therefore have to confirm that Taiwan could be made impregnable against an assault from mainland China. There were powerful strategic arguments for doing just this. Many months earlier, the Joint Chiefs had already warned that the loss of Taiwan would severely damage America's interests in the region.

If Taiwan fell into Communist hands, Japan would lose an essential source of food supplies. And if and when Mao created a new air force, aircraft based on the island would threaten not only Okinawa and the Philippines but also the sea lanes southward to the British in Malaya. If the Joint Chiefs were asked a direct question—Could the island be defended?—they would have to reply that it could. Whether Taiwan *had* to be defended, whether it *should* be defended, and whether the Joint Chiefs had the budget to do so: those were different matters, but as the end of 1949 drew near they remained a subject for fierce controversy that Acheson had so far failed to put to rest.

Meanwhile the politics continued to ferment. Among those senators who used the recess for foreign travel were a trio of Republicans who went to Asia. The first to return was Alexander Smith of New Jersey. He had seen both Chiang Kai-shek and General MacArthur and sought an audience with Acheson to tell him what he had learned.

No one could call Senator Smith a troublemaker. A devoted son of Princeton, where he had studied under Woodrow Wilson, Smith was nearly seventy and had come to electoral politics late in life. In foreign policy he wished to remain bipartisan. But he insisted to Acheson on November 30 that the United States must hold Taiwan "by any means short of actual war." If that meant military occupation, then so be it. The following day Smith told the press that this was what MacArthur wanted. He went further and urged the president to override Acheson and Jessup and make the general America's mastermind of Asian strategy.[11]

Lose the support of a moderate such as Alexander Smith, and you might as well concede that bipartisan consensus was doomed. It suffered another blow when another Republican flew home, Senator Homer Ferguson of Michigan. He, too, had visited MacArthur in Japan. On December 6, Ferguson repeated what Smith had said and framed another question for Acheson to answer. Where should America place its perimeter in Asia? From Japan to Indonesia, by way of Okinawa, Taiwan, and the Philippines, said Ferguson. "When I get back to Washington," he told the press in Honolulu, "I'm going to see Louis Johnson and lay the cards on the table."[12]

This was just what Johnson wished to hear. In late November an exhausted Harry Truman had left Washington to recover with a break at Key West. While he was in Florida, sly stories began to circulate to the effect that he had lost confidence in the secretary of defense. In the wake of his feud with the navy, the press was beginning to turn against Louis Johnson. As December wore on, the man who had lifted up a Model T Ford prepared for the inevitable: a test of strength against Acheson with Taiwan as the pretext. Once again Johnson would draw Lightning Joe and General Omar Bradley into a quarrel and expect them to give him their full support.

The issues became still more pressing when Chongqing surrendered. Now that China was all but overrun by the People's Liberation Army, in London the foreign secretary Ernest Bevin was keen to recognize Mao's republic as soon as possible, and probably early in the new year. With Hong Kong to be protected, British businesses still clinging on in Shanghai, and the Chinese diaspora so prominent in Malaya and Singapore, the Labour government had every reason to do so. In international law their case for recognition was solid. The British had also lost all sympathy for the Kuomintang, whose aircraft had attacked their merchant ships.[13]

Would Acheson follow suit and ask the president to recognize Mao's regime? He would not, and even if he had, Truman would have said no; but this was another question Acheson's enemies were keen to make him answer. On December 7 the last of the roaming Republicans landed in America after a long flight from Asia. At forty-one, the same age as Joseph McCarthy, Senator William Knowland of California was as youthfully fiery as his colleague from Wisconsin. To add fuel to his flames, Knowland also had the funds for the China region that he had extracted from the Democratic senator Tom Connally during the negotiations about the NATO arms package. Accusing the British of appeasing a dictator, as they had done at Munich in 1938, Knowland called for the money to be spent to defend Taiwan. Three days later, Chiang and the KMT made the island their official home.[14]

In the weeks that followed, Knowland toured the West Coast, telling his listeners how he had escaped from Chongqing just before it fell. He called for Acheson to fire all the Asia specialists on his staff. "The policy the State Department has been following in China," said the senator, "has given aid and comfort to the Communists." From here it was not so great a leap to the charge that Taft would bring, that the department had consciously encouraged Mao's victory; and then, if the atmosphere in Washington grew still more poisonous, it would require only another modest jump to reach McCarthy's claim that Foggy Bottom was a nest of Soviet spies.

That would not come until February. In December, Knowland's rhetoric was strong but still restrained. Above all, he wanted a debate on every aspect of the Asian crisis the moment the Senate met again. On his travels he had visited not only China, Taiwan, and Japan; he had also touched down in Seoul. Behind the Taiwan question there loomed, like the next peak in a mountain range, the question of Korea. Meanwhile, the State Department labored to clarify its thinking about the Far East.

Mr. Kennan and Professor Jessup

Philip Jessup liked to be methodical. Months had passed since the end of July, when the ambassador had begun his review of the United States' Asia policy. Not until January would he and Mrs. Jessup travel to Tokyo to meet General MacArthur and tour the region. He was "taking a slow boat to China," in the unkind words of Senator Knowland. In the meantime Jessup proceeded with academic caution. Although he had long taken a close interest in Asia affairs, serving on the board of a research foundation, the Institute of Pacific Relations, he had never lived or spent much time in any Asian country. In mid-August he issued a call for papers from a list of experts, all of them Americans. And then, but not for another seven weeks, Jessup held a seminar at the State Department, an event which—like his ties to Alger Hiss—would come in time to be used against him.[15]

"We covered," Jessup would later tell a Senate hearing, "practically every question, I should think, that you could think of in connection with Asia." Jessup deemed three days in October sufficient for this purpose. Neither the British nor the French were asked to attend the seminar, which was understandable perhaps, since they would have brought along their colonial axes to grind. More damaging was the omission from the list of invitees of any native speaker of Chinese, Hindi, Japanese, or Malay. In the Washington of 1949, it did not seem necessary to seek the opinions of Asians about the future of their region.

The twenty-five experts at the China Round-Table, as the seminar came to be known, had among them one great veteran, George C. Marshall, who had spent the whole of 1946 in Chongqing striving to make peace between the KMT and the Communists. They also included Harold Stassen, the Minnesota Moose, apparently there to keep Republicans involved. Other than that, the experts consisted of businessmen, scholars, and a Christian missionary. The most controversial of the academics was a long-standing Jessup acquaintance, the outspoken Professor Owen Lattimore of Johns Hopkins University in Baltimore.

Born in China in 1900, Lattimore knew the country intimately. He had met Mao Zedong, authored fine books about Mongolia and Xinjiang, and edited *Pacific Affairs*, a journal published by the institute of which Jessup was a trustee. Professor Lattimore's politics were less clear. Earlier in 1949, he had published a book titled *The Situation in Asia*, written with panache and a command of detail but strewn with barbed asides about America's stance since the war. Making short shrift of the Truman Doctrine, Lattimore called it "baffling" and "defective." In the book he criticized the Marshall Plan as "risky and makeshift," and then he said oddly sympathetic things about collective farms in Russia. At the China Round-Table Lattimore alarmed the Minnesota Moose by advocating swift recognition of Mao's China.[16]

Was Owen Lattimore a Communist, or at least a fellow traveler? In the months to come his enemies would sift through every word he wrote or uttered, in an effort to prove that he was a Soviet agent as treacherous as Alger Hiss. Not until 1955 would Lattimore clear his name entirely of the charge. One thing is certain: that in proceeding as he did, assembling experts whom he could not be sure he could trust, Jessup was politically naïve. Like Acheson, Jessup performed at his best when he came well briefed to a negotiating table where he faced a foreign counterpart. Neither Acheson nor Jessup had ever run for office. Neither one had been trained to endure the cross fire of American democracy. In Congress the following spring, the Lattimore connection would become a cause célèbre, and in time—together with his ties to Alger Hiss—it would almost wreck Philip Jessup's career.

While the politics seethed around him, Jessup refused to be hurried. Another six weeks went by. Not until November 16 did he deliver his first written report to Acheson. When it came, it either stated the obvious or merely reaffirmed views that the secretary of state had already formed. Taiwan was not mentioned; Jessup gave only one brief paragraph to Korea; and India and Pakistan received little more.

The following morning Jessup formally presented his report to the president. Then, with his flair for condensation, Acheson saw Truman in private and summarized the document's message about China policy. He saw it as a choice between two clear alternatives. One course of action, said Acheson, might be for America to oppose the Communist regime: "harass it, needle it, and if an opportunity arose attempt to overthrow it." The other—and this appealed far more to Acheson and Jessup—would be "to attempt to detach it from subservience to Moscow and over a period of

time encourage those vigorous influences which might modify it."
In other words, they meant to wean Red China from the Kremlin,
and then, with trade, education, and perhaps more missionaries,
gradually help the Chinese nation to become another Western
Europe.[17]

Behind all this there lay a view of Asia that was deceptively
simple to articulate. Across the region a revolution was occurring.
Lattimore had said this in his book, others had said the same, and
Jessup agreed. It was, wrote Jessup, "a deep-seated movement,"
driven both by discontent with misery and by nationalist revolt
against the old colonial powers. So deep were the roots of the crisis, both social and economic, that instability in Asia might endure
for decades. There could be, said Jessup, no "quick panacea."

The immediate danger was this: that in China and in Vietnam especially, the Communists had captured the revolutionary
struggle. In response, Jessup wrote, America had to contain the
Communist threat not by force of arms but by convincing the
people of the region that they were better off without the Marxists. "The basic attitude of the peoples of Asia towards the United
States"—here was the core of the matter for Acheson and Jessup.
To win over the people and show its sympathy for nationalism,
America had a list of tasks to undertake: it had to rebuild Japan as
a peaceful democracy, it had to pressure France to show wisdom
in Indochina, and it had to give some economic aid to Asia, promote social reform, and bring Jawaharlal Nehru's India into the
anti-Soviet fold.

Ideas such as these—above all, the emphasis on hearts and
minds—would become familiar in the years ahead. By the end of
1949 any reader of the press could already find them expressed by
opinion formers seeking to define America's role in Asia. But the
vision of the region that Jessup and Acheson developed was very
much an overview, like a vast landscape painting without much
light or shade or detail in the foreground. And like so much of the

discourse of geopolitics in every era, the long view they took failed to connect with events as they unfolded month by month.

By now the United States was rapidly losing its last listening posts in China. Since the fall of 1948, Mao's officials had been arresting and abusing US diplomats such as Angus Ward, the consul in the Manchurian city of Mukden. Ward was still in captivity, subjected to brutal treatment which caused outrage in America. After the fall of Guangzhou in December, the State Department found itself bereft of reliable sources of Chinese information and came to depend all the more on hearsay, conjecture, and ideology.

If Jessup and Acheson both believed that China could be weaned away from the Soviets, it was because they also believed that the USSR was intent on building its own empire. "The Communist drive, particularly in China," Jessup wrote, "is now the tool of traditional Russian imperialism in the Far East." Once the Red Chinese saw that this was so, and that Stalin meant to take control of Inner Mongolia, Manchuria, and Xinjiang, a rift would surely open up between them and the Russians, a rift that America could exploit.

Was any of this true? You could certainly try to trace a line of continuity between the Asian policy of Russian tsars and the path that Stalin appeared to be pursuing. Fifty years earlier, as it completed the Trans-Siberian Railroad, Russia had sought to dominate Manchuria and make the north of China its exclusive sphere. It had abandoned the attempt only after losing its war with Japan in 1905. Forty years later, in their offensive known as August Storm, the Russians had occupied Manchuria again at the end of World War II and begun to ransack the factories and steel mills the Japanese had built. This seemed to be consistent with the old Russian pattern of bullying China into subservience. Or perhaps this sort of argument merely led into a trap. It was all too tempting, as it remains today, for observers to look at Russia's long and complex history, with its twists and turns and its competing ideologies, and to pluck from it whatever lessons they might wish to find.[18]

It was also all too easy to forget that Stalin was a Leninist as well as a Marxist. On the one hand, he believed in the dialectic of class struggle, occurring at a different pace in each nation across the globe, but inevitable all the same as capitalism stumbled from one crisis to another. But Lenin, his inspiration, had been equally obsessed with the short-term tactics of the revolution. He had written scores of articles and pamphlets, all of them studied avidly by Stalin, in which he responded to events with a ruthless flexibility.

If this was also Stalin's technique, then overviews like Jessup's or Dean Acheson's could be dangerously misleading. If Stalin was capable of changing his tactics and making them swerve in a new direction—something he had often done in the past—then all the talk of tsarist history and traditional Russian policies might be irrelevant. It might be that the Soviet dictator had a new approach to China that differed from the aggression of the Romanovs. And all the time Stalin had two other great advantages over his American opponents.

One was his knowledge of the Chinese revolution; the other, his intelligence from the United States. For nearly thirty years, since even before the Soviet debacle in 1927, when Chiang Kai-shek all but destroyed the Communist Party in Shanghai, Stalin had been studying Chinese affairs. Although he treated Mao Zedong with suspicion, he knew more about him than Americans ever could. Stalin also held the high ground of information about events inside the United States.[19]

Of course, he had his British spies, especially Donald MacLean, who had recently left the British embassy in Washington, and Guy Burgess at the Foreign Office in London. But leaving aside the Cambridge traitors or his other secret agents, Stalin had his official envoys at 2650 Wisconsin Avenue Northwest, the Soviet embassy in Washington. To assess America's stance in Asia, the Russian diplomats merely had to read the morning papers, where members of Congress and Truman's cabinet sniped at each other using leaks and counter-leaks as a tool of politics.

On the topic of Asia, the surreptitious briefings to the press grew all the more plentiful as Christmas approached: so plentiful that the secretary of the army complained to Acheson about the endless leaks from Foggy Bottom. There was a reason why they were taking place. At some point, the wrangling about Asia would have to culminate in a test of strength between Dean Acheson and Louis Johnson. Each side strove to chip away at the other.[20]

The showdown between them could not be delayed much longer. It would have to take place at the National Security Council and before the looming deadline of early January. Besides the Jessup review, the paper trail that led to it contained a memorandum—NSC 48/1—composed by George Kennan. Here was another global overview that, combined with Jessup's, would shape the Asia policy that Acheson devised. Although it was meant to be top secret, its conclusions would soon be widely known.

Weary, frustrated, and not always on the best of terms with the secretary of state, Kennan was shortly to leave Foggy Bottom and move to academia. Like a memo he was also drafting about the Super Bomb, 48/1 was a brilliant piece of work, composed in the subtle, elegant prose that was unmistakably his. Kennan had a vision of the world not so different from the one the British had adopted. Like the British, he thought of the Soviet Union as a state both blessed and cursed by its geography.[21]

"Operating from the center of the Eurasian continent," Kennan wrote, the USSR "may advance or retreat in the east or the west as the occasion demands." This was something the Russians understood themselves, one of the lessons they drew from their past when they studied their medieval forebears, heroes such as

Alexander Nevsky in the thirteenth century, who had to cope with the Mongols and the Teutonic Knights at one and the same time. Kennan reached the same conclusion as his British counterparts, and insisted that control of the Rimland of Eurasia must not be allowed to fall into Russian hands.

In London, this sort of thinking led straight to a focus on the Persian Gulf and the Suez Canal. Not only was this region part of the Rimland; it also contained what the British now called the "wells of power," the Iraqi and Iranian oil fields they were coming to rely upon. Since the Gulf was not quite yet an overriding American obsession, Kennan preferred to emphasize the strategic importance of Japan.[22]

In the Kennanite vision of the globe, the decisive assets were the great industrial zones—what he called "war-making complexes"—centered on coal and steel and engineering. These included the German Ruhr, American industrial cities such as Pittsburgh, and the Soviet mines and factories created by Stalin's Five-Year Plans. World War II had been a battle not only between armies but also between these hubs of industry.

In Japan George Kennan saw another war-making complex that had to be preserved from Russian influence. "The industrial plant of Japan," he wrote in 48/1, "would be the richest strategic prize in the Far East for the USSR." Japan had to be defended as well as the countries that supplied the Japanese: Malaya with its tin and rubber, Indonesia with its oil, and Burma and Indochina with their rice. Like Philip Jessup, Kennan did not see the task of holding them as chiefly military—in his view it had more to do with hearts and minds and economic aid—but even so a defensive perimeter had to be secured.[23]

This was precisely the question the Joint Chiefs of Staff had been grappling with since the end of World War II. To answer it, Kennan revived a concept the Joint Chiefs had adopted in 1947, an offshore line of strongpoints to act as bases for ships and aircraft. To protect Japan, America had to maintain what Kennan called "a minimum position," which lay along the island chain nearest to the coast of Asia. "The first line of strategic defense," he wrote, "should include Japan, the Ryukyus, and the Philippines," and by the Ryukyus he meant Okinawa. Kennan saw no reason to make the defensive perimeter encompass Taiwan or South Korea, since at the time neither one ranked as an industrial hub. Nor did Kennan think that Mao's victory on the mainland had decisively altered the military balance.

The Jessup and Kennan views of Asia flowed into Acheson's decision-making. And yet from both memoranda two crucial elements were missing. Neither paper offered an informed analysis of what might be happening in Beijing or Moscow. It was simply assumed that Mao was currently a pawn of Stalin, but that in time this would change, when Red China came to see how imperialist—from Acheson's point of view—the Russians really were. The other thing they did not mention was American public opinion, or rather, public attitudes as they were voiced in Congress.

In the years before Pearl Harbor, Congress had hampered and confined what Franklin Roosevelt could do overseas. FDR's foreign policy in the 1930s had been a long compromise imposed upon him by lawmakers and by an American public inclined to neutrality even in the face of fascists on the march in Abyssinia and Spain. In 1950 the issues would be different, and neutrality could not be an option, but in other ways the two situations were similar. Truman's grip on Congress was even weaker than FDR's; both the Senate and the House were ready to dispute his leadership in foreign affairs; and emotions were quite as inflamed as they had been a dozen years before.

Herbert Lehman's election victory in New York had served only to make the Republican Party more determined to cut the ground from beneath the feet of Harry Truman. Throughout 1949 the Republicans had been fighting a long rear-guard action. By the time the president returned from Key West on December 20, they were ready to take the offensive.

CONFUSION AND GRAVE DANGER

In 1951 Secretary of Defense Louis Johnson would tell a committee of Congress, convened to investigate the origins and the conduct of the Korean War, that he had done everything he could to urge Truman to step up to the defense of Taiwan. He would claim that he had abandoned the attempt three days before Christmas 1949 when the president made it clear over lunch that he would do no such thing.

In his testimony, Johnson was seeking to clear himself of blame for budget cuts and other errors that had left the army fighting a war for which it was unprepared. His evidence was scarcely objective. Nor was Acheson's version of events in the memoirs he wrote in the 1960s. Neither one would readily admit that they had made America's Asia policy the subject of a quarrel between their rival factions.[24]

For the grand old men of bipartisanship, Senators Tom Connally and Arthur Vandenberg, the situation had become alarming. Between them they patched together a foreign policy platform that they hoped might unify the warring sides in Congress. On December 21, frail and gaunt after the operation on his lung, Vandenberg, the Republican, spoke at a press conference and called for unity. Knowing as he did that Taft was trying to lead the party along a different route, he sketched out three measures intended to keep its members in the fold.

Deep cuts in Marshall aid, a refusal to recognize Red China, and a restoration of diplomatic ties with General Franco's despotism in Spain: these policies should be enough, Vandenberg hoped, to keep the bipartisan consensus alive. The following week, Tom Connally followed suit for the Democrats, giving the press an identical package of suggestions. With this he hoped to win over not only the Republicans but also the economical likes of Senator Walter George and his fellow southerners, who wielded so much power in the Democratic Party.[25]

What neither Connally nor Vandenberg could do was solve the Asia riddle. That task had to fall to the National Security Council, which was due to assemble on December 29. Meetings and decisions of the council were supposed to be as secret as Kennan's memos, at least until the president divulged their contents. In this case they were nothing of the kind.

Both before and after this critical session of the council, the maneuvering continued, and it included more leaks and counter-leaks. Some of the news stories were garbled and misleading, others accurate, but the overall effect was ambiguity and muddle, relayed swiftly through the wires to London and to Moscow. Truman was obliged to try to clear the air, chiefly about Taiwan, by making a definitive statement of his position. When this failed to do the trick, Acheson went further with statements of his own; and in doing so he deepened the confusion.

This Washington intrigue began on December 23. That was the day when the president left the city to spend Christmas in Missouri. Secretary Johnson had already left the capital: he was on his way to Florida, intending to remain there until after the meeting on the twenty-ninth. As subsequent events would show, Johnson absented himself not because he had lost the Taiwan argument but because he wished to prolong it.

While Truman was flying to Kansas City, the State Department remained intensely active. On the morning of December 23, a cable arrived from the US consul in Taipei giving a gloomy new assessment of the situation on the island. Inflation was out of control and the Taiwanese people hated the KMT regime. Without more American money, Taiwan would be bankrupt in six to nine months and Chiang Kai-shek's army would disintegrate, leaving the island open to invasion. The consul saw only one ray of hope. Fearing Communism quite as much as they loathed the KMT, the people of the island would welcome General MacArthur and a military occupation by America.[26]

That same afternoon, with uncanny timing, Ambassador Wellington Koo appeared at Foggy Bottom with Chiang's list of what he needed. It included US military advisers, economic aid, and equipment for six army divisions. He received another firm refusal from Acheson's staff, which insisted that Taiwan had all the resources it required. Acheson did not tell Koo that the State Department had prepared a confidential memorandum to be circulated that day among its press officers and sent to US diplomats abroad.

"Loss of the island," said the memo, "is widely anticipated." If the press or anybody else asked questions about the prospects for Taiwan, they were to be given background briefings to the effect that the island had "no special military significance," America would not intervene in its defense, its loss would not damage the United States or its allies, and any blame should be attached to Chiang Kai-shek.[27]

With six days still to go to until the NSC convened, it was rash of Dean Acheson to issue such a document. Nor did it tell the whole truth. On December 15, Truman had received a note from Secretary Johnson setting out MacArthur's position. "It would be fatal," MacArthur had said, "for Taiwan to fall into predatory hands," because from there an enemy could bomb US air bases located on Okinawa and the Philippines. He ruled out putting US troops on Taiwan; but he wanted Truman to declare that any attempt to invade it would be an act of war and America would fight to save it.

General Bradley and the Joint Chiefs could not go that far; but from their wartime planning they knew that Taiwan could be made secure from invasion without sending US troops to hold it.

Accepting the view from Tokyo that the island was essential, that week they called—"as a matter of urgency"—for a new program of military supplies and advice for the KMT. It would be based on MacArthur's and the navy's view of how best to defend Taiwan without ground forces.[28]

Safe in his Florida retreat, Louis Johnson expected Bradley to argue the matter out with Acheson. But far from giving up the struggle, as he later claimed, the defense secretary was also fighting back himself, by mobilizing the press in the form of Washington's sharpest reporters. One of them was Drew Pearson, who for nearly forty years wrote the syndicated column Washington Merry-Go-Round and broadcast weekly on the radio.

As one of those who regarded Truman's team as mostly mediocre, in 1949 Pearson had led the press campaign against Harry Vaughan. He had seized on the five-percenter story, he fed McCarthy with material, and in the process he helped the secretary of defense with his economy drive. While other columnists began to abandon Louis Johnson, Pearson remained his staunch supporter. In return he received, apparently from Johnson's deputy Steve Early, the details of the feud about Taiwan, including the Joint Chiefs' decision—prompted by MacArthur—that the island could not be allowed to fall. Twenty-four hours before the Joint Chiefs officially made up their minds, Pearson ran the story.

Christmas came and went. On December 28 the president flew back to Washington, with a week to go before his State of the Union address. It would be devoted to domestic policy, which meant the Fair Deal, poor though its prospects were. Although the winter was mild, Lewis and the miners were out on strike again, coal stocks were falling, and the railroads were starting to cancel trains. Again reporters were writing about corruption: Pearson claimed that Frank Costello had a lobbyist working on Capitol Hill.[29]

It was against this background of pervasive skepticism about his administration that Truman would chair the NSC's crucial meeting about Asia, set for 2:30 p.m. on the twenty-ninth. Before it began, Acheson had to face down the challenge from the Pentagon; and so that morning the Joint Chiefs assembled in his office. It was a tense, demanding session. Acheson interrogated General Bradley and his colleagues as though they were on the witness stand. Charging them with being inconsistent, he delivered a lecture filled with Jessup's and Kennan's views of Asia.

As he always did, Acheson tried to cut through the details to reach the points of principle. For him, one thing mattered above all: to stop Communism from swallowing the region. To do this, the United States must put itself on the side of nationalists, yearning to be free of what he called "the dead hand of European colonialism." If America sided with the KMT, corrupt and decadent as Acheson thought it was, then America would be an imperialist power, arousing the hatred of the Chinese people and their neighbors. Nehru's government in India was about to give the People's Republic of China diplomatic recognition; the British would not be far behind; and while it might be a year or two before America did the same, it would have to be done in the end.[30]

Behind Acheson's ideas there lay his dubious assumption about the Sino-Soviet relationship. Convinced that Russia planned to strip away the northern provinces of China, Acheson saw what he called "the seed of inevitable conflict" between Mao and the Soviets. This looming rift between the Kremlin and Beijing was, he believed, the ace in America's hand; and it would be squandered if the president committed the United States to Taiwan and made itself, and not the Russians, an imperialist menace to China. General Bradley saw all this for what it was. He bluntly told Acheson that the State Department "had decided to let Formosa go for political reasons." Bradley might have added what he knew full well: that if it had not been for the Pentagon budget cuts, he might not have hesitated about protecting Taiwan.

In Truman's hierarchy, Acheson ranked higher than the generals; and when the NSC met that afternoon his opinions prevailed. They put their seal on NSC 48/2—"The Position of the United States with Respect to Asia"—a document embodying the Jessup and Kennan line. By way of diplomacy, free trade, and a smaller version of the Marshall Plan, America would lead the Asian peoples along a path to prosperity, and eliminate what the paper called "the preponderant power and influence of the USSR." Taiwan would have to fend for itself while the USA strengthened its defensive line from Japan and Okinawa to the Philippines. That afternoon, the president ordered the navy to reinforce the Seventh Fleet in the western Pacific.[31]

NSC 48/2 was clearly marked "Top Secret." But with Louis Johnson still away in Florida, his aide Steve Early had gone to the meeting in his place. Now sixty years old and a veteran of World War I, in which he had fought in the trenches with a machine gun, Early had first met FDR in 1912 when Truman was still working on his father's farm. Wily and abrasive, more loyal to Roosevelt's memory than he was to his successor, Early refused to allow the Taiwan question to subside. He ignored the instruction to keep the meeting confidential.

On the morning before the NSC convened, an account of its agenda appeared in the *New York Herald Tribune*, written by Drew Pearson's leading rival. This was Bert Andrews, a reporter who in 1948 had helped to build Richard Nixon's career with his coverage of Nixon's pursuit of Alger Hiss. Andrews's story, which could only have come from Early, claimed that the Joint Chiefs had called for a team of military advisers to be sent to the island to organize its defense.[32]

In the days that followed, Congress and the press scrambled to find out what the NSC had decided. Conflicting versions appeared, some of them pro-Acheson and some the opposite, some of them claiming that the president agreed with the Joint Chiefs and others saying he had slapped them down. The best-informed correspondent—James Reston of the *Times*—ran a story on January 1 that precisely captured the message of NSC 48/2. He called it a "detailed Asia paper," correctly stating that Truman had decided not to defend Taiwan. But Reston's report clashed with other stories and in the public mind the confusion continued. The Truman administration appeared to be a house divided.

In London the mixed signals from America caused consternation. By now Ernest Bevin was determined to sever Britain's last links with the KMT. Chiang's warships had mined the approaches to Shanghai, endangering the British trading companies still in the city. Bevin did not wish to see America commit itself to Taiwan; but still he did not know just what his ally meant to do.[33]

The atmosphere grew still more feverish when the State Department's internal memo of December 23 became public in Tokyo, leaked perhaps by someone on MacArthur's staff. The details of Koo's request for arms and money were made public, too, after Acheson's spokesman denied that any such request had been submitted. An irate Senator Knowland accused the department of lying and called for help from Herbert Hoover, who gave, as a former president and an old China hand, his opinion that Taiwan must be held. When India recognized Mao's China, the temperature rose still further. Republicans began to argue that if London did the same, Britain's share of Marshall aid should be reduced.

It was at this fraught moment that Senator Taft intervened. On the day of India's announcement, Taft spoke for an hour to the *Dayton Journal Herald* to set out his foreign policy position. The full text of the interview would be held back for three weeks, to be released at an even more opportune time. But two items could not wait and were published at once: Taft's call for the US Navy to put a base on Taiwan and make it as secure as Okinawa, and his claim—to be amplified relentlessly in the months ahead—that the loss of China had been caused by pro-communist attitudes in Acheson's department.[34]

By now the bipartisan consensus about Asia had only a few days left to live. It finally collapsed on the morning of January 5. To end the confusion, Truman would have to make a plain declaration about Taiwan's future. Addressing Congress the previous evening, he had avoided foreign affairs, but his first press conference of 1950 was due at 10:30 a.m. and this would have to be the venue. The president read the reporters a statement ruling out any military aid or advice to Chiang Kai-shek or the use of US forces to protect the island. Refusing to take questions, he told them that the secretary of state would answer any they might have.

As Truman spoke, the bipartisan consensus was breathing its last in Acheson's office. The Republican senators William Knowland and Alexander Smith had arrived at 10:35, to receive another of his lectures. Acheson said again that the Soviets had seized Manchuria and meant to subjugate China as a whole. America would neither risk war for Taiwan nor take control of the island and reveal itself as an imperial power. This was too much for Knowland, who branded Acheson a defeatist for abandoning the island and accused him of following "a policy of grave danger to the American people." Senator Smith—angered by the administration's failure to consult the Senate—warned Acheson that he could no longer be bipartisan.[35]

Although Acheson meant to draw a line under the affair, he merely made himself the target of direct attack from hostile forces determined to make Taiwan their battle cry. In 1949, even amid the quarrels about NATO, he had largely been free from personal abuse, but this was to be the outcome as the secretary of state drove home with little tact what he thought was a victory. When

Acheson met the press that afternoon, he scolded his opponents for what he called "their amateur military strategy" and insisted that "no responsible person in the government" had ever believed that US forces should go to Taiwan. If his words were a rebuke to Hoover and Taft, they could also be taken as an insult to Mac-Arthur. Parts of the press began to call for Acheson's dismissal.

The following day, the British did what everyone expected and recognized the People's Republic of China. In doing so they kept the Taiwan question at the top of Washington's agenda. In the *Herald Tribune* on January 8 Bert Andrews ran a story describing the months of wrangling between Acheson and Louis Johnson, with details that again could only have been given by Steve Early. Meanwhile, Senator Vandenberg had been briefed by John Foster Dulles about a detail that Acheson had brushed aside.

As Dulles pointed out with his usual rigor, Taiwan had become a part of the Japanese Empire in 1895 by virtue of the treaty that had followed Japan's first war with China. And legally this was still the case, because the United States, its allies, and Japan had not yet signed a peace treaty to end the war that began with Pearl Harbor. Under the UN Charter, the people of Taiwan had the right to reject their retention by Japan or their absorption by the KMT. Instead they might vote for independence from both China and Japan, something that Acheson knew would most likely be the first choice of the Taiwanese. And if they did vote for self-rule, then under the terms of the Truman Doctrine of 1947 America could not refuse to protect them.[36]

The attempt to define an American policy for Asia had descended into a mess of inconsistencies and contradictions. On the Senate floor, Taft took up the Dulles line, advocating the one thing Mao's China could never accept: autonomy for Taiwan. He urged the president to use the Seventh Fleet to block the Taiwan Strait. This left his fellow Republican Arthur Vandenberg in a quandary. On the one hand, he could no longer trust the administration; on the other, he had to restrain the China hawks in his own party. "The whole thing is desperately complicated," Vandenberg wrote to a constituent in Detroit. He could not have foreseen that seventy years into the future the Taiwan question would remain precisely that. Some might also say that Chiang Kai-shek, with so many years behind him of devious maneuvers, had outwitted a State Department that failed to appreciate his sheer talent for survival.[37]

Under pressure but still believing that he controlled the agenda, Acheson made one last effort to close down the debate that his rivalry with Johnson had made so acrimonious. He was due to speak at the National Press Club at lunchtime on Thursday, January 12. Although intended to be definitive, his address that day would prove to be the most contentious of his career.

THE PRESS CLUB SPEECH

It was a speech the secretary of state should not have needed to give. In hearings earlier that week, Acheson had testified about Asia to both the Senate and the House, giving them almost verbatim the findings of NSC 48/2. Although both meetings were in private, Tom Connally told the world the essential details. The secretary of state also had Truman's full support. If the president had invoked the prestige of his office and made a definitive statement of policy about Taiwan, he might have quelled the last dissenters in his ranks. But on the morning of the twelfth, when Truman met the press again for his weekly session, he failed to grasp the opportunity.[38]

With the reporters chiefly asking questions about the coal strike and organized crime, the president said nothing about Asia. Instead he left the subject to Acheson, who again was in no mood for tact. At the press club that day, the secretary meant to crush his opponents with a speech intended to make the maximum effect both at home and, perhaps more to the point, among those who heard or read it overseas. Six hundred guests were at the luncheon: not only journalists and members of Congress, but also the diplomatic corps. Voice of America recorded it for radio transmission around the world.

George Kennan saw a first draft and described it in his diary as "dull and sanctimonious." Acheson rewrote the speech himself, mastering it so thoroughly that he gave it without reading from a script. Because of this, the State Department never released the text in full, making do instead with a shortened version that left out his scathing asides about Taft and his other critics. But the reports in the press the next day were copious, with extracts displaying Acheson's sarcasm about opponents whose intellects he saw as weaker than his own.[39]

"I am frequently asked," Acheson told his audience, "has the State Department got an Asian policy? And it seems to me that that discloses such a depth of ignorance that it is very hard to begin to deal with it." Speaking for sixty-one minutes, including ten for questions, Acheson called his critics charlatans and fools and accused Chiang Kai-shek and the KMT of "the grossest incompetence ever experienced by any military command."

Acheson wished to avoid the slightest trace of ambiguity, in a speech intended to resonate abroad and end the misunderstandings that were rife in London and Paris. In the section that dealt with Indochina, he included an elegant tribute to Robert Schuman; but he also hoped to send a message to Stalin and to Mao, a message that might prize open the rift between the two that Acheson believed was inevitable.

That summer, after the Korean War began, Senator Taft would claim that in the press club speech Acheson had invited Kim Il-sung's invasion of the South by appearing to leave it outside America's perimeter of defense. Eisenhower would say the same in 1952 during his election campaign. Casting a perennial

Together in London in 1950 (left to right): US Secretary of State Dean Acheson; Ernest Bevin of Great Britain; and Robert Schuman, foreign minister of France. *STF / Agence France-Presse via Getty Images.*

shadow over Acheson's reputation, this charge has been debated many times, and rightly so. The facts of what he said are not a matter for dispute. The problem lay in what Acheson did not say as firmly as he might have, in what he did not know, and in the shifting political context in which he spoke. Acheson simply had no means of assessing the true state of play between Stalin and Mao; but without due caution he pressed ahead.

Acheson defined, with the utmost clarity, America's perimeter of strongpoints in Asia. On January 13, the *Baltimore Sun*—whose staff were close to Acheson—illustrated his words with a detailed map that showed the American line of defense snaking down through the sea to the west of Japan and the Philippines but excluding both Korea and Taiwan. In Congress the map was assumed to be the work of the State Department, which indeed it might have been. The map precisely matched the section of the speech where Acheson spoke directly about the Pentagon's military posture.

Nor was this statement new. The papers could have printed the same map the week before the speech, using the content of Senator Connally's briefings, or even in the spring of 1949, when the US Army had begun its withdrawal from South Korea. Elsewhere in the speech Acheson made it plain that the perimeter line referred to America's network of air and naval bases. He did not make it a frontier beyond which the Communists could do what they pleased. He said that if areas outside the perimeter were attacked, the United States would rally the United Nations to defend them; and this is precisely what it did when North Korea invaded the south.

But Acheson did not give that point the emphasis it deserved. He devoted far more time to what he saw as his principal message to the Kremlin. "The most important fact in the relations of any foreign power with Asia," Acheson said, was this: that the USSR was planning to annex the northern provinces of China and above all Manchuria with its rich resources. It was an old Russian policy, he claimed, with its origins in the era of the tsars. "Communism," he said again, "is really the spearhead of Russian imperialism."

This claim about the Soviets had been central to the Jessup and Kennan reviews; but Acheson had little evidence to support it. Apart from what could be found in history books, his material chiefly amounted to dispatches in the late summer from his ambassador to Russia and the US consul-general in Shanghai, who saw Stalin imposing what he called "a totalitarian monopoly" in Manchuria. By January 1950 the situation had moved on. Mao was still in Russia, where the US embassy had no clue about the progress of his talks with the Kremlin. In Shanghai, the consul—under constant watch from the authorities—could send only brief telegrams, and he would soon be evacuated to Hong Kong.[40]

Acheson had also failed to convince the skeptics from Congress who sat at the tables in the press club. Among them was Senator Alexander Smith, compelled to listen while the secretary poured scorn on what he called the "foolish adventures" with regard to Taiwan that Smith, Knowland, and Taft had urged upon him. By now their patience was exhausted. Nothing Acheson could say would appease a GOP mostly bent on his destruction. He also antagonized fellow Democrats by paying too little heed to their opinions.

The following week the House of Representatives would debate a package of economic aid for South Korea. The Senate had already approved the measure, which, although large—worth $150 million—should have been uncontroversial, consisting mainly of supplies of cotton, lumber, and fertilizer for the country's farms. Instead it provoked another rebellion by the Democrats in Congress, one still more damaging than the revolt about aid for NATO in the fall. This would raise more doubts about America's support for Syngman Rhee.[41]

A statesman at the mercy of his own divided party, Acheson failed to reckon with the cunning of events that were lurking in ambush around him. As he gave his speech, and while in Moscow the atmosphere was improving between Mao and Stalin, in New York the second trial of Alger Hiss was nearing its conclusion. Meanwhile, but as yet unknown to Acheson, a shocking development had occurred in London. Following a lead from the FBI, the British had uncovered a Soviet spy in the most secret enclave of the nation. For Acheson the Anglophile, this would be an embarrassment as grave as the fate of Alger Hiss.

MAO IN MOSCOW—2

*I*n his Moscow dacha at the turn of the year, Mao Zedong felt his health improve. His dizzy spells went on, but he was sleeping well, and his anger had subsided. On January 1, Ivan Kovalev arrived from the Kremlin bearing what appeared to be an olive branch. He wanted the Chinese leader to approve a public statement, in the form of an "interview" he was deemed to have granted to the Soviet news agency TASS.[1]

It was brief and bland, but enough to prove to the world that Mao was still alive and making progress in Russia. It was also a good omen for China, because it mentioned talks about a treaty of alliance, that gift that so far Stalin had refused to offer. The "interview" ran in Pravda *on January 2, and that evening Molotov returned to the dacha. What did Mao want? he inquired. Above all, Mao replied, a treaty of friendship and assistance. Molotov said yes. It was decided that Zhou Enlai, Mao's foreign minister, would come to Moscow to negotiate the terms. Once it had been announced that Zhou was on his way, there could be no turning back; and so at last the prize seemed to be within Mao's reach.*

What had happened to change Stalin's mind? It might be that he did not change his mind at all, but had always intended to strike a deal with Mao after first giving him a cold reception, as a way to put him in his place. If Stalin had meant to deny him a treaty, he would not have invited Mao to Moscow to begin with. In any case, Stalin still held the upper hand, making no promises about the treaty's contents. It might address the ports in Manchuria, the Chinese Changchun Railroad, the terms of loans or military aid, or the future role of Russia in Chinese regions close to the border. All of this was on the table, but nothing yet agreed. Even so, the mood had altered, and so, perhaps, had Stalin's thinking. In that first week of January, Pravda began to publish items that supplied some clues. They advocated more wars of liberation like the one that Mao had led, or like the fighting under way in Vietnam.

First Pravda reprinted a speech that Mao's deputy Liu Shaoqi had given in Beijing in November, calling for armed struggle against the old colonial powers, or what Liu described as their "semi-colonial" successors. Delivered at a conference to delegates from thirteen countries, from Iran to the Philippines, at first Liu's speech had met with disapproval from Moscow. Now it had the Kremlin's blessing. Next there came in Pravda articles in praise of Mao and the Communists in China, urging other nations to follow their example and to free themselves from their oppressors.

Moscow also wished to toughen the stance of the Communist Party in Japan. On January 6, another organ of the Soviet press issued a condemnation of Nosaka Sanzo, the man who had wanted to come to power only by way of the ballot box. Beijing condemned him in the People's Daily ten days later. The Japanese Communists bent to the Soviet wind. On January 19, General Secretary Tokuda Kyuichi officially repudiated Nosaka's peaceful line. Instead he called for a struggle like Mao's in China against the government in Tokyo and General MacArthur.

What did all this mean? It appeared to suggest a growing confidence on Stalin's part about the prospects for more Asian revolutions. Mao had told him that China intended to give diplomatic recognition to Ho Chi Minh. Stalin had his misgivings, doubting Ho's chances *of victory. He also knew that recognition of Ho would antagonize France. Even so, he promised Mao that the USSR would follow suit.*

All of this had its relevance to Stalin's new mood toward the Chinese leader. It seems that other factors also played their part. Now that India had recognized the People's Republic, with Britain about to do the same, Stalin would not wish to see such contacts develop into closer ties. To preempt such a thing, the Soviet Union had to be China's best friend; and this would have to mean a treaty with Beijing. Nor did Stalin wish to hear more speculation in the outside world about a schism between himself and Mao.

The United States loomed largest of all. It has been argued that perhaps Stalin's spies fed him the details of NSC 48/2, with its hands-off approach to China and its decision not to defend Taiwan. But espionage was scarcely required. Since late summer, the American press—so carefully studied in Moscow—had chronicled not only the fumblings toward an Asia policy but also the wrangling at the Pentagon, first about the B-36 bomber and then about Taiwan. Stalin had all this at his disposal.

Not only did Stalin now possess Beria's atom bomb. He also had his air defenses, including the new jet fighter, the MiG-15, that the NATO allies had glimpsed over Berlin. During the hearings in Congress, in October, the US Navy had discussed the vulnerabilities of the American B-29 bombers of World War II vintage and the limitations of the B-36. The MiG-15 could shoot down both kinds of aircraft. While this might have had no direct bearing on Stalin's attitude toward Mao, it had important consequences. In his decision-making, Stalin could take a measured view of the nuclear threat he faced. He had no cause to find it terrifying.

America's stance toward Asia was also becoming clearer. James Reston's story in the New York Times *on January 1 could have told Stalin all he needed to know about NSC 48/2. Within thirty-six hours of the story's appearance, Molotov appeared at Mao's dacha. More clarification soon arrived, first in Truman's press conference statement of*

January 5, and then in Acheson's press club speech. Stalin responded to both, and in ways that revealed more about his ideas.

Truman's refusal to defend Taiwan could certainly be read as an American attempt to divide Mao from Moscow. This seems to be how Stalin saw it. He did his best to wreck any chance of America drawing closer to Beijing. First he sent his new foreign minister, Andrey Vyshinskiy, the prosecutor in the show trials of the 1930s, to make a suggestion to Mao. The Kremlin wanted Mao to demand that the United Nations expel the KMT and give him their seat on its Security Council. Mao leaped at the idea, and Zhou Enlai made the request. When the UN rejected it, the Soviet delegation walked out, vowing not to return until Mao was given what he asked for. That same day, Mao ordered the seizure of the remaining US diplomatic compounds in China.

The press club speech had also included Acheson's statement that Russia was trying to absorb Manchuria and Xinjiang. Since the 1920s the Soviet Union had resented any claim that in China it behaved like tsarist empire builders. Molotov and Vyshinskiy returned to Mao and asked him to issue a statement refuting this Western libel. Moscow would tell the press the same thing. Both statements went out, and then Zhou Enlai arrived in Moscow for the treaty talks.

Stalin had now appraised Mao at first hand. He had found him suitable to be the flag carrier for Asian Communism and to serve as a conduit through which he could support other revolutions elsewhere. Stalin could also be sure that if and when Mao tried to invade Taiwan, the United States would not intervene. Throughout this process, Stalin was several steps ahead of the Americans. Knowing far more than they could about Chairman Mao, he also knew far more about what Washington thought than Washington could know about him. He had outsmarted the United States; or so perhaps Stalin believed.

CHAPTER SIX

MOTORAMA, COAL, AND THE HYDROGEN BOMB

The American industrial machine is a unit, just like an automobile. . . . What, short of economic insanity, would prompt us to trade our streamlined, free-wheeling, competitive system for some outmoded Old World jalopy?

—BENJAMIN FAIRLESS, *president of U.S. Steel, 1950*[1]

As Washington grew more agitated by the week, the rest of the country went in search of a different kind of spectacle. Across the Northeast it was almost the warmest January on record. Although the nation still had its five million unemployed, crowds thronged the streets and the department stores. With the recession long since over, they had money to spend. Furniture sold well. So did the new electric ovens that were in so much demand; and if the shoppers lined up for a movie, the one most of them chose had nothing to do with angst or with foreboding.

Instead the film was an epic of ostentation and erotica featuring the charms of Miss Hedy Lamarr. *Samson and Delilah*, directed by Cecil B. DeMille, would be by far the most successful movie of the year, seen by nearly sixty million people. While some critics called it an old-fashioned movie, with its opulent sets and costumes and its archaic dialogue, a motion picture could not be as popular as this unless it spoke to the mood of the nation. What DeMille gave the public was glamor, lust, and luxury, all in Technicolor. This was as essential an aspect of the era as the anger aroused by the trials of Alger Hiss.

At one and the same time Americans could worry about Communism and corruption while they also felt a yearning for extravagance and a surge of optimism. Since the end of World War II the public mood had fluctuated between periods of high morale and intervals of gloom amid shortages, inflation, strikes, and scares about the Soviets. If there was a moment when a new and more durable spirit of confidence began to set in, it occurred in the winter of 1950. At last, the standard of living was beginning to improve. The previous summer a powerful rally had begun on Wall Street, with the Dow Jones Industrial Average led sharply upward by the automakers. American consumers entered the new year in a buoyant frame of mind, and so did the nation's industrial elite.[2]

Of all the many festivals of corporate America, the most lavish and the most revealing of its age took place that same month at Forty-Ninth Street and Park Avenue in New York. A nine-day equivalent of *Samson and Delilah*, the event was another orgy of color and the tactile, paid for by the largest company in the world.

Only the Waldorf Astoria could host something so splendid. The hotel's ballroom, the grandest in the city, was the venue of choice for socialites and statesmen, the space where Cardinal Spellman in his scarlet robes threw his Christmas parties. The ballroom also had an elevator that could lift automobiles up from the street. General Motors could find no finer setting for its 1950 celebration of the car.

The GM MidCentury Motorama opened on January 19, and cost more than a million dollars to stage. A company that did everything by the numbers, General Motors logged the footfall through the show. Frank Costello was away in Miami Beach, and so the gangster missed the party in his favorite hotel; but this was an event for the multitude. By the time the Motorama ended, more than 320,000 people had passed through its doors. They gazed and gawked at Pontiacs and Buicks while actors performed a musical review of half a century of rubber tires and carburetors. Television visited as well, to convey to millions more what GM called "the drama of America."[3]

The company's chairman, Alfred P. Sloan Jr., came down from his apartment on Fifth Avenue to open the proceedings; but their guiding light was Charles E. Wilson, GM's president. Fifty-nine years old, portly and white-haired, Wilson was known to his peers as "Engine Charlie." Born in a small town in Ohio, where his parents were teachers, Wilson had trained as an electrical engineer and invented an early form of starting motor for automobiles. Later he joined GM, and as he rose through the company's ranks he acquired a salesman's talent for a memorable line.

Early in 1953, President Eisenhower would summon Engine Charlie to become his secretary of defense. During the confirmation hearings in Congress, he uttered words that would become notorious. "For years," Wilson said, "I thought what was good for our country was good for General Motors, and vice versa." To Wilson's annoyance, the sentence was endlessly garbled and recycled to make him the emblem of the overmighty corporation, but it captured the essence of what he believed. It was also the message of the Motorama.[4]

When Ike chose Engine Charlie to lead the Pentagon, he did so because—apart from knowing how to run a huge enterprise—Wilson had values that the president shared. For Eisenhower, Wilson, and Alfred Sloan, America stood for freedom, progress, and democracy, and they saw GM's cars as a manifestation of all three. The automobile, said Wilson, was "an extension of liberty itself." And since you could not have freedom without aspiration, he filled the Motorama with objects to be envied.

"There is no competition," Wilson told the television viewers, "to the desire to own a Cadillac." For the Motorama his engineers produced the ultimate example of the brand. A car that a modern Delilah might drive, the gaudiest attraction at the show was a Cadillac convertible painted tawny cream, with fittings in gold plate and an interior lined with the fur of fourteen leopards from Somaliland. Since GM believed in the feminine mystique, they chose to call the car "the Debutante." A reporter asked what the company had in mind when it designed its vehicles. "I would say," came the reply from Engine Charlie, "that our objective was to obtain a blonde who could cook."

The "Pillar of Progress," centerpiece of the General Motors Motorama at New York's Waldorf Astoria Hotel, January 1950. *Associated Press / Shutterstock.*

At the center of the ballroom, a column of glass rose thirty feet into the air to form the "Pillar of Progress," containing replicas of each generation of cars made by GM since the company was founded. At the foot of the pillar, five giant wheels revolved to show the latest models at their gleaming best. Among them was the one that Wilson meant to be the biggest seller of the year ahead, the Chevrolet Bel Air. With its chrome and its curves and its attractive sticker price, the car embodied everything he aimed for: innovation, style, and affordability. If you wished, you could drive it as a manual; but pay just $150 more and you could have an automatic version of the Chevrolet. And if you did so, you would make your modest mark on history. You would take to the road with a Powerglide transmission, a feat of ingenuity that said as much about its era as the films of Cecil B. DeMille.

When Charles Wilson made his gaffe about GM and the voters, the fuss he caused led people to forget that Engine Charlie knew his business. He and Alfred Sloan might have their limitations, but they understood aspects of America that many commentators barely grasped at all. In predicting the shape of the postwar world, they had been right when others had been far too pessimistic.

While economists worried that America would stagnate, GM prophesied something else: rising incomes, bigger families, and the exodus from cities to the suburbs, where, said Mr. Sloan, a car would cease to be "an option" and instead become "a must." At a time when the Allies had not yet entered Paris, Sloan had forecast what would happen after the war was won. Far from a return to mass unemployment, in his speeches in 1944 Sloan predicted a surge in consumer demand. For a while—for years perhaps—it might produce inflation, with strikes and bottlenecks while industry converted back from war production; but if GM invested in new plants and equipment, it would emerge into an era of lasting expansion.[5]

Plans were laid before victory in Europe, and in 1946 Sloan and Wilson issued stock and borrowed money. In the next two years GM spent almost $600 million on new machines and factories, a huge sum at the time. By the end of 1949 the company was selling as many cars each month as it had in the year before Pearl Harbor. A few weeks before the Motorama opened, GM repaid the final tranche of the debt it had taken on. The company's cash flow could easily finance a dash for growth in 1950.[6]

"I see no reason," Engine Charlie said at the Motorama, "why the next ten years should not be increasingly prosperous." For Wilson and for Sloan, the future seemed to be an open road filled with opportunity. Their confidence rested on more than just the demographics of the nation. It also arose from their understanding of what had transpired in the 1930s and during World War II. An engineer himself, Wilson knew full well the value of the technical advances that GM and America had made before and after Pearl Harbor, advances that could now be set to work in peacetime.

The Powerglide transmission was a case in point. The system it employed, known as a fluid torque converter, first appeared in Germany in the early 1900s but for decades it was thought far too expensive to be mass-produced. In 1937 GM had found a way to put it into buses, and in wartime it was fitted into heavy tanks. Reengineered and refined, this kind of automatic transmission was suitable at last for a passenger car. As part of the company's drive for postwar expansion, GM opened a factory in suburban Cleveland solely to make Powerglides for the Chevrolet.[7]

Plants such as this were shrines to productivity, that other factor that did so much to shape the 1950s. Output per worker was leaping ahead as a consequence of automation, better skills, and the coming of age of a workforce with solid years of high school behind it. Here there was another battle to be fought, about how to share the benefits between price cuts for the customer, profits for GM, and higher wages for employees. Even this was some-thing Engine Charlie thought he could resolve.

As General Motors entered 1950 with a confidence not seen for more than twenty years, other corporations felt the same: Ford, Chrysler, DuPont Chemical, General Electric, and above all U.S. Steel and its competitors. They too were spending heavily on new plants and machines. For an observer such as George Kennan, this—and not the army, the navy, or the Bomb—was America's strongest card against the Soviets.[8]

What Kennan had called the nation's "war-making complex" began the new decade with strong balance sheets and rising divi-dends. Battered by the Great Depression, corporate America had striven for many years to reduce the crushing burden of debt it had run up in the 1920s. By the end of 1948, the total borrowings of companies amounted to only 30 percent of the nation's income, less than a third of the same ratio at the time of the Wall Street crash of 1929. Despite the recession of 1949, corporate profits grew that year and the payouts to shareholders rose as well.[9]

If visitors from overseas took the turnpike through New Jersey and crossed the Delaware at Trenton, they would pass in 1950 a huge construction project that bore the name of U.S. Steel's CEO. The Fairless Works was the largest mill his company would ever build. No foreigner who saw the steel mill, the crowded railroad yards, or the DuPont plants nearby would conclude that here was a nation going to the dogs, the victim of a conspiracy of leftists. And yet this was precisely what many Americans believed.

It was the strangest of ironies that the most famous of the country's anti-communist crusades would occur at just the moment when corporate America had least to fear from such an enemy within. There were conflicts aplenty in the nation, deep rifts and wounds that needed to be healed and might never be so, but American capitalism had no cause for alarm. Of course, it had its flaws and its disputes; and to see these as they were, free from ideology, you had to travel farther west to the coalfields south of Pittsburgh.

Another irony was this. History remembers the early weeks of 1950 for Truman's decision to start the process that led to the building of a hydrogen bomb. In fact the president devoted more hours of work and worry to the coal strike that has been forgotten.

Haunted Men

Television had already come to western Pennsylvania. Steel antennae appeared on the roofs of wood-frame houses, bringing *Texaco Star Theater* to the Monongahela. In the houses lived the miners of the region. Their television sets were a visible reminder that they were, in dollars and cents per hour, among the best-paid manual workers in America. But the story could never be as simple as that. The wages they earned had to be measured against the nature of the work and the length of time they could endure it.

The average coal miner was forty-five years old, which meant that he had first entered the pit when Warren Harding was the president. Safety had improved, and new machinery had transformed the business; but the miner who had lived through the 1920s and 1930s would not think he belonged to a privileged segment of the workforce. He would know that he owed his rates of pay to the campaigns he had fought led by John L. Lewis. He would also know that in the coalfields, prosperity might not last.

In the years that followed World War I, the United Mine Workers had been forced into retreat. Because of shrinking output, foreign competition, and aggressive tactics by the owners of the mines, the union's membership had fallen steeply, reaching its nadir in 1932; but even before the Great Depression began, the mining counties of the Appalachians had known hardship at its most extreme. It had taken the New Deal era and Lewis's alliance with FDR to bring the UMW's strength back to a peak and for wages to recover.

Only in the spring of 1946 had the miners returned to what they thought of as fair parity with other occupations. The seven years or so after World War II would come to be described as "the reign of King Coal," a period when America gorged itself on fossil fuels. The average American used seven times more energy than his or her equivalent abroad. With output rising and the union strong, the miners became what their British cousins used to call "aristocrats of labor"; but it was a fragile species of nobility.[10]

"Miners are haunted men," said a government report in 1947. "Their minds are vexed with the memories of bloody struggles. . . . [T]heir hearts grow weary repressing the importunate warnings of the dangers that lurk underground. Their families silently share these burdens." That same year, an explosion at the Centralia coal mine in Illinois took 111 lives. The Centralia disaster helped to make Adlai Stevenson the governor and gave Lewis a fleeting period of popularity. It also underlined a point that Lewis never tired of making. Injuries, lung and heart disease, and daily wear and tear meant that America's 400,000 miners died, on average, at the age of fifty-six, eight years younger than the national norm.[11]

For the UMW, the long dispute of 1949 and 1950 was an effort to defend the gains they had made—above all, their pensions and their welfare fund—and to push them further before oil and gas and European rivals eroded their bargaining power. Lewis, with his love of Napoleonic history, called the stoppage "the Marengo campaign," referring to a battle that Bonaparte had nearly lost and then rescued with a daring counterattack. In fact, the strike more closely resembled trench warfare. It was an exhausting struggle drawn out over a period of almost a year.[12]

As he tried to deplete the nation's coal supply while keeping the miners with at least some income, Lewis began his series of on-off stoppages in the spring of 1949. He called the miners out, then led them back to work, then he did the same again, until finally, in December, the UMW told its members to go to the mines for only three days a week. As the short-time working took effect, the stocks of coal began to run down; but the mild winter weather prevented the crisis from coming to a head. By the middle of January, the miners were reaching the limit of their stamina.

It was still the custom for the miners and their families to shop at company stores owned by their employers, a practice that was convenient but open to abuse. As the miners' unpaid bills began to mount, the stores cut back their credit. Unable to survive for many more weeks, they defied Lewis's instructions and stopped work entirely. By January 16 thousands of miners had begun to stage wildcat strikes, held without a ballot and therefore exposed to sanctions from federal courts. "We might as well starve to death quickly as starve to death slowly," one miner told a reporter as pickets began to roam the coalfields shutting down the mines.[13]

The center of the wildcat stoppages lay in two Pennsylvania counties, Fayette and Greene, where the miners were locked in combat with the giants of corporate America. From the outset, Lewis had aimed to focus his attack on the so-called "captive mines," meaning those controlled by steel companies, which required coke for their blast furnaces. The largest operator of the kind was H. C. Frick, owned by U.S. Steel, whose flagship was the new, mechanized Robena mine in the Monongahela Valley. More mighty still was Pittsburgh Consolidation Coal, the largest private coal producer in the world, whose mines lay hereabouts and in northern West Virginia.

Under a different name the company still mines coal today, with a tenth of the workforce it had in 1950. At the peak of its strength its influence reached deep into the heart of government. The company had as its chairman a Cleveland lawyer and steel executive by the name of George M. Humphrey. A stalwart of the Ohio GOP, close to Senator Taft, he would go on to serve in Eisenhower's cabinet as secretary of the treasury. There he would sit alongside John Foster Dulles and Engine Charlie of GM. And so the dispute in the mines brought into play some of the most powerful forces in the United States. In that sense it resembled the quarrel about Taiwan, another chessboard where the knights and rooks of politics maneuvered against each other. While the details of the coal dispute were intricate and hard to follow, beneath the surface of events there lay another narrative whose theme had to do with the future of America.

For George Humphrey and his colleagues, the prospects for the nation looked as bright as they did for General Motors. Like GM, Pittsburgh Consolidation had embarked in 1945 on a spending program to expand and modernize with a view to maximizing output at the lowest cost. It was, said the company early in 1950, "an American policy of plenty."[14]

By holding out against the UMW, Humphrey intended not to destroy the union's power but instead to bring about what he and his board called "stability." By this they meant long-term labor contracts that would allow them to invest, fight off competition from other fuels and from overseas, and still pay higher benefits and wages. All of this amounted, the company said, to "a common goal for labor and for management."

This was just the sort of thing that people were saying in Britain, West Germany, and France, where it belonged to the centrist philosophy that the Marshall Plan promoted. Indeed, Humphrey was one of the Marshall Plan's principal advisers. With its talk of common goals to be achieved by way of higher productivity, this kind of thinking was the industrial equivalent of the middle way that so many were looking for in politics. Would it work? It might be feasible in industries such as coal, steel, and autos, where there was strength on both sides—management and labor—and there were gains to be made from technology. It would be a far harder project to complete in those parts of the American economy where unions were weak or barely existed, or where advances from technology were likely to be meager or lay largely in the past.

In the meantime, the coal strike had to be resolved. Keen to see the dispute settled, Truman had the power under Taft-Hartley to intervene and make the parties come to the table: but since his stated aim was to repeal the act, he did not wish to invoke it if he could avoid doing so. Lewis kept his own counsel, with many suspecting that the union was secretly encouraging the wildcat strikes. The mine owners waited, equally reluctant to have the president involved. General Motors forecast that if the dispute dragged on, by early March its assembly lines would come to a halt.

All the while, the politics continued to seethe in Washington. Serious debate about the country's destiny fell victim to partisan rhetoric and strife. There were now only two subjects on which the rival forces arrayed in Congress could agree. One was a domestic measure that relieved the burdens of the poor and the aged, but which, because it lacked the charisma of foreign policy and weapons, has faded into historical oblivion. This was the long-delayed overhaul of FDR's social security system. The other subject where consensus beckoned was the hydrogen bomb.

"A NEW AGE OF NIGHTMARE"

The Super Bomb belonged to that species of decisions that appear to make themselves. "He had no choice," said Senator Brien McMahon, after Truman ended the suspense about the H-bomb by announcing on January 31 that research would be authorized to assess its feasibility. McMahon had done as much as anyone to contrive this outcome, trying to wedge the president into a corner with only one exit route. He portrayed the hydrogen bomb as the inevitable consequence of a divided world in which the United

States had to stand against what the senator called "alien forces of evil."[15]

So perhaps it was; and up to a point Truman seems to have agreed. In 1956 an academic researcher named Warner Schilling visited the former president to ask him how he had reached his decision. He found Truman baffled that anyone should pose such a question. For the president it appeared to have been the only prudent step he could take. Endorsed on all sides in Congress, his decision also pleased the public. In February 1950 a Gallup poll showed 77 percent of Americans in favor of building the new bomb.[16]

From Truman's perspective, the choice he made at the end of January merely authorized the acceleration of Super Bomb research that had been fitfully underway at Los Alamos since the early 1940s. As the president saw it, his announcement followed smoothly from an earlier decision, the one he had taken in October 1949 to speed up the nation's atomic weapons program. Although this came about in response to the Soviet bomb test, it had already been recommended by the Joint Chiefs of Staff months earlier.

If Truman could make his Super Bomb decision so swiftly, it was partly because he had the benefit of Secretary of State Dean Acheson's guidance in the process. This was another of those situations where Acheson the lawyer was in his element: a debate between expert professionals. Here again Acheson could apply the Brandeis method, slicing through the minutiae to draft an opinion that the president could adopt. But while the decision was one thing, the sequence of events that led to it was quite another.

The outcome owed as much to politics as it did to science and to strategy. At the time, Truman resented the way the ambitious McMahon and his Senate colleagues had tried to manipulate him. As the president said to his aides and to Acheson, it was only because Senator Edwin Johnson of Colorado had told a television audience about the Super Bomb, stirring up excitement, that they had to make a public announcement at all. If the senator had been more discreet, the decision might have been made quietly as just another step in the evolution of the US nuclear arsenal.[17]

Truman knew that his predicament was far from ideal. Because of the publicity about the Super Bomb, he had no choice but to tell America what he had decided, just as he had to make a statement about Taiwan. But his announcement about the hydrogen bomb created new risks of its own. It might set up a political chain reaction, making it impossible to halt the project wherever it might lead. Public pressure to move from research to construction of the bomb would become irresistible, leaving no room for second thoughts, or for some attempt—far ahead of its time though this would have been—to negotiate a strategic arms treaty with the Soviets.

Indeed, since the summer of 1949 such a chain reaction had already taken place in an atmosphere of acrimony. Schilling, the academic researcher, interviewed not only Truman but also another sixty-five people who had been involved in the H-bomb discussions. Time and again he was taken aback by their recollections of the anger with which the debate had been conducted. These arguments had begun in late September and then unfolded in parallel with the feud at the Pentagon between the navy and the air force.[18]

In the face of the revolt of the admirals, General Omar Bradley had been emphatic—more emphatic than perhaps he might have wished—about the central role that strategic bombing had to play in America's military posture. This could scarcely be otherwise. The Pentagon was confined to a tight budget, and atomic weapons—or the Super Bomb—seemed to be the best way to deploy scarce resources. Eisenhower agreed. And development of the Super Bomb had the extra appeal that its cost would fall under a separate line in the federal budget earmarked for the Atomic Energy Commission (AEC).

Bradley knew the shortcomings of the B-36. He also knew the difficulties of precision bombing, a subject that the British and the Americans alike had studied intensively before and after 1945. A Super Bomb that could lay waste to one hundred square miles would require a far less accurate drop than the Hiroshima or Nagasaki bombs. Added to that, the Joint Chiefs had some intelligence about the new Russian jet fighter, which would make Soviet defenses all the harder to penetrate.

The evidence given to Congress during the row with the navy had also touched on the need for long-range missiles, which was where debate was heading. The term "intercontinental ballistic missile" had not yet entered the lexicon, but during the Super Bomb controversy it came close to appearing in newspaper columns by the Alsop brothers. Apparently fed with information by the air force, they speculated about an intercontinental missile tipped with a hydrogen bomb as the future of warfare.[19]

From the Joint Chiefs' point of view, all these factors converged to build the case for the H-bomb. Elsewhere the politics did the same. In early October 1949, a few weeks after the news of the Soviet atom bomb test, a powerful coalition came into being to support it. While Brien McMahon was its most vocal member, with Edwin Johnson and fellow Senate Democrats from the "economy bloc" closely aligned, the strongest impetus came from two other forceful characters. One was Lewis Strauss, a member of the AEC, who began to press for the new weapon. The other was the defense secretary, Louis Johnson.

Now fifty-three, Strauss had begun his working life as a traveling shoe salesman and risen by force of intellect to become an investment banker. He had become a partner in the firm of Kuhn Loeb, which later would merge with Herbert Lehman's family

firm. By the 1940s Strauss had entered the kind of Jewish phil-
anthropic circles in New York to which Senator Lehman also
belonged. Their politics could not have been more different.

A Republican, Strauss regarded Bob Taft with something near
to adulation. The two men had been close since 1917, when they
had both worked for Herbert Hoover in the US Food Administration created during World War I. Their friendship deepened
when they worked together to create a new railroad terminal for
Cincinnati. By the late 1920s, the young Strauss had become one
of Wall Street's principal experts on financing for railroads and
steelmakers. His clients included George M. Humphrey of Ohio,
the same man who played so central a role in the coal strike and
then after 1952 in Eisenhower's cabinet.[20]

These personal connections lead us into the core of the
Republican Party as it was at the time. The GOP of the 2020s is
so different from the party of seventy years ago that it requires an
effort of imagination to conceive of it as it once was. In those days,
the mightiest elephants in the Republican herd took the form
of men whose industrial interests lay concentrated in Cleveland,
Chicago, and the other cities of the heartland. Corporate lawyers
or magnates in iron and steel, they preserved the party's continuity with the GOP of the 1896 election and Presidents McKinley
and Taft. Their kind of party has ceased to exist; but in 1950 it was
still thoroughly alive.

With Strauss on the side of the Super Bomb, it could be guaranteed that Senator Taft and his group in Congress would support
it. So would the Thomas Dewey wing of the party, which had no
reason not to. Across the aisle, Brien McMahon brought with him
the bulk of his fellow Democrats, including the battalion from
the South. That being so, nobody could have halted the hydrogen
bomb. In this sense, too, Truman had no choice.

And yet there were those who tried to frustrate the project.
The AEC turned for scientific counsel to its General Advisory

Committee. Chaired by the physicist J. Robert Oppenheimer, it gathered in conclave at the end of October and heard from General Bradley and the Joint Chiefs. On October 30 Oppenheimer drafted the committee's report, which concluded that the Super Bomb should never be produced. The project would consume resources and reactor time, delaying the rest of the atomic program. Committee members were also horrified by the prospect of what they called "a weapon of genocide."[21]

Six of the committee's members signed Oppenheimer's draft. "The extreme dangers to mankind inherent in the proposal," they wrote, "wholly outweigh any military advantage that would come from this development. . . . [I]ts use would involve a decision to slaughter a vast number of civilians." Their report infuriated Senator McMahon, leaving him—it was later said—"almost in tears." He saw the document on October 31. It was surely no coincidence that the following day Senator Edwin Johnson spoke on television about the Super Bomb.

This was the point at which the anger began to grow. The advisory committee had not been unanimous, and there were other scientists keen to challenge its findings: above all, Edward Teller, formerly of Los Alamos and now at the University of Chicago. Into the fray stepped Lewis Strauss, whose brilliant mind had long been fascinated by physics. In the second half of November, he and McMahon each gave the president memoranda pressing for the development of a thermonuclear fusion weapon. On Truman's orders, Acheson and Louis Johnson formed their working group to assess the issues. Its other member was David Lilienthal, an FDR liberal and chairman of the AEC, who was of a mind to oppose the project.[22]

Since Lilienthal had already handed in his resignation, his doubts were unlikely to prevail. And so again—as with the Taiwan question—Acheson and Louis Johnson served as the protagonists. But while Acheson played by the rules, methodically listening to different points of view, the secretary of defense had already chosen his ground in favor of the hydrogen bomb.

His economy drive at the Pentagon left him unable to follow any other course. Conducted though it was to comply with Truman's budget, Johnson had gone at the task with such public gusto that the $13 billion cap had become his own. If any gaps appeared in the nation's military armor, Johnson would be blamed. The surest way to seal them up was to build a new and devastating weapon.[23]

Secretary Johnson had taken steps to ensure that the hydrogen bomb project would go ahead. He had been conferring with Strauss since September; and he had also made a curious appointment to his staff. As its interface with the Atomic Energy Commission, the Pentagon had a body called the Military Liaison Committee. To chair it Johnson chose one Robert LeBaron, who served as his deputy secretary for atomic affairs.

A chemical engineer, married to a former chorus girl from the Ziegfeld Follies, LeBaron had played no role in the Manhattan Project to build the atom bomb. He left no mark on World War II, he held no university post, and his business career had lacked distinction. Before Johnson promoted him from obscurity in the fall of 1949, LeBaron merely served as the research director of a little-known chemical company in Virginia. His appointment at the Pentagon was approved by Truman only on October 19. Ten days later, LeBaron sat alongside the Joint Chiefs as they met Oppenheimer's committee; and by mid-November he had forged an alliance with Senator McMahon in favor of the Super Bomb.[24]

LeBaron was evidently there merely to act as the mouthpiece for opinions that Louis Johnson had already formed. Once again, the secretary of defense was waging a war of maneuver to get his way. Once again it was fought out with leaks and counter-leaks to the press. Some went to the journalist Drew Pearson; others—apparently from Strauss—flowed to the *New York Times*. The coverage reached a remarkable peak with the syndicated columns that Joseph and Stewart Alsop wrote about the new weapon.

On January 2 the Alsop series began to run in the *Washington Post* under the headline "Pandora's Box." Splendidly written and carefully balanced, the columns covered the story from every angle, strategic, scientific, and philosophical. No American who read them could fail to appreciate how immense the issues were in what the Alsop brothers called "a new age of nightmare." As they put it on January 18, "the mere possibility that this terrible weapon may be built in two or three or four years alters the whole face of world affairs."

The Alsops wrote of what they called "a cruel, circular dilemma." Since it had to be expected that the Russians would learn how to make a hydrogen bomb, an American refusal to do so would amount "to acceptance of ultimate surrender to the Soviet Union." On the other hand, they wrote, "it is equally intolerable for such a weapon to be competitively manufactured by two hostile world systems." They ended the series with the stark conclusion "that the old assumptions of world politics and strategy are now obsolescent."

With press coverage so intense, Acheson and his team had to complete their work swiftly. More than a decade before *Doctor Strangelove*, strategic thinking about the implications of a weapon such as the Super Bomb remained in its infancy. Acheson and his staff did the best they could in the time available, but it was short. Although Truman had not set a deadline for their report, it could hardly be delayed beyond the end of January, now that the Alsop brothers and their rivals had aired the subject so thoroughly.

George Kennan produced another brilliant paper on January 20. It was his valedictory item, as his time at the State Department had only weeks left to run. A prophetic piece, it warned against what he called "this mortal error" of anchoring America's foreign policy in the threat of using the hydrogen bomb. It would, he believed, act as a form of "hypnosis," sealing minds against other options. Kennan wanted to open secret talks with Stalin and Molotov similar to those that had led to the lifting of the Berlin blockade, with a view to obtaining some international agreement to control atomic energy and atomic weapons. Only if such negotiations came to nothing, he said, should America proceed with the Super Bomb.[25]

Two days earlier, James Reston of the *Times* had run a story reporting similar views held by Lilienthal of the AEC. But by this time Truman was already close to making up his mind. One question kept coming into the foreground of debate: *What do we do if the Russians get an H-bomb?* It is impossible to quantify the effect of the Alsop columns, but, like most of the comments in Congress and the press, they insisted on a definite answer of some kind. The decision Truman reached was as firm as it could practically be. At his final meeting with Acheson before he made his announcement, the president cut the discussion short after only ten minutes by posing the same question: *Can the Russians do it?*[26]

If the mood had been less heated, perhaps there might have been more time. But by now, with the help of the simultaneous controversy about Taiwan, Senator Taft was building his attack on the State Department and finding many allies in Congress. Whatever Stalin thought about the press club speech, it had made its impact in Washington; but not the one that Acheson intended. Instead it provoked more hostility and another bout of protest from the Democrats on Capitol Hill.

THE KOREAN SCUTTLE

As if to capture the plight of the administration, beset by the Asia question and unable to revive the Fair Deal, an accident took place that some evil spirit might have conjured up to embarrass Harry

Truman. It occurred off the coast of Virginia. On the morning of January 17, at high tide and in clear weather, the USS *Missouri*—the navy's only battleship in service—misread the buoys marking a channel that led to the open sea. Traveling at fifteen knots she struck a sandy shoal in Hampton Roads.

Her bow lifted six feet into the air. The *Missouri* slid for half a mile across the mud, ripping a gash in her hull. For two weeks, the battleship bearing the name of the president's home state lay beached on the shoal. The navy received thousands of letters from the American public offering advice. In Moscow, *Red Fleet*, the Soviet navy's magazine, blamed the grounding on "the low level of American naval technique." At home there were those who compared the stranded *Missouri* to Truman's policy program.[27]

None of this amused the president. Using tugs, divers, dredgers, and explosives, the navy prepared for an attempt to free the ship. With its reputation at stake, the admirals or their aides sent individual replies to each letter writer, including the comedian who suggested using blimps to lift the battleship off the mud. No words of encouragement came from the White House. In the end, the navy with the utmost good humor transformed the incident into something of a triumph, pulling the *Missouri* clear of the shoal while on deck the band played "Anchors Aweigh." Still Truman declined to offer his congratulations.

Transcripts of his news conferences during these weeks show him replying to questions with terse, irritable answers. When pressed about the coal strike, Truman could only insist that "the national emergency is not here." It was noticed that his voice was growing hoarse. Bereft of new initiatives, Truman was also about to lose his closest adviser, the lawyer Clark Clifford, who served as his special counsel. Even critics of the administration made an exception for the shrewd and suave Mr. Clifford. At the end of January he would be leaving the White House to earn fees in private practice.[28]

Clifford, who came from St. Louis, had been the only member of Truman's Missouri Gang fully committed to the Fair Deal. In Clifford's blond and handsome form Truman had possessed his sole equivalent to the guileful lawyers whom FDR had mustered to great effect during the Washington battles of the 1930s. Clifford's departure could be seen as a tacit admission that the Fair Deal was done for.

He was leaving at a moment when the president was asking for new tax revenues and sending a special message to Congress on the subject. As Clifford must have known, Truman had little prospect of obtaining them while the House Ways and Means Committee led by Muley Bob Doughton of North Carolina controlled the public purse. And with the Fair Deal all but dead and buried, the anti-Truman skirmishers were also gathering on another front. The Brooklyn rackets scandal drew ever nearer to the mayor of New York. Clark Clifford had described, in a perceptive memorandum of 1947, the political risks posed to the Democratic Party by its big-city machines. Now the issue was coming to a head. The stories about Frank Costello and the Mob, and the national campaign by other mayors for a federal probe, had produced a Democratic senator keen to take up the matter. This was the young Estes Kefauver of Tennessee. He was seeking funds from Congress to pay for an inquiry into organized crime and its influence in politics.[29]

Embarrassing though this might be in an election year, Kefauver had every reason to pursue such an investigation. With no word yet from Truman about his intentions for 1952, Kefauver had the makings of a candidate for president; but as yet he lacked a national reputation. In his state he also had to reckon with an egregious political machine, the so-called Crump regime in Memphis, from which he was estranged. Kefauver pressed ahead, with some Republicans keen to assist him in a project that might weaken the Democratic Party. Among them was Joe McCarthy, who in January was prowling Washington in search of a new cause to adopt.

The day after the *Missouri* struck the shoal, the Senate published its report on the five-percenter scandal. Harry Vaughan escaped with his reprimand, and Truman refused to fire him. Having lost that battle, McCarthy assembled the press to tell them he was joining Kefauver to demand a Senate probe of the rackets. A little later, McCarthy also called on Congress to impeach the secretary of the navy, not because of the battleship on the mud, but instead because of the firing of Admiral Louis Denfeld.

Neither of McCarthy's interventions aroused much interest. He was simply too junior and too wild a card. Besides, the principal excitement of the month remained the Asia question, where Taft was still at work. The Republican National Committee was due to meet in Washington in early February to approve a new manifesto covering topics foreign and domestic. The senator wished the document to bear his imprint.

The *Dayton Journal Herald* released the full text of Taft's interview about foreign policy on January 23. It ran for the whole of a page. Still opposed to NATO, Taft called instead for a second Monroe Doctrine: this time, however, America would declare that if the Soviets invaded Western Europe, it would mean World War III. Again he urged the United States to defend Taiwan, saying it should place the navy in the Taiwan Strait and build a base on the island.

In later years Acheson would find a phrase to convey his contempt for those who savaged him in Congress in 1950: he would call their onslaught on the State Department "the attack of the primitives." But Acheson's account of what transpired was neither full nor entirely fair. Read in its entirety, Taft's critique of foreign policy was thoughtful and cogent. The formation of NATO, he believed, would make war with Russia more likely, because it would provoke the Soviets to attack before the allies were rearmed, a view that resembled something Kennan had been saying privately. Nor did you have to be simple-minded to harbor doubts about the State Department's China stance.[30]

The interview contained Taft's comments about fellow travelers of Moscow. "We had for some reason," he said, "this pro-Communist attitude in the State Department growing out of the New Deal idea that Communism was a kind of democracy and the pro-Communist idea that the Nationalist government of Chiang Kai-Shek of China was fascist." As a consequence, said Taft, "we never gave China what it needed at the time." This view did not belong to Taft and his friends alone.

No one could describe the erudite Joseph Alsop of the *Herald Tribune* as a primitive. And yet—despite his personal esteem for Acheson—he held the same opinion as Bob Taft. While the Alsop columns about the Super Bomb were appearing, the *Saturday Evening Post* ran a series in which Joseph Alsop also leveled an accusation of pro-communism against the State Department. Alsop felt that America had come close "to offering China up to the Communists, like a trussed bird on a platter."[31]

Acheson's press club speech had settled nothing. By now, too many influential people had lost confidence in the administration, and the Asia question supplied a focus for their discontent. It was against this backdrop that Acheson aroused the revolt about South Korea among Democrats in Congress. On January 19 the House of Representatives debated the Korean aid bill. Although the bill was widely expected to pass, it went down to defeat. The majority against it was tiny—only one vote—but the language was extreme. The Republicans made the debate a motion of no confidence in Acheson, referring again and again to the press club speech. Both Taiwan and Korea lay outside the perimeter of defense—so why ship money to Seoul if it was not to be given to Taipei?

Into the proceedings there crept the name of the China scholar Owen Lattimore, alleged to be one of the leftists who had sabotaged Chiang Kai-shek. If this was an ill omen for Truman, Acheson, and the State Department, another was the effort the GOP made to mobilize its forces. Eighty percent of the Republican members of the House came to the chamber to scupper the bill. With sixty-one Democrats voting the same way, mostly coming from the South, this was just enough to kill it off.[32]

The defeat horrified Walter Lippmann, who called it "the Korean scuttle," a grievous blow to America's side in the Cold War. Since the debate had also been about Taiwan, the situation could be rescued by adding some economic help for the island. A little later this was done, and South Korea received its funds. But the affair was a precursor to a still more strenuous campaign against the administration.

On January 21, the jury returned with its verdict in the second trial of Alger Hiss. They found him guilty of perjury. The judge required a few days to consider the sentence, and while he was doing so the Taft interview appeared. When the sentence came, there would commence four extraordinary months for American democracy. In the winter and the spring of 1950, the many strands of the politics of the era would be woven into a knot that Truman could not untie.

THE GERMAN QUESTION

*F*or France and its leaders the German question had come to seem almost insoluble. Left to themselves, they might have opted for intransigence, a blank refusal to give West Germany the means to make itself a powerful nation. But this the French could not do. They still had to reckon with the danger that restless Germans might tire of their impotence and turn eastward to join the Soviet bloc. Nor could the government in Paris ignore a fact of postwar life: that it had to satisfy the United States.[1]

"What do they really want, these Americans?" inquired Vincent Auriol, the president of France. He was another politician whose ideas had been formed before World War I. A socialist, first elected to the French Assembly in 1914, Auriol had been a disciple of Jean Jaurès, the leader of his party, assassinated three days before that war began. In that distant time, it would have seemed inconceivable that one day America would set France a diplomatic test the country had to pass. And yet this was now their situation.

To fulfill his promise to Secretary Acheson, the French foreign minister, Robert Schuman, had to find a means to restore West Germany to the fellowship of Europe. Some progress had been made in November, at Petersberg near Bonn, but it was only a small step along the way.

Acheson, Ernest Bevin, and Schuman had agreed with Chancellor Konrad Adenauer that the industrial dismantling of the Ruhr would be curtailed. West Germany would also be invited to join, as a junior member, the Council of Europe, set up in 1949 as what Schuman hoped would be a nucleus for European union. In fact the council remained an impotent body that only dealt in words. Bevin and the British joined it with reluctance, wary of any move that might dilute their national autonomy.

At home in France, the Petersberg Accord aroused the usual anxieties. The Communists railed against it, as they did against everything that had America's support. For them this agreement, like NATO and the Marshall Plan, signified the imperialism of capitalists in Washington and on Wall Street, eager to colonize the assets of the Ruhr and then wage war against the USSR. On the right, another fear was heard. Would Germany rise again, rebuild its industrial might, and crush its rivals in Europe economically?

Schuman won a vote of a confidence from the French Assembly, but only after four days of debate. To survive, he had to set himself another test. If France was to be safely reconciled with the new West Germany, their economies would have to be integrated. And this, he told the assembly, could only be achieved by absorbing both into some larger economic structure that no single nation could dominate. This would have to be, said Schuman in words that need no translation, "une structure commune, collective, Européenne." What this meant in practice he could not yet say.

As one writer put it, Schuman was "a man of the frontier." Raised in the border region between the Moselle and the Rhine, college trained in Germany, he was French by choice. After World War I he might have opted to practice as a German lawyer. Instead Schuman settled in the eastern French province of Lorraine. Horrified by German atrocities in Belgium, he had come to hate the militarism of the Reich. If Schuman wished to break down borders, it was to ensure that nothing of the sort occurred again.

His Catholic faith played its part as well. For him this did not mean, as it did for some French Catholics, allegiance to the sterile totems of royalism and reaction. Instead it made for a belief in fairness and equality: in the 1930s, Schuman had voted with the left for workers' rights. It also meant that Schuman understood that other glaring fact of life, the relative poverty of France. In Washington he gathered evidence about America's high wages and brought it back to President Auriol. To raise the French standard of living closer to America's was another challenge, inseparable from the German question.

At the heart of everything lay coal and steel. In 1946 France had begun to implement the Monnet Plan, drafted by Jean Monnet, banker, diplomat, and disciple of American techniques. The plan called for modernization, a program of investment in electric power and basic industries. This was how France spent much of its Marshall aid. By 1950 the Monnet Plan was running into difficulties, hampered by inflation and by Franco-German antagonism.

In West Germany, Chancellor Adenauer saw France's situation as what he called "a psychological problem." It was practical as well. To make its steel, France required coal and coke from the Ruhr, while the Germans needed the iron ore that the French mined in Schuman's homeland of Lorraine. Tariffs and other kinds of protectionism impeded trade between the two.

With the Ruhr still under British occupation, schemes were afoot to "internationalize" its resources; but the parties differed on how this might be achieved. America wanted the Ruhr to thrive again, as a German Pittsburgh at the heart of a Europe free from the Soviets. The British were not so sure. The Labour government in London hoped to see the Ruhr in socialist hands, but their ideas were vague. For France, one outcome was still entirely unacceptable. They could not allow the Ruhr to be what it had been for Hitler, a weapon to be used against them. West Germany also had its demands to make. Next to Lorraine were the coalfields of the Saarland, German territory now overseen by France. This Adenauer wanted to regain.

In January 1950 Schuman tried to end the impasse. His staff were suspicious of the Germans. Adenauer they could not fathom out; but they abhorred the leader of the socialists, Kurt Schumacher. Him they saw as "a Hitler of the left." Even so, the French diplomatic corps had to fall in step that month when Schuman crossed the Rhine on his first visit to Adenauer's new republic.

His mission was to try to find some common ground. As Schuman arrived in Bonn, the West German press vented its spleen against the French, accusing them of plotting to annex the Saarland. Schumacher was hostile, and Adenauer mostly aloof. One of his ministers proclaimed in public that France must share the guilt for World War I.

Schuman seemed to return from his mission empty-handed, except for one detail. He and Adenauer had spent two hours alone together. Adenauer was a fellow Catholic. Had this, or their shared experience of persecution by the Nazis, enabled them to build a rapport? Perhaps; but any formula they found would have to please so many different people. Dean Acheson, the British, and French and West German public opinion: all of them they would have to bring within the fold. The coal and steel problem would also have to be solved. One more fact of life was this: that not everyone could be satisfied. In the end the British were to be the ones left out.

CHAPTER SEVEN

LOYALTY AND SCHISM

Our political system was out of joint. . . . [I]nstead of two healthy parties we had one party bloated with a too long tenure and another party reduced to dark frustration. In this unwholesome state some Republicans turned to extremism.

—CONGRESSMAN JOSEPH MARTIN JR., *Republican House minority leader, 1949–1953*[1]

On the morning of Wednesday, January 25, from Boston down to Delaware a fog as thick as those described by Dickens settled over land and sea. It grounded the planes at Idlewild Airport and kept ocean liners far from their moorings. To the south, although the fog was sparse, it drifted in strands around the dredgers lifting yellow mud from beside the USS *Missouri*. In New York the fog descended everywhere, filling the avenues and the railroad yards where the stocks of coal were dwindling.

Many Americans were better off that morning, because at midnight the new federal minimum wage had come into force. But on Wall Street the markets were falling. Bad news had come from Detroit, where an all-night meeting in a downtown hotel had failed to settle a dispute at Chrysler. At 10 a.m., a stoppage would begin. In Washington, the Bureau of Mines confirmed what most Americans already knew: that a coal emergency was near. Only four weeks' supply of fuel remained aboveground.

At about the same moment that Chrysler went on strike, a man and a woman emerged from a subway exit in Manhattan. The husband was tall, lean, handsome, even elegant in his long tweed overcoat. He looked far younger than his age, forty-five. His wife was slender too, wearing a green woolen dress beneath her winter coat while in the style of 1950 her hat was plumed with feathers. Alger and Priscilla Hiss were arriving through the mist to hear the sentence of the court.

Alger and Priscilla Hiss leaving the federal courthouse in Lower Manhattan on January 25, 1950, after Hiss was sentenced to five years in prison for perjury. *Anthony Camerano / Associated Press / Shutterstock.*

When he was a college senior in Baltimore, his classmates had voted Hiss "most popular fellow" and "best all-round man." At Harvard Law School, where he walked in sunshine, he was one of the editors of the law review. Hiss found a mentor at the school in the same Professor Felix Frankfurter who had so enthralled the young Dean Acheson. He went on to the Washington of the 1920s, where he enjoyed—again like Acheson—the honor of clerking for a justice of the Supreme Court. Later there followed thirteen years of government service, including ten at the State Department.[2]

On this wintry day Alger Hiss stood convicted of a federal crime. Among the reporters in the courtroom was a Briton, Alistair Cooke, who had seen him many times before. That day, Cooke wrote, Hiss "was as erect as always, but at a distance you could see how a strong emotion inside him could give an almost violent, jagged definition to his fine bone."[3]

It took only twenty minutes for the judge to hear some arguments and then pass sentence: five years in prison on each of two counts, the terms to run concurrently, but stayed to allow for an appeal. As they left the courtroom, Cooke noted, "Hiss swept a long, broken face through the rush of newspapermen." In the street a crowd had gathered. They chased the couple through the fog until, a block away, the Hisses found a taxi.

This had been a long story, and the most sensational charge had come at the beginning. In August 1948, a committee of Congress had heard Hiss accused of helping to create a Communist cell at the State Department in the 1930s. Two Republicans, Senator Karl Mundt and Congressman Richard Nixon, had seized upon the allegation, which made all the more enticing reading because of the connections of the man they concerned.

Not only were Hiss and Acheson friends, but Acheson's law-firm partners had included Hiss's brother Donald. More alarming still was the fact that Hiss had been at the Yalta Conference in

1945 as part of FDR's delegation. At that meeting, Stalin, Churchill, and Roosevelt had settled much of the future of postwar Europe, awarding the Soviets their huge sphere of influence in the east. For those who saw Yalta as a betrayal of Poland and other countries of the region, Hiss's presence at the conference seemed to confirm their deepest suspicions.

All of this had been well aired long before the verdict of the court. The evidence had been labyrinthine, and the charges Hiss faced were gravely serious. Although never indicted for espionage, he was convicted of lying under oath to a grand jury about his contacts with the principal witness against him, Whittaker Chambers, an avowed ex-Communist. Chambers had claimed that in 1938 Hiss had given him State Department documents that Chambers then passed to the Russians. The grand jury had heard Hiss deny that this was so; but this was a lie, the trial jurors decided in January 1950. And yet none of this had so far amounted to a lethal blow against the State Department or the White House.

Three months after the scandal first erupted, Harry Truman and his party had won the 1948 election. In January 1949, the Senate confirmed Acheson's appointment with only six Republicans voting against. For nearly eighteen months the Hiss affair had rumbled on, complete with its colorful details—above all, Chambers's use of a pumpkin to hide strips of microfilm—but so had Acheson and Truman, under fire from many directions but making good progress in foreign policy. Senator Herbert Lehman's victory in New York seemed to some to prove that the Democrats could survive the Red Scare without sustaining lasting damage.

The Hiss affair exploded with its full force only after Alger Hiss was sentenced. Partly this was due to an error that Acheson was about to make, albeit with the best of motives. It also seems that something more profound occurred that winter: that change in the prevailing mood of public opinion whose early signs observers such as Senator Arthur Vandenberg had detected months earlier. It was this change of mood that gave the Hiss affair its salience.

In the circumstances of the era, it could not be measured precisely. By the late 1940s opinion polls were a familiar feature of the landscape, but they were still far less frequent than they are today and they were far from adequate. Sampling methods were crude. The polling data at the time lacked a fine grain of detail, without a breakdown by way of age, gender, region, occupation, income, ethnicity, or religious affiliation. Hence—for example—the different views that scholars hold about the reasons why Harry Truman triumphed in 1948.

Fortunately the situation is not hopeless. Although in 1950 political science had yet to become a fixture on every college campus, there were some pioneers. One was an enterprising journalist, Samuel Lubell; another an academic, Valdimer Orlando Key Jr. at Johns Hopkins University and then at Yale. They made the best of assets that Americans have always possessed but which they tend to take for granted.

Americans inherit a time series of census data longer and far more comprehensive than those of most other nations: the census taken in April 1950 was a fine example, immensely informative about its period. They also have a plethora of numbers from their many and frequent congressional, state, and city elections, down to ward level. These often tell us more than those that come from presidential contests.[4]

Lubell and Key both used this kind of data to explore the politics of their day. If we look again at their work and at the electoral map, we might come closer to understanding the forces that made McCarthyism what it was. Far from being a demonic force of nature, or some kind of emanation from America's psychic depths, Joe McCarthy came about for rather more mundane reasons. He was part of a revival of the GOP that could and should have been predicted.

If we examine the details of the 1948 election and compare them with those of the general election of 1952, the midterm ballot of November 1950, and the primaries in the spring of the same year, the following conclusion appears: in the principal battleground states and cities, half of the swing that gave Eisenhower the White House had already occurred in the minds of voters before the Korean War began.[5]

If this is so, then the change in the political mood must have taken place in the first few months of 1950. This is truly the hidden history of the McCarthy era. Because McCarthy took the anti-communism of his age to new extremes, he has cast a spell over recollections of the period. But he could not have done what he did if there had not been a preexisting mood and a set of circumstances that gave him his moment.

As far as McCarthy the person is concerned, perhaps the best that we can say of him is this: Joe McCarthy was a man of talent but also of turbulent emotions, who came to be betrayed by ambition, by liquor, and by scheming people who claimed to be his friends. A man who inflicted suffering on others, he died an early, sordid death of a kind that should invite pity and not scorn. But if McCarthy was a flawed human being, he was also an event, a point of intersection between the forces at work in the America of his time.[6]

Although he did so much to create what we call McCarthyism, he was also its product and its victim. Sensing that the mood of the nation was changing, he seized what he thought was his chance to shine. Pushed along by people more powerful than himself, McCarthy started on the path that led to his destruction.

THE UPSTART FROM OUTAGAMIE

McCarthy's era began at about five o'clock in the afternoon of January 25. In the Senate, Karl Mundt was on his feet, heaping insults on the head of Alger Hiss. While there were those who described the gentleman from South Dakota as "a windbag," this relentless onslaught on Hiss was part and parcel with the new aggression the Republican Party had displayed since Congress had reconvened. Senator Mundt spoke for three hours to denounce the man who had been sentenced that day, mentioning Hiss's Harvard accent and the sharp crease in his trousers. One of those hours had passed, and Mundt was recounting yet again the details of the affair—the pumpkin papers, Yalta, and the role he had played with Nixon in bringing it all to light—when Senator McCarthy intervened.[7]

Was the gentleman aware, McCarthy asked, of "a most fantastic statement" that the secretary of state had just made? Quoting from a brief report on the wires, McCarthy repeated words that Dean Acheson had spoken at a press conference that afternoon: "Regardless of the outcome of the appeal, I shall never turn my back on Alger Hiss." As Mundt proceeded on his way, McCarthy rose again. Was Acheson, he inquired, "also telling the world that he will not turn his back on any of the other Communists in the State Department?"

And so McCarthy's moment came, but it had been a long time in the coming. Since 1945, anti-communism had already passed through several mutations in America, moving to and fro between different targets—the labor unions, Hollywood, the followers of Henry Wallace, and of course the leaders of the Communist Party of the United States—without McCarthy playing a conspicuous part. The claim that Yalta had been a betrayal not only of Eastern Europe but also of Chiang Kai-shek had been current almost from the moment the conference ended. And yet McCarthy had been silent on the subject.

Nor had he been a vocal critic of Truman's foreign policy. In early 1949 Joseph McCarthy had not been among the six Republicans who objected to Acheson's appointment. He had supported the NATO treaty and the arms for Europe. He had said next to nothing about Taiwan. And while McCarthy would vote against Truman's Fair Deal, he did not make reflective speeches like those of Bob Taft about the socialistic threat it posed. Here was another irony: that McCarthy, who would come to be remembered for an ideological crusade, was never much of an ideologue himself.

The path that led him to intervene against Dean Acheson had been erratic, but it had an underlying pattern. "Joe," a friend of his told a reporter in 1947, "was so ambitious it was terrifying." Five feet eleven and weighing close to two hundred pounds, McCarthy could be physically intimidating, but he also had charm and stamina. Above all, he knew how to thrust himself into a situation and grab attention, seizing whatever opportunity arose without thinking through what might come next.[8]

The first full-length magazine profile of McCarthy called him "the Senate's remarkable young upstart." Born the fifth child of seven to an Irish farming family near the town of Appleton in Outagamie County, Wisconsin, he had tended cows, raised chickens, and dropped out of high school at the age of fourteen. He went back at age twenty, graduated in a year—McCarthy was far cleverer than his adversaries would admit—and then studied law at Marquette College, a Jesuit school in his state.

He paid his way with many different jobs, most of them blue-collar, but he also knew how to be a salesman. "His success," it was said, "grew out of a knack he had of making people feel good and of turning himself into a social focus." He drank with gusto, played poker for money, sold his blood to hospitals, and he boxed. McCarthy felled some of his opponents with hammering blows, but he lost to others who had finesse as well as brawn.[9]

Because of the lengths to which people have gone to unearth his secrets, we know more about McCarthy's early life than we do about the formative years of almost every other politician of his era, the exceptions being those who reached the White House.

The central question about him, but one that tends to go unasked, is simply this: *Why was Joe McCarthy a Republican?* His allegiance to the party came about not as the product of a personal creed but as a consequence of being from Wisconsin. Here was a divided state, both industrial and rural, but with an economy closely integrated with Chicago's: and these features of McCarthy's territory would come to shape his destiny.

After many years as a Republican stronghold, Wisconsin had swung to FDR in 1932. With his Irish background and his college years of manual work, McCarthy might easily have gone the same way. The first time he ran for office, hoping in 1936 to become a district attorney, he did so as a New Deal Democrat. But when he first won an election, at the age of only thirty in 1939, party loyalties played no role at all. McCarthy swept to victory to become a circuit judge for three counties. Some thirty-five thousand people voted in the ballot, five thousand more than in the previous contest in 1936. The means by which he brought so many voters to the polling booths set a pattern for the rest of McCarthy's career.[10]

There exists a certain species of politician for whom executive office or the task of making laws hold no attraction. For them, the lure of politics lies in the thrill of the campaign. Turnout at the ballot box is everything, since maximizing turnout is the proof they crave of their talent for the chase. And that was the kind of politician Joe McCarthy was, a perennial competitor who loved the hubbub of elections and tried to carry it with him into Congress. He forgot that the Founders never meant to make the Senate an arena for excitement.

To win his judgeship in 1939, McCarthy had fought a highly personal contest, depicting his opponent—who had sat on the bench for more than twenty years—as pompous, old, lazy, and unsympathetic to the people. Visiting every precinct, McCarthy presented himself as what he was, a local boy made good. He also did something new: he organized a mailshot of handwritten postcards and sent them to each voter by name. To finance all of this, he broke campaign rules and went deeply into debt, another trait he would retain in later life.

Only in 1944 did McCarthy become a Republican. He was finishing his tour in the Pacific, where he had served as a marine intelligence officer and flown eleven bomber missions, manning a tail turret and strafing the palm trees. Later he embellished his war record; but he was not alone in that on either side of the Atlantic. What McCarthy did or did not do in wartime matters much less than his decision to join the GOP and to run for the Senate.

The only motive people could think of at the time was that in his region Joe McCarthy saw no future for a Democrat after the war. His style of electioneering could only work in a state where he knew the terrain and the voters could see him as one of their own. So he was tied to Wisconsin, which was swinging back Republican again. He lost in the primary in 1944, and then in 1946, starting from close to zero, he used his youth and his status as an ex-marine to gather around him the state's Young Republican organization. McCarthy, one reporter wrote, "literally pushed himself into the GOP endorsement, so vigorously . . . that no other candidates appeared." He beat the sitting senator, Robert La Follette Jr., in the primary and then easily won the election in November, taking every county except one.[11]

Two months later, McCarthy went to Washington, a bachelor whose political creed was ambivalent. Much the same was true of his state, where the Republican Party faced both left and right. Although in 1946 La Follette was a Republican, for fifty years he and his family had been the midwestern leaders of the Progressive movement in politics. Isolationist but liberal, in the 1930s the La Follettes had been allied with Roosevelt's New Deal. Their strand of opinion remained strong in Wisconsin. Although McCarthy won his race with a conservative message, calling for curbs on the unions, as soon as he was elected he veered the other way. He came out for his fellow midwesterner Harold Stassen, backing him to be the next Republican candidate for president. "I am for Stassen," McCarthy said in December 1946, "because of his liberal policy on foreign affairs and his middle of the road views on domestic policies."[12]

After so publicly supporting the Minnesota Moose, McCarthy had to stick with him. At the Republican National Convention in 1948, Stassen's defeat left him out in the cold, close neither to the Taftites nor to Governor Dewey's followers. As a junior senator, McCarthy could not expect prestige assignments to committees, but he did not make the best of those he had. "Four freshman senators rate in the dunce-cap class," the columnist Drew Pearson wrote in August 1947. Among them he included Joe McCarthy.[13]

McCarthy found himself accused of being a stooge for Pepsi-Cola as well as a construction company called Lustron. The mud clung to McCarthy's hide. Then, in the spring of 1949, his career descended into the bizarre when he took up the cause of the Waffen-SS, or rather, the cause of some of its members who had been convicted of the murder of American prisoners at Malmedy in Belgium. A Senate subcommittee was investigating claims that the convictions had been obtained by torture. McCarthy barged into the proceedings, alleged a cover-up, and insulted the subcommittee's chairman, a Connecticut Republican, in a speech on the Senate floor.[14]

All the time, McCarthy was trying to balance competing interests in his state. In elections he ran up by far his largest majorities in a belt of rural counties that cut a slash across Wisconsin from Green Bay down to the border with Iowa. Here, where dairy and sugar beet farmers had suffered from wartime price controls and rationing, and wanted free markets instead, McCarthy's support grew as the years went by. But their populations were small. To win his Senate seat, he had to take the lakeshore industrial counties surrounding Milwaukee. This meant that he could not neglect old La Follette supporters. Nor could he attack the labor unions head-on; but here another complication arose.[15]

While McCarthy's origins pushed him toward the liberal wing of his party, other elements in Wisconsin prodded him toward the right. He could not have gained the Republican nomination without the backing of the party's local elite. Known as the Republican Voluntary Committee, it was led by Tom Coleman, the party's most prominent member in the state. Coleman ran an engineering company that supplied the automakers of Detroit, and his committee was dominated by industrialists. They had every reason to want to see the national party throw its weight behind Bob Taft. In 1946–1947, the Milwaukee area witnessed a long strike at Allis-Chalmers, a farm equipment maker. The dispute became a national cause célèbre when it was alleged that Communists controlled the company's union local. Allis-Chalmers helped to fund Coleman's committee, which drew McCarthy toward the Taftite camp.[16]

Caught between these rival spheres of influence, McCarthy also had a religious constituency to please. He never wavered in his Catholic faith. Politically this served him well, because in and around Milwaukee Catholics accounted for more than a third of the electorate. But even this raised complicated questions for McCarthy, since the Catholic Church spoke with more than one voice. For every Catholic bishop who inclined toward the right, there was another who preferred to preach a social gospel. Among the union leaders, Phil Murray of the CIO was as convinced a Catholic as Joe McCarthy.

McCarthyism would arise out of this complicated matrix. His first three years in the Senate saw McCarthy zigzag to and fro, seeking to appeal to the different groups he had to satisfy. He also acquired a reputation as a partygoer. In Washington, that rare commodity—a senator without a wife—had his uses at the dinner table. But the summer of 1949 found him adrift from his senior colleagues in the chamber, with no clear direction to his career.

And then his fortunes began to revive. In August the five-percenter scandal gave McCarthy headlines, an alliance with Mundt, and—for a while—a working partnership with Drew Pearson. That summer the Catholic question also became rather easier to answer. Although Pope Pius XII had never been anything but anti-communist, in 1949 his statements on the subject acquired a new urgency. On July 1, in response to the persecution of the church in Poland, Hungary, and elsewhere, the pope declared that any Catholic who adopted Communist views must be excommunicated.[17]

It would be hard for any Catholic as devout as McCarthy to ignore the wind that blew from Rome. At the same time, he heard the call of a voice from closer to home. We might describe Joe McCarthy as the Macbeth of American politics, a man led on to ruin by promises of greatness to come. In McCarthy's case, the witches on the heath took the shape of the newspaper interests controlled by Colonel Robert J. McCormick of Chicago.

Among the press barons of the era McCormick was the most powerful. Sworn enemies of Truman and everything for which he stood, McCormick and his family owned the nation's two papers with the largest circulation, the *Chicago Tribune* and the *New York Daily News*. Like General Motors, they were awash with cash, as the surging sales of cars and televisions and the like fed their advertising revenue.

It was said of the *Chicago Tribune* at the time that "it is impossible to understand America without knowing something about it." Colonel McCormick liked to see himself and the *Tribune* as the voice of Chicagoland, the chain of cities that curved around Lake Michigan from South Bend to Milwaukee. Some Republicans in the region tried to keep their distance from McCormick, but McCarthy was not among them. His alliance with McCormick proved to be the turning point of his career, as McCarthy became a willing tool of the colonel's project to recapture America's industrial core for the GOP.[18]

McCormick's appeal grew all the more seductive when in 1949 the colonel found a new mouthpiece in the nation's capital. At about the same time that the pope issued his anti-communist decree, the *Chicago Tribune* bought the *Washington Times-Herald*. To act as the paper's general manager the colonel chose his niece, Ruth McCormick Miller. Otherwise known as Bazy, she was twenty-eight, with passions that included breeding Arabian horses and ousting the Democratic Party from the seat of power. Bazy Miller had been the leader of "Twenties for Taft," a national movement of Republican young women determined to put the senator into the White House. One of the *Chicago Tribune*'s chief Washington reporters, Willard Edwards, later remembered her as "a puppet for McCormick." In 1950, Edwards would be one of McCarthy's principal sources of anti-communist material.[19]

Miller joined the *Times-Herald* on October 8. At the time, the paper was pushing the stories that arose from what so many called "the loss of China." Eleven days later, McCarthy inserted a written statement into the *Congressional Record* quoting at length from a *Times Herald* column. The column was the work of Austine Hearst, daughter-in-law of William Randolph Hearst, McCormick's counterpart on the West Coast. Austine Hearst related the story of John Stewart Service, a foreign service officer who had served in China in wartime. He had been accused of leaking documents to a New York foreign policy magazine, known as *Amerasia*, that had connections with America's Communist Party.[20]

By the fall of 1949 the *Amerasia* story had been running intermittently for nearly five years. Using every means at its disposal—wiretaps; tailing of suspects, including Service; and break-ins to *Amerasia*'s offices—the FBI found that the magazine had obtained hundreds of government documents dealing with British and American activities in Asia, some of them secret. Six men, including Service, were arrested in June 1945. A grand jury cleared Service of wrongdoing, but the *Amerasia* case ended inconclusively. Although three men were indicted for stealing official property, the Justice Department never brought them to a full criminal trial.

Because of this untidy outcome, the *Amerasia* affair remained an embarrassment for the Truman administration, to be revived periodically by journalists and by Republicans in Congress. McCarthy entered the field very late and his comments went unnoticed; but they represented the first time the senator had raised the subject of Communism in the State Department. "Perhaps it is," McCarthy's statement said, "that some of the personnel . . . are more sympathetic to certain foreign ideologies than our own."

While Congress was in recess, the senator expanded on the theme: first with his verbal attack in November on the *Madison Capital Times*, and then with a talk at his old college. Amid the Jesuits at Marquette in December, McCarthy blended the language of Pius XII with that of Austine Hearst. He described a global war between what he called "the Communistic atheistic world and the Christian nations." It was a war America was losing, he said, in part because the State Department was "shot through with Communists."[21]

These speeches made no national impact, but by January McCarthy had made his choice. He abandoned the middle of the road, discarded the Wisconsin of La Follette, and went all out for the Colonel McCormick line. Although McCarthy was gambling with his future, he seems to have had the same intuition as Bob Taft. In his tour of Ohio, Taft had seen a pool of apathy waiting to be stirred into life, and McCarthy saw it too. Addicted to campaigning, he meant, like Taft, to electrify the voters with a startling message that could not be ignored. It would be as sharply personal as his race for office as a judge in 1939.

The sentencing of Hiss took place at a moment in 1950 when the new mood in the GOP was coming to a head. With the Republican National Committee due to meet for a convention in early February, the drafting of its manifesto had begun. McCarthy's Wisconsin ally Tom Coleman, a leading member of the RNC, was among those who wrote the document. Much of it played the same tune—"liberty versus socialism"—that had failed to win New York for John Foster Dulles. But the RNC also inserted a section headed "Loyalty." Describing Communism as an "international conspiracy" which "corrupts ideals . . . destroys the fiber of man and denies the existence of God," it deplored "the dangerous degree to which Communists and their fellow travelers have been employed in important government posts." It called for the "prompt elimination" of Communists and their sympathizers from the federal payroll.[22]

If McCarthyism required a founding text, then here it was. Another date was approaching, Lincoln's birthday, on Sunday, February 12. RNC chairman Guy Gabrielson wanted Republican speakers to disperse across the nation that weekend bearing the message of the manifesto. West of the Mississippi, both Nixon and Mundt would be featuring in starring roles. McCarthy had speaking engagements too, but the RNC did not mean him to be a center of attention.

As he had so often done before, McCarthy would force his way into the picture, this time with a script supplied by Colonel McCormick's newspapermen. It would be far easier than McCarthy could have imagined. For this, Dean Acheson and the British would bear some of the blame.

THE MOUNT OF OLIVES

Like Acheson's speech at the National Press Club, his words of support for Alger Hiss were carefully prepared. Usually, his briefings to the press were discreet affairs with no verbatim quotes permitted. On the afternoon of January 25, Acheson encouraged them. He spoke slowly and repeated his phrases so that his listeners could take them down exactly. Going beyond the lines that McCarthy had reported to the Senate, Acheson the bishop's son referred his listeners to the Bible. He quoted the verses from the Gospel of Matthew where, before the crucifixion, Christ reminded his disciples on the Mount of Olives of their duty to care for the afflicted and to visit those in prison.[23]

Acheson knew the risks that he was running by refusing to disown Alger Hiss. That morning he had warned his wife that if he spoke out as he did he would be vilified; and vilified he was, in the press and in Congress, where Mundt called him "poor, befuddled Acheson." Like the plight of the USS *Missouri*, Acheson's statement drew forth a flood of letters from the public. While some were supportive, others called for his impeachment, and it seems that even the president had his doubts. Truman brushed aside Acheson's offer of resignation; but when reporters asked him if he approved of what Acheson had said the president replied—as he had done about the battleship—with a terse, ambiguous "no comment."[24]

What did Acheson think he was doing? His sincerity cannot be questioned, but at the time Acheson also believed that he could ride out the storm he knew his words would cause. "This too will pass," he wrote to his daughter on January 27. Acheson knew he could not be fired; and from his point of view, he was still advancing on every front.

That week he delivered the official advice about the hydrogen bomb to Truman. The president duly followed it up with his announcement that research into the weapon would proceed. As for the aid to Korea, this was being salvaged with the modest concession of some money for Taiwan. Meanwhile, Ambassador Philip Jessup had arrived in Vietnam, where he was making progress in persuading the French to grant wider powers to the new government led by Bao Dai. The arms for NATO would soon be flowing across the Atlantic, after Paris and London agreed to guarantee that none of them would be shipped to their colonies.

Acheson had a weaker grasp of politics at home in the United States. Although in his memoirs he would blame McCarthy and other people he called "primitives" for the assault against him and his department, things were not so simple. Even without McCarthy his remarks would have provoked a furor from a Republican Party now moving along the path that Taft, who was no primitive, wanted it to follow. With their political backs to the wall, and midterm elections approaching, many in the party felt they had no choice but to adopt the new spirit of aggression. If McCarthy had said nothing, his colleagues Taft and Mundt would have led the attack on the State Department, with the *Chicago Tribune* urging them on.

A few days after Hiss was sentenced, the *Tribune* opened a new front in its war on Truman. Months earlier, the paper had highlighted the allegation that former FBI agent Larry Kerley had leveled against the State Department, when he had said that during the war it had protected Soviet agents and their fellow travelers. With this story now a fading memory, on January 29 the *Tribune* switched to a new variation on the same theme. It published the first of a series of six articles describing a Communist infiltration of the government, chiefly written by McCarthy's friend Willard Edwards.

"Shields 74 on US Red List: White House Orders Names Suppressed," ran the headline to the piece. The *Tribune* claimed to have seventy-four names of government insiders—including "one cabinet member"—with Communist affiliations. It was, said the story, only one of a number of similar lists of hundreds of names that Truman was refusing to disclose. The rest of the Edwards series would run on either side of Lincoln Day.

Stories like this had appeared before—with differing degrees of plausibility—but the truth or falsehood of what the *Chicago Tribune* said mattered less than the timing. Beginning in March, Acheson would have to persuade Congress to extend the Marshall Plan for another year, with another rebellion likely in the Senate. And beyond that there lay the primary elections in the spring and early summer. In two of the big states where the Republicans had the most to gain or lose—Ohio and Illinois—they already possessed energetic candidates for the US Senate who were sure to be nominated: Bob Taft and Everett Dirksen. In California, with its open primary system, Richard Nixon could hope to do more than merely win the backing of his party's loyalists. If he built upon the Hiss affair, he might achieve an impregnable lead and then cruise to victory in November.

Even in states where the Democrats ruled supreme, the primaries posed a threat to Truman's leadership. The party had split in the South in 1948, when the enemies of Truman's platform for Black civil rights chose their own presidential candidate, Strom Thurmond of South Carolina, to carry the rebel flag for states' rights and the Jim Crow laws. Two years on, the Democrats of the region aimed to heal the rift within their party, even at the cost of crippling what remained of the Fair Deal. In three states in particular—Alabama, Florida, and North Carolina—the primaries might sabotage the president, if the GOP could set the terms of debate and push it to the right.

The Republicans had every incentive to stir the cauldron of politics. All they needed was a story or two that would run for a few months and cause the maximum embarrassment. If Truman's Fair Deal had been genuinely popular and making steady progress, then the president might have had little to fear. But apart from the new minimum wage and the prospect of some social security reform, his cupboard stood empty. With no money to spend, Truman had no means to fill it up again. As for Acheson's foreign policy, so far all its achievements lay in Europe. Although a Franco-German deal would be a coup he could be proud of, it would not speak loudly to an American electorate.

It seems that none of this entered into Acheson's calculations when he spoke up for Alger Hiss. Both he and Truman knew that the mechanics of Congress favored the use of wrecking tactics by their opponents. But at this sensitive moment, both at home and overseas, they allowed events to slip away from their grasp. And while McCarthy prepared for the Lincoln Day weekend, when he would take the *Chicago Tribune* stories and turn them into a sensation, the Democratic Party began to slide into another debacle on Capitol Hill. It arose from that same issue—segregation and Jim Crow—that would overshadow the party's primaries in the South.

Since his victory over Tom Dewey, the issue of Black civil rights had receded from Truman's priorities, sacrificed to his efforts to keep the rest of the Fair Deal alive. Three years earlier, police in South Carolina had savagely beaten a Black veteran, Isaac Woodard Jr., blinding him for life. The assault had so outraged Truman that he had appointed his presidential committee on civil rights. The report it produced in 1947, *To Secure These Rights*, spoke of a moral crisis in the nation and shaped the program for racial justice that Truman carried with him into the election of 1948. But then the president's initiatives lost momentum.

With his two executive orders in July of that year, Truman had begun to desegregate the federal civil service and the armed forces. While the former made progress, the latter, chiefly the army, dragged their bureaucratic feet. In 1949, the crisis deepened on the streets and in the countryside, with more incidents as shocking as the fate of Sergeant Woodard.[25]

The housing shortage in so many cities supplied a pretext for new kinds of atrocity. The Ku Klux Klan returned in Alabama with bombings of Black families who tried to move into white neighborhoods in Birmingham. In Chicago, rioters turned out to stop people of color from buying homes beyond the South Side. Even the new minimum wage contained a form of apartheid, since it excluded farmhands and domestic servants, occupations where so many workers were Black. And meanwhile, criminal justice in the South produced a stream of abuses: above all in Lake County, Florida, with the case of the Groveland Boys, four young Black men falsely accused of the rape of a white woman.[26]

In July 1949 a sheriff's posse had killed one of the four, and a mob, including Klansmen in their robes, had driven four hundred Black residents from their homes. In September an all-white jury convicted the other three, and two of them faced death in the electric chair. For a while the Groveland case received some attention nationwide, but chiefly because the governor sent in the National Guard. After that it faded from the headlines, but in Florida the case would influence the upcoming Democratic primary.

In the fall of 1949, the civil rights movement began to call the situation "an emergency." In an attempt to break the deadlock in Washington, activists gathered forces for a campaign that— although it failed—would look forward, like the elections in New York, to the politics of the 1960s.

Defending the Indefensible

Thirty blocks north of the White House stood the capital's most spacious Unitarian church. Its clergy had preached to Lincoln and cared for wounded soldiers in the Civil War. In 1950 the congregation at All Souls had for their minister a British liberal in exile. He had made the church a fortress for civil rights, striving to end the segregation that still scarred the city and the nation. In January the Grecian columns of All Souls provided the venue for a rally born from a sense of deep frustration.

Its principal organizer was Roy Wilkins, acting secretary of the National Association for the Advancement of Colored People. Eager to rid the NAACP of any taint of Communism, Wilkins was engaged—like Philip Murray at the CIO—in a purge from its ranks of suspected party members or their fellow travelers. Since the New York conspiracy trial he had felt compelled to be ruthless, even if it meant splitting the movement that the NAACP aspired to lead. And so on January 15, when more than four thousand delegates arrived at All Souls, their credentials were checked, and those who might be too far to the left were turned away. Wilkins refused to invite Paul Robeson.[27]

Even so, the rally represented something radical. Compared with the mass meetings of a later time it might have seemed small. Most of the press ignored it: the period's newspapers were almost as segregated as the state of Alabama. But in the Washington of Truman's era, where swimming pools were barred to people of color and the police arrested Black men for "incommoding the sidewalk," a gathering as large as this had the shock of the new.[28]

The rally marked the start of three days of lobbying Congress and the president. Calling the campaign the National Emergency Civil Rights Mobilization, Wilkins meant it to be sharply focused. In 1949, Congress had blocked—as it always did—an anti-lynching bill, but it also blocked a measure to end the poll taxes that in six southern states kept more than eight out of ten Black adults off the voting register. This outcome left two angles of attack still open. On the one hand, Wilkins would try to change the congressional rules of procedure that stifled so many bills at birth; on the other, he and his allies would push for a specific civil rights bill that had wide support from both parties on Capitol Hill. The debates that followed would persist until the spring, giving Republicans yet another means to lay bare the schisms on the Democratic side.

To get civil rights bills into law, Wilkins and his allies in Congress had to find a way to break the filibuster in the Senate, a weapon the Democrats from the South had used three times since 1945 to abort legislation of such a kind. Meanwhile, in the House, the Mobilization and its friends had to prevent the chamber's Rules Committee from murdering bills by refusing to allow them to come up for a vote. This might just be feasible in 1950, when a clear majority in Congress wanted to end an obvious form of inequality that it had helped to prohibit during World War II.

In 1941, three days after Hitler invaded Russia, FDR had issued an executive order creating an agency to end racial discrimination in the hiring of workers in the war industries or in federal programs. With Congress providing the money it required, Roosevelt's Fair Employment Practices Committee (FEPC) had survived for five years. When peace returned, Congress starved it of funds and allowed it to die, with the Georgia Democrat, Senator Richard Russell, as the engineer of its demise.[29]

Truman wished to legislate to revive the FEPC, make it permanent, and use it to enforce a ban on discrimination in every industry. New York State had led the way in 1945 with just such a law, signed with enthusiasm by Governor Dewey, and six other states had done the same. In 1947 similar bills were introduced in Congress, but they came up against the brick wall that Russell and his southern caucus had erected. In the fall of 1949 the moment came to try again. With backing from both sides of the aisle, Adam Clayton Powell Jr., the Harlem congressman and Baptist preacher, brought in a bill for a new and stronger FEPC to regulate every business or government body with more than fifty employees.

If Congress passed the Powell bill, the nation would turn a corner in its history. For the first time since 1875, the end of Reconstruction after the Civil War, a federal civil rights measure would enter the statute book. Since most Republicans supported it, the bill started well, sailing through the Labor Committee in the House. On the Tuesday after the rally at All Souls, Roy Wilkins and his colleagues went to see the president. It was the morning the *Missouri* ran aground; the coal strike was vexatious too, and Truman had no time to waste. "You don't need to make that speech to me—it needs to be made to senators and congressmen," the president said, cutting Wilkins short, but he endorsed the bill all the same.[30]

The following week, as the jury in the Hiss trial retired to decide its verdict, Powell's FEPC fair employment bill cleared a technical hurdle in the House. Twelve months earlier, when Congress had reassembled after Truman's election victory, Speaker Sam Rayburn had coaxed his colleagues into a procedural reform to reduce the blocking power of the Rules Committee. Only by doing so could Rayburn hope to pass those items of the Fair Deal that he could support. Early in 1950 the conservatives in Congress, mostly Democrats but also some from the GOP, tried to reverse the Speaker's change in the rules. On January 20 the effort failed when the House decided to leave his reform in place.[31]

It was a triumph for the Mobilization, "the first concrete evidence of its effect," in the words of Clarence Mitchell Jr., the NAACP's chief lobbyist in Congress. Fourteen years later, Mitchell would help secure the passage of Lyndon Johnson's Civil Rights Act of 1964. But at this much earlier stage in his movement's history, he could only be cautiously optimistic. Mitchell had no illusions about the difficulties he faced.[32]

As a young reporter in the 1930s, Mitchell had seen racism at its worst in one of the trials of the Scottsboro Boys in Alabama, that notorious affair that so resembled the case of the Groveland Four. His Washington career took the shape of a long, circuitous march around the many obstacles that Congress put in his way, a march in which one step forward was all too often followed by two steps back. In 1950, despite the good omens, Mitchell and his allies would go down to defeat as new barriers sprang up in their path.

During one of the meetings at All Souls, Powell had banged his fists on the preacher's lectern, pledging what he called "his sacred word" that he would bring Congress to a halt if his bill was blocked from a vote. But on January 23, when it was due to come to the House floor, Speaker Rayburn simply ignored it. He refused to call the FEPC bill up for debate, preferring to discuss a futile measure with no hope of passage, a bill to give statehood to Hawaii. And there matters rested, with four weeks to wait until the Powell bill would have another chance of a vote.[33]

Throughout the winter and into the spring the Powell and Mitchell campaign would continue. First in the House and then in the Senate, the battle for an FEPC bill would be fought out in parallel with McCarthy's assault on the State Department, the debates about Asia, and the skirmishing ahead of the elections in November. All of these events shared a common structure that derived from the balance of forces in Congress and the nation.

THE POWER OF THE NEGATIVE

Whether he spoke in the language of Woodrow Wilson or that of FDR, Truman called for change and renewal. In the winter of 1950 it seemed that America had lost what appetite it possessed for either one.

Now that the economy was growing once again, with the increasing confidence that GM's booming sales epitomized, why should the country opt for anything the least bit radical? Here was a question as awkward for the right as for the left. Meager though the polling data were, they did not show a public eagerness either to extend Roosevelt's New Deal or to roll the nation back to the days of Calvin Coolidge.

In January a Gallup poll gave a thousand Americans a list of the nation's problems and asked them which would be the biggest issues in the year's elections. Only one in twenty-five named civil rights. A quarter, 25 percent, said high taxes, and another 23 percent chose public spending and the budget deficit. Fifteen percent said foreign policy and 11 percent chose labor unions and strikes. Although none of this would comfort Harry Truman, another Gallup poll that came in April contained bad news for the Republicans. What did people think about the party's slogan "Liberty versus socialism"? Three-quarters of the public had never heard the phrase.[34]

In the light of numbers such as these, a strategist might have counseled either Truman or Taft to go for moderation and the center ground. This was precisely what they could not do. Committed as he was to the Fair Deal, Truman also had to try to maintain his voting coalition: labor unions and farmers, urban Blacks in the North, Jewish liberals such as Herbert Lehman, and old Progressives in the Midwest and beyond the Rocky Mountains. If shifting to the center meant disowning civil rights, or the Brannan farming plan, or promising never to raise taxes, it was a price Truman would not pay. And besides, the president thought he *was* a centrist, a man from the heart of the country, chosen to be FDR's running mate for just that reason. After his election wins in New York, Truman did not see why he should change course.

For a GOP where conservatives were gaining the upper hand, the center ground held no attraction. It had proved to be a trap for Thomas Dewey. What Republicans beheld was a Democratic Party at war with itself, unable to cohere around Truman's program and led in Congress by stale old men addicted to power and patronage. While this might be a caricature of Truman's Democrats, it contained a grain of truth. The Republicans could play on something else as well: the gap between the president's rhetoric of fairness and his party's defense of the indefensible in the South.

In this situation the Republican Party did not require a positive program of its own: if the polls were correct, the nation did not demand it. All they needed to do was to be negative. They could try to widen the cracks in the administration, such as the feud about Taiwan. Ready to hand they also had the case of Hiss and others like it, rich with detail and apparently so frightening. The FEPC bill offered them another opportunity. If it failed to pass, then Truman would be damaged and the Democrats might lose votes in the North in November.

Most Republicans supported civil rights reform; but if it came to a choice between that and weakening the president, their leadership would opt for the latter. They handed the Democratic Party the means to wreck Truman's agenda. Even if the Powell bill survived the House, which was now unlikely, it would collide in the Senate with a filibuster mounted by the friends of segregation. As a minority party pledged to defeat the Fair Deal, the Republicans had every reason to retain or even strengthen the mechanism by which filibusters worked. And this was precisely what they had done, with a deal struck between Dick Russell the Democrat and the GOP's most histrionic senator.

In the Republican ranks in the Senate Bob Taft usually took the lead, but in second place was Kenneth Wherry of Nebraska. To his critics Ken Wherry was an object of derision. They called him "the merry mortician," because his string of business assets at home in Pawnee City included a funeral parlor. Senator Wherry would leap to his feet in the chamber and beat his chest as he denounced Acheson, NATO, the Marshall Plan, and anything other than low taxes and free markets. But again it would not do to dismiss him as a "primitive."

As Wherry often pointed out, although he knew how to embalm a corpse he also practiced as a lawyer, and he had studied at the Harvard Business School. Behind him, as he saw it, there stood many millions of Americans. While Taft could be regarded as the voice of heavy industry, Wherry spoke for another great Republican constituency, small-business owners. His colleagues in Congress found him irresistible. "Taft they respected," it was said at the time, "but Wherry they loved."[35]

While Wherry was one of those who favored civil rights legislation, he would never willingly yield ground to Truman. And so the previous year he had reached out across the aisle to Senator Russell. They found a common cause in the Senate's Rule XXII, which laid down the procedure for a cloture vote to end a filibuster. In March 1949 this alliance between a Republican and a southern Democrat engineered a change in the cloture rule, and with it Russell and Wherry destroyed that year's attempts at civil rights reform. In the future a filibuster could only be cut short if two-thirds of all the members of the Senate voted for cloture, rather than merely two-thirds of those present in the chamber at the time.

Ten months on, the Russell and Wherry amendment to Rule XXII remained in place, making a filibuster all but impossible to break. Unless the rule were changed again, the Powell bill was doomed. Wherry would have to play his hand adroitly to ensure that the Democrats bore the blame; but if the FEPC fair employment bill came to a Senate vote in April or May, and the southerners filibustered it to death, the timing would be ideal. Truman would be humiliated on the eve of the midterms.

Seeing everything to gain as the primaries drew near, the Republican Party made ready for a fight on all fronts. With his statement in support of Hiss, Acheson had offered them one opening; and then, nine days after the sentencing of Hiss, the British supplied them with another. And after that came Lincoln Day, and then the storm aroused by Joe McCarthy.

STALIN AND KOREA

*N*ew faces were appearing in the front rank of the Soviet elite. In December 1949 Stalin had ousted the mayor of Moscow, who was accused of offenses including building too many dachas for his colleagues. His replacement would be Nikita Khrushchev, summoned back from governing Ukraine. Another rising star was Nikolai Bulganin. Placed in charge of Russia's military industries, he would take a special interest in those essential tools of air defense: radar and jet engines.[1]

These two favorites of Stalin stood onstage at the Bolshoi on January 21 for the anniversary of Lenin's death. A picture ran in Pravda *showing Bulganin between Mao Zedong and Stalin, with Zhou Enlai a few feet away. Khrushchev stood close to Georgy Malenkov in this array of Politburo members, men who maintained continuity with 1917 but also appeared to point toward the future.*

Unwise though it was to speculate about what might happen after Stalin's death, the symbolism seemed clear. The picture displayed China and the Soviets united in devotion to the memory of Lenin. With it went the implication that the new generation of leaders, with Malenkov, Khrushchev, and Bulganin prominent among them, would take the Sino–Soviet alliance forward to new triumphs.

The following day the talks about a treaty began in earnest. There were points of disagreement, especially about the railroad in Manchuria; but after so much prevarication the progress now was rapid. Within a week they had a draft treaty of friendship that both Mao and the Kremlin could accept. Stalin relinquished the assets won from China in 1945, agreeing to surrender the railroad, the naval base at Lushun, and the port at Dalian by the end of 1952.

In a separate, secret document that they did not wish Dean Acheson to see, Stalin insisted on one concession that Mao did not want to make. Only one foreign nation—the USSR—would be permitted to trade or to invest in Manchuria and Xinjiang. This Mao had to swallow. Other than that, the treaty was a coup for China. With it came hard currency and supplies that Mao badly needed: a dollar loan from the Soviets and a pledge of more military aid.

At this moment Stalin turned again to North Korea. He had changed his mind about an invasion of the South. On January 17 at a party in Pyongyang, Kim Il-sung had been excited, even passionate— and a little drunk—as he pressed the Soviet diplomats for their help in persuading Stalin to give him the green light. He told Ambassador Terentii Shtykov that he "was always thinking about how to launch an attack." Kim wanted to visit Russia again to discuss this matter with Stalin.

Shtykov relayed all this to Moscow; and on January 30, with the Sino-Soviet treaty almost finalized, Stalin replied by telegram. An invasion would be fraught with risk, but he said he understood Kim's point of view. Yes, Kim could come to Moscow; but the crucial line was this: "Inform Kim Il-sung," Stalin told Shtykov, "that I am prepared to help him in this matter."

This fateful message delighted Kim Il-sung. The Kremlin followed through at once by sending a Soviet general to Pyongyang. This veteran of Stalingrad would become chief adviser to the North Korean army. There were other hurdles yet to jump and no final decision was yet taken, but Stalin had accepted Kim's core argument: it was time to reunite Korea by force.

A switch of tactics so momentous demands an explanation. The crudest way to interpret Stalin's change of mind would portray it as a response to Acheson's National Press Club speech. By appearing to leave South Korea outside America's perimeter of defense, Acheson had invited an attack; or so it might be argued. Stalin's telegram would not be published for another five decades; but even without it, many people—starting with Bob Taft—had long since reached this conclusion. It was the common currency of the 1950s.

Was this view correct? The timing suggests that the press club speech must have played some part in Stalin's thinking. But Acheson's speech was only one piece in a larger puzzle. When Congress voted on January 19 to withhold economic aid for South Korea, some of the language was just as unwise as Acheson's was later deemed to be. The Ohio Republican who opened that debate in the House called the aid for South Korea "strictly rat-hole money that we cannot afford." This was not a helpful comment, and the vote spoke for itself.

The reality seems to be this. On the one hand, Stalin had persuasive reasons to wish to see South Korea taken militarily. On the other, any foreign observer—and not only Stalin—who studied America in 1950 might well think that here was a nation unwilling or unprepared to go to war to save the southern regime of Syngman Rhee.

For Stalin, Korea was too valuable to lose. The North, integrated by Japan into connection with Manchuria, might help to build a new Chinese industrial machine that he would wish to see flourish. North Korea had its excellent port at Wonsan, but it also had a land border with the USSR only eighty miles from the Soviet naval base at Vladivostok. If there was any danger that South Korea might invade and conquer the North, then action had to be taken to forestall it.

Added to that were the attractive assets of the South, if they could be acquired. Rice and grain, the ports at Inchon and Pusan, and a long littoral facing Japan and putting it in reach of air or submarine attack: these also had their value to Russia. And if Stalin saw prospects of a Communist rising in Japan, as it seems he did, South Korea was all the more worth having. If Syngman Rhee's government was as weak as Stalin's envoys in Pyongyang reported it to be, then the task of defeating it would be feasible.

As for the United States, Stalin would see the following: an army weakened by budget cuts; a Pentagon apparently eager to focus on the defense of Western Europe; and confusion in high places about the nation's strategy for Asia. Once US troops left Korea in 1949, it seemed unlikely that they would return. Stalin probably also thought he could discount the US nuclear threat. Then Truman ruled out the protection of Taiwan, Acheson made his press club speech, and Congress said its negative piece about Korean aid.

All Stalin needed now was to be sure of Mao, not least to guard the rear of Kim Il-sung. With the Sino-Soviet treaty in place, Stalin could tell North Korea that invasion plans could be laid. He had reasonable grounds to think that America would not intervene. Such perhaps was the logic of Stalin's change of mind.

CHAPTER EIGHT

THE NINTH BOURBON

In the age of atomic energy, transmuted into a
weapon which can destroy great cities . . . a serene
president of the United States sits in the White
House with undiminished confidence in the triumph
of humanity's better nature.

—ARTHUR KROCK *of the* New York Times,
February 1950[1]

T he British did things differently. Not for them the theater
of the trials of Alger Hiss. Instead they tried to muffle the
publicity when the atomic spy Klaus Fuchs first appeared
in the dock. His arraignment on February 3 at Bow Street Mag-
istrates Court in the heart of London was as understated as the
British so often chose to be.

From time to time the justices at Bow Street heard sensational
cases, gory murders of the kind that entertained the country. But
mostly the crimes that came to the court were as drab as postwar
London itself, with its grime, its smog, its rubble from the Blitz,
and the ration books still required for daily items. The crime rate
had fallen steeply since the end of World War II, leaving the mag-
istrates to deal with drunks, petty thieves, or restaurant owners
who dealt in contraband.[2]

Among the routine clientele at Bow Street, Klaus Fuchs attracted little interest. He was thirty-eight years old, a former refugee from Nazi Germany, thin and bespectacled with a receding hairline. With only the usual shorthand reporter standing by, the police led Fuchs to a small courtroom on an upper floor to hear the charges against him. The newspapers carried merely a few brief paragraphs, barely hinting at the scale of Fuchs's espionage.

Ten days earlier he had confessed to spying for the Russians since 1941. Not only was Fuchs the head of theoretical physics at Harwell, the British atomic research facility, working on the building of a British atom bomb. He had also spent three years in the United States at Los Alamos as part of the Manhattan Project. There, he had been privy to the early work on a thermonuclear device.[3]

When Fuchs came up for trial in March, the case would be fully reported, but the British did not wish to provoke a furor before they had to. As luck would have it, on January 10 Prime Minister Clement Attlee had called a general election. The king dissolved Parliament on the day that Fuchs first came to court. Attlee faced no awkward questions in the chamber about the lapse of security that had allowed Fuchs, a former member of the German Communist Party, to flourish undetected for so long. Nor did fears of Russian spies feature in election speeches.[4]

Even when more details emerged, British reticence and public ignorance about the British bomb prevented the Fuchs affair from causing a nationwide alarm. News of Fuchs's confession had appalled his Harwell colleagues and the government, because it jeopardized their hopes of atomic cooperation with America; but the wider waters of British politics remained untroubled. As voters went to the polls, they mostly had domestic issues in mind. The Labour Party wanted to nationalize more industries, while the Conservatives promised to do the opposite and to accelerate the end of rationing.

If weapons of mass destruction figured in the campaign, it was only because Sir Winston Churchill—troubled by the way the Cold War was unfolding—gave a speech calling for talks with Stalin to find some means to control the Bomb. As for the Red Scare, it did not seize the attention of the voters. The British people were used to having Communists about the place, but mostly they saw the Marxists for what they were: a spent force at the margin of debate. In 1945, the Communist Party had won two seats in Parliament, and because of this in 1950 its leader had the privilege of making an election broadcast on the BBC. At the ballot box both Communists were voted out.[5]

It was a different story in Washington, where reticence was rare and the thought of Communists aroused such fear and loathing. While the British kept the Fuchs affair from troubling the voters, in America two powerful men wished to do just that. One was Senator Brien McMahon, who had won his victory for the hydrogen bomb but intended to maintain his momentum. The other was J. Edgar Hoover.

The FBI director had known the name of Fuchs since the previous September, when the bureau had given the British the intelligence that ultimately led to his confession. The day before Fuchs appeared in court, the British told the FBI that he had been arrested. By another stroke of fortune, Hoover was due to testify on February 3 to a Senate committee. He was asking them for funds for many more agents, to hunt for Soviet infiltrators and to cope with a crime wave that seemed to the FBI to be surging out of control.

The news from London could not have arrived at a more suitable moment. While Hoover was seeking more money and more G-men, McMahon also had a project he wished to advance. Like Churchill across the ocean, the senator called for diplomacy with Stalin. Even before Fuchs was arrested, McMahon had warned that the Soviets would build a hydrogen bomb; and now he proposed an ambitious scheme for arms control. To go with it and to smooth its path he called for a successor to the Marshall Plan, this time a fund to pay for peaceful work on atomic energy and to give economic aid to nations that might include the USSR. For McMahon, the revelation of Fuchs's treachery seemed to make this all the more essential. Like the FBI director, he made the most of the news.[6]

Fuchs was arraigned on a Friday, and Hoover testified to Congress three times in the days that followed. McMahon summoned Lieutenant General Leslie Groves—who had led the Manhattan Project—to tell the Joint Atomic Energy Committee how much damage Fuchs might have inflicted. By Monday evening, February 6, the American public knew the fearful truth.

With Fuchs's help, the Soviets had tested their first atomic weapon much earlier than Groves had predicted in even his most pessimistic mood. Fuchs might have also given Russia vital secrets of the H-bomb. Were more atom spies at large? Hoover hinted that they were. Pressed for an estimate of the number of subversives in America, he said nearly 600,000: "54,000 card-holding Communists . . . and ten times that number of fellow travelers and sympathizers." It was one of many numbers that would circulate in the days that followed.

Eager to display what he knew about Fuchs and to give the FBI the credit, Hoover went so far as to mention—before the spy had made a guilty plea in court—the existence of his signed confession. On only one subject did Hoover observe the strictest secrecy. He did not reveal the source of the information that had led to Fuchs. It had come from the VENONA project, the US Army's wartime decryption of radio traffic between Moscow and Soviet embassies abroad.[7]

Goodness knows how fierce a blaze Hoover might have ignited if he had revealed that one decrypt seemed to point to Alger Hiss as a Soviet agent at Yalta. But this was scarcely required in an atmosphere already so incendiary. The *Chicago Tribune* was continuing its series by Willard Edwards exposing alleged Communists in the seat of government. Meanwhile, the paper had sent a reporter to Cambridge, Massachusetts, in search of leftist renegades in Harvard Yard. And by one more coincidence, on Monday night, in a sports arena in Washington, the Republican National Committee held a rally to launch its manifesto—with its section about loyalty calling for a purge of federal employees.

Beneath a huge portrait of Abraham Lincoln, eleven thousand delegates ate chicken and potato salad out of boxes and listened to the party's leadership. There were senators and congressmen at the liberal end of the GOP who found the manifesto reactionary. The prevailing spirit was the other way, however, with Bob Taft as the hero of the evening.

Each speaker was allotted less than a minute. They hammered on relentlessly, not only at Truman's socialist Fair Deal, but also at Klaus Fuchs and Alger Hiss. Russia had created its atom bomb, said one senator, "through treachery within our ranks." The administration, he went on, "through stupidity or through design, has coddled Communists and shielded traitors."[8]

A Difficult Week

The week started badly for Truman, and it would finish in a mixture of calumny and farce. Whatever the president knew or did not know about VENONA, neither he nor Secretary Acheson were given the full contents of its decrypts. To that extent both men, far from being wise overseers of events, were captives of a process they could not fully comprehend. If they were unaware of what the decrypts had revealed, they also had no means to verify or to refute the estimates J. Edgar Hoover gave of Soviet subversion. The arrest of Fuchs struck Truman without warning. Again he had no comment to make. The president was grappling with a crisis nearer home.

This was the moment when Truman privately said that the coal strike was the gravest challenge he had faced as president. By now it was reckoned that the country would run out of coal in fourteen days' time. The winter weather, that fickle ally of the United Mine Workers, had so far been benign, but it was expected to worsen. On the day Truman made his announcement about the Super Bomb, he had appealed to both sides to resume production while a board of inquiry reviewed the miners' claims. The union ignored him.

Their leader, John L. Lewis, was about to turn seventy; and as if to celebrate his birthday, the wildcat strikes became a national stoppage. On Monday morning, February 6, everywhere but in southern West Virginia the miners stayed away from work. "This will hurt Harry Truman," said the leader of the union local at the industry's showpiece, the Robena mine in western Pennsylvania. "The men are madder than hell," said another of the strikers. As the FBI director testified on Capitol Hill, and the GOP unveiled its manifesto, pickets swarmed across the coalfields.[9]

Left with no choice, at noon the president invoked the Taft-Hartley Act, the Republican statute he did not wish to use. Truman appointed a fact-finding board and gave them a week to report. If they said the nation's health and safety were in peril, Truman would ask a federal judge to halt the strike and make both sides bargain in good faith.

"The Emergency Is Lewis," ran a Pittsburgh headline. So far the victory was Taft's, as Truman turned to the law the senator had created. Because he passed away in 1953, before reaching the age of sixty-four, even Bob Taft has receded into that historical oblivion that overtakes most members of Congress. Much the same can be said of Senator Ken Wherry, who died still younger, in 1951. And yet at this moment they had more power than the president to shape America's national conversation. Everyone knew where Taft and Wherry stood. Events had conspired to give them two angles of attack upon the president. One was the threat from Communists within; the other, the allegation that Truman had failed the test set by the coal strike by allowing it to continue so long before he intervened.

Amid the stories about Hiss, Fuchs, and Lewis, the Republicans seized control of the discourse of the country. Sensing this shift, Truman made a series of attempts to wrest it from their grasp. His first futile effort began while the Republican delegates were munching their chicken at the rally in the sports arena.

That evening, the president and First Lady dined at the F Street Club, the guests of Senator and Mrs. McMahon. In those gracious days it was still the after-dinner custom of the capital for ladies to leave the gentlemen to their port and brandy. While the sexes were separated, two veterans of the club—Fred Vinson, chief justice of the Supreme Court, and Arthur Krock, Washington bureau chief for the *New York Times*—discussed the hostile press that Truman was receiving. Vinson beckoned to the president to join them, and it was agreed that he would give an interview to Krock.[10]

When he met Krock a few days later, Truman spoke about peace, the economy, the Fair Deal, and the budget deficit, for which he blamed his enemies in Congress. He did not mention the coal strike. As for the pursuit of Communists in Washington, the president repeated an old line, calling the story a "red herring." Krock rose to the occasion, writing up their interview in lyrical prose that cast Truman as a calm, serene statesman with gravitas unshaken by the cares of office. "The penumbra of doubt and fear,"

Krock wrote, "stops short of him. . . . Mr. Truman is the kind of American who must be observed at first-hand, free to speak with the candor and natural piety of his make-up."

Far from restoring sweetness and goodwill, Krock's piece merely aroused more indignation. The president's pun about red herrings went down badly. Truman also made the peculiar mistake of saying that the country could prosper even with so many workers still unemployed. And by granting an exclusive interview, the president had flouted the unwritten rules of the era. The reporters heckled him at his next press briefing. In later years Truman would pretend that the interview had never taken place, a lapse of memory or a fib for which he had to apologize to Krock and to Congress.

In the weeks and months that followed, Truman would try repeatedly to turn back the tide of opinion. Each time he would fail. The hour belonged to voices less august than that of Arthur Krock. As Lincoln Day drew near, Congressman Richard Nixon and Senator Karl Mundt rehearsed the speeches they were due to make. Nixon was to go to Idaho and Utah to talk about Hiss and the Communist conspiracy before circling back to California to pursue his campaign for the Senate. Mundt would speak in his home state of South Dakota as well as in one of the industrial towns the Republicans had to capture, South Bend, Indiana. Meanwhile, Joe McCarthy, less favored by his party's leaders, had arranged his own more modest speaking tour.

McCarthy's schedule had only four engagements, two of which were in Nevada, a state with only one seat in the House, three electoral college votes, and no Senate contest that year. The trip would take him first—on Thursday, February 9—to a place where the election in November was expected to be close. And then, in a hotel in Reno on Saturday night, McCarthy would bring the week to its chaotic end.

McCarthy's Wheeling Speech

Only sixty miles from Pittsburgh and still nearer to the coal-fields there stood the steel town of Wheeling, West Virginia. It lay within a congressional district that switched back and forth between the two parties. For the time being it was held by the Democrats. Eager to displace them in November, the Republicans of Wheeling had invited Joe McCarthy to speak at their women's club's Lincoln Day dinner.

On Thursday afternoon, February 9, McCarthy arrived in Wheeling with two speeches in his briefcase. One dealt with the nation's housing crisis, a subject on which McCarthy differed from Bob Taft but where he had made little impact. His hosts preferred to hear the other speech, about subversives in the heart of Washington. It would combine the themes that McCarthy had developed since October.[11]

That was when he had formed his connection with Bazy Miller and the *Washington Times-Herald*. Her journalists helped McCarthy's office write the Wheeling speech. Some of the material came from the Willard Edwards series in the *Tribune*, and some of it recycled McCarthy's Wisconsin material from the fall. Into the mix went the betrayal at Yalta, *Amerasia* and John Stewart Service, Larry Kerley's testimony to Congress, and fragments of the evidence against Alger Hiss. Going further than Senator Mundt, McCarthy called Acheson a "pompous diplomat in striped pants with a phony British accent."[12]

"Today we are engaged," ran McCarthy's text, "in a final, all-out battle between communistic atheism and Christianity." It may be that he never uttered this sentence in Wheeling, because—notoriously—the only press reports of the occasion followed the typescript of his speech and not the words McCarthy actually spoke. But this only became a matter of controversy because of the startling claim the typescript contained about a spy ring in the State Department. "The bright young men who are born with silver spoons in their mouths are the ones who have been most traitorous," McCarthy said. "I have here in my hand a list of 205—a list of names that were made known to the Secretary of State as being members of the Communist Party."

Later McCarthy would deny that he said 205 in Wheeling, and he would qualify the figure and change it to 207 before switching back to 205. Then he would fasten on 57 as the number of card-carrying party members at large at Foggy Bottom. In fact, as yet he had no list of names at all; but then neither did the other people—Willard Edwards and even perhaps J. Edgar Hoover—who had already tossed so many numbers into the air. In the days to come, Senator Mundt would add to the confusion by saying that the FBI had 4,000 Communists under surveillance.

In the early hours of February 10, a report of the Wheeling speech—headlining McCarthy's assertion that there were 205 party members working for Acheson—went out on the news wires. Reprinted across America, but not yet by the big-city dailies, it vied for attention with the more shocking news from El Paso of Ingrid Bergman's Mexican divorce. The State Department issued a rebuttal, saying that it knew of no Communists among its staff.[13]

And here the trouble started. While McCarthy pushed his story, it dragged him along in its wake, leaving him unable to pull back. On Friday, February 10, he flew to Utah to meet his friend and Senate colleague George Malone of Nevada. When his airplane paused in Denver, reporters told McCarthy what the State Department had said. He replied with a bluff, challenging Acheson to call him that evening when he would read him the list. Then McCarthy gave as clear a statement as he ever would about the meaning of his figures. According to him, there had been—"some time ago," and he did not specify when—some 289 people identified as security risks in the State Department. Of these, he claimed, 207 still worked there, and 57 had Communist Party cards.[14]

In Denver, McCarthy said something still more revealing. He intended, he informed the press, "to tell this story over and over until the public gets tired of it." Feeble though his sources were, his timing was ideal. Amid the distrust created by the New York conspiracy trial and then by the cases of Hiss and Fuchs, the most McCarthy had to do was to repeat the story endlessly, keeping it running until some other scandal intervened. All the while he held some advantages over the administration. They had to do with the Loyalty Review Board that the Truman administration had established to cleanse the federal payroll of Communists and others deemed unfit to serve.

By an executive order in March 1948, the president had sealed the loyalty files of federal employees, refusing to share them with Congress. From a radio studio in Salt Lake City on Friday afternoon, McCarthy demanded the disclosure of the files the State Department had accumulated. He knew Truman would reject any such request; but for as long as the files were sealed, McCarthy could claim that any errors he made were honest ones, and blame them on a secretive administration. And if one day the president relented under pressure and released the files, then McCarthy would have won a victory. In the meantime, the story would not die. To keep it alive, he could, if necessary, resurrect the *Amerasia* affair, whose messy outcome could be made to look suspicious.

It was all the harder to refute McCarthy's claims because the federal government had grown so large. Two million people worked for Harry Truman. By the end of 1949, the review boards had processed more than 6,400 cases of suspected disloyalty, and 201 employees had been fired. But the government was always hiring, the FBI was always conducting checks, and new cases for investigation were always appearing, at a rate in 1950 of as many as 200 a month. Neither Truman nor his officials could ever say for sure that they had no lurking Communists yet to be dismissed.[15]

That weekend McCarthy could not know how events might unfold. His first task was to get his party on his side. If Taft and Wherry had the power to mold the state of mind of the GOP and the nation, then McCarthy had to acquire it too. And so he did, gradually pulling his party into orbit around him. The biggest Republican speeches of the weekend were supposed to be by Ken Wherry in Los Angeles and by Guy Gabrielson in the Truman heartland of Missouri. Apart from Hiss and Fuchs and Communism, they spoke about the wider issues: socialism versus liberty, corruption in the cities, and the evils of the Brannan Plan. With his extreme language and his constant repetition, McCarthy narrowed down the focus to just Communism. Soon his colleagues began to do the same.

At first McCarthy could only call for help from Senator Malone, a loyal fellow Irishman but a weak campaigner. Malone preferred to speak about the evils of Great Britain and his pet scheme for extra tariffs to protect American jobs; but this would not do for McCarthy. Speaking that Friday night in Salt Lake City, with McCarthy nearby but taking the evening off, Malone mentioned Fuchs and condemned the British for their leftist ways. Then he drifted off the point to talk about his tariff.[16]

McCarthy had something more pertinent to say. Seizing a chance to talk to the press, he told reporters that his list of Communists might grow. "There may be many more," he said. "We just have the names of 57." He and Malone were flying to Reno the next day for a speech by McCarthy that they had scheduled five weeks earlier. At that time, before the jury convicted Hiss, and when Taiwan remained the pressing issue, there had been no obvious reason to bring McCarthy to Nevada. Perhaps the trip was merely meant to be a jaunt with some of the gambling that

McCarthy so enjoyed thrown in. He turned it into yet another opportunity.

In Reno McCarthy raised the stakes. Waiting for him in the city was a cable from Acheson's staff demanding the list of Communist Party members in their ranks. Ignoring the request, the senator sent a telegram to Truman urging him to ask Acheson for the names and insisting that the president unseal the loyalty files. That evening in Reno McCarthy gave the Wheeling speech a second time.

This was the day—February 11—when the coal strike entered its climactic phase and Truman declared a national emergency. When the fact-finding board reported that the dispute was endangering the country, Truman asked a federal judge for an injunction to halt the stoppage. Issued against the union that afternoon, the injunction would dominate the next day's headlines. McCarthy pressed ahead regardless.

Again, McCarthy went after John Stewart Service, who was now en route to India to serve as a US consul, coming close to accusing him of treason. Opening another line of assault, this time against the Ivy League, McCarthy also named the astronomer Harlow Shapley, director of the Harvard Observatory, accusing him of Communist subversion. McCarthy ended the evening in the hotel bar with reporters who needled him about his list of names, which he seemed unable to produce. McCarthy lost the list, remembered one of the reporters, "between his eighth and ninth bourbons."[17]

Shambolic though the situation was, McCarthy had already clinched one victory. Despite the coal strike, he was making the impact he desired. In speeches that weekend four more senators from the GOP, including one from the party's liberal wing, also stressed the threat from a Communist enemy within. Among them was Ken Wherry, who in California switched his focus from attacking the Fair Deal to the case of Alger Hiss. But if

McCarthy were to maintain his grip on the Republican agenda, he would have to take his campaign to the Senate floor. This he would do ten days later.

In the face of this barrage of defamation, the Democratic Party should have been united, a solid phalanx in support of Truman and the State Department. In fact, the Democrats remained as divided as they had been at any time since 1937. Some might say that the party required younger chieftains from a rising generation, with fresh ideas and a different style of leadership. Arthur M. Schlesinger Jr. felt that this was so—it was one reason why he wrote *The Vital Center*—and others agreed. Perhaps the Democrats also had to recognize that the rifts within their ranks could not be repaired.

It may be that Truman accepted this analysis. But if he were to act upon it, he would have to carry through an anti-conservative purge of just the kind that FDR had tried and failed to accomplish. Truman had briefly considered doing such a thing after his election triumph in 1948, only to be talked out of it by Speaker Sam Rayburn, who knew how risky such a purge would be. Instead the Democratic Party continued as it was.

At odds with itself, it could not mount a robust defense against the kind of politics that McCarthy represented. The bitter truth was this: that if McCarthy wrought the havoc that he did, much of the blame lay with the Democrats themselves.[18]

DINNER AT THE ARMORY

Six months on from Labor Day, the moment came for yet another festival. Since the age of Andrew Jackson, Democrats had gathered at this time of year to celebrate the memory of Thomas Jefferson. In 1950 the Jefferson-Jackson Dinner, as it had come to be called, would be held on February 16 at the National Guard Armory in Washington. Built like an aircraft hangar, it covered two blocks on the edge of the city. Like GM's Motorama, the event would capture the flavor of its time.

It was another awkward day for the president. The coal strike continued, as the miners ignored the injunction and the telegrams from Lewis telling them to return to work. Krock's interview story had appeared, bringing down on Truman's head the fury of a press corps that resented such exclusive access. "You seem to be in a kind of disgruntled mood," said the president as he met them that morning for their weekly briefing.

Again and again, Truman replied with "no comment" when asked about the coal strike, Mao's visit to Moscow, and Churchill's call for fresh diplomacy with Stalin. On one subject he was emphatic. This was his first press conference since McCarthy's Wheeling speech. There was, said Truman, "not a word of truth in what the senator said."[19]

Perhaps the president meant to keep his powder dry for his speech at the Armory that evening. The Jefferson-Jackson Dinner would be a revealing occasion, one that displayed the condition of the Democratic Party with its flaws but also its remaining strengths. Nobody who saw the pictures taken at the event could fail to note one curious detail: that while Republicans were said to be the party of the rich, it was the Democrats who seemed to be the ones with money.

Ten days earlier at their Washington rally the Republicans had eaten their chicken and potato salad at $1 a head. For the Armory dinner each ticket cost $100, at a time when the average American worker earned less than $60 a week. Commentators noted the contrast between the two occasions. So did Senator Taft, who also objected to another feature of the proceedings. He accused Truman of "nationalizing the airwaves," since his speech would be broadcast on all four radio networks and televised on another two.[20]

Expensive though the tickets were, all of them were sold. The diners were to number 5,300, packed so tightly into the hall that some of them had to sit on the floor. And since the budget for the evening was variously quoted at figures of up to $200,000, anyone could see what it might yield in funds for the Democratic National Committee (DNC). How much of the money came from lobbyists for corporations, the labor unions, or other interest groups? Here was another question members of the press were keen to raise.

At the Armory the decor told a story of its own. To organize the dinner the DNC chose an architect and businessman, Charles Luckman. As the president of Lever Brothers, which sold soap and margarine, on New York's Park Avenue in 1949 Luckman had commissioned one of those postwar skyscrapers, built with steel and glass, that were to make the street a showcase for modernity. He meant to do something similar at the Armory event.

Luckman hired the greatest industrial designer of the age, the Frenchman Raymond Loewy, who gave his style to streamlined trains and to cars built by Studebaker. With Loewy's genius to guide it, the Armory dinner and its setting conveyed a thrilling message about what it meant to be a modern Democrat. Here was a party—or so the decor seemed to say—in touch with its past but advancing with confidence into a future bright with promise.

Along one side of the building, the top table extended for hundreds of feet, in curves that flowed like the wings of a luxury automobile. Here sat the dignitaries—governors, senators, and Truman's cabinet—but also leaders from the labor unions. Nearby was FDR's favorite film actor, Myrna Loy, one of those Hollywood liberals who aroused the ire of the right. It was rumored that she was about to run for Congress, perhaps to fill the seat to be left empty by Nixon. Miss Loy denied that this was so. To evoke the party's history, heroes from the past appeared. High above the top table Loewy had placed the images of Jefferson and Jackson, shown in classical profile as if they were two ancient Romans.

To feed the five thousand, more of his expertise came into play. Since the Armory had no kitchen of the size required, the filet mignon and the *pommes rissoles* had to be brought four miles across the city from two hotels, the Statler and the Mayflower. To keep the dinners warm and serve them to the guests, Loewy had installed a system of charcoal heaters with electric timers. Lanes marked out with flashing lights guided six hundred waiters to the tables.

The Jefferson-Jackson Dinner spoke of glamor and prestige; but did it really speak to the nation or the moment? At the Mayflower that same evening, John L. Lewis was in talks with the mine owners in a fruitless effort to end the dispute. With states and cities beginning to ration coal, in New York the lights on Broadway were due to be switched off in four days' time. The president was about to ask the federal judge to hold Lewis and the UMW in contempt of his injunction. But when Truman rose to address the diners at the Armory, he gave a speech almost identical to the one he had made on Labor Day in Pittsburgh.

Truman dealt with neither Communism nor the H-bomb, as if they were not the talk of the country. The coal strike also went unmentioned. Instead, Truman's target was the GOP, and again he used the line about the "scare words" they were flinging at the voters. Republicans, said Truman, were like "the cuttlefish that squirts out a black cloud of ink whenever its slumber is disturbed." But by this he meant their attacks on his Fair Deal, the subject that Wherry and McCarthy left on one side as they turned the spotlight to the menace from the Reds.[21]

If Hiss had been acquitted and Fuchs had never spied for Russia, the issue of the hour might have been taxation. Still unable to reverse the Republican tax cuts of 1948—at the Armory, Truman called them "asinine"—the president had sent to Congress a few weeks earlier his package of measures to raise a billion dollars. The package would end tax breaks, close loopholes, and increase the rates paid by corporations, while reducing excise taxes as the South required. But among the diners in the hall, Truman would see many who in fiscal and other matters were distinctly unreliable.

Scott Lucas, for one, the Senate majority leader, who had voted for the Republican tax cut that the president viewed with such contempt: he was just about to offer his opinion on Dean Acheson. Senator Lucas would tell Chicago a few days later that the secretary of state should not have uttered words of comfort for Alger Hiss. Elsewhere at the top table sat Speaker Sam Rayburn. Without Rayburn's help, Truman could do little, but he was unreliable too.

At the age of sixty-eight, with thirty-seven years in Congress behind him, Rayburn owed his rank as Speaker largely to his record as a unifier of his party. "We're going to have only one kind of Democrat in Congress," he had said in 1949. This was a promise he could not keep. A few weeks after the Jefferson-Jackson Dinner, where Rayburn spoke as well, both the Senate and the House were due to vote on a bill that exposed the sectional rift within the party. The bill, which concerned the price of energy, would stir Rayburn into revolt against his president.

Time and again in the postwar years the politics of energy divided Truman's party. Four months earlier, Rayburn's protégé Senator Lyndon Johnson had won the gratitude of the oil and gas producers when he helped to destroy the president's nominee, Leland Olds. Now the same lobby hoped for a second victory over the Federal Power Commission (FPC). As coal lost ground to natural gas, delivered by pipeline nationwide, the FPC tried to regulate the trade. The giants of the business—Shell, Standard Oil of New Jersey, and the rest—fought back with the Kerr Natural Gas Bill, named for Senator Robert Kerr, the Oklahoma Democrat who introduced it in the Senate.[22]

Intended to bar the FPC from controlling the price of pipeline gas, the Kerr bill split both parties in Congress, but the rift among the Democrats was the more visible. On one side stood the consumer states and cities of the Midwest and the North, especially New England, where the economy was relatively weak. Against them were arrayed the gas and oil interests of the Southwest and the Gulf of Mexico. In March, after weeks of debate, the measure passed both chambers of Congress by thin majorities. Rayburn and Lyndon Johnson were among its staunchest advocates.

"This bill," Rayburn said, "will not raise the price of natural gas by one red penny." Truman disagreed. Inspired as he was by the ideas of Justice Louis Brandeis, he refused to surrender his right to regulate a powerful industry. In April he would veto the Kerr bill, opening a breach with Speaker Rayburn just when he required his full support. Among the tax breaks the president wished to end, the costliest by far was a subsidy for oilmen and gas drillers: the depletion allowance that helped them finance new wells. FDR had tried and failed to put this to an end. In 1950 Truman lost what meager chance he had of doing so.[23]

This was typical of the Democratic Party at the time. Riven by conflicts that it could not lay to rest, the party lacked a unifying vision of the future. Among the victims of its internal feuds was the bill to create a permanent Fair Employment Practices Committee, which was now as unlikely to pass into law as Truman's revision of the tax code. Six days after the Jefferson-Jackson Dinner, again Sam Rayburn blocked the version of the FEPC bill proposed by Adam Clayton Powell. He replaced it with one that was far weaker.[24]

At the Washington Armory that evening, civil rights amounted— as so often in this era—to a topic too embarrassing to mention. The DNC was about to appoint a Black vice-chairman, William Dawson from Chicago's South Side, the other Black member of Congress. He did not speak that evening. Besides the waiters at the tables, the guests included two hundred people of color, and Lena Horne came to sing for the diners; but Truman

"The Hard Way," by Daniel Fitzpatrick, from the *St. Louis Post-Dispatch*, February 23, 1950. *St. Louis Post-Dispatch Editorial Cartoon Collection, State Historical Society of Missouri, Columbia Research Center.*

said not a word about this part of his program. And yet that very morning something had occurred that should have been on everybody's lips.[25]

In two cases pending before the Supreme Court, the Justice Department had filed briefs calling for an end to segregated education. One of the cases, *Sweatt v. Painter*, concerned H. M. Sweatt, a Black mailman from Houston, who had been refused admission to the University of Texas School of Law and instead relegated to a new school set up for people who were not white. The other, *McLaurin v. Oklahoma*, involved George W. McLaurin, a Black graduate student at the state university at Norman. A federal judge had ordered his admission to the college, but the faculty insisted that he sit—in class, at the library, and in the cafeteria—in separate spaces marked "reserved for Negroes."[26]

Brought by Thurgood Marshall of the NAACP, the Sweatt and McLaurin cases would be argued before the court in April. They would test the court's long-standing doctrine of "separate but equal," and then they would pave the way for the more famous case of *Brown v. Board of Education* in 1954. But they failed to qualify for comment at the Armory. At Truman's uncomfortable press conference that day, a reporter inquired about the Justice Department's intervention in the two cases. "I haven't read the brief," the president replied, "and I don't know what is in it, and I can't answer your question any more than I could last week."[27]

And so, at the outset of the McCarthy era, despite the funds it could raise and its Hollywood flirtations, the Democratic Party failed to locate its vital center. It might at this moment have renewed the commitment to civil rights that Truman had made in 1948. If this could not be achieved with new federal laws, then the other option was the more determined use of the Justice Department in cases similar to those of Sweatt and McLaurin. The Democrats might also have pursued the same issue in all those cities outside the South that the party controlled. Instead they often did the opposite, in Chicago and elsewhere.

Too long in power, too wealthy, too divided, and too distant from the voters, Truman's party found itself outflanked by events and new opinions that were leaving it behind. No disciplined party would have permitted an enemy as flawed as Joe McCarthy to cause as much trouble as he did.

Nor was he their only adversary. While McCarthy scattered buckshot with his reckless energy, elsewhere the politics of the right were developing in another new direction. It would put an emphasis on ideology and culture that went beyond the Taftite call for free markets and low taxes. In time this would present as much of a challenge to the Democrats as the effects of McCarthy's Wheeling speech.

NEHRU, BENGAL,
AND PAKISTAN

A mong *the leaders of nations, the one most given to philosophy was Jawaharlal Nehru. Imprisoned nine times by the British, he had been in jail in 1944 when he wrote a masterpiece called* The Discovery of India. *In the book he reflected on the world that would follow the war. For Nehru it had seemed that only two choices lay open to humanity. Either the world would pursue peace and cooperation, or it would revert to what he called "the old game of power politics on a gigantic scale," with America and Russia creating new forms of imperialism that would cause another cycle of destruction.[1]*

Six years on, as Nehru read about the hydrogen bomb, Indochina, and Taiwan, he was coming to believe that perhaps the choice was already made. "The world is drifting," Nehru wrote in February 1950, "towards major conflicts and possibly war." A few weeks earlier, India had at last become a republic, but Nehru's celebrations had been brief. His nation was close again to hostilities with Pakistan. Nehru felt that he might have to resign as India's prime minister.

A ceasefire the previous year had brought a fragile peace to the disputed state of Kashmir where, soon after winning their independence from Britain, India and Pakistan had fought each other for fourteen months. But early in 1950 bloodshed returned elsewhere. In East Bengal, Pakistan's security forces raided a Hindu village in search of a suspected Communist. The inhabitants fought back. The police went on a rampage, villages were burned, women raped, and men were killed. In February on both sides of the border riots began. They spread to the cities of Kolkata and Dhaka, where Muslims and Hindus murdered each other.

The number of deaths ran into hundreds and perhaps even more in the worst episodes of communal violence in India and Pakistan since the horrors at the time of Partition in 1947. "We appear to live," Nehru wrote, "somewhere near the top of a volcano and any spark tends to waken it into eruption." By the middle of March 1950, two hundred thousand Hindu refugees had fled from East Pakistan into India, converging on Kolkata, and one hundred thousand Muslims escaped the other way.

To some it might appear that the world was now at peace, with the ideological divide between Moscow and the West the principal source of future conflicts to be feared. For Nehru the binary antagonism between America and the USSR told only one part of the story. In The Discovery of India *he had warned of the persistence of ethnic and religious strife and rivalry and what he called "group emotions and conscious or subconscious urges." With his vision of a modern, secular India, committed first and foremost to ending poverty, Nehru meant to show his country how to escape these features of its past. It was this secular vision that he saw in danger.*

As March began, the talk of war grew louder in both Pakistan and India. An attempt had failed at UN mediation in Kashmir. Neither Britain nor the United States could or would intervene to help: both wished to see India and Pakistan settle their differences by themselves, so that together they could defend the periphery of Asia against the Soviets. With the Kashmir question unresolved, the violence in Bengal threatened to cause the fighting to resume.

In India, the extremists, the Hindu Mahasabha, implicated in the murder of Mahatma Gandhi, began to bay for confrontation. In Pakistan, the prime minister, Liaquat Ali Khan, warned that "if India wants war, she will find us fully prepared." Among his supporters some hinted that Pakistan might reach out to the Kremlin as an ally. That year, despite his wish to be nonaligned in the Cold War, Nehru privately considered doing the same.

Within Nehru's Congress Party, dissident voices questioned his authority. His deputy and rival, Gandhi's closest follower, Sardar Vallabhbhai Patel, the "Iron Man of India," as he was known, met with the dissenters and seemed to call for a tougher line than Nehru's against Pakistan. Nehru toured Kolkata and wondered how he could continue in office.

The violence was worst in the railroad town of Howrah across the Hooghly River from the city. A Hindu crowd killed a British businessman as he tried to defend his Muslim servant. Seeming to reveal an India in chaos, the incident brought matters to a head. At the risk of antagonizing Patel, Nehru cabled Liaquat Ali Khan, and urged him to come to Delhi for talks. They reached an agreement—a joint declaration that India and Pakistan would both protect their minorities—which averted war. But if the peace held, as it did, this was only because Patel, despite his skepticism, lent it his backing, and because of the harsh tactics Nehru employed. Howrah fell under martial law, with the army called in to deal with rioters. Meanwhile, the tide of refugees continued to flow across the border.

In 1950, as throughout the rest of the Cold War, the old game of power politics played out in ways that could not be reduced to a struggle between Communism and its opponents. Even without the Cold War, the "group emotions" and religious strife that Nehru described would have taken their toll in South Asia. But neither could they be disentangled from the global divide. India and Pakistan each feared that the other might throw in its lot with either Washington or Moscow.

Across the subcontinent there also fell the shadow of China. In the autumn of 1949, while visiting America, Nehru had made it clear to Truman that he intended to opt for early recognition of the People's Republic. It had to be done, and the sooner the better; but behind this there also lay Nehru's sympathy for China's revolution, land reform, and socialist planning, and his dream of a Pan-Asian space of peace and equality freed from the colonial yoke.

Patel, wary of Chinese aspirations as a great power and its intentions in Tibet, urged Nehru to be more cautious. In these events and debates of 1949 and 1950, much of India's future could be found in genesis.

CHAPTER NINE

THE COMING STRUGGLE

After the disaster in China and the Soviet atomic explosion . . . it is one's duty to sound the alarm, to rouse what of the public can be reached to the prospect of total defeat, enslavement, and death.

—JAMES BURNHAM, The Coming Defeat of Communism, *February 1950*[1]

I n the final week of February, the weather took the side of John L. Lewis and the miners. As Governor Dewey began to ration coal in New York State, freezing rain and snow swept across the region and bore down on the Yale College campus in New Haven, Connecticut. The storm reached its peak on February 22, just as the men of Yale were assembling for their 1950 Alumni Day. They would eat lunch, hear speeches, and dedicate a memorial to classmates who had given their lives in World War II. The occasion would also mark, though few of the alumni knew it at the time, the inauguration of a new style of politics. This came about in a curious way, as things sometimes do at the Ivy League.

So much had happened since the fall of 1949 to endanger the liberal program for which Truman was the advocate. Stalin's bomb, the strikes, the Taiwan question, the cult of Frank Costello, the Sino-Soviet pact, and then the stories about Hiss and Fuchs:

each new development had damaged the president's position. To many he appeared to be caught unprepared. Had the time come to create some new alternative movement from the right? In their different ways, Senators Bob Taft and Joe McCarthy had both felt public opinion swinging in their favor. While the Democratic Party lost its way, its opponents seized their moment and a new conservatism began to emerge.

At Yale it would find its spokesman in a college senior by the name of William F. Buckley Jr. Even at the age of twenty-four, Buckley meant to be a shaper of debate. He was already acquiring that style of writing and of oratory, so elaborate and so distinctive, that would make him such an unnerving foe. With the help of the authorities at Yale, he was also about to achieve a degree of celebrity that would launch him on his career.

By a touch of serendipity, the organizers of Alumni Day had invited Stuart Symington, a Yale graduate and the secretary of the air force, as their keynote speaker. He flew into New Haven in a Lockheed Constellation to talk about atomic warfare, a theme that could not have been more timely. Truman's H-bomb announcement had raised new questions about America's military stance. Just how large did the air force have to be to win a war in which both sides would use atomic weapons and both might soon have Super Bombs as well? Much larger, said Symington, to retain the nation's air supremacy.[2]

The Russians, the secretary told the alumni, were building combat aircraft at a rate far faster than America and its NATO allies. If America fell behind, he would know whom to blame: "those who clamor for a balanced budget." This was one of a series of speeches Symington gave that winter openly accusing his masters, the president and Secretary of Defense Louis Johnson, of weakening the nation by capping spending by the Pentagon.

Symington said his piece and struggled home through the snow on one of the trains not yet halted for lack of fuel. But while his speech made headlines next morning, behind the scenes at New Haven another drama was played out. The authorities at Yale had barred the young Bill Buckley from speaking at the celebrations. This Buckley would reveal in 1951, when he published the book that made his name.

Seventy years after it first appeared, *God and Man at Yale* retains its power to challenge and provoke. When Buckley indicts his alma mater for what he calls its "violent, all-consuming search for money," when he accuses Yale of teaching godless socialism, and when he calls for leftist professors to be fired, he might be dismissed as a troublemaker or as a McCarthyite intent on killing free inquiry. Some of Buckley's critics said so at the time; but there was more than this to *God and Man at Yale*.[3]

Like the young senator from Wisconsin, Buckley was a Catholic. Like McCarthy, he believed that, as he put it, "the duel between Christianity and atheism is the most important in the world." And if McCarthy named the Harvard scientist Harlow Shapley as a fellow traveler with Moscow, so did Buckley in *God and Man at Yale*. But the book was not a rant like the senator's. On the contrary, it was eloquent and closely argued, and it made one telling point that Yale could not refute without some self-examination.[4]

This was Buckley's charge of hypocrisy. When it asked its alumni for donations, Yale declared that it stood for Christianity and the liberty of the individual. How could it do so if, as Buckley alleged, its professors and its textbooks said the opposite, preaching secularism and praising the good deeds of a regulating state? There were cogent answers Yale could give, but not without debate of a kind that powerful institutions such as this rarely wish to have in public. Yale also claimed to believe in academic freedom; but it refused to allow Bill Buckley to call the college to account.

The address Buckley would have given appeared as an appendix to *God and Man at Yale*. As Buckley told the story, he submitted it to the president's office two days before he and Symington were due to speak. The president objected to the text, saying it would "upset the visitors." When Buckley refused to rewrite it, they agreed that he would quietly stand down.[5]

Containing in embryo the arguments of *God and Man at Yale*, this undelivered speech perfectly conveyed the Republican mood at the time. "The liberal," Buckley wanted to tell the alumni, "is the absolute dictator in the United States today." This comment would have puzzled Truman, who knew how hard it was for liberals to win a point in Congress. But if Buckley was being provocative, he was also conveying the sense of deep frustration that had settled over the Republican Party after the 1948 election.

To Buckley, a Taftite supporter of the GOP, it seemed that Yale had succumbed entirely to the liberals when the college's largest debating society voted to endorse the Fair Deal and then the campus Republican Club collapsed. In 1949 Buckley became editor in chief of the *Yale Daily News*, where he tried to turn back the tide. In his columns he condemned Truman, Acheson, and Hiss, defended the Taft-Hartley Act, and decried the Brannan Plan and Adam Clayton Powell's FEPC bill. His Alumni Day speech would have said much the same, and it would also have aligned him with Senator McCarthy.

"Suppose," ran Buckley's text, "the administration of Yale . . . were to formulate its educational credo. . . . Suppose it asserted that it considered Communism, socialism, collectivism, government paternalism inimical to the dignity of the individual and to the strength and prosperity of the nation." Suppose all this, wrote Buckley, and Yale would have to rid itself of those faculty members who disowned the official creed and still sought to expound their liberal or leftist views.

Sinister though Buckley's words might sound to many, he belonged to a segment of opinion whose influence was spreading. If his speech had been delivered and reported in the press, it might have been recognized for what it was. Buckley's speech placed him in the ranks of a new form of intellectual anti-communism that was gathering momentum. Late 1949 and early 1950 produced a stream of books that looked again at the Communist threat and struck a note of increasing alarm.

TAKING THE OFFENSIVE

This new wave of anti-communist writings came as a delayed response to events in Europe in 1947 and 1948. Those were the years of a general strike in France and the Russian coup in Prague, episodes that had displayed the wide range of tactics the Kremlin could employ to extend its reach and subvert the West. These books all strove to make the same point: that Soviet infiltration took many forms, some of them blatant and some of them insidious.

The most famous of the titles—*The God That Failed*—appeared in New York and London in January. Its editor, Richard Cross-man, a member of the British Parliament on the left of the Labour Party, would have been horrified if anyone had said that he helped prepare the ground for Joe McCarthy. A book of the highest literary quality, *The God That Failed* consisted of essays by famous writers who had been Communists or fellow travelers in the 1930s and then broken away, appalled by Stalinism. But the book had an obvious relevance to the case of Alger Hiss, who—if the jury's verdict was correct—had been a 1930s Marxist who had *not* renounced the faith.

While the book had many messages, one of them was this: that Communism tapped deep roots of spiritual angst. Lenin and Marx appealed to educated people, lost and in search of something to believe. Arthur M. Schlesinger Jr. had said the same in *The Vital Center*, but Crossman made the point more forcefully. "The Communist novice," he wrote, "subjecting his soul to the Canon Law of the Kremlin, felt something of the release which

Catholicism also brings to the intellectual, wearied and worried by the privilege of freedom."[6]

The new anti-communism of 1950 dealt in psychology as well as politics, often citing the novels of Dostoevsky for their exploration of the revolutionary mind. It also delved into the minutiae of Communist subversion, drawing on firsthand research in Paris of the kind that Schlesinger had undertaken. At about the same time, another book appeared, much less widely read than *The God That Failed* but quite as relevant to Buckley and the new conservatism. It came from Buckley's mentor at Yale, a political science professor named Willmoore Kendall.

Written by a Frenchman but translated by Kendall, who also gave it an introduction, the book—*A Communist Party in Action*—examined how the Communists functioned in France: their recruitment of members, their party cells, and their grip on labor unions and intellectuals. Anyone who read the stylish prose of Kendall's introduction could find there the source of Buckley's way with words. The professor would also supply what Buckley regarded as some of the sharpest lines in *God and Man at Yale*.[7]

Kendall had another close friend, James Burnham, a New York philosophy professor and former Trotskyite. Six days after McCarthy's Wheeling speech, Burnham brought out his book *The Coming Defeat of Communism*, which caused almost as much of a stir as *The God That Failed*. That summer Kendall would arrange for Buckley and Burnham to meet, an encounter that gave birth to an enduring collaboration. When Buckley founded his magazine, the *National Review*, Burnham provided much of its backbone of ideas. Another vigorous, challenging writer, in 1950 he already commanded attention. In a skeptical review in the *New York Times*, James Reston called Burnham "the cloak-and-dagger philosopher." Even so, Reston devoted two full pages to his appraisal of the book.[8]

Chapter 1 of *The Coming Defeat* bore the title "The Catastrophic Point of View." "The Third World War," wrote Burnham, "is already taking place." Fifty years before the coinage of the term "hybrid warfare," Burnham described America's struggle to defend the world against the Kremlin as "a kind of war for which we have no name." It was, said Burnham, "a political, subversive, ideological, religious, economic, resistance, guerilla, sabotage war, as well as a war of open arms."[9]

Fought out not only in Europe and in China but also in America's backyard—Burnham was worried about Communists in Chile—it was a war America could only win if it acknowledged that it was taking place. The nation could not hope to prevail merely by *containing* the Soviets. Instead, Burnham called for a forward strategy, taking the battle to the Russians by way of what he called "political-subversive warfare." He demanded the use of every kind of tactic—overt, covert, and "unorthodox"—to chisel away at the edifice of Communism. He wanted the "unorthodox" operations to be overseen by the Central Intelligence Agency. On the home front he urged corporations, charities, and universities to cut off funding to writers, artists, teachers, and academics if they proved to be what Burnham called "apologists for Communist causes." Among them he also cited Harlow Shapley.[10]

How new was all of this? Some of what Burnham wrote— such as his attack on liberals in Hollywood—had often been said in the past; but this was an aside, not Burnham's central theme. Reston of the *Times*, who was well placed to judge, found the book striking and original, much as he disagreed with what it said. The novelty lay in Burnham's assertion that the Cold War was a *real* war, not a figure of speech, that it was happening *now*, and that America was losing and had to change its tactics.

If Burnham had been an isolated voice, his message might have fallen by the wayside. But a few weeks later another book began to circulate, the one by John Foster Dulles, *War or Peace*. Dulles had no connection with Burnham or with Buckley, but he echoed Burnham's plea for a new, more determined policy abroad. Carrying more authority than Burnham's, his book helped to tilt the scales of debate still further against the president. Dulles also warned that the Cold War was real and America faced the prospect of defeat. "It is time to think," wrote Dulles, "in terms of taking the offensive."[11]

Dulles's proposals were vague compared with Burnham's, but the drift was the same: something was rotten in the state of foreign policy. Dulles also meant to keep the Taiwan question alive. He saw Asia as the place where America was weakest, with no adequate response to the challenge posed by Mao and Ho Chi Minh. Nor would he let the president dismiss the talk about government subversives as a red herring. Dulles squeezed in a reference to Hiss and Fuchs, when he mentioned cases of "treasonable cooperation" with Moscow involving "highly educated persons who, by birth and environment, were . . . steeped in the traditions of our western society."[12]

And so the tide of opinion boiled up around Truman. It may be that Joe McCarthy never read any of these books: the *Chicago Tribune* gave him most of what he needed. But he could feel the waters rising and carrying him with them. At Wheeling he had taken what Taft had said about the State Department and pushed it much further. In response, Acheson and his aides could try to rebut each detailed allegation. They could also try to counter their critics by developing a new strategy to rally the nation for the coming struggle with the Soviets.

At Foggy Bottom they were already doing so, starting work on the policy document that would come to be known as NSC-68. But if Acheson were to regain the high ground of debate, he would require a united chorus of support from the elected politicians of his party. This was something he had not enjoyed even at the peak of his success.

That winter the Truman administration faced critics on all sides. McCarthy was merely the most violent and least sober. While Burnham and Dulles sounded their alarm, another controversy nearer home continued to escalate. In America, foreign and domestic policy could never be kept separate; instead, the heightened language of division passed back and forth between the two domains. As the Fair Deal floundered, one of the great questions it addressed—health-care reform—gave rise to rhetoric almost as extreme as McCarthy's.

THE BATTLE OF ARMAGEDDON

In October 1949 Truman had captured one objective in his campaign for health care for all. Congress agreed to spend more federal money on building hospitals, extending a program it had created four years earlier. The rest of Truman's health-care plan had been wrecked on the shoals of politics. Because it never came to pass, it has mostly been forgotten, except as a distant prelude to Lyndon Johnson's Medicare and Medicaid. At the time, the fierce opposition it aroused spilled over into other spheres, helping to create the tension and the anger so widely felt.

His enemies called Truman's plan "socialized medicine." In doing so they used an emotive slogan. By now the phrase was old and familiar, first slung at Franklin Roosevelt in 1934 and then repeated endlessly thereafter. Taken up by politicians, and most of all by Senator Taft, it was thrown again at Truman even when his plan was already doomed.

Aware that his scheme would be hard to engineer, Truman had chosen to be as cautious as FDR had often been. If Roosevelt had lived, he would have made federal health care a centerpiece of his fourth term; but he never set out his program in detail, because he would have to wait for the time to be right. Truman took FDR's tentative plans and developed them into a program with three key elements, one of which was sure to bring down the wrath of the nation's doctors. Apart from the federal funds for new hospitals, Truman's program would have paid for larger medical schools to meet a shortage of physicians, most acute in the South. The third leg of the scheme, and the one that caused the most trouble, would have been a national system of health insurance, to be financed by a federal payroll tax. It would have been compulsory for all but a few.[13]

Truman knew that progress would have to be gradual. After a year in office, he saw a hospital bill go through Congress, the Hill-Burton Act, that used federal money to meet one-third of the cost of new facilities. This was the program, which even Taft supported, that came to be renewed in the fall of 1949. The rest of Truman's plan had to wait. Three times between 1943 and 1947 his and FDR's allies in Congress tried to pass an omnibus health-care bill. Each time they fell at the first hurdle, with the medical profession applauding their defeat.

The nation had 190,000 doctors, organized in the American Medical Association (AMA). With their money and their intimate connection with the public, the doctors were a lobby still more effective than the labor unions, much as they detested the comparison. Truman's insurance plan appalled the AMA, which saw it as a form of federal dictatorship over their working lives and perhaps their fees. Taking their side, Taft called the Truman health plan "tyrannical and inefficient," and warned that if it were enacted America would become a totalitarian state.[14]

In the spring of 1949, returned to office with labor on his side, Truman tried again. He sent a health-care message to Capitol Hill covering his essential goals but without proposing a bill of his own. Tactically he meant to let Congress do the work while he kept up the pressure for reform, in the hope that each element would fall into place. While this might require a third term in the White House, step by step the job might be done.

By September the lawmakers had four health-care bills to choose from, ranging from another omnibus package to a modest bill cosponsored by Taft that would pay for health care for the poor. None of the four could pass. The AMA rejected all of them, including Bob Taft's. The doctors preferred either the existing medical prepayment schemes, Blue Cross and Blue Shield, or policies sold commercially by insurance companies. But although enrollment in plans like these had grown rapidly since the 1930s, the coverage was limited and mostly bought by city dwellers. The South and the rural West lagged far behind. Fewer than four million Americans had comprehensive health insurance of the kind Truman wanted. Even so, the AMA defeated Truman's plan, with southern Democrats among the association's strongest allies.[15]

If, as seemed likely, the Truman payroll tax would take as much as 3 percent of everybody's wages, his health-care plan had no hope of approval by Congress; but the doctors' campaign against it became still more ferocious in December 1949. All year the AMA had been locked in combat with Oscar Ewing, the leader of Truman's health-care team. That month, when Ewing went to England to study the Labour government's National Health Service, the AMA called his trip "a bureaucratic mission at the taxpayers' expense" and warned that the fight would continue. The new year would witness, said the association, "the battle of Armageddon—the decisive struggle which may determine not only medicine's fate but whether state socialism is to engulf all America."[16]

Since Ewing was by trade a Wall Street lawyer, it was as silly to denounce him as a socialist as it was to brand New York's Herbert Lehman a friend of Communism. But, as Ewing later recalled, the failure of the Truman plan could not be blamed entirely on the medical profession. In the form presented to Congress, the plan had raised too many questions that neither he nor the president could answer.

How would responsibility be shared between Washington and the states? How large a bureaucracy would the plan create? What freedom would it give to patients to choose their physicians? Only as the system developed over time could issues such as this be addressed. But leaving aside the details, Truman's health-care plan suffered from another fatal flaw. Neither Truman's party nor the president had built a popular movement to support it. Gradually, Ewing came to see that a project so ambitious would require the backing of organized consumers nationwide, and above all from a vocal coalition of senior citizens. Campaigns such as this still lay far in the future.

As 1950 began, the AMA looked to the midterm elections, when it hoped to bury Truman's plan forever. For help the association turned to another new book, this time called *The Road Ahead: America's Creeping Revolution*. Back in 1944, its author, John T. Flynn, had promoted the idea that FDR had provoked the Japanese attack on Pearl Harbor as a ploy to bring America into World War II. The *Chicago Tribune* had seized on that story, and then five years later it also heaped praise on *The Road Ahead*.[17]

In language like Senator Taft's, the book attacked the British form of state-provided medicine and said that this was Truman's inspiration. "Our American system is being destroyed," wrote Flynn. "Russian communism is the grand terminal. British socialism is a station on the line." Issued cheaply in paperback with a bright pink cover, *The Road Ahead* became for a while the most widely distributed book in the nation. Advertised in the press across the country, it was bought in bulk by surgeons and physicians. The AMA sent copies to every member of Congress, and it also began to appear in doctors' and dentists' waiting rooms. Nearby on the coffee tables there would be found the usual copies of *Readers' Digest*. In the month of McCarthy's Wheeling speech, the magazine—which had fifteen million subscribers—printed a condensed version of *The Road Ahead*.[18]

As the health-care controversy raged throughout the year, it burst its banks and overflowed into other fields and became, like Joe McCarthy, a hostile force the president could not contain. As Flynn's book made its rounds and Truman wrangled with the press, McCarthy did what he had promised. Forty-eight hours before Yale's Alumni Day, he took to the floor of the Senate to defend what he had said in West Virginia.

In response the Democrats made an error that would cost them dearly. They did what Yale refused to do for Buckley and gave McCarthy a platform from which to speak. He would make the most of it, prolonging the fracas about his allegations until, like Flynn's *Road Ahead*, they became an issue in the primary elections.

THE FIFTH COLUMN

Senator Scott Lucas thought he knew how to crush the upstart from Wisconsin. It should not be difficult, or so the majority leader believed, to expose the lunacy of the Wheeling speech. On the evening of February 20 Lucas stood almost alone on the Senate floor to confront McCarthy. The senator from Illinois had told his Democratic colleagues not to expect votes in the chamber that night. Most of them had headed home or to social gatherings. Senator Lucas had only one ally at his side, the tireless worker Herbert Lehman.[19]

On his desk McCarthy had placed a pile of photocopies, which, for more than five hours, he would pick up, put down, and wave at his opponents as he pledged "to root out the fifth column in the State Department." All Lucas had to do, or so he thought, was to demand the names of the card-carrying Communists at Foggy Bottom and then watch McCarthy wither up in silence. It was a fatal mistake, but one which displayed not just the majority leader's miscalculations but also the weaknesses of the Democratic Party at the time. Lucas came poorly prepared and failed to see how ugly the situation was.

Although much older than McCarthy—the previous day Lucas had turned fifty-eight—Lucas bore him a curious resemblance. Six feet two, a former college athlete, Lucas liked to fish and shoot, and he shared McCarthy's taste for the masculine culture of the Senate. "Plain solid food, good bourbon, and male talk": those were said to be Lucas's diversions, not so very different from his opponent's.

A farm boy like McCarthy, the youngest son of a family with little money, Scott W. Lucas came from Havana, between Peoria and Springfield. It had a reputation as a gambling town, something that later in 1950 would come back to hurt him. There, like McCarthy, he had practiced as a country lawyer. He served a short spell as district attorney before the New Deal brought him into Congress in 1934. Far smoother than McCarthy, Lucas had the "clean-cut profile and tanned skin," said one detractor, "of a country club Romeo."[20]

His fellow Democrat from Illinois, Adlai Stevenson, called Lucas "workmanlike, conscientious, and enlightened." He also felt he was overpromoted, "a small town boy . . . who'll never set the world on fire." Others said the same. Chosen to lead his party in the Senate at the start of 1949, Lucas had struggled with the task, worn down by the southerners with their filibusters or their threat to use them. They gave Lucas a stomach ulcer that put him in the hospital.

A senator had to function as a sort of microcosm of his state. This was as hard to do in Illinois as it was for McCarthy in Wisconsin. Competing interests pulled Lucas in different directions, as he tried to please the party machine in Chicago while maintaining his grip on rural voters downstate. A similar problem beset him in the Senate. A little like Truman, though he had much less resilience, Lucas rose to the top of the party because his colleagues thought he could mediate between its wings and factions. Conservative by nature, Lucas believed in balanced budgets, he kept his distance from the labor unions, and he opposed Truman's plan for universal health insurance.

Lucas looked back with pride to a speech he had made in 1937, when in the House of Representatives he had condemned FDR's plan to pack the Supreme Court with liberal justices. In the course of his five-minute oration, he had warned that if Roosevelt's plan went ahead, "the Democratic party will be split in twain and probably destroyed." Thirteen years later, that was still the problem: party unity was missing. As a moderate, Lucas could reach out in the Senate to the likes of the powerful Dick Russell and Walter George. But he also believed in Black civil rights and the FEPC fair employment bill, and he was an enthusiast for the Marshall Plan, NATO, and arms for Europe, subjects that so divided the Democratic Party.[21]

To defeat McCarthy, Senator Lucas needed all his soldiers on the front line, firing at the enemy and not at each other. This he did not have. Nor did he see how dangerous it might be to underestimate his adversary. That evening McCarthy won the battle of the headlines. He did so by repeating a simple message again and again. There was, he said, "a bunch of twisted-thinking intellectuals" who had seized control of the State Department and made a fool of Truman. The Communists had to be "cleaned out," a phrase McCarthy kept repeating; and the job could only be accomplished by a committee of Congress. The committee must be granted full access to the government's loyalty files, with the power to ensure that subversives were dismissed.

McCarthy stormed and blustered. He made gross exaggerations and told some outright lies. While Taft had merely spoken about left-wing influences at the State Department, and Senator Karl Mundt had focused on Alger Hiss, McCarthy invented an "espionage ring" embedded at Foggy Bottom. He made up conversations he claimed to have had with the FBI, or the CIA, or the Treasury Department—he did not say which one—about the commies with top secret clearance. But he could not be caught out because he refused to name names, other than the few he had mentioned in Reno. He would give the full list of party members, McCarthy said, to the Senate subcommittee he wanted convened.

Lucas tried to tie him down by pointing to discrepancies between the various numbers he had quoted. Like the boxer he had been, McCarthy ducked and weaved, evading the question, and then he struck back with an obvious reply. "Instead of there being 57 Communists in the State Department," he said, "let us say that there are only one or two." That would be bad enough, if the Communists in question could be shown to have played some role in shaping policy.

In fact, by now McCarthy *had* obtained a list of suspects, sketchy though it was, with each name redacted and instead assigned a number. The photocopies he brandished came from the so-called Lee list, compiled in 1948 by a House staffer named Robert E. Lee. Working for a House committee, before Truman sealed the loyalty files from scrutiny by Congress, Lee had read a summary provided by the State Department. From this Lee took a list of 108 questionable employees, including 57 who were still working at the department that year. Lee's report was the only list McCarthy had, and it said nothing about a ring of spies, but it contained just enough detail to keep him on his feet.[22]

A few months later, when Congress published the Lee list, with the names still omitted, it would show how flimsy McCarthy's charges were. He had entirely misrepresented the contents of the list. But even so, he had caught Scott Lucas off guard, as he described each case of alleged disloyalty, again without naming names. Some of them McCarthy called Communists, others "members of Communist front organizations." He spoke of "psychopaths," "fellow travelers and pseudo-liberals," and he labeled one "flagrantly homosexual." Although Lucas had a large Senate staff, it did not occur to him or to them to place a call to Acheson's deputies. They could have revealed the provenance of the list and shown how McCarthy was misusing it.[23]

Two of McCarthy's allegations made the biggest splash in the press, though both were travesties of the truth. One case was McCarthy's No. 9, whom he described as a White House speech writer who belonged to an organization with Communist links. In fact, the man in question had never worked for the government but merely applied for a job; and the body to which he belonged was Americans for Democratic Action, the liberal but anti-communist ADA. Unable to check what McCarthy said, the *New York Times* printed the allegation the next day. They headlined the story with a piece of pure invention: McCarthy's claim that one of America's "foreign ministers," still in his post in 1950, had passed information to Moscow. The Lee list did not mention this at all.[24]

After two hours, Lucas tried to put the session into recess, only to be outflanked by the mortician from Nebraska. Seeing merely a handful of senators in the chamber, Ken Wherry suggested a quorum call. McCarthy agreed, and the summons went out for absentees to return. Back came the heavyweights, among them the sociable Democrat Brien McMahon, returning from a Georgetown party and still in evening dress. Senator Mundt arrived as well, to reinforce McCarthy with his expertise on Alger Hiss.

As McCarthy repeated his slogans and spoke of "three big Communists" in the State Department, the anger grew on the Senate floor. The burly McMahon surged over to Karl Mundt's desk, waved his fist in his face, and accused him of "trial by Star Chamber." The incident helped to guarantee precisely the outcome McCarthy desired: more column inches the next day.

After five exhausting hours, Lucas made his fatal error. With his back to the wall and unable to bring the debate to a close, he agreed to appoint a subcommittee to examine McCarthy's claims.

"The whole evening," Lucas said wearily, "has been rather point-less." In reality, the Republicans had achieved everything they wanted. Not only would the hearings give McCarthy his plat-form; they would also place the president in the firing line. The GOP's subcommittee members would demand the loyalty files, and Truman would refuse to release them. A few months before the midterms, the Republicans would make the issue a direct challenge to the president's authority.

Just before midnight, the Senate recessed. Again, no one had spoken in direct support of Acheson. In the weeks to come, only one Democrat in the Senate would offer a personal defense of the secretary of state. This was New York's Herbert Lehman. With his long experience of antisemitism, Lehman knew a bully when he saw one. As Senator Lucas fell silent that evening, Lehman and McMahon led the rejoinders to McCarthy.[25]

It was said by some at the time, and many have said so since, that McCarthy strayed onto perilous ground by making alle-gations he could not sustain. This is an exaggeration. Even if everything he said that night had been entirely false, he ran lit-tle risk of wrecking his career. In front of the subcommittee that Lucas had promised, McCarthy would have to substantiate *some* of his claims, although as yet he could not do so. But—as he had pointed out—all he needed was *one* plausible case of a Kremlin fellow traveler connected to the State Department. In the year of Hiss and Fuchs, that would be enough.

In reserve he had the *Amerasia* affair, whose complexities could be spun out for weeks. And if McCarthy did fall flat, what penalty could he suffer? He would look foolish but no worse. He would not have to face the voters in Wisconsin until 1952; and if a week is a long time in politics, two years feel more like an eternity. *In extremis* the Senate could censure a mem-ber who abused its proceedings, but this had occurred only five times since 1810. McCarthy's censure would not come until the late autumn of 1954.

He also drew strength from his party's new mood of aggression. That evening McCarthy had merely expanded on the new Republican manifesto, with its call for a purge of Washington leftists. While some members of the GOP, including Richard Nixon, had doubts about McCarthy's tactics, they would not disown him. Meanwhile, Wherry and Mundt had committed themselves to his support. All across the country he would find activists and newspaper editors who would follow every word he spoke.

That night McCarthy had skillfully managed the press. He liked to drink and mingle with reporters, and in these early days many of them liked him. He understood their deadlines and how hard they competed for news. He knew how swiftly a story phoned in to a copy taker by a wire-service reporter could be relayed across the country with no time for verification. But if McCarthy used the press, the press could use him as well, as the *Chicago Tribune* had discovered. Columnists on the right supplied him with new material and urged him to carry on. This process of mutual manipulation pushed McCarthy down a road of no return. That would be one component of Joe McCarthy's tragedy. Alcohol would be another.

For the president who, like his party, could not foresee the harm McCarthy would inflict, so far he amounted only to an irritation. The subcommittee Lucas had agreed to form would begin its hearings in the second week of March. In the meantime, the president's eyes were turned elsewhere, toward the coal crisis that he viewed with such anxiety.

THE CHANGING TIDE

Harry Truman never lost the virtue of humility. Fifty years later, one of his closest aides would recall a day at Key West when they sat on the beach and watched the waves roll in. "Do you realize," Truman had said, "if you and I walked out there and we drowned, this great country would go right on without us?"[26]

America was always moving on, driven by cycles of economic change that wise politicians did not claim to understand. Two great shocks to the system since 1929, the Great Depression and World War II, had made normality all but impossible to define. The president had no doubt that American growth would continue. Having endured those arduous decades, he did not try to predict the path it would follow. His task, as he saw it, was twofold.

First, he had to create the preconditions for prosperity. At home this meant measures such as dams and river management, the St. Lawrence Seaway, and land reclamation in the West. It would also include open markets abroad, chiefly in a unified Western Europe remodeled—as the Marshall Plan envisaged—in America's image. Another precondition of a sound economy was, from Truman's point of view, his goal of a balanced budget, that target he had adopted partly out of what he saw as common sense, partly out of his fear of inflation, but also because it was forced upon him by Walter George and his allies in Congress.

Truman's second task was this: to share the wealth. It was a phrase the president could never use, because it would have conjured up the prewar ghost of Huey Long. Even so, and however crudely, it might have summed up what the Fair Deal meant to do. But Truman had lost control of fiscal policy. With Congress against him in the matter of taxes, he could take only halting steps to realize his dream of social justice. If his payroll levies for health care were treated as insurance premiums and paid into a fund, then technically they would fall outside the federal budget. Like most of the rest of the Fair Deal, the plan lay stranded on Capitol Hill all the same.

For better or for worse, the sharing of the wealth was a puzzle that industry and labor had to work out for themselves. While

Truman did what he could to shape the negotiations between management and unions, often he found himself merely a spectator to their disputes and the bargains they would reach. The same was true of two other vast constituencies who looked on from the sidelines: that large majority of workers in America who lacked a union, and the owners of small businesses for whom Senator Wherry claimed to speak.

They, too, were spectators as the long, strenuous coal strike finished in a rush. On March 2 the federal judge found in favor of Lewis and the United Mine Workers, refusing to hold them in contempt of his injunction. The Taft-Hartley Act had failed to end the dispute. With no end in sight to the stoppage, schools were closing for lack of heat, and half the nation's steel mills had ceased to operate. Truman sent a message to Congress asking them to pass a law to let him seize the mines as he had done in 1946. "The coal industry," he said, "is a sick industry," an industry that could not give the country what it needed.[27]

Truman's message arrived in the Senate on a Friday afternoon, March 3; and then suddenly, as if Lewis had been waiting for precisely this, a deal was done. By Sunday evening the coal strike was over. At 5:30 p.m. at the Statler Hotel, Lewis signed a new contract with the mine owners. He paused to tell reporters in his rumbling voice that the UMW had achieved a victory for all Americans. Lewis called the Taft-Hartley Act an "abomination," and then he sent telegrams to the union's three thousand locals telling them to go back to work. By midnight the first miners were underground in West Virginia. The railroads hurried freight cars to the coalfields to begin the refueling of the nation.[28]

It was a curious end to the affair. It left the American people wondering how the dispute could grind on for so long and then be concluded so swiftly. Had Lewis planned the whole thing from the outset, with the aim of discrediting the Taft-Hartley Act? Many suspected that he had. This perception could only harm

John L. Lewis, president of the United Mine Workers of America, speaking in Chicago during the 1949–1950 national coal strike. *Associated Press / Shutterstock.*

the president. Much as Truman disliked Taft-Hartley, calling it "a slave labor law," he could not afford disruption on such a scale. Even Truman's admirer Arthur Krock of the *New York Times* felt the president had mishandled the crisis. Krock saw his conduct during the affair as "a major political liability" that might give the Republicans control of Congress.[29]

Meanwhile, the contract looked like a triumph for the miners. The union obtained an increase of only 5 percent in the basic wage, but this had never been the principal issue. More important was the extra sixty cents a day each miner would receive in royalty payments to the welfare fund that Lewis controlled. This was a much bigger win for the UMW. But while Lewis boasted of success in his Marengo campaign, the companies seemed satisfied as well.

At Pittsburgh Consolidation, which had led the talks on the owners' side, George Humphrey and his board did more than show signs of relief. They spoke of the deal as a victory for free enterprise, free markets, and management's right to manage and negotiate. The contract would run for twenty-eight months, bringing the stability they sought. "I hope . . . that we will do away with coal strikes in the future," said Humphrey's number two, George Love, who would go on to lead Chrysler in the 1960s.

History would show that Love was correct. In the fall of 1952, with the war in Korea still being fought, once again wildcat strikes closed many of America's mines; but these were protests against Truman's wartime controls on wages and prices, not a battle between the miners and the companies. The Statler agreement marked the end of half a century of national coal disputes which, since the great anthracite strike of 1902, had posed a political threat to one White House after another. The rest of American industry had also entered an era of relative tranquility. With the exception of steel, where there would be national strikes again in 1952 and 1959, a graph of the days lost in strikes, measured against the number of days worked in the economy as a whole, would show a steep decline after the spring of 1950.[30]

This age of industrial peace would endure until the rekindling of inflation in the mid-1960s. If 1950 marked a turning point, the precise explanation differed from one business sector to another; but Lewis and the companies had found a formula that others sought to emulate. The UMW accepted automation, while the companies accepted the creation of his partial, private replica of Britain's welfare state.

Critics could find fault with the way John L. Lewis led his union. Not only was he secretive and autocratic. He also condoned violent tactics against nonunion mines. As for Lewis's welfare fund, it lacked a sound actuarial basis, built as it was on the royalty for each ton of coal. Later, the medical benefits had to be reduced as oil and gas and foreign mines took more market share and sales of American coal began to fall. But in 1950 Lewis had delivered for his members. He had little time for intellectuals such as Schlesinger; and yet Lewis produced a practical version of a vital center at a moment when the Democratic Party could do no such thing.

The labor leader Schlesinger knew best was Walter Reuther of the United Auto Workers. That union's strike at Chrysler continued into the spring of 1950, to be followed perhaps by a dispute with General Motors. Lewis saw the moment as an opportunity to strengthen labor as a whole and to reclaim the standing he had enjoyed in the critical years of 1936 and 1937 as its uncrowned king. He publicly offered the UAW a $1 million loan. Reuther, far too seasoned a campaigner to trust Lewis, turned the offer down.[31]

In the year of the GM Motorama, the autoworkers did not require allies. With the economy reviving and GM going all out for volume, Alfred Sloan and Engine Charlie Wilson would not want to see their factories turn into battlefields. The new Chevrolet sold in its hundreds of thousands, fueled by gasoline costing no more in real terms than it had in the grimmest year of the Great Depression. With demand so strong for what the workers made, the tide seemed to be running in the union's favor.

Although Reuther could not get what he would always strive for, a voice in the planning of the business, he could see that GM's finances would permit a contract still better than the UMW's. His 1950 contest with the company would center, like the coal strike, upon those fundamental questions of the postwar era: not only how to divide the spoils of America's surging productivity, but also how best to ensure that it would persist.

CHINA AND VIETNAM

*I*n Moscow the Sino-Soviet treaty had at last been signed. That evening, February 14, Mao Zedong hosted a reception in a monument
from the last years of the tsars, the city's Metropol Hotel, fitted out with
ornate columns with a hint of ancient Rome. Following protocol, Mao's
staff had invited Stalin's wife as well as the dictator. Perhaps they did
not know that she had shot herself in 1932. Three days later, Mao and
Zhou Enlai began their long journey home by rail.[1]

The China to which they returned was not yet a country at peace.
The People's Liberation Army was preparing an April offensive against
the island of Hainan, to be followed perhaps by Mao's invasion of
Taiwan. In the interior, rebels and diehards from the Kuomintang
were still on the loose. A telegram arrived from Deng Xiaoping, who
now led the Communist Party in Chongqing, warning of bandits
threatening the western province of Sichuan.

While Mao was in Moscow, Stalin had advised him to continue to
be prudent with the advance of the revolution. As the Kremlin hoped,
coalition government remained the official Beijing line. Mao planned
to retain what he called "the national bourgeoisie," meaning private
enterprise in Chinese hands. "Some people believe," Mao would say in
a speech to Communist Party members in June, "that it is possible to

eliminate capitalism and implement socialism at an early date. Such an idea is wrong."

By March inflation had begun to ease, but Mao still saw years of preparation ahead before the transition to socialism could commence. Government spending had to be cut, industry reorganized, and although land reform continued it would be gradual and cautious. In line with Stalin's recommendations, on March 12 he sent a circular to the party chiefs in those parts of China that the PLA had taken from the KMT in 1949. Feudal landlords had to be dispossessed, wrote Mao; but as yet he did not wish to touch "the semi-feudal rich peasants," whose support he still needed.

Even so, a harder line could also be seen. The following year, 1951, would bring the campaign known as zhenfan, an onslaught against "counterrevolutionaries" that would lead to at least seven hundred thousand executions. The campaign had its roots in events soon after Mao arrived home from Russia. On March 18, his colleague Liu Shaoqi ordered the suppression of the bandits and other opponents of the regime, leading some local officials to keep registers of KMT members and other "hostile elements." In the coastal provinces of Zhejiang and Shandong, the registers listed almost a quarter of a million names.

While Mao began to build his new China, military history unfolded too. As he and Zhou were passing through Manchuria, far to the south a meeting occurred on the border with Vietnam. The previous month, both China and the USSR had done as they had promised, recognizing the Vietminh as the country's government. Now Ho Chi Minh's commander, General Giap, met with a liaison team from the PLA and asked for supplies and help with the training of his troops.

In time, this would result in a catastrophe for France. In Paris the war with the Vietminh was controversial and unpopular. To some it was a waste of money and of soldiers' lives. Others saw it as a crime. In 1949 journalists had started to reveal the details of what came to be called "the dirty war," a catalog of torture and other atrocities committed by the French army. The Communists said it was a bankers' war, fought to protect the profits that accrued to France from the rubber plantations and the rest. In the French Assembly, both left and right spoke of the webs of corruption that the Affair of the Generals had laid bare.

Despite all this, the government of Georges Bidault still hoped to secure military aid from the United States. This aim of French policy had become more realistic in January, when in Paris the National Assembly had voted, after a long hesitation, to approve the new regime in Vietnam, semi-independent and led by Bao Dai. On February 4 the United States officially recognized not only his government but also the kingdoms of Cambodia and Laos. Events were moving toward US involvement in Vietnam, but still not quickly enough for the French. They began to press more urgently for military help while their position worsened.

Although France still controlled Hanoi and Saigon, much of the hinterland was already lost. After studying the Rapport Revers, the army at last decided to abandon most of Route Coloniale 4 and the posts that it connected. The most vulnerable was Cao Bang, in the far northeastern corner of Vietnam. By the spring of 1950 it was all but cut off by the Vietminh, relying on parachute drops of supplies. Evacuating Cao Bang would require sending a relief column up RC4 from the French base at Lang Son. The Foreign Legion would have to hold the road while airborne troops provided reinforcements with landings along the route. The French commanders delayed this difficult operation. Meanwhile, General Giap laid his plans for an attack.

Kim Il-sung was doing the same in North Korea. The Soviet general that Stalin had given him arrived in Pyongyang, and Kim drew up a list of the arms and ammunition he would need for his invasion of the South. Kim sent the list to Moscow on March 14. By the end of that month, intelligence was flowing to Seoul and Tokyo about ominous signs of activity north of the 38th parallel. These reports were not ignored by General MacArthur's staff, but neither were they seen for what they were.

CHAPTER TEN

IN DEEPEST PERIL

*The Truman administration has not had for over a
year a single new, interesting, and constructive idea
to which the nation can rally.*

—WALTER LIPPMANN, *March 1950*[1]

A t Christmastime it had seemed that Dean Acheson
would win his feud with Louis Johnson. As the spring
approached, both men were swiftly losing ground. Ahead
of them lay questions they could not resolve.

Even without the hyperbole or the vivid clash of personalities, grappling with the nation's new ascendancy could only give
rise to stresses and strains that would test the strength of America's body politic. Decisions had to be made, whether wisely or
not, but within a range of choices bounded by two conditions.
The United States could not be a global leader on the cheap; but
neither could it maintain a consensus view of its policy overseas
if it could not agree on what to do at home as well. The consensus
had to include agreement about taxes and the budget. In 1950,
as the possibility of consensus vanished, both Acheson and Johnson found themselves impaled on the horns of these national
dilemmas.

The secretary of defense was the man in deeper trouble. While no one painted Louis Johnson as the dupe of Communists in his department, he had begun to lose the president's support. He opted for bravado, insisting that despite his Pentagon economy drive he could still defeat the Russians. "I want Joe Stalin to know," Johnson told a college audience in early February, "that if he starts something at four o'clock in the morning the fighting power of America will be on the job at five." His words would come back to haunt him when the war in Korea began.[2]

Even when Johnson made his speech, his words carried little conviction. When Stuart Symington, the secretary of the air force, had warned that America was losing its air supremacy, he had revealed the military's doubts about Johnson's stewardship. Dwight Eisenhower grew ever more anxious; and in the press the Alsop brothers relayed what their Pentagon sources told them about unrest in the building. A few days after Johnson's message to Stalin, the Alsops began a series of columns in the *New York Herald Tribune* expressly aimed at ousting the defense secretary from his post. Openly accusing Johnson of lying about America's military readiness, they warned that his spending cuts would lead to defeat in the global struggle.[3]

For the Joint Chiefs, unable to challenge the budget ceiling the president and Johnson had imposed, the most pressing question remained the hydrogen bomb. So far Truman had only authorized research. In the wake of Klaus Fuchs's arrest, the Joint Chiefs finalized a memorandum warning that the Russians might already be ahead in the race to acquire a thermonuclear device. They urged the president to go all out to build the H-bomb.

Johnson agreed, and so did the National Security Council— which meant Dean Acheson—and on March 10 Truman gave his approval. It was the outcome the critics of the Super Bomb had feared: that once a first step had been taken, the process would become irreversible, with both the United States and the Soviet Union committed to this new and terrifying weapon. But the president's decision, welcome though it was to Louis Johnson, failed to solve the other problems Johnson faced.

The H-bomb would be useless without missiles or bombers to deliver it, aircraft far more capable than the B-36 that Johnson backed with such fervor. The Alsop brothers poured as much scorn on the B-36 as they did on the defense secretary. As the pressure mounted for more cash for the air force, Johnson was pushed into a corner from which there was no escape. If he admitted that he had cut the Pentagon's spending too severely, his position would be untenable. It was almost an open secret that Truman was asking for a still deeper reduction, to perhaps as little as $9 billion in 1952. This seemed to be the only way to fulfill his pledge of a balanced budget before the presidential election. Even Johnson could see how impractical it was.

Although Acheson retained the president's backing, his problems were accumulating too. Western Europe, the scene of his diplomatic triumphs in 1949, could not be painlessly rebuilt. There remained that intractable issue, the dollar gap and America's huge trade surplus. Even with their currencies devalued, Britain, France, and the other nations lacked the competitive edge to sell their goods in dollar markets to earn the hard currency they needed. The Marshall Plan could not be ended; but to secure its smooth renewal by Congress that spring, Acheson had to show that the money was well spent.

He had to prove that the Europeans were doing what they should. Since the fall, Acheson and his colleagues had become still more convinced that Western Europe could neither prosper nor rearm without a single economic market, freed from internal tariffs and trade barriers, with even perhaps a single currency. But the British remained reluctant, with Prime Minister Attlee, Sir

Stafford Cripps, and Ernest Bevin resisting any move that might harm their Commonwealth partners or interfere with socialist planning at home.

On February 23, Britain went to the polls, and the outcome created still more complications for the State Department. With rationing so unpopular, and the unemployment of the 1930s now a receding memory, the middle-class voters of Outer London and the nation's other suburbs deserted the socialist flag. The Labour Party's majority in the House of Commons crashed from 146 seats to just 5.

From Paris in March, Averell Harriman assessed the implications. During a visit to London he had talked to Cripps and Bevin and seen still more of Churchill. Most likely the next twelve months would produce another general election, which would bring Churchill back to power; but until then the Labour government would have to stagger on, a hostage to its parliamentary left wing. While Bevin would strive to maintain the Atlantic alliance, Harriman saw little likelihood of the British taking steps to integrate their economy with Europe's. Meanwhile Field Marshal Bernard Montgomery, Britain's most senior soldier, was freely telling visitors that NATO was a sham, far too weak to hold the Rhine against the Russians.[4]

Would Acheson's strategy unravel? It seemed that it might. In Congress bipartisan foreign policy for Asia had already broken down, and Europe might be next. In Congress, Taft and his anti-British allies would argue yet again that the Marshall Plan merely subsidized socialism. To fend off attacks such as this from the Republican right, Acheson had to strengthen his position by placating the party's East Coast internationalists, whose organ was again the *New York Herald Tribune*. They were restless and dissatisfied.

While the Alsop brothers harried Louis Johnson, in the same newspaper Walter Lippmann charged Acheson with a lack of direction. Like Churchill, he wished to see new talks with Stalin to find some formula for peaceful coexistence. For Lippman, the problem also lay with the president, whom he accused of a loss of grip. In the middle of March Truman appeared to prove him right, when, suffering from headaches and fatigue, he took the First Lady's advice and cruised down the coast to Florida to spend three weeks at Key West.

Although Lippmann and others saw scope for diplomacy, Acheson found himself besieged by hawks who tried to push him the opposite way. James Burnham, outspoken though he was, had captured what was coming to be a common emotion: an impatient yearning for a firmer stance against the Soviets. One Republican in Congress said that America should "draw down the Iron Curtain on our side."

The phrase belonged to Christian Herter, one of those northeastern members of the GOP whose support Acheson had to preserve. Herter sat in the House for the western side of Boston, later he would serve as governor of Massachusetts, and he had worked hard to help the Marshall Plan come to fruition. While Truman was in Florida, Herter stopped by at Acheson's office, described the Russians as "barbarians," and called for what amounted to an ultimatum to the Kremlin.[5]

Herter wanted one last effort at negotiation, and then, when Stalin rejected America's terms, a clean break with the Soviets, forcing Russia and its satellites out of the United Nations. Acheson warned that this path would lead to war. On one thing they agreed: that Americans suffered from "a false sense of security" in the face of a Kremlin bent on world domination.

In his strident way Burnham had said just this. So had John Foster Dulles in his book; and seeing how isolated Acheson had become, Dulles reached out to the secretary of state with kind words by letter and by telegram. Listening to people such as Herter or Dulles had its risks, given their hawkish views about

Asia and the Taiwan question. But Acheson believed that he could give them a hearing and still retain control of foreign policy. In fact, it was gradually falling away from his grasp. In early April, two weeks after he met with Herter in private, the congressman revealed their conversation to the *Boston Globe*, an unfriendly act that added to the pressures on the State Department.

Unlike Louis Johnson, whose position bordered on the hopeless, Acheson had room to rethink with a new initiative. As yet, it could not be disclosed in full; but Acheson's aim was to unite the nation and its allies against the Communist menace. Acheson coined a phrase—"total diplomacy"—which he began to feed into the public domain.

The phrase first appeared in February in a talk he gave at another private session with people of influence. His audience at the meeting was the Advertising Council, which FDR had formed in 1942 to put Madison Avenue to work in the service of a nation at war. Inevitably—and this must have been Acheson's intention—the phrase began to circulate in Washington. The text of his talk was released, and then, at Berkeley, California, on March 16, Acheson put his full weight behind it. "The times call," he said, "for a total diplomacy equal to the task of defense against Soviet expansion."[6]

Just what did this mean? The answer would be set out at great length in NSC-68. In February and March, the document was taking shape in the State Department under the leadership of Paul Nitze, whom Acheson had made his head of policy and planning to succeed George Kennan. For more than two decades, NSC-68 would remain officially top secret. Only in 1975 was it declassified, when Secretary of State Henry Kissinger released it as part of an array of early Cold War papers. By then its existence and its contents had already been known for many years to anyone who took an interest. In this it resembled so much else in Washington that was supposed to be confidential.[7]*

Amid the fraught politics of 1950, Truman dared not publish anything as ambitious or as controversial as NSC-68, whatever he might think of its vision of the world. But although the document could not be released verbatim, neither Acheson nor Nitze meant its conclusions to be hidden away. To keep them from Congress and the public would defeat the purpose of its drafting.

THIS REPUBLIC AND ITS CITIZENS

If Nitze and Acheson had had their way, the fall of 1950 and the early months of 1951 would have been a turning point for America. So they proved to be, when military spending soared during the war in Korea, but this occurred without the calm and careful planning and diplomacy that the authors of NSC-68 intended. They had in mind something the United States had failed to do in the late 1930s, that era that had left such a mark on the secretary of state.

Acheson's speech at Yale in 1939 might have served as a preface to NSC-68. Like that speech, the document called for a supreme effort to resist a dictatorship seeking mastery of the globe. This time, however, America would achieve its goals without a world war. In the face of the Soviet threat, the free world would have to unite, mobilizing all its resources, economic,

---

*Referring to NSC-68 by name, the Alsop brothers discussed the document in a newspaper column as early as May 1953. In 1961 and 1962 in separate books, two scholars—Samuel P. Huntington and Paul Y. Hammond—examined it in detail. Even while NSC-68 was being drafted, a shrewd reader of either the Alsops or James Reston could have seen how the State Department's thinking was developing.

military, and cultural too, in a great endeavor that Acheson believed would win the peace.

The Pentagon's annual budget would treble to $40 billion, a number the document discreetly omitted but that Nitze thought was necessary. The Marshall Plan would go on and on, and, as Ernest Bevin had suggested, it would reach out to encompass Asia. The NATO allies would receive more arms, Americans would pay higher taxes, and spending on their social services would fall. All of this would amount, said NSC-68, to "a comprehensive and decisive program . . . to frustrate the Kremlin."[8]

Above all the authors called for national cohesion. Like so many others, including Eisenhower at Columbia and de Gaulle in France, they saw this as the first battle to be won. Instead of the discord that Roosevelt endured before Pearl Harbor, Nitze and his colleagues hoped to create a new American consensus to meet a threat as alarming as Hitler. Here was the definition of "total diplomacy," a policy that Acheson would have to sell at home and abroad, because without the NATO partners it would be doomed to fail.

He was hoping to meet them in London in May, with his Berkeley speech preparing the ground. Britain, France, and the other allies would also have to spend far more on defense; and if Acheson could win their support, then at home in America in the summer and the fall the work of consensus building would begin in earnest. Or so it might have done, if the war in Korea had not intervened.

Although Nitze did not set a firm timetable, its outline can be found in the raft of not-so-secret papers that Kissinger released so many years later. The basic premise of NSC-68 was simply this: that the Soviets, by giving their people guns instead of butter, and steel mills and coal mines instead of housing and higher wages, were swiftly catching up with America's military and economic might. The year of maximum peril would be 1954. If Truman accepted this conclusion, he would have to be ready three years earlier with a federal budget that might break the promises he had given to the voters.

Why was 1954 such a critical date? Because by then, said the authors of NSC-68, the Russians would have two hundred atom bombs, and possibly an H-bomb as well, with the secrets Fuchs had stolen helping them on their way. Coupled with their huge superiority of ground forces in Europe, an atomic arsenal of such a size would give the Soviets something close to Cold War victory.

At that point, they could, if they chose, make a thrust across the Rhine, obliterate the British and their airfields, and overrun France and the rest of the continent, and do so with the means to retaliate against an American nuclear strike. More to the point, the Russians would not *need* to start a war. By 1954, said NSC-68, their strength would be such that West Germany and the other countries most in danger would see no choice but to peel themselves away from the United States and enter the Soviet orbit. In the meantime, said the document, the Russians already had the power to make nonsense of America's strategy of containment.

No one had yet used the phrase "flexible response," but the concept lay close to the heart of NSC-68. On the ground, the Soviet army or forces allied to Stalin might make local offensives—against Yugoslavia perhaps, or maybe in Asia—that would test America's resolve. Would America risk a global war, fought with atomic weapons, for the sake of Belgrade or French Indochina? To counter such localized attacks, and meet each crisis without resorting to the ultimate sanction, nuclear war, America required a flexible range of options—more marines, more airborne divisions, and stronger allies with troops and aircraft of their own.

NSC-68 did not go into such detail, but this was its clear implication. By 1954 America and its allies would have to be ready with far larger armed forces and a stronger industrial base to meet the enhanced challenge from the Soviets. The extra spending would have to begin in the federal budget year ending in June 1952, which meant that Truman would have to put it into his State of the Union message in January 1951. And since the president could not do so without a guarantee that Congress would support him with a new bipartisan consensus, the story would have to be sold to Capitol Hill and to the nation still earlier. The authors of NSC-68 hoped that Truman would announce the new strategy in June 1950.

"Hope" is the word, because—in the first half of that year, before the fighting started in Korea—their prospects of success were remote. In the decades since its drafting, NSC-68 has had many critics. It has been seen as the point of origin of America's national security state, a view that makes its drafting a fateful episode that closed off diplomatic options, embedded a huge military in the fabric of the nation, and froze the world into a Cold War that would last for forty years. At the moment of its birth, its gravest flaw was something else. In the spring of 1950, the trouble with the document was this: NSC-68 was politically absurd.

"This republic and its citizens," wrote Nitze, "in the ascendancy of their strength stand in their deepest peril." This resembled the language of the weeks and months after Pearl Harbor. To describe the Soviet threat in such a way might win the endorsement of hawks on all sides, but it was the opposite of what Truman had been saying in public since the previous fall. And while the document clashed with the serenity he had projected to the journalist Arthur Krock, it would also humiliate Louis Johnson. The secretary of defense had been telling the nation something very different as he strove to keep his budget down to $13 billion. "Our military strength," NSC-68 went on, "is becoming dangerously inadequate." Johnson could not admit such a thing and remain in office.[9]

On March 22, as the document neared completion, he exploded with fury in Paul Nitze's office. Dean Acheson was in the room. Johnson called NSC-68 "a conspiracy" against him, refused to be briefed about it, and threatened to resign. Acheson would later recall the episode as a sign that Johnson was mentally ill; but in the atmosphere of Washington that month anger was commonplace, and in public members of Congress were flying into fits of rage. For weeks the Alsop brothers had been calling Louis Johnson a liar and a danger to America. Their columns contained phrases oddly similar to some of those in NSC-68. Even a politician less beleaguered than Johnson might have seen this as part of a conspiracy.[10]

If he had kept his temper, Johnson might have reminded the State Department of political reality. The economy bloc in Congress, to which Johnson was so close—including Democratic senators such as Walter George and Harry Byrd—could scarcely approve so drastic an increase in spending, or the taxes that would finance it. The cost of that year's arms shipments for the NATO allies had already upset them enough. Even in summary form, repackaged to go to Congress, NSC-68 and Truman's next budget message would have to include vast sums for overseas aid. These could be portrayed—in the language of Truman's opponents—as money down another bottomless rat-hole.

On the Republican side, Bob Taft, with his doubts about NATO, could not endorse such a thing. Neither could Senator Wherry. While they might sign up to the NSC-68 view of the world, depicting an epic struggle that America must win, they would prefer a victory that came more cheaply. It would have to consist of homeland defense built from atom bombs, H-bombs, and more aircraft. In this they would have the support of the conservative Democrats. In any event, Taft and Wherry were focusing on the upcoming elections in November. If their strategy was based, as it seemed to be, on breaking up bipartisan consensus, they could hardly be expected to help create a new one.

Would the document please more amenable Republicans, should they come to read it? Christian Herter, Arthur Vandenberg, and John Foster Dulles—who was now sounding so friendly—might see its appeal. But they could not align themselves in its favor without some concessions elsewhere. NSC-68 begged two obvious questions. If its authors wished to deter the Soviets from local offensives, why had Acheson washed his hands of Taiwan? And how could America spend $40 billion a year on defense and foreign aid and still afford Truman's Fair Deal? To win the full support of Dulles and others like him, Taiwan would have to be defended. The Fair Deal might have to be scrapped.

This question—*What could America afford?*—was the one so many people were asking at the time, whatever they thought about foreign policy or Stalin. All the time it lurked in the background of events, arising in the coal strike, in the debate about health care, and in the 1949 elections in New York. Walter Reuther of the UAW, the deepest thinker in the labor movement, knew that this issue lay at the heart of everything. The board of General Motors and some of the leaders of other corporations knew it too.

How much—or so the question might be put—could America spend on all the things it had to do? How much on defense and foreign aid, how much on health, public housing, roads and bridges, and social security? And how much, when all this had been addressed, could the nation leave to consumers and to businesses to invest or to spend as they saw fit? Economists might argue, and they did, about the figures and the theory, the right mixture of borrowing and taxes, and how much inflation America could tolerate. From the point of view of politicians, the question had to be posed in simple terms.

In NSC-68 Nitze and his colleagues tried to give a simple answer. To help them with their thinking, on March 16 they spent four hours with Robert Lovett. In 1941 at the War Department, Lovett had taken on the role that Louis Johnson had played before him, overseeing the expansion of the air force. Later he served as George Marshall's deputy at the State Department. By profession Lovett, like Nitze, was an investment banker, a partner in Brown Brothers Harriman, and a Yale friend of Averell Harriman's. In business, his special subject had been railroads. That day he spoke with all the confidence of Wall Street in a year when the Dow Jones is soaring.[11]

There was, said Lovett, "practically nothing that the country could not do if it wanted to do it." He saw "no financial problems worthy of the name" in the surge of spending that NSC-68 would involve. The program would be hard to sell to the public, that he knew, but it could be done with the help of what he called "a group of elder statesmen." They would study the findings and audit the plan. When the moment came for the president to rally the nation, they would give him their support.

Lovett was correct about the economics, but not about the elder statesmen or the prospects for national unity. Like Alfred Sloan and Engine Charlie Wilson at General Motors, or Benjamin Fairless at U.S. Steel, Lovett understood that industry was not yet working at its full potential. Since the bank he co-owned made its money issuing stocks and bonds for corporations, Lovett knew that their balance sheets were strong with ample scope to borrow and to build. He also knew America's productive power, and the returns still to come from the nation's investment since the early 1930s in technology, science, and education. These insights help explain Lovett's bullish mood.

Later, during the Korean War, when Lovett served as defense secretary, the Pentagon would spend far more than Nitze was proposing. After 1953, when Engine Charlie was running the department, worried about the strain on America's resources, the military budget fell, but it still remained three times larger than it had been in 1949. As Lovett had predicted, the economy continued to thrive. But in the spring of 1950 his case remained unproven and there was ample room for doubt.[12]

Nitze and his colleagues tried to forestall their critics with a crude formula that had the merit of making the issues plain. They compared America's economy with Stalin's. The Russians, they estimated, spent 14 percent of their economy on the military—more than twice as much as America did—and another 25 percent on capital investment. The United States, they argued, could do the same or spend still more. If America could grow to make its annual output worth $300 billion—a figure the president's economic advisers had themselves published in January—then it could afford NSC-68. The boost the program would give to the economy would make every American better off.

In wartime this might work. In peacetime it could not. Edwin Nourse had resigned as chair of the Council of Economic Advisers and been replaced by Leon Keyserling, a New Deal liberal. Keyserling also wanted a program for expanding the economy; but while he was receptive, he was also cautious in his comments on NSC-68. To pay for the program, but also to ward off inflation, raising taxes would not be enough. There would have to be planning, price controls, limits on consumer credit, and possibly wage controls as well: the return of measures used in World War II, measures that Congress had dismantled and shown no desire to resurrect.

The fate of the program would depend, wrote one of Keyserling's aides, on "the imponderables of political faith and action." And here the prospects were poor. When Lovett mentioned the need for elder statesmen to endorse the plan, he gave no names, but one man in particular was indispensable. These were the months of "the second Eisenhower boom"—the first had been in 1948—when in public and in private the general was surrounded by admirers urging him to run for president. Without his approval of the concept of NSC-68, it would be futile to propose it.

Would Eisenhower sign up to support the plan? Although Ike still sat on the political fence, his views about the military budget were easier to determine. While the general felt that the Pentagon's spending had fallen too far, neither he nor the Joint Chiefs would wish to see a surge that could not be sustained. If Eisenhower were asked in the spring of 1950 to endorse NSC-68, he would also have to trust the Democratic Party to deliver it. And that, the general's diary shows, was something he could not do. As Eisenhower put it on April 5, "I believe we must have a Republican victory in '52."[13]

As for Congress, there was nothing much to ponder. If it would not vote for items from the Fair Deal or for Truman's modest revision of the tax code, then it could not vote for anything as grandiose as NSC-68. Barring the outbreak of a war, the Acheson and Nitze plan had only one hope of coming to fruition. In the elections in November, the Democrats would have to make big gains, repeating their victory in New York in other places across the nation. Only this could restore the authority the president and Acheson would have to command.

While the date for his London meetings drew closer, although not yet confirmed, Acheson soldiered on, seeking to instill the concept of "total diplomacy" into hearts and minds. The primaries were also drawing near, with the first due in the South in May and then the more important contest in California in June. While the writing of NSC-68 continued, the campaigning had already begun in a committee room in Congress, where Senator Joseph McCarthy obtained the attention he had sought.

THE NOISY ANTICS OF A FEW

In March, within the space of just twenty-three days, Joe McCarthy struck the depths of ignominy and then rose again, rescued by his colleagues and by events. With his intuitive grasp of the public mood—or with the devil's own luck—he had picked an ideal time to challenge Truman and his form of politics.

John T. Flynn's *The Road Ahead* and the wider trend of opinion of which it was a part had, together with the coal strike, created a moment of acute vulnerability for the president. It suited McCarthy's operating style. He knew how to present himself as a radical of a kind, a young outsider who broke rules in pursuit of truth. Fraught with risk though this strategy was, it succeeded for Joe McCarthy. As the next few months would show, it also appealed to voters disenchanted with a Democratic Party so long in power.

McCarthy's three weeks of melodrama began on March 8. In the Senate caucus room, full of reporters and tobacco smoke, the inquiry Scott Lucas had promised met for its first session. Because Acheson's department was the focus, the investigation fell under the aegis of the Senate Foreign Relations Committee, thought by many to be the most eminent committee in Congress. Its chairman, Tom Connally, delegated the affair to a panel led by Millard Tydings of Maryland. "I have more important things to do," Connally is said to have remarked, "than go to a skunk hunt."

Senator Tydings should have been a perfect choice. He could not be seen as some docile instrument of Truman's or the secretary of state's. A decorated hero from World War I, in 1918 Tydings had led a machine-gun battalion that took a vital ridge near Verdun, an exploit that helped propel him into Congress as a Democrat four years later. Roosevelt had tried to purge him from the party in 1938, because Tydings opposed the New Deal's second phase. Like Walter George he had survived, a dogged conservative. A month before Pearl Harbor, Tydings had voted with Taft and other Republicans to try to stop FDR from arming American merchant ships in the North Atlantic. On that occasion he called his president "Hitlerian."[14]

Tall, gaunt, sarcastic, and—said one observer—"thoroughly capable and logical," Tydings was about to turn sixty. He was also, or so it was thought, impregnable in Maryland. To help him confront McCarthy, the leadership had given him the powerful Senator Brien McMahon, who was more of a Truman loyalist but highly effective. With all this in his favor, and McCarthy floundering for proof of his accusations, how could Tydings fail? Only because other factors were at work to frustrate the Tydings Committee.

The committee would not produce its report until July. It would refute every charge McCarthy made; but while this amounted to a tactical victory for the Democrats, the process as a whole was a strategic defeat. By then the damage had been done. McCarthy had achieved the only thing he had required. Although he could not prove his central charge that Acheson's department contained a Red fifth column, he had kept the story alive while Truman was in difficulties on all fronts.

Although the phrase "McCarthyism" was coined at the end of March, his movement had not yet taken the form that would make it so notorious. Memories of McCarthy have come to be shaped by its most sensational episodes, the televised hearings in 1953 and 1954, when he led his own committee with his investigating counsel, Roy Cohn, at his side, and they hunted for Communist subversion in the army and elsewhere. By that time the Republicans controlled the White House and both chambers of Congress, and McCarthy had the intimidating weight of the majority. In 1950—when the GOP was still an insurgent party—the dynamics were entirely different.

At the peak of his power, McCarthy would lash out in all directions. At the time of the Tydings Committee, he and most of his party kept their focus on two principal targets: the State Department and the elections that were so close. However discreet Nitze tried to be in drafting NSC-68, it was common knowledge that Acheson was seeking new policies to shore up NATO and to end the lingering controversy about the Taiwan question. To

Senator Millard Tydings, chairman of the subcommittee investigating McCarthy's allegations of Communism in the State Department (left), and Senator Joseph McCarthy (right), in one of their many verbal confrontations, in the Senate Caucus Room on March 8, 1950. *Bettmann / Getty Images.*

salvage his position Acheson would have to reach out to Republicans with some bold gesture. Even those who wished to help could drive a hard bargain. As for those who did not, they would want to see McCarthy make the Tydings hearings as embarrassing as possible. And this was precisely what McCarthy did as he mastered his techniques of persecution.

The hearings began with taunts from Senator Tydings while McCarthy bluffed, played for time, and called the committee a tool for the State Department. As yet he had still not laid his hands on the names of the suspects on the list compiled by the staffer Robert E. Lee, and so Tydings kept demanding them. Behind the scenes, McCarthy called for help from friends old and new, including not only his ally from the Wisconsin GOP, Tom Coleman, the national committee man, but also reporters from the McCormick newspapers, a former FBI agent, and members of the China lobby. Between them they raised funds and assembled material that McCarthy fed to the press.

Again McCarthy named John Stewart Service and Harlow Shapley, although the Lee report had referred to neither one. He mentioned Owen Lattimore, who had belonged to *Amerasia*'s editorial board, and he threw in an innuendo about Philip Jessup, saying that he had an "unusual affinity for Communists causes." This gave the *Washington Times-Herald* a pretext to libel the ambassador in a headline as a "pal of Reds." In his first four days of testimony, McCarthy gave nine names in all, and he added one anonymous homosexual who he claimed was an official at the CIA. Apart from Jessup and Service, mostly the names seemed irrelevant to the case he was trying to make.[15]

Seven were people unconnected to the State Department of 1950, and the details he cited came chiefly from newspaper cuttings or from the dusty recesses of the *Congressional Record*. Although the Jessup connection with Alger Hiss might be promising, as yet McCarthy had nothing concrete to add. To link some of his other names to Communism or to organizations with Communist ties, he had to delve back into the 1930s, and shift his tactics away from his central charge about espionage in Washington.

While in February McCarthy had talked about "spies" in the State Department, in these early hearings he spoke far more vaguely about what he called "security risks." A phrase as loose as this could mean almost anything; but in the aftermath of Hiss and Fuchs it sounded all the more unnerving. McCarthy used it first to attack the New York attorney and feminist Dorothy Kenyon. A sixty-two-year-old from a family of lawyers, Kenyon had spent more than three decades campaigning for women, labor unions, and the city's disadvantaged.

Until the end of 1949 she had been part of America's mission to the United Nations, serving on its commission for women. Her post brought with it a State Department salary of $12,000 a year, a large sum at the time, which McCarthy mentioned twice. Other than that, Kenyon had no government role, and Acheson had never heard of her. It was absurd to suggest, as McCarthy did, that she belonged to a clique of Red sympathizers with influence over America's foreign policy.

McCarthy labeled her a traitor nonetheless. "The Communist activities of Miss Kenyon," McCarthy said, "are not only deep-rooted but go back many years." She had ties, or so he claimed, with twenty-eight organizations that at one time or another had been called fronts for Communism. They included the Consumers Union and the League of Women Shoppers. Kenyon replied by calling McCarthy a coward and a liar, while her friend Eleanor Roosevelt came to her aid in her newspaper column. "To imply that she is a Communist, or in any way subversive," the former first lady wrote, "is one of the funniest things ever suggested."[16]

In the 1930s and 1940s Kenyon had inhabited the New York that the writer Mary McCarthy would portray in her novel *The Group*. Her Manhattan was the New Deal town of rallies in Union Square, Orson Welles and the Mercury Theater, and Mayor Fiorello La Guardia's efforts to promote progressive causes. Kenyon had served under La Guardia as a city judge. In the New York of that era, and most of all during the Spanish Civil War, no one active as a liberal could fail to meet or perhaps to share a platform with people who had some Communist affiliation. Those ties might be close or distant, fleeting or innocuous, but in the 1950s they could be unearthed as ammunition for Joe McCarthy.

These tactics were ugly but effective. Cases such as Kenyon's helped McCarthy paint a picture of a social stratum, privileged and affluent, with interests and values that set them apart from ordinary Americans. Privately educated, she had been to Horace

Mann, an expensive school in the Bronx, and then graduated from Smith College. This, too, was made to count against her; and so was a statement Kenyon had made of sympathy with Alger Hiss. On March 14 she came to the committee to deny that she had ever been a Communist. "I am," she said, "an independent, liberal, Rooseveltian Democrat." An hour later one of the Republicans on the committee quoted a speech in which Kenyon had called the Hiss trials "an example of hysteria."[17]

With material such as this, McCarthy and his allies wove a tapestry of connections between FDR liberals, the Democratic Party, Hiss, and the Kremlin. McCarthy placed Kenyon among those he called "fellow Communists, fellow travelers, suckers, and just plain dopes," people who through malice or naïveté were endangering America. The Tydings report cleared Kenyon's name, but by the time it appeared McCarthy had already made his impact: not so much on Dorothy Kenyon, in whom he swiftly lost interest, but rather on the atmosphere of an election year.[18]

He came closest to disaster when he tried the same technique against Philip Jessup. By March 20, when the ambassador took the stand on the fifth full day of hearings, many observers saw McCarthy as a busted flush, unable to substantiate his accusations against the State Department. So far, as Tydings kept reminding him, McCarthy had failed to name a single proven Communist. As a Senate veteran, Tydings stuck to the rules, refusing to allow McCarthy—who was only a witness himself—to cross-examine those who testified. Instead, McCarthy filtered questions through a fellow Republican, Senator Bourke Hickenlooper, a former governor of Iowa. Hickenlooper made much of an ancient Smith College yearbook in which, at the age of thirty-two, Kenyon had confessed to socialist sympathies. But he lacked McCarthy's aggressiveness, and Jessup left him fumbling for words.

The ambassador had just returned from his Asian mission, pursued by Radio Moscow and Radio Beijing. Both denounced

Jessup as an arch imperialist, charging that his visits to Saigon, Bangkok, and the other capitals belonged to "an American policy of aggression." Jessup had all this put into the record, plus his speeches attacking Communism. With McCarthy now looking vulnerable, Tydings delivered what seemed to be a fatal blow. He read out two letters he had received expressing horror that anyone should question Jessup's integrity. One of the letters came from General George C. Marshall, and the other from Eisenhower.[19]

McCarthy's plight appeared to be terminal when, a few days later, the *New York Times* published a third letter from a hero renowned for his wisdom. It was the eternally Republican Henry L. Stimson, Herbert Hoover's secretary of state and FDR's trusted guardian of the atom bomb. "This is no time," Stimson wrote on March 24, "to let the noisy antics of a few upset the steady purpose of our country." Praising the achievements of Dean Acheson, he castigated Joe McCarthy, calling him a little man. Two days later, the *Washington Post* cartoonist Herbert Block created the phrase "McCarthyism," in a cartoon showing a tottering pile of slimy buckets with a barrel of tar at the top.[20]

If that week marked the low point of McCarthy's campaign, it also saw the start of his recovery. People who knew him well found that far from being chastened or humiliated, he thrived on the derision and the anger he aroused. If columnists such as Drew Pearson or the Alsop brothers attacked him, it only spread McCarthy's name around the nation. When he aroused the wrath of an older generation, he replied by depicting them as complacent members of a moribund elite. For every enemy McCarthy made in high places, he attracted a crowd of new friends. Letters began to fill the mailbags in Congress voicing support for his defiance.

McCarthy also found allies whose hard evidence of Soviet infiltration went far beyond the *Amerasia* case or the minutiae from the trials of Hiss and the leaders of the CPUSA. Drew Pearson had heard a curious story: that McCarthy was receiving information from an officer in military intelligence, Brigadier-General Carter Weldon Clarke. While Pearson was aware that Clarke had supervised in wartime the breaking of Japanese codes, he knew nothing of Clarke's more sensitive role as an architect of the VENONA decryption of Soviet radio traffic. That was a secret even Pearson could not uncover. Nothing McCarthy said in public required details from VENONA; but Clarke could give him something almost as valuable. Clarke might offer moral support from a military expert who gave him the confidence to press ahead.[21]

Pearson also registered the changing mood. While his sources in the Senate told him that Taft was urging McCarthy to keep the rumpus going, his readers besieged him with hostile letters when he criticized McCarthy. "It looks as if he has ignited a potent though irresponsible segment of our public opinion," Pearson wrote in his diary as early as March 19. Day by day he felt pro-McCarthy sentiment continuing to build. Meanwhile, Taft, Wherry, and their colleagues in the conservative wing of the GOP swung in behind McCarthy, privately at first and then with speeches stepping up the assault on Acheson.

Growing ever bolder, McCarthy the gambler also stood to gain from another lapse of judgment by Scott Lucas. To convene the Tydings Committee, the majority leader had required a resolution on the Senate floor. In his zeal to finish off McCarthy, Senator Lucas had wanted the vote to be unanimous; and so he unwisely accepted a Republican amendment. This gave the committee the power to subpoena Acheson if the State Department refused to hand over its loyalty files. Injured though McCarthy was by the letters from Eisenhower and Marshall, his ally Senator Hickenlooper intervened to pull him clear by demanding their release.

Although Tydings knew that Truman would plead executive privilege and withhold the files, the senator was duty bound to use his powers to ask for them. With Jessup still at the witness table, and Hickenlooper making such a fuss, Tydings had no choice but to promise to send in the request. Since the president was sure to object, the wrangling about the loyalty files would keep the story running far into April or even into May. And then, after Tydings held a press conference to taunt him yet again, McCarthy went for broke. On the morning of March 21, he told reporters that he had the name of America's top Soviet spy.

The name was Owen Lattimore's. Fellow traveler or not, Lattimore had certainly played at least a walk-on role in the *Amerasia* affair of 1945, and since then he had from time to time advised the State Department. Harold Stassen, whom McCarthy knew well, had met Lattimore at the China seminar that Jessup had convened in October. No one could deny that at the seminar Lattimore had advocated for recognition of Red China. Anyone who read the professor's most recent book could also find him urging America to abandon Taiwan and give China's seat on the UN Security Council to Mao, the very thing Beijing and Moscow were now demanding.

None of this made Lattimore a Russian agent; but it was enough to open a breach in the State Department's defenses. At first, McCarthy refused to identify Lattimore in public, but on that afternoon of March 21, he told Tydings in private that the professor was the master spy. Washington being what it was, Lattimore's name sped around the city, taken by some as the proof McCarthy needed of a Soviet fifth column. Others saw the accusation as a sign that McCarthy was close to defeat.

While McCarthy called for yet more files, from the FBI as well as Foggy Bottom, Richard Nixon offered him a line of retreat. Like J. Edgar Hoover—who did not wish to share the bureau's secrets with mere politicians—the scourge of Alger Hiss was trying to keep McCarthy at a distance, apparently alarmed by his reckless style. On March 22 Nixon called for an end to the Tydings Committee. He suggested instead an independent, non-political commission, led perhaps by Eisenhower, to investigate

McCarthy's allegations. This looked like what it probably was: an attempt by Nixon to position himself, ahead of his Senate primary, as the calm, responsible anti-communist, a safer pair of hands than his rival from Wisconsin.

The political weather was shifting too violently to allow anything so middle-of-the-road. Bob Taft, who kept close to his voters in Ohio, sensed the same vibrations that Pearson had detected. On the day that Nixon asked for moderation, Taft met his fellow leaders of the Senate GOP. He emerged to tell reporters what Pearson already knew: that McCarthy was winning over hearts and minds. The reaction, said Taft, was "pretty good on the whole, except here in Washington." He wanted McCarthy to "keep talking and if one case doesn't work out he should proceed with another."[22]

If this was cynical, it was also shrewd. When Eleanor Roosevelt or Henry Stimson made their pleas for sanity, they spoke to only part of the nation. Since Labor Day, the drift of events and commentary had eaten away at the president and his party, giving McCarthy a receptive public. Three hundred miles away in North Carolina, the anxieties McCarthy played upon would reappear in a midterm primary where the Democratic Party was tearing itself in two.

Planners and Plotters

Each southern state had its peculiar chemistry. Each one formed a prism of its own, where the great questions of the era were filtered and refracted by local personalities, histories, and politics, so that in each one the picture that emerged was subtly different from the picture seen elsewhere. Held though it was by the Democrats, North Carolina gave a home to what was, compared with the rest of the South at the time, an unusually large number of Republicans. More than a third of the voters regularly turned out for the GOP. They could, if they wished, vote in Democratic primaries, which meant that here the outcome was far from a foregone conclusion. In the spring of 1950, the McCarthyism that was growing nationwide fastened its grip on the primary season in the state. The episode would show how McCarthy's movement became as powerful as it did, by drawing on old animosities from the FDR years.

The Democratic senator up for reelection had long been a national figure. Although Frank P. Graham was as liberal a Rooseveltian as could be, he had made his name not as a politician but as an educator. *Time* magazine had described Senator Graham as America's finest leader of a public university; another writer called him "the best loved and the best hated man" in the Tar Heel State. For nineteen years he had been president of the University of North Carolina (UNC), making Chapel Hill the academic jewel of the South. Graham was sixty-three, a teetotaler, slender, and only five feet five. In the Senate he was sometimes seen munching a carrot as he hurried between meetings. Yet there were also those who saw the liberal Graham as a friend of the Communists.[23]

In 1934, when a national textile strike had closed the cotton mills, Graham had helped arrange bail for a student protester with what were said to be ties to the CPUSA. Because of this, and because of other stories that swirled around Frank Graham, the FBI had opened a file, which became still bulkier when Roosevelt appointed him to the nation's War Labor Board during World War II. J. Edgar Hoover had reviewed the Graham file himself and seen nothing subversive in its contents. Truman admired Graham, and in 1947 and 1948 he served on the president's commission on civil rights. Still the murmurings went on about the presence of Communists on campus and about Frank Graham's leanings to the left.

The rumors reached a peak early in 1949. Questions were asked about his appointment to a part-time role with the Atomic Energy Commission. An AEC review board had raised doubts about Graham only to be overruled; and when this became known, via a networked radio show, politicians called for his dismissal. In Congress a Louisiana Democrat labeled Graham "disgraceful" and "an incubus" and urged UNC to fire its president.[24]

The storm might have passed if Frank Graham had not found himself in Washington in March of that year. When his predecessor died unexpectedly, North Carolina's Democratic governor appointed Graham to serve as senator until the 1950 election. And here the politics became a blend of the local and the national as the issues and the climate of opinion that produced McCarthy came to mingle with Tar Heel rivalries and old divisions in the state.

The governor, a dairy farmer named Kerr Scott, had swept into office at the end of 1948 with a program that resembled Governor Jim Folsom's in Alabama, tailored for the postwar South. Like Folsom, Scott wanted highways instead of dirt roads, more schools and higher pay for teachers, and better rural hospitals with more doctors. But his victory came at the expense of the Democratic Party's dominant machine in North Carolina. This was the so-called Shelby dynasty. Its leaders were lawyers linked to banking, insurance, the power utilities, and the textile plants clustered around the cities of the Piedmont. They remembered not only the strikes of the 1930s but also the attempts by Phil Murray and the CIO to unionize the South in the postwar years.[25]

Kerr Scott had broken the Shelby group's hold on the state, and his choice of Frank Graham for the Senate angered them still more. Graham's name had been suggested by Scott's ally Jonathan Daniels, editor of the *Raleigh News-Observer*. The son of Josephus Daniels, Woodrow Wilson's secretary of the navy, Jonathan Daniels had briefly served in 1945 as FDR's and then Truman's press secretary. His newspaper continued to speak for the president and his program in North Carolina, and he wrote one of the earliest full-length accounts of Truman's life. An authorized and flattering biography titled *The Man of Independence*, it was published in 1950. With both Graham and Daniels so obviously close to Truman, that year's Democratic primary turned into a fight for and against the president's Fair Deal.

On the day Taft came out so strongly in public for McCarthy, the Shelby dynasty made its move against Senator Graham. As their candidate to oust him they had chosen a different kind of Democrat, Raleigh's most powerful corporate lawyer. The conservative Willis Smith, six feet one and the former president of the American Bar Association, chaired the board of trustees of UNC's rival college, Duke University. Smith was also—and this came to be significant—general counsel for North Carolina's medical society, which represented physicians. When Smith gave his first campaign speech on March 22, it read as though it might have been composed by John T. Flynn.

In *The Road Ahead*, Flynn had given a page to Frank Graham, calling him a "National Socialist Planner . . . up to his neck in Communists." Besides the stories that had dogged him for so long, the case against the senator consisted, like McCarthy's case against Dorothy Kenyon, of his membership or affiliations with groups that were said to be Communist fronts. Among them was a New Deal offshoot, the Southern Conference on Human Welfare (SCHW). Often seen as the region's liberal flag carrier, it pressed for Black voting rights and wanted to see the labor unions grow in the South. In 1950 the conference also advocated that idea so controversial in Congress, a permanent Fair Employment Practices Committee to enforce civil rights in the labor market.[26]

Almost from the moment it was founded in 1938, with Eleanor Roosevelt as its first keynote speaker, the SCHW's opponents had condemned the organization as a Trojan horse for Communism. Twice in Congress the House Un-American Activities Committee had branded it subversive. By now most of the labor unions, and Eleanor Roosevelt, had long since parted company with the group; but not Graham, who remained its honorary president.

Without naming the SCHW directly, or even naming Graham, Willis Smith placed it at the heart of his campaign. "We hear of the delusions," Smith said in his first speech, "being suffered by otherwise good and honorable people who are unwary of dangers that lie ahead in socialism, communism, and the so-called welfare state." Smith condemned "social planners and plotters who seek to change the American way of life," and he spoke against the "evils" of an FEPC. "I do not now nor have I ever belonged to any subversive organizations," Smith said; and he promised that he would never be "duped" into lending them his signature. It was an obvious jibe at his opponent.[27]

And so North Carolina's Democratic primary developed into a personal but also an intellectual feud between two eminent men so visibly different, coming from opposite sides of a divided party. The politics of race were thrust into the center of the picture. Time and again Graham would deny that he was a socialist. He would distance himself from a permanent FEPC. He would disown the plan for health care that Truman and Oscar Ewing had proposed. But all the time his opponents portrayed him as an extremist from the left. County committees for Smith placed advertisements in the press, throwing the Southern Conference at Graham and listing its objectives: "state and federal FEPC laws, abolition of segregation, socialized medicine, and social equality and association for whites and negroes." Doctors joined the fight as well, producing their own campaign ads supporting Willis Smith.[28]

It would take a while for Washington observers to notice what was happening in the South; but by the end of March the threat to Truman was plain to see. With so many Republicans registered as Democrats to make their mark on the party's primaries, the contest was bound to be close. If—like the elections in New York the previous fall—it served as a Truman referendum, the issues here were still more emotive.

Into the Tar Heel primary there flowed so many tributary streams some of them with sources in the 1930s or even long before: the threat that Truman might pose to segregation, fear of the unions, fear of a bureaucratic state, and the administration's failure to build wide support for its most ambitious programs. Even fear of the Soviet Bomb had its relevance, after the scare about Graham's access to atomic secrets. Senator Graham became the emblem of all these sources of anxiety.

Something similar occurred in Florida, a state that already had a multitude of retirees. Here, the warnings about the dangers of "socialized medicine" carried all the more resonance. Here, too, Graham's liberal ally in the Senate, the New Deal and Fair Deal stalwart Senator Claude Pepper, was facing his equivalent of Willis Smith. His conservative foe was George Smathers, who in January had launched his campaign with a speech in Orlando that led with an attack on Truman's health-care plan. The Florida primary would be as raucous as North Carolina's and produce as bad an outcome for the president.

Since Truman loathed Claude Pepper, he would shed no tears to see him go; but strife such as this in his party could only harm his program. In Alabama the situation differed, because the Democrat up for reelection to the Senate, Lister Hill, had no strong opponent. And yet the same themes appeared in this primary too. The voters in Alabama also had to select the delegates to the state's Democratic committee, who would—in 1952—pick their candidate for president. Here again choices had to be made about what it meant to be a Democrat.

Joe McCarthy had not created the atmosphere in which these and other primaries were fought. Even without him, they would have been bitter and divisive; but his influence made itself felt nonetheless. While McCarthy said little or nothing about civil rights or health insurance, and while he still avoided frontal attacks on the labor unions, his tactics were otherwise identical to those deployed against Frank Graham. As McCarthy began to cast his spell upon America, he drew into his following people already aroused by other issues and other kinds of talk that could combine with anti-communism. The influence flowed the other way as well, as many more letters arrived in McCarthy's office and urged him to continue.

None of this could help the cause of the administration's foreign policy. As Nitze and his team finished drafting NSC-68, the question still remained: *How could Dean Acheson sell it to the country?* With a national consensus seeming ever more elusive, he and the president reached out to Republicans with gestures they had no choice but to offer.

THE DIPLOMACY OF FEAR

Arthur Vandenberg, frail and awaiting more surgery, looked on with growing dismay at the antics Henry Stimson had described. The senator's cancer had moved from his lung to his spine. His wife was also close to death. In Washington one Republican after another followed McCarthy's lead, speaking of a "master spy" in the State Department. In the words of Walter Lippmann, a "fearful quarrel" was now raging in the capital; and although Lippmann despised McCarthyism, he remained a skeptic about the State Department. He traced the quarrel back to America's mishandling of the China question. Senator Vandenberg, despite his afflictions, intervened to try to calm the storm.

His first task was to see the Marshall Plan renewed by Congress. On March 24, Vandenberg wrote a public letter to Paul Hoffman, the plan's administrator. Calling it "this unpartisan concept," and using words like those of NSC-68, the senator said that it had, as he put it, "smoked out Soviet Russia's sinister plan for world domination." Truman rejoiced at the letter and sent his thanks to Vandenberg; but this was scarcely enough to rescue the consensus the senator had labored to build.[29]

Cracks were appearing elsewhere in the edifice of policy. The British, so attached to Iranian oil and the Suez Canal, were selling weapons to Egypt and the other Arab nations. This angered Israel's many friends in Congress, and some of them threatened to reduce London's Marshall aid. On March 29, in what was called the Irish revolt, the House of Representatives voted to end Marshall aid entirely if Britain refused to accept a united Ireland. Eisenhower raised still more doubts about the administration when, in a speech in New York, he said that America had disarmed too far.[30]

The Senate called Ike to testify. Eisenhower's wartime general Joseph Collins had recently told Louis Johnson that he could accept no more cuts in the army budget. Eisenhower, cool and courteous, made no jarring pleas for extra money, but he made it plain that he agreed with Lightning Joe. On the day the *Washington Post* ran its McCarthy cartoon, which was also the day of the Irish revolt, Eisenhower warned the senators that America's defenses were at risk. He spoke of Soviet paratroopers threatening Alaska, while Russia's fleet of submarines prowled the high seas. Off the coast of California and with excellent timing, a navy pilot promptly sighted what was thought to be a Russian periscope. Meanwhile, the press ran photographs of Truman relaxing in the sunshine at Key West.

In so much trouble in so many ways, Acheson chose that week to try to pacify the GOP. Little time remained in which to do so. In his radio show, Drew Pearson had named Owen Lattimore as McCarthy's master spy. The professor, who had been in Afghanistan, was flying home to America; and in early April he would go before the Tydings panel to try to clear his name. Taft, Wherry, and their friends were already demanding Acheson's dismissal, and McCarthy intended to make Lattimore's appearance another show trial. On March 28, with the help of Ernest Bevin and Sir Winston Churchill, Acheson made his preemptive move.

At that moment it might have seemed to Acheson that he had more friends in London than in Washington. McCarthy's campaign had become an international incident, its every stage closely followed by the British. His tirades against the State Department filled them with alarm. For Churchill, now perhaps the prime minister in waiting, the situation seemed especially worrying, since he could not do without Dean Acheson. The future of the West depended, Churchill believed, on European unity with at its heart some form of Franco-German union, that project to which Acheson was also committed. Churchill had admired his "total diplomacy" speeches, and that afternoon in Parliament he made one of his own. It was one of his most important since the war.

Churchill praised Acheson and Vandenberg—"that great American statesman"—and called for a United States of Europe with Britain, France, and West Germany joining in its creation. In response, Bevin closed the debate with the confirmation that Acheson would come to London in May to meet the NATO allies as he hoped. With the Labour Party so wary of a federal Europe, Bevin could say no more; but it was clear that he and Acheson and Robert Schuman would also discuss ideas, however tentative, for a Franco-German rapprochement.[31]

When Bevin's words reached Washington that day, they allowed Acheson to make his move and attempt to restore some harmony between the parties. He revealed that he was appointing a Republican, John Stewart Cooper, a former senator from Kentucky, to act as a senior adviser during the London talks. An old comrade of Vandenberg's, Cooper would help Acheson and Jessup in their efforts to secure the anti-Soviet alliance.

But if Acheson hoped to outflank his critics and pave the way for NSC-68, again he underestimated McCarthy and his

colleagues. Nor could eloquence from Churchill appease a Republican Party that thought it had found another Alger Hiss. While
Churchill was on his feet in Parliament, the news came through
from Florida that Truman had refused to release the loyalty files.
Senator Tydings spoke to his colleagues and immediately applied
for subpoenas. McCarthy prepared for another verbal brawl, with
Professor Lattimore as his target.

In the closing days of March all the different currents in the
politics of 1950 converged. Bob Taft, determined to bring matters
to a head, had written yet another manifesto. Once again it warned
of creeping socialism. "Is Truman taking us down the British
road?" the senator inquired in a piece for *Collier's* magazine, echo-
ing John T. Flynn. That week the publisher bought space in the
nation's leading papers to carry Taft's question in large headlines.
Meanwhile, the president was reaching his limits of exasperation.
So far in public Truman had kept his temper about McCarthy.
His explosion would come on the afternoon of March 30.

Earlier that day, while a US warship in search of submarines
scoured the waters off San Francisco, McCarthy had taken to the
floor of the Senate a second time. His enemies still saw him as
a wounded beast who might be finished off with ridicule. His
list of friends was growing all the same, joined by Styles Bridges,
an ex-governor of New Hampshire, who with Taft and Wherry
formed their party's leadership in the upper chamber. With
Bridges and Wherry to protect his flanks, McCarthy embarked
on another verbal marathon.

For more than four hours he held the floor until he was sweat-
ing and disheveled. With again a heap of documents beside him,
McCarthy spoke about perverts, degenerates, crackpots, and traitors, about "phony diplomacy" and the loss of China, and about the
people he called "bad policy risks," all of them members of what
he said was the "pro-Soviet bloc in the Far Eastern Division of

the State Department." Under the influence of Owen Lattimore, they had, he claimed, sold the Chinese people into slavery. When Herbert Lehman crossed the aisle and asked to see his evidence, McCarthy loomed over him and snatched the documents away. "Go back to your seat, old man," reporters heard McCarthy say.[32]

At times when McCarthy paused, older Republicans came forward with a different script. For East Coast senators such as the New Jersey moderate Alexander Smith, with his genuine concerns about Taiwan, McCarthy's diatribe might be embarrassing, but it also offered them an opening. Keen to push the nation's Asia policy in the direction they preferred, they took up the cause of John Foster Dulles, urging Acheson to appoint him as another bipartisan adviser. Dulles was in Washington that day, visiting Arthur Vandenberg and calling on Acheson as well. His threatening undertone was this: that in New York in November, when Lehman had to stand for reelection, he might run against him once again.

Such is the way that foreign policy is sometimes made. While Professor Lattimore traveled home from the Middle East, the president, harassed and frustrated, prepared to assemble the press in Florida.

THE KREMLIN'S GREATEST ASSET

It was one of those occasions when, as though the politicians were acting out a scene from Shakespeare or Ibsen, conflicts long in the making burst into open view. Over the course of the preceding week McCarthy had pulled onto the stage in one role or another the most powerful characters of the Western world. The one person missing was General MacArthur, despite Republican attempts to drag him as well as Eisenhower into the political arena. All of them knew, as Churchill did, that they were peering into a future dark with hazard. The H-bomb was leaving the realm of theory to become a weapon that might one day be deployed. How could they not be liable to anger?

Truman's fury with McCarthy, when at last it came, sprang from genuine alarm about the vanishing of what remained of consensus. The coal strike, when John L. Lewis had exhausted Truman's patience, seemed to have thwarted his hopes for peace in industry. His party was just as difficult, obstructive, and schismatic. As for foreign policy, Truman had not yet seen the final text of NSC-68, but he knew its gist. If Paul Nitze was right about the scale of the Soviet threat and the need for unity and resolution, then McCarthy's tactics were all the more hateful.

With all this in mind, the president met the press that afternoon. While McCarthy said his piece in Washington, Truman's staff served lemonade and hot dogs on the lawn. The weather at Key West was turning cold. Truman's shirt was open-necked and five minutes into the proceedings his naval aide slipped his coat around his shoulders. The press knew all the issues—McCarthy, the possible return of Dulles, the warnings about defense from Eisenhower, and the elections soon to come—and each one was addressed.[33]

Harry Truman spoke of saboteurs in Congress and a "fiasco" in the Senate. He named Wherry and Bridges as two of the ringleaders, but most of all he blamed the man at work that afternoon. "I think," said Truman, "the greatest asset the Kremlin has is Senator McCarthy." Four times in different ways Truman said this same thing, with the reporters—who knew what a storm this would create—eager to quote him precisely. The president and the press settled on a milder form of words, replacing "Senator McCarthy" with "the partisan attempt in the Senate to sabotage the bipartisan foreign policy," but even so McCarthy's name would fill the headlines.

While Truman's detonation was controlled, his anger was evident, but so, too, was something else: that McCarthy had driven the president onto the back foot, where he had to defend not only Acheson and Jessup but also his Pentagon budget, which he insisted was sufficient. Truman tried to steer the conversation to economics and the dollar gap—"the greatest problem with which we are faced," he called it—and said he hoped to close it with another bipartisan initiative, this time to reduce America's trade surplus in some way yet to be determined. Again he quoted from his speech on Labor Day, accusing the Republicans of using scare words, "socialism" and the rest, to stir up the voters in the midterms.

By the end of the day, it was clear that Philip Jessup would be sacrificed. While remaining with the State Department he would be moved sideways from his post, to be replaced as ambassador-at-large by a Republican recommended by Arthur Vandenberg. And since both Vandenberg and Acheson wanted Dulles for the role, his was the only name that would do.

As the reporters at Key West left to file their copy, McCarthy was still on his feet in the Capitol with another hour of talking yet to finish. He could claim to have taken Jessup's scalp, and in April he would also start to win the battle of opinion. It would be another bad month for Truman, and still worse for Mayor William O'Dwyer of New York. Old predators reemerged, this time Frank Costello and the Mob, forcing the Democratic Party up against the ropes. While the president found himself the target of more vitriol, O'Dwyer was obliged to contemplate the likely end of his career, wrecked by the underworld of Brooklyn.

SAKHALIN ISLAND

*R*emote *though it was, the island of Sakhalin in the Soviet Far East had its fascination for Stalin. The same had been true of his fore-runners in the tsarist era. In the 1850s they had striven to bring it into their empire and done so at last in 1875. For those twentieth-century observers who chose to use the new idiom of geopolitics, Sakhalin could be seen, like Korea, as part of the Rimland of Eurasia, a frontier asset poised between Siberia and the northern tip of Japan.[1]*

After its defeat by the Japanese in 1905, Russia had been forced to share Sakhalin with its enemy, and the island was divided along the 50th parallel. At Yalta, Stalin extracted from Roosevelt and Churchill an agreement that he could take back the southern half and also annex from Japan the long chain of islands, the Kurils, that curved away to the northeast toward the Russian territory of Kamchatka.

All of this Stalin had done in 1945, when the Soviet army swept through Manchuria and occupied South Sakhalin. Settlers, including miners from the Donbas and peasants from the west of Russia, were sent to colonize this new possession and replace the Japanese, who were deported.

In 1946 the Communist Party chief from Sakhalin came to Moscow and Stalin plied him with questions about the island's resources. "Nature there is even richer than in the Crimea," the official claimed. He talked about oil, coal, and the abundant forests for making paper, and Stalin listened. Four years later, on March 26, 1950, when the strategic value of Sakhalin had become still more apparent, Stalin called one of those nocturnal meetings of which he was so fond. He told his Politburo about an ambitious project.

To help defend the Kurils and the Soviet Far East, they would use workers from the Gulag to dig a railroad tunnel linking Sakhalin and Siberia. Passing beneath the Strait of Tartary, six miles wide at its narrowest point, it might take five years to complete. The project, later abandoned after Stalin's death, was one more sign of the importance he attached to Northeast Asia.

The timing of the meeting was significant. Six days earlier, Kim Il-sung had sent word from Pyongyang that he wished to come to Moscow. Stalin agreed, and on April 10 Kim met him to discuss the invasion of South Korea. Stalin gave his approval, but with a condition. Although Stalin thought it unlikely that the United States would intervene, he insisted that Kim must obtain Mao's backing for the plan.

Meanwhile, Philip Jessup had returned from Asia troubled by what he had learned in his visits to America's allies. At the State Department on March 23 he spoke of what he called "the weaknesses of our friends." So few had yet embraced the democratic values that Washington wished to implant. Thailand was autocratic and feudal, and Burma run by the military. While Jessup now agreed with the French that Indochina was the key to Southeast Asia, he retained doubts about Vietnam's Bao Dai. The worst of all the Asian leaders was Syngman Rhee in South Korea.

Rhee, Jessup said, was "about as bad in this respect as anyone we have had to deal with." He arrested or bullied members of his parliament and was threatening to postpone an election due in May. With such coercive tactics, Rhee might, Jessup feared, drive his people into the arms of the Communists. His colleagues at Foggy Bottom were equally frustrated by the economic policies that Seoul was pursuing.

Inflation was spinning out of control, as Rhee's government ran up a budget deficit and printed money to finance it. Taxes went uncollected, and spending was too high. Dean Acheson lost patience with the situation and on April 3 he issued a rebuke. In a note he gave to Rhee's ambassador in Washington, he told Rhee to bring inflation down or face the consequences.

Acheson wanted something that resembled the rigorous Dodge Line in Japan; but while Prime Minister Yoshida Shigeru had swiftly put that economic policy into practice, Acheson doubted that Syngman Rhee would do the same. He said that if no firm steps were taken, America might have to reduce its economic aid, which that year was due to run at $100 million. Rhee must also hold the elections as planned.

And so for the third time in 1950—the first had been the press club speech, and the second the vote in Congress in January—America left its commitment to South Korea open to doubt. The State Department released the text of Acheson's note, and it ran in the press on April 8, while Kim was in Russia. Senator Knowland, the China hawk from the GOP, fell into line with Acheson and endorsed what he had said.

Preoccupied with Europe, Acheson left South Korea on one side as he focused instead on his "total diplomacy" campaign and his forthcoming talks in London. Later that month the US ambassador John Muccio came back from Seoul for sessions at the State Department. Although, in Jessup's words, "a hot war" was already taking place on the peninsula, with more clashes along the 38th parallel, Muccio gave his briefings to second-tier officials but not to the secretary of state.

The contrast with Moscow was profound. Stalin's intricate dealings with Mao, his Sakhalin tunnel project, and his personal attention to Kim Il-sung showed how closely he engaged with his strategic swerve to Asia. Even in his seventies, with his faculties declining,

Stalin remained a fearsome adversary. His concern for detail did not diminish. Still as well informed about the China region as he had been since the late 1920s, Stalin also retained his flexibility, as he did when he authorized Kim's invasion. Nor did Stalin have to cope with the erratic politics of Capitol Hill. Instead he could demand careful plans for war and expect to see them carried out.

CHAPTER ELEVEN

CALIBAN UNLEASHED

The debris cast up by this rushing tide of events,
much of it corrosive, will confront the President on
his return.

—ARTHUR KROCK *of the* New York Times,
April 1950[1]

Ernest Hemingway's new novel, his first for a decade, ran as a serial that spring in *Cosmopolitan* magazine. If readers had hoped for another *For Whom the Bell Tolls*, a tale of heroism and a call to arms, instead they were given a litany of contempt by an author disillusioned with the postwar world. In *Across the River and into the Trees*, a book most critics would dislike, Hemingway jeered at Dwight Eisenhower and mocked the singing career of Harry Truman's daughter, Margaret. He also wrote perhaps the most vicious words that the president would attract in 1950.

"I am not, nor have ever been, an unsuccessful haberdasher," said Hemingway's central character in the novel, an aging army colonel. "I have none of the qualifications for the Presidency. . . . [N]ow we are governed in some way by the dregs. We are governed by what you find in the bottom of dead beer glasses that whores have dunked their cigarettes in."[2]

This was just another way of saying what had been said so often—that Truman was no match for Franklin Roosevelt—but rarely with such poison. While Hemingway's book offended readers at the time, it also showed how frantic and overblown America's discourse had become. The novel began its serialization in the week before McCarthy's Wheeling speech. Hemingway drew on that other source of slurs against the president: not the charge that he was soft on Communists, but the taint of what the Alsop brothers had described as "courthouse mediocrity."

In April this familiar accusation returned. Arthur Krock of the *New York Times*, who had once been so supportive, could already feel, like Drew Pearson, the erosion of Truman's authority. The president seemed impotent and weary, unable to escape from shadows of the past. Neither he nor his party could afford more hints of scandal; but their big-city machines and the Mob supplied that very thing. While Truman took his working holiday at Key West, Mayor O'Dwyer of New York preferred a spring break at Key Largo. The two men came back from Florida on the same day, April 10, amid new sensations that threatened to cast around them yet again the odor of organized crime.

The gambling rackets, so hard to quantify but ever present, formed a trap that might disable any Democrat who held high office in their territory. In Illinois Adlai Stevenson saw this as his most urgent concern as governor. If bookies and number runners were rife in Chicago, he could blame his fellow Democrat the mayor, but not when the gambling took place in profusion in the far-flung counties just across the Mississippi from St. Louis. That spring pressure grew for a purge in Illinois, while in New York one was already underway.[3]

In January, with the Brooklyn rackets story continuing to build, Bill O'Dwyer had made a bold or desperate plea for gambling to be legalized in New York State. This, said Governor Dewey, would be "fundamentally immoral." The mayor was left defenseless as proof emerged of corruption in his police department.

Miles McDonald, the Brooklyn district attorney, began a series of raids in the first week of April that brought his investigation of the borough's bookmaking syndicates to a climax. In gambling joints close to that fertile terrain, the Navy Yard and the army base, among the betting slips his men found lists of payments to the cops. On O'Dwyer's arrival home from Florida, the police commissioner hurried to his office, keen to take over the investigation. McDonald refused to cooperate, because in Brooklyn he could trust almost no one in the NYPD.[4]

If this were not embarrassing enough, something still more atrocious had occurred in Truman's Kansas City. It came to light on April 6, the day the State Department named John Foster Dulles as Dean Acheson's ambassador-at-large. The previous evening, witnesses had seen Charles Binaggio, a Democratic ward boss and numbers racketeer, and Charlie Gargotta, his enforcer, drinking at the Last Chance Tavern, Kansas City's most notorious gambling den. On the morning of the sixth, the police found their corpses in Binaggio's headquarters, the Democratic Club on Truman Road: each man had four bullets in his head. Gazing across the room, above the bodies and the pools of blood, there hung a giant photograph of Harry Truman.[5]

Whoever killed Binaggio and Gargotta had an obvious motive: the two gangsters had recently been called to testify about the city's rackets to a federal grand jury. But besides the Mob, suspicion also fell on local politicians, because Binaggio allegedly controlled the Democratic Party apparatus on Kansas City's North Side. Some said he had connections with Frank Costello; others remembered a party dinner in Missouri the previous fall where Truman was the guest of honor. At that event, a photographer had captured a shot

"Crime, Politics and Co.," by Daniel Fitzpatrick, from the *St. Louis Post-Dispatch*, April 7, 1950, the day after the discovery of the corpses of Charles Binaggio and Charlie Gargotta. *St. Louis Post-Dispatch Editorial Cartoon Collection, State Historical Society of Missouri, Columbia Research Center.*

of Binaggio sitting three seats away from Stuart Symington, the air force secretary.

The Kansas City slayings revived those old tales of corruption that the *Chicago Tribune* had worked so hard to attach to the president. Everyone knew that in the Prohibition era Truman had owed his first important role in politics, as a Jackson County judge in 1923, to the convicted tax evader Tom Pendergast, the city's fixer-in-chief. In the postwar years, Kansas City politics continued to be infamous for payoffs, rigged contracts, ballot-box stuffing, and—in 1947—the theft from the courthouse of a safe full of ballot papers. For Senator Taft and his fellow Republicans, the murders presented an opportunity almost as fruitful as the furor about Alger Hiss.

Even before the killings, it had been all but inevitable that the Senate would mount the national investigation into organized crime that the Democrat Estes Kefauver had demanded. But its funding, its membership, and its terms of reference had yet to be agreed. Scott Lucas, tossed back and forth by his Senate colleagues, had his doubts about entrusting the inquiry to the ambitious Kefauver, who had only been a senator for fifteen months.

While Senator Lucas dithered and delayed, worrying about the imminent debates on Marshall Plan renewal, on the Republican side Binaggio's death aroused new fits of rhetoric. "The land is filled with blood and the city is filled with perverseness," said Senator James Kem, a Republican from Missouri, quoting from Ezekiel the prophet as he called Kansas City "indescribably corrupt." Until Lucas gave Kefauver what he wanted, this sort of attack would continue. In parallel with the rise of McCarthyism, that other accusation—current since the fall—became all the more common: that Truman and the Democratic leadership were dragging their feet for fear of what might be revealed about Costello, O'Dwyer, and their other big-city machines.[6]

Apart from Richard Nixon's run for the Senate in California, the elections that mattered most in 1950 would be those fought out in the cities of the arc of prosperity, Chicago and Cleveland above all. Their voters would decide the fate of Senators Lucas and Taft. If and when the Kefauver Committee began its national probe, it would have to explore both towns. But while Cleveland had its rackets, Chicago, that Democratic fiefdom, was the more likely of the two to produce revelations that would ambush Truman and his party. Besides the sheer size and notoriety of both its underworld and its Democratic machine, Chicago also still possessed an unrivaled influence over the nation's anxious vision of itself.

You might think that by now, twenty years on from the heyday of Al Capone, nothing new was left to say about gangsters and lowlife in the city on the lake. In fact the subject kept all its somber fascination, and in 1950, at the peak of the popularity of film noir, Chicago had if anything enhanced its power to fashion the image Americans formed of their country. That spring you could take your choice of different ways to conceive of Chicago's asphalt jungle, but none of them conveyed a message helpful to the Democratic Party.

The 1950 Oscar for Best Picture went to *All the King's Men*, with its theme of political corruption in a rural state; but in March a Chicago novel won the National Book Award for fiction. The winner was Nelson Algren for *The Man with the Golden Arm*, his account of Frankie Machine, an ex-con and morphine addict trapped in Algren's neon wilderness along Division Street. An epidemic in the use of heroin had indeed begun in Chicago after World War II. It reached its peak in 1949 and 1950 and prompted the city to begin a crackdown on Black youth.[7]

A subject that engendered fear, the trade in narcotics also brought with it the specter of the Mob. And here another book— *Chicago Confidential*—cast the city as the perennial capital of gangland. The work of two newspapermen, Jack Lait and Lee Mortimer, it appeared at the end of February and sold well. Since the book had mentioned Charles Binaggio, linking him to the national crime network said to be run by Costello, the authors captured all the more attention.

A book that was easy to mock and parody, it described in hurtling prose a Chicago filled with "juve delinks," a "scarlet sisterhood," and "degenerates in the twilight zones of sex." But Senator Kefauver read *Chicago Confidential*, he took it seriously, and he befriended its authors. The book would leave its imprint on his committee's findings. Organized crime in Chicago, said Lait and Mortimer, was part of "the Mafia, the Unione Siciliano, the super-government which now has tentacles reaching into the Cabinet and the White House itself." Minus the mention of the White House, this would be Kefauver's own conclusion.

Was it true? Was there really a Mafia, an Italian American hierarchy of crime, systematically constructed all across the nation? Even if the Cosa Nostra were a myth made by the tabloids—and that was a question still up for debate—illegal gambling was real enough in the Windy City, and documented by the Chicago Crime Commission. So was police corruption. That spring the commission was collecting evidence of graft in the North Side precincts where Algren's novel had been set.[8]

In neither New York State nor Chicago could this kind of thing remain a merely local matter. Their populations were too large, their politics too close to call, and if corruption stories swung their voters against the Democratic Party, the national implications might be decisive. In 1948 four million people had gone to the polls in Illinois. Although they gave Truman their twenty-eight seats in the electoral college, his winning margin had been thin. Only thirty-four thousand votes had separated him from Tom Dewey. In the governor's race, Adlai Stevenson had polled far ahead of the president, but a familiar pattern had recurred: the two parties neck and neck downstate, a huge Democrat plurality in the city of Chicago, but a Republican majority in the Cook County suburbs that surrounded it. And there in the metropolitan fringe the tales of sleaze at the heart of the city might be especially potent.[9]

In 1950, with Lucas up for reelection, the Democrats might lose if too many of their voters stayed at home in the city and if the Republican Everett Dirksen made the most of his rural and suburban base. In his primary in April he won an easy victory with one ominous feature for the Democrats. Dirksen drew a high voter turnout in precisely the Chicago suburbs that he would need to capture in November.

In the city the Democratic machine was eager to have Truman come to Chicago for a rally. A date had been announced—May 15—but this would plunge the president into the midst of the controversy about rackets and the Mob. Like most of the rest of the GOP, Dirksen was moving to the right. He was likely to campaign not only against the alleged drift to socialism but also about two kinds of immorality: leftists and homosexuals in the State Department, and gambling and corruption in the cities. With this and other challenges looming up ahead, the president returned from Key West.

FERMENT AND THE LURE OF POWER

So much was going wrong for Harry Truman in the spring of 1950. Eight months on from the end of the recession, an expanding economy seemed only to aggravate the wrangling. There appeared to be no subject on which people could agree, or that could not be made the pretext for an ideological squabble. Housing, taxes, natural gas, schools, and farming subsidies: the list of topics for dispute went on and on, until strife became a habit that Congress refused to shake off.

Truman wanted federal help for middle-income housing, something that surely every district could put to good use; but this idea died its death on Capitol Hill. Federal aid for schools was gridlocked as well. Catholics, Protestants, and nonbelievers still differed about the inclusion of schools run by churches. Even that innocent tuber, the American potato, could produce a fight between left and right.

As part of the battery of farming policies the New Deal and the war had left behind, the government had spent half a billion dollars since 1945 to buy surplus potatoes and keep up their market price. During World War II the farmers had dug for victory with the help of great strides forward in techniques and machinery. In peacetime they did not wish to stop. They produced glut after glut. In the fall of 1949, rotting heaps of green potatoes had piled up in the freight yards of Idaho and Maine. All the signs were that 1950 would yield another enormous crop and another exorbitant bill for taxpayers to pick up.

The price support regime had to be abolished or reformed, but this would be hard to accomplish. The Truman cabinet hoped to revive parts of the Brannan Plan, that complicated scheme that Congress had already rejected. Intended to cope with a new peacetime world when gluts were frequent, partly because America's farmers were so productive, and partly because foreign nations lacked the dollars to buy what they grew, the plan had some merits. But in a year when nothing that smelled even faintly of socialism had a chance of passage into law, the Brannan Plan was blocked again. Congress kicked the potato problem into 1951 and the farmers went on planting more tubers.[10]

The political conflicts seen in 1950 followed a pattern. An old order of things was coming to an end and a new one had yet to be born. This did not yet endanger the New Deal institutions and programs that FDR had built. Social security, the federal minimum wage, the might of the labor unions, expanded federal agencies, and landmarks such as the Tennessee Valley Authority (TVA): these were either permanent, or safe at least for many years to come. So was much of Roosevelt's farm policy of 1938, which Congress kept alive when it rejected Truman's attempts at reform. Instead the old order nearing its death was the political balance of forces that had existed in Roosevelt's lifetime and had begun to decay long before 1945. This was what the Republican Party was seeking to replace as it gnawed away at Acheson and Truman and the Fair Deal manifesto.

Bob Taft led the Republican pack. His adversaries, including not only Truman but also writers such as Walter Lippmann, still tried to portray him as a relic of the years before Pearl Harbor. That spring they summoned up the old phrase "isolationism" to dismiss the senator and his colleagues as outmoded troublemakers. In doing so they failed to see the point. When Republicans demanded the defense of Taiwan, or when they reached out to Douglas MacArthur in Japan, they could not be described as isolationists. In any case, their real target lay elsewhere. It could be seen in Dirksen's campaign in Illinois. Taft, Ken Wherry, and Styles Bridges, with the help of McCarthy but in other ways as well, were trying to split and break open the old alliances and affinities on which Roosevelt's power had been based. In this, Taft and his allies were thinking—like the young Bill Buckley at Yale—about the future rather than the past.

Guy Gabrielson, the chairman of the RNC, was talking about the Republican capture of parts of the South. He saw Virginia as the state his party might take, because it was fiscally conservative, one of the homes of the "economy bloc" of Harry Byrd and Walter George. Here the RNC's leaders were getting ahead of themselves, but the South was definitely in play. In the region the Democrats were fighting each other, with the help of nudges from the GOP. The nudges had to do with civil rights, socialism, and fear of Moscow, the same topics that had destabilized Frank Graham in North Carolina.

Soon after the president's return to Washington, these issues crystallized in Alabama too, in a form that again displayed Truman's frail position in the South. Long before Selma and the era of George Wallace, this was a locality always to be watched. In 1947 the journalist John Gunther had called Alabama "a state in ferment." Its Democrats had swung so enthusiastically for Strom Thurmond for the White House in 1948 that Truman could not win a single vote—the states' rights Dixiecrats blocked his name from appearing on the ballot. Two years later Alabama contrived another rebellion when Lister Hill, the Democratic senator facing reelection, chose to spring a trap on Truman. The manner in which he did so spoke about the shift in politics nationwide and the fate of Truman's form of liberalism.[11]

There had been a time when Hill and Truman were as one. In 1932, when Alabama went all out for FDR as part of that southern tide that would help sweep him to the nomination in Chicago, Lister Hill had been a New Dealer before the phrase existed. The TVA had its roots in his bill, vetoed by President Hoover, to create a dam at Muscle Shoals. He was close to Senator Hugo Black, Roosevelt's trusted Alabama friend, and after World War II Hill had remained a liberal. As the Hill of the Hill-Burton Act, he put federal money into building hospitals; and although he spoke out against "socialized medicine," he still wanted the government to do more. He hoped to use additional federal cash to expand Blue Cross and Blue Shield plans for those unable to afford them.[12]

That spring, however, Hill had another task to accomplish: to end the rift of 1948 and reclaim his party from the rebels of that year. The Alabama Dixiecrats were fielding candidates for every office. Running for governor was Eugene "Bull" Connor of Birmingham, who in 1963 would turn his city's fire hoses and police dogs on the protesters led by Martin Luther King Jr. Bull Connor and his faction knew what they were for: segregation, Jim Crow, better roads, and better old-age pensions. They also knew what they detested: an unbalanced budget, federal bureaucracy, and what they called, again in the language of John T. Flynn's *The Road Ahead*, "the National Socialist Democratic Party of Harry S. Truman and Lister Hill." In the wake of the Kansas City murders they copied the language of the GOP, accusing the president of making Washington the tool of the big-city political machines.

To prevent the likes of Bull Connor from controlling the party in the state, Lister Hill stole some of their Dixiecratic language. Hill had always been a friend of segregation, but hitherto he had not made it the core of his appeal to the voters. On April 12, speaking to Alabama by radio from Washington, he embraced it fervently. "I am a States Rights Democrat," Senator Hill proclaimed. Only a united Democratic Party in the South, he said, could defeat the FEPC fair employment bill and the rest of what remained of Truman's program for Black civil rights. This was the price to be paid for preserving those liberal policies, such as expanded health care, that Hill still wished to promote. Widely reported nationwide, his words could only help to deepen that great rift in the Democratic Party: the split between its southern echelon and its very different cohort in the industrial north. Hill's intervention also posed another question that could not be indefinitely ignored.[13]

In the primary in May his allies won what was seen in the state as a victory for liberals, who swept the Dixiecrats aside and recaptured Alabama's Democratic committee. In 1952 they would form the state's delegation to choose a nominee for the White House. Whom would they select? As the Eisenhower boom continued, with Republicans pressing the general to declare his allegiance, this question began to edge its way into the political arena. An answer would eventually be found, and one that would suit Lister Hill. His Alabama colleague, Senator John Sparkman, would become the running mate of Adlai Stevenson when he ran against Eisenhower.

The shrewdest observers already foresaw what was coming. In the *New York Herald Tribune*, Stewart Alsop saw the events in Alabama for what they were: a contest for the soul of the Democratic Party. By routing the Dixiecrats as they did, Sparkman and Hill acquired a more powerful voice in the party nationwide. In doing so, they drew it ever more deeply into the realm of fudge and compromise. This was another legacy of those early days of Joe McCarthy.[14]

For Truman, back from Florida, the prospects for 1952 were even now a theme for meditation, vying for his attention with the choices that Acheson and Paul Nitze were trying to thrust upon him. On the day Lister Hill gave his radio talk, the president replied to the final draft of NSC-68. Because the document failed to include detailed plans or a budget, it could not be approved as it stood; but Truman was reluctant to give it his consent even in principle.

Passing no judgment on its view of the world, or on the military stance it advocated, Truman referred the report back to the National Security Council, asking for the numbers and an analysis of what NSC-68 would do to America's economy. Since Truman wanted Nitze to confer with the White House budget office, the Treasury, and his Council of Economic Advisers—a process that would consume the spring and summer—this would probably be enough to postpone a decision, pro or con, until after the elections in November. Delay was Truman's only option.

With the Marshall Plan yet to be extended, and the House so reluctant to raise taxes, bold talk of bigger budgets would be futile. Nor could he expect Democrats to fight their primaries on the domestic issues of the day only for the White House to spring

NSC-68 upon them. Given how adamant Truman had been that the Pentagon's budget was sufficient, he could not tell America that he had been wrong. Meanwhile, the new ambassador Dulles had his own priorities, including taking a stand on Taiwan, which might carry more weight than Acheson's grand strategy.

As Truman made his calculations, he also had to reckon with his own timetable. By its very nature NSC-68 was a medium- or long-term program that set 1954 as its pivotal date. Most of it would have to be overseen, if it came about at all, by whoever was sworn in as president in January 1953. It would be pointless to launch such a program without a strategy for keeping the White House in Democratic hands. And at just this moment in the spring of 1950, five years almost to the day since he first took the oath of office, Truman decided not to run again for president.

On April 16 he wrote a brief memorandum to himself. It was eloquent, deeply felt, and private, so private that it might not have been definitive, since he might later have changed his mind. "I am not," he wrote, "a candidate for nomination by the Democratic convention. . . . [I]n my opinion eight years as president is enough and sometimes too much for any man to serve in that capacity. There is a lure in power. It can get into a man's blood just as gambling and lust for money have been known to do." For Truman the reader of history, a president who yearned to go on and on in office would resemble a Roman tyrant. "When we forget," Truman wrote, "the examples of such men as Washington, Jefferson and Andrew Jackson, all of whom could have had a continuation in office, then we will start down the road to dictatorship and ruin."

If Truman had shared his memorandum with the other leaders of his party, they might also have seen it as a response to the circumstances of the moment. There were some who already saw the republic in danger. In the amphitheater of the Senate caucus room, scenes were unfolding that a Roman audience might have recognized.

BITTERNESS AND FANATICS

Returning from the Middle East, Owen Lattimore had bounded off the plane at Idlewild weary from the flight but filled with the determination of a man who thinks he has many friends. At his side was the editor of the *Baltimore Sun*, who had flown to London to meet him and to show his solidarity with a neighbor. Confident that he could trounce Joe McCarthy, the professor meant to do more than clear his name. Lattimore also intended to show that he was correct about Red China and the rest of Asia.

In New York he summoned the press. "No one," said Lattimore, "likes to be splattered with mud, even by a madman." Flanked by his lawyers, he called McCarthy's charges false and libelous, but then he displayed the kind of vanity to which scholars are sometimes prone. It was Lattimore's way of denying that he had ever been an architect of anything at Foggy Bottom. "If the State Department had followed the approach that my books have suggested," said the professor, "we would be in a much better position . . . and China would not now be in the hands of the Communists."[15]

That was on April 1. Two days later and in the same unrealistic vein, he released a memorandum he had written for Philip Jessup's seminar the previous fall. Besides the recognition of Red China, Lattimore wanted America to make friends with Ho Chi Minh, discard South Korea, and allow Japan to go its own way, trade with Mao, and choose its own stance toward the Cold War. These were views precisely the opposite of those that Dulles held and that the State Department could accept.

That month in Washington three battles were being fought, impossible to disentangle from one another, with the Republican

Party gradually winning each one. Lattimore would become a civilian casualty trapped between the warring sides. One of these battles had to do with Truman's Fair Deal, and one with McCarthy's accusations. The third was the dispute about America in Asia that had become so fierce after the fall of Shanghai and the China White Paper. This last was a policy battle that Lattimore's side had already lost; but it was the combination of the three that gave McCarthy his advantage.

It seemed that with each passing week the conservative triumvirate of Taft, Wherry, and Bridges clung more tightly to McCarthy. Senator Bridges went to the Senate floor to rebut what Truman had said in Key West and to denounce what he called "the appeasers, the subversives, the incompetents, and the homosexuals who threaten our security." In Portland, Maine, Taft said that only a Republican Congress could end the "creeping socialism" in the country, and that only a Republican White House could rid the State Department of its Communists. Meanwhile, those in his party who stuck close to Chiang Kai-shek looked forward to seeing Dulles win the day in their favor. Seizing on Lattimore's memorandum, they added their voices against him.[16]

On the morning when the police found the Kansas City corpses, Lattimore appeared before the Tydings panel. For five hours he would sit at the witness table in a Senate caucus room filled to overflowing. For the first time, the hearings would be televised, and the viewers were given a spectacle almost as exotic as a scene from *Samson and Delilah*. The audience heard Lattimore call McCarthy's charges "base and contemptible lies." Nearby, with a film camera poking over one shoulder, sat a Mongolian monk in a long red robe. The Living Buddha, as the press had come to call him, was a friend of Lattimore's. The professor had brought him from China to teach at Johns Hopkins. From the top table McCarthy glared at Lattimore but was barred from speaking.[17]

The session would reach its climax with what appeared to be another defeat for the young man from Wisconsin. Senator Tydings revealed that the FBI director had called the subcommittee to his office and given them a précis of the Lattimore file. Nothing in it suggested that he had ever been a Communist or a spy. From the chair Tydings gave Lattimore the cleanest bill of health he could. "The FBI file puts you completely," he told the professor, "up to this moment at least, in the clear."

Nothing however could be so simple when FBI director J. Edgar Hoover was involved. Although he did not think that Lattimore had been a party member, in private Hoover felt that the professor might have been manipulated by those who were. If under oath a witness testified to something of the kind, then McCarthy would have what he needed to keep his case alive. During the session, Lattimore had himself confirmed that he had been close to two of the *Amerasia* defendants.[18]

Lattimore had also declared war on America's friends of Chiang Kai-shek. In front of the press and Chiang's advocate Senator William Knowland, the professor had devoted half his time at the witness table to insulting the China lobby. McCarthy was "their willing tool," he said, the "instrument or the dupe" of "bitter fanatics" who would tolerate no criticism of Chiang. With their brutality and their corruption, the professor claimed, Chiang and his cronies had lost China. Lattimore urged America not to make the same error again by supporting what he called those "little Chiangs," Syngman Rhee in South Korea and Bao Dai in Vietnam.

This was dangerous ground for Acheson and Truman. At the time, the China lobby had two wings. One wing dealt in conspiracy theories, while the other, which was more moderate and included Knowland and the Alsop brothers, cited reasonable grounds to criticize America's record in the region. By antagonizing both groups, Lattimore revived a controversy that should have been concluded.

Lost amid the uproar was a simple truth. By appointing John Foster Dulles, Acheson had already acknowledged that he needed help with his Asia policy. In doing so, he had been magnanimous and humble. He had also awarded his department's Far Eastern brief to a new assistant secretary, Dean Rusk, who in 1945 had proposed the partition of Korea along the 38th parallel. Despite the flaws of Syngman Rhee, Rusk would work closely with Dulles to develop America's support for his regime. It was also now the case that sooner or later America would have to protect Taiwan, since Dulles would not flinch from its defense, and Rusk was coming to agree with him.[19]

Although Acheson had gone as far as he could go, it seemed to count for nothing. Provocative and indiscreet, Lattimore invited a rejoinder and an inquisition that would cloud the Asia question yet again. The China lobby had a weapon against Lattimore, a witness who would once more disinter the loss of China and seek to expose the guilty parties.

Their weapon was Louis Budenz, an FBI informant who taught economics at the Jesuit university at Fordham in the Bronx. A Catholic who had lapsed, spent ten years as a Communist, and then rejoined the church of Rome, Budenz had become in 1948 a celebrity of anti-communism. Apart from testifying against Alger Hiss, he had also been the government's star witness in the conspiracy trial in New York, spending ten days on the stand to reveal the secrets of the CPUSA. Budenz caused another sensation when he gave the Tydings Committee evidence against Lattimore.[20]

It was April 20, more than two months after the Wheeling speech and awkwardly close to primary season. A few weeks earlier, Budenz had finished writing another of that year's many books about the Red menace. *Men Without Faces* told a familiar story about what Budenz called "the poison of fifth column influence," but it contained one chapter that gave McCarthy what he had to have. In Chapter 10—"Cloak and Dagger"—Budenz claimed that the Communist Party had infiltrated the Institute of Pacific Relations, that think tank where Jessup had been a trustee and Lattimore had edited a journal.

His evidence was hearsay; but in the caucus room Budenz repeated it under oath. Lattimore and the editors of *Amerasia*, had belonged, Budenz said, to a party cell that subverted the institute, making it a propaganda tool for Mao. "This game of Red deceit," wrote Budenz in his book, "began the rout of Nationalist China." Under questioning he faltered. He admitted that he had never met Lattimore, that he had no incriminating documents, and that he had never discussed the professor with the FBI. Even so, Budenz had done enough.

When Congress starts an inquiry such as the one the Tydings Committee was assigned, it sets up a process that acquires an impetus of its own. The inquiry, once begun, can slide away from its original purpose at the risk of causing collateral damage on all sides. This is all the more so when the panel is given wide terms of reference and is chaired by a senator as diligent as Millard Tydings. Once Budenz had testified as he did, Tydings had no choice but to recall Lattimore to give his response. He would also have to enter the maze of *Amerasia*. This line of questioning would stretch out the proceedings to the end of May, with McCarthy still unvanquished. Although his fifty-seven Communists had failed to materialize, he grew ever more outspoken, amplifying his message with every speech or press briefing he gave.

Perhaps Richard Nixon had been right. An independent commission, neutral and separate from Congress, might have been the best way to go. Or, at the outset, Senators Scott Lucas and Tom Connally might have asked Truman to turn McCarthy's charges over to the FBI and tell it to investigate the State Department. Now it was too late.

Each day the pressure grew for the president to unseal the loyalty files. But what might they reveal? And if they gave Foggy Bottom a clean bill of health, would McCarthy merely claim, as he had claimed already, that the files had been tampered with by the same homosexuals and leftists who had betrayed Chiang Kai-shek? Even Tydings, who had fought the Germans at Verdun, became anxious and alarmed, besieging the president with pleas for help.

Senator Lucas had failed to see how the process he had begun might spin out of control. Now he and his party would incur its consequences. Senator Tydings summoned Lattimore to appear again on May 2. That would be the Tuesday when four states voted in their primaries: Alabama, Indiana, Taft's Ohio, and Florida where a conservative tide was breaking over the Truman Democrats. In the meantime, the secretary of state strove to explain his concept of total diplomacy.

The View from Foggy Bottom

From his office Dean Acheson surveyed the globe. With his journey to London now only a few weeks away, he was preparing another speech to promote the message of NSC-68. It would be given on April 22 in front of a demanding audience, the nation's newspaper editors, meeting for their annual convention. Since all of them had run McCarthy's allegations, Acheson would have to rebut them; but most of all he wished to share his vision of America's role in the world.

Although Truman had forbidden any publicity about Nitze's document, Acheson worked its ideas into this speech and his private briefings to Congress. That month, the flow of news seemed to confirm NSC-68's grim warnings about the global struggle with the Soviets. As it did so, it also maintained the tension now so tangible in Washington.

The Kremlin was as difficult as ever. While more reports arrived of Russian submarines in the Pacific, an incident occurred in the Baltic. On April 8 a bomber from the US Navy had taken off from the Rhineland bound for Denmark, strayed over the sea, and been shot down by Soviet fighters. In their perverse way the Russians chose to make a diplomatic protest about the violation of their airspace. Two weeks later, they added a demand for the withdrawal of NATO forces from Trieste, the Italian enclave on the Adriatic that Stalin had tried to claim as his own.

A diplomat as experienced as Dean Acheson does not rattle a saber in response to provocation such as this. He was used to crises. He tried to look beyond them, into the patterns underlying the shifting surface of affairs. By now he could define with the utmost clarity the challenges he saw overseas. From time to time, as he described them, he summoned up a word—"disintegration"—that had appeared in his Yale speech of 1939, when he had warned of the threat from Hitler and Japan.

For Acheson, Europe had to be America's first priority. "If anything happens in Western Europe," he told Tom Connally and the Foreign Relations Committee in a private session, "the whole business goes to pieces." Here the German question loomed larger than any other. West Germany had to be transformed from what he called an "ex-enemy" into a willing ally, securely anchored in the Western alliance, with its economy rebuilt. The issue of reunification with its eastern half he saw as something to be indefinitely postponed.[21]

The military men, not only the British field marshal Montgomery but also the Joint Chiefs in Washington, were talking of the need for West Germany to rearm as part of NATO. Any hint of such a thing alarmed the French, who took grave offense in April when Chancellor Adenauer visited West Berlin and his audience sang "Deutschland über Alles." This meant that possibly for years to come the German contribution to Europe's defense would have to be solely industrial, above all by supplying its neighbors with steel and coal, those two commodities so central to postwar politics. But this would leave unsolved that other great problem, the defense of West Germany's eastern frontier against a Soviet Union so mighty. Should America send ground forces back to Europe, where it now had only one army division? Some voices in Washington wanted to add another five. Acheson agreed. He also admitted that this was a decision he had no power to make.

If Europe had to be America's focal point, what of the rest of the world? "We cannot scatter our shots equally," Acheson told the senators. "We just haven't got enough shots to do that." In Asia the United States would have to mount chiefly what he called "a holding operation." Here, too, he saw the risk of collapse at either extreme of the great crescent that curved from the Punjab to the northern Pacific.[22]

At one end was Japan, where another "ex-enemy" had to be made a friend, but fully independent, to retain the loyalty of a people tired of occupation. This would require the long-delayed peace treaty with Tokyo, a delicate task of negotiation that Acheson would give to John Foster Dulles. The other end of the crescent contained perils of its own. Nonaligned though it was, India, with Nehru as its leader, formed what Acheson saw as a crucial force for stability in Asia. Or so it might, if it were not for the poverty and food shortages the British had left behind. The possibility of war between India and Pakistan deeply worried Acheson, and the pact the two countries signed in April did not bring it to an end. While it might bring peace to Bengal, it did not resolve their disputes over Kashmir.

Along the rim of the crescent lay Southeast Asia. Acheson now accepted France's case for military aid to hold Indochina. Truman had given his consent, and on April 27 the State Department told the French that they agreed in principle; but this could not be made public. There still remained the problem Jessup had identified: that America was having to rely on regimes, such as Bao Dai's, whose credentials as bastions of democracy were weak.

Even the British could not be trusted entirely. For Acheson the Middle East chiefly mattered as part of the frontier of containment of the Soviets, with oil as a secondary concern. For the British it was the other way around. They could not do without their oil from Iran, Kuwait, and Iraq, to feed the refineries they were building in England with funds from the Marshall Plan. The Suez Canal had to be held, with thirty thousand British troops in the zone around it, but Acheson was all too well aware that Egypt wanted them gone. He also knew of Iran's resentment of the profits the British were extracting. That issue would blow up in 1951, and the warning signs were already plainly visible.

Acheson was America's fifty-first secretary of state. None of the fifty who held the office before him had been obliged to think so deeply about so many parts of the globe. With his gift for cutting through the detail, he had arrived at one central conclusion that tied everything together. If one word on his lips was "disintegration," then "mobilization" was another. It was the theme of NSC-68; and although the document remained a secret, the concept could be found everywhere that spring in Acheson's pronouncements.

More resources had to be found, military but therefore also economic. Again Western Europe and its productivity occupied the foreground. If NATO were to be a genuine front line, the additional forces required from Britain, France, and the other partners would strain their taxpayers to the limit. "A very great effort is called for by the West," Acheson told the senators. "You have got to have larger tax revenues, and that means a much greater productive base in Europe to carry that on."[23]

This was also the message of NSC-68. In May he would have to prod the Europeans once again to unravel the array of tariffs and exchange controls that he saw impeding their prosperity. Acheson would do so in the expectation that the British might be incapable or unwilling and the French perhaps still unprepared. In return he would promise America's best efforts to import more and export less. He knew this objective might take years to accomplish. In the meantime, the dollar gap would still be yawning wide.

From all of this, Acheson drew another conclusion. Marshall aid would have to go on and on, beyond its expected end in 1952. Early in May, as he left for London, the renewal of the Marshall Plan would be entering its final stage in the grinding machine of Congress. The votes were expected to be close: so close that even a few lost seats in November would jeopardize the plan's survival.

American politics at their highest level were reaching an impasse. What Acheson had said about foreign affairs—"We just haven't got enough shots"—applied with equal force to domestic policy. It was essential for Acheson to regain momentum, as Truman had tried and failed to do with his interview with Arthur Krock. In this frame of mind Acheson drafted his speech for the American Society of Newspaper Editors. As he did so his thoughts traveled back to Labor Day weekend.

A MADMAN WITH A GUN

Mass shootings, those incidents that would later become so familiar, happened in Truman's America only between hoodlums. The sole exception was the case of Howard Unruh, the ex-soldier who had killed so many random victims in Camden, New Jersey, on September 6, 1949. It was so unusual an episode that it led to no national self-interrogation. Declared insane, Unruh spent the rest of his days in a New Jersey hospital. The country moved on; but Unruh's crimes left their mark on Dean Acheson.

Until now he had kept his temper in public about Joe McCarthy's charges. When Acheson's explosion came, three weeks after the president's, it was a sign of how wounded he felt that he would turn to the Camden murders to express his feelings about the senator's campaign. Acheson did so in his speech to the editors on April 22, when his message about foreign affairs struggled to be heard amid the noise created by the Tydings inquiry.

Earlier that week, on the day Budenz testified against Lattimore, the newspaper executives had heard from Joe McCarthy. By now some people who met him thought the Wisconsin senator might be mentally unhinged. In private, McCarthy was drinking heavily and threatening to break Drew Pearson's ribs. Pearson replied in his radio show with a comparison that would become commonplace. Three years before the playwright Arthur Miller, he likened McCarthy's campaign to the witch trials at Salem.

In front of the newspapermen McCarthy ranted again. He labeled Acheson "incompetent" and denounced what he called "the egg-sucking phony liberals . . . those who hold sacrosanct those Communists and queers who have sold 400 million Asiatic people into atheistic slavery." McCarthy's invective turned the stomach of some of those who heard him; but he was gaining ground. Although he could be called hysterical, a blunderer, or a partisan terrorist, his charges still had to be answered. This was becoming all the harder now that Budenz appeared to confirm them.

At the editors' convention, Acheson wanted to talk about "total diplomacy." He offered the phrase as he talked about global free trade, the Marshall Plan, and ending poverty in Asia, where hunger gave Communism its appeal. In the language Churchill also used about the United States, Acheson spoke of the nation's "belief in freedom and tolerance, its great productive power, its tremendous vitality." All of it, he said, must be brought to bear in the struggle with the Kremlin.[24]

Acheson could not ignore McCarthy. A man of honor, loyal to friends and colleagues, the secretary of state did not shirk his duty to defend them. He named names of his own, twenty-one staffers and advisers at the State Department, Rusk, Jessup, and many more, praising their fortitude and—with his sarcasm—dismissing the idea that they were tools of Moscow. At this point Acheson was speaking without a formal script but with emotion.

He called McCarthy's charges "trash" and "a filthy business," compared the senator to Shakespeare's Caliban from *The Tempest*, and then he came to Howard Unruh. McCarthy reminded him, Acheson told the editors, "of that horrible episode in Camden . . . when a madman came out on the street in the morning with his revolver. With no purpose and with no plan, as he walked down the street he just shot people . . . without sense, without purpose, without direction."

His audience stood and clapped and cheered; but many of them had also applauded McCarthy's speech. As they dispersed across the country, the confusion deepened. To some it seemed that Acheson had lost his cool. While Truman's enemies alleged a cover-up at Foggy Bottom, his friends grew restless too. The administration and the Democratic leadership in Congress were pushed toward the surrender of positions they had vowed to defend.

With Senator Tydings now so traumatized, the moment could not be far off when the president would have to give him the State Department loyalty files. Nor could Congress postpone the reckoning with Frank Costello and what he signified. The arch-mobster had appeared on Capitol Hill to deny all knowledge of illegal gambling, a comic touch that only made the Senate look foolish. At almost the same moment, Secretary of Defense Louis Johnson was at last admitting to another committee of Congress that he had to have more money for the air force. With the Joint Chiefs on the brink of an uprising, he had little choice.[25]

Meanwhile, the American people were making their voices heard. George Gallup, the nation's leading pollster, chose to dismiss

Republican prospects of large gains in November, when he found in April that only 37 percent of Americans intended to vote for the GOP. But he ignored the trend his own data displayed, showing a five-point Republican improvement since the fall of 1949. Strip out the effect of the Democrats' overwhelming majorities in the South, and the two parties were evenly matched in the rest of the country. The Democrats were polling at 40 percent and the Republicans at 39, with a fifth of the voters undecided. Meanwhile, Truman's approval rating had sunk to its lowest level since the summer of 1948.[26]

The most striking feature of the polls was the impact that McCarthy was making. At a time when fewer than six out of ten Americans could correctly define the term "Cold War," he achieved far greater recognition. In the first week of May, Gallup asked Americans if they had heard of McCarthy's charges about Communists at Acheson's department. Eighty-four percent said yes. Of these, two-fifths thought his campaign was good for the country, while only 29 percent thought it was bad. Half of all Republicans welcomed the stand McCarthy took. Even among Democrats, McCarthy's supporters outweighed his detractors. But some of his strongest backing came from the college educated. Forty-six percent of this group approved of his campaign.

The Gallup results would not be released for weeks, but the Republican leadership had already chosen their ground. Another floor debate about McCarthy would occur in the Senate on May 3. Scenting victory in the war for public opinion, Wherry uttered one more diatribe against Dean Acheson. From the opposing side, only one senator spoke up with kind words for the secretary of state. Again it was New York's Herbert Lehman. If the Democrats in Congress were demoralized, it did not help that they had just suffered a blow from the South.

Red Pepper's Defeat

In the Alabama primary on Tuesday, May 2, Lister Hill won his Pyrrhic triumph, sweeping away the Dixiecrats to regain control of his party. But while the implications of this result would take time to assess, there was nothing ambiguous about the news from Florida. In the Democratic primary, the Fair Deal loyalists went down to abject defeat. In the early hours of Wednesday morning, already trailing by fifty thousand votes, the liberal Senator Claude Pepper hoisted the white flag. The winner, George Smathers, called his victory "a repudiation of extremism."[27]

Although the outcome was entirely clear, opinions differed about why it had occurred. The result might be seen as Truman saw it, as the triumph of a young rising star over an eccentric who had long been losing support. For years, Pepper had tempted political fate as he struck poses that placed him out on a limb. Not only had he visited Stalin in Moscow soon after the war; he had also urged America to scrap its atom bombs and cooperate with the Russians. Now forty-nine years old, Pepper had been close to Henry Wallace. He had tried to block Truman's nomination in 1948, and he had touted himself as a possible successor in the White House.

In contrast George Smathers, who was thirty-six, had a pretty wife, a wartime record as a marine in the Pacific, and sound credentials first as a federal prosecutor in Tampa and then as a congressman. Others saw the Smathers campaign as a matter of dirty tricks, similar to those used against Frank Graham in North Carolina. Smathers's supporters produced a pamphlet—*The Red Record of Claude Pepper*—that contained a photograph of Pepper with Paul Robeson. On the front cover a picture of the senator showed him with bad teeth, bad skin, and staring eyes that made Pepper look, wrote one columnist, "like a cross between a startled alligator and a patent medicine salesman."[28]

From the outset, however, the primary had also been a battle of ideas. On one subject—Black civil rights—Pepper had equivocated, first endorsing Truman's program of 1948 and then later calling it "a snare and a delusion." Embarrassed by the case of the Groveland Four, he refused to give a view on their guilt or innocence even when clear evidence emerged of a miscarriage of justice. This hesitation might have cost Pepper some liberal votes. But the rest of Truman's Fair Deal had Pepper's full support, above all universal health insurance and the repeal of Taft-Hartley, and so again the campaign was a referendum on the president's program.

When Smathers announced his candidacy in Orlando in January, he had given what amounted to an anti-Truman manifesto. His speech was long, detailed, and couched again in the terms of John T. Flynn's *The Road Ahead*. "Florida will not allow herself," Smathers had said on January 12, "to become entangled in the spiralling spider web of the Red network." Since Smathers said this weeks before the Hiss conviction and the Wheeling speech, he owed nothing to McCarthy at this stage. Instead he referred to that other sensation, the Communist Party conspiracy trial in New York. But as McCarthyism began to flourish, so the issue became as potent as it was in North Carolina; and like Willis Smith in that state, Smathers blended it with his attack on creeping socialism.[29]

While Pepper had the labor unions on his side, mustered by the CIO, Smathers had the medical lobby, most of the press, and Florida's business interests big and small. He aimed his fire at Truman's health plan, Taft-Hartley repeal, and the president's wish to see a permanent Fair Employment Practices Committee. All of them Smathers denounced. Although he avoided the crude racist language heard in Alabama and North Carolina, Smathers called the FEPC bill the work of "misguided zealots" who would sow discord between Black and white.

In the days after Pepper's defeat, some observers called Smathers a Republican in disguise. Was his success in Florida a warning that the GOP might be about to conquer the South? This question would be far too premature, because a political earthquake on that scale still lay more than twenty years in the future; and anyway, this was scarcely a typical southern state. "Florida is different," wrote the leading analyst of southern politics, Professor V. O. Key.[30] Urbanized and relatively wealthy, with its chain of suburbs between Miami and West Palm Beach, the state might instead be seen as an island of the North that had somehow floated down the coast. But if that were so, then Pepper's ejection from the Senate might still carry a bleak message for the Democratic Party.

It might be a sign of a broader shift toward the right that also encompassed the North and the Midwest. Truman, ever more beleaguered but still optimistic, refused to accept any notion of the kind. He brushed aside those critics who saw the Florida primary as a plebiscite against his Fair Deal. Others might view the outcome as a conservative "revolt of the suburbs" of the kind that overtook the Labour Party in Great Britain. Professor Key's northern counterpart, Samuel Lubell, felt that this was taking place. As for the role of McCarthy, the timing and the sequence of events told perhaps a story of their own. A conservative swing in the nation came first and helped to create his receptive audience, and then he reinforced it with his rhetoric.

In those early days of May 1950, calm analysis would have to wait. Despite the work of pioneers such as Key and Lubell, the study of voting patterns and political opinion remained a subject in its infancy. Impressionism still prevailed among those who tried to read the country's mind. And besides, too much was happening too quickly to permit a detached observer to stand back and survey the panorama.

From Detroit there came word of a truce between capital and labor. The strike at Chrysler, three months old, ended with a partial victory for Walter Reuther and the autoworkers. Stories from this industry, lying as it did at the heart of the economy, always commanded attention; but on this occasion they had to compete with a crowded field of rivals.

There was still no sign of any armistice in Washington. On May 3, as Congress absorbed the news from Florida, the House Ways and Means Committee voted to defy Harry Truman by slashing the excise tax on cigarettes. Elsewhere a New York Republican who had been a staunch defender of the Marshall Plan changed his mind and called for a cut in the program. Owen Lattimore testified again, and again his efforts to clear his name sank into the mire of *Amerasia*. Despite the president's efforts to calm the country's nerves, Senator Tydings prophesied a shooting war with Russia.

Scott Lucas read a message from the State Department saying that McCarthy had so far presented "not a shred of evidence" to prove any of his charges. All he did was draw forth the onslaught from Ken Wherry, who claimed that Lucas was breaking Senate rules by calling McCarthy a liar. When calm returned to the chamber, the senators voted to create the inquiry into organized crime that Estes Kefauver had demanded. He would lead it in pursuit of Frank Costello and the Mob.[31]

In this hectic atmosphere the president and his allies could not hold every point on their perimeter. With Acheson about to fly to London, the White House made a tactical withdrawal. Late on May 4, Tydings revealed that Truman had agreed to give him the State Department loyalty files.

The president had no choice. Too many issues were pressing on him from all sides. While Truman was promising more cuts in the Pentagon budget, a position now untenable, he also had yet to see the final vote on Marshall Plan renewal. A space had to be cleared, so that he could devote his energy to a further attempt to rise above the turmoil.

Eight months on from Labor Day Truman was about to make another journey across the country. By railroad he would travel nearly seven thousand miles in a reenactment of those campaigning tours that had helped to bring him victory in 1948. The climax was to be his appointment in Chicago.

THE SCHUMAN PLAN

*I*n France the spring of 1950 brought the return of familiar troubles. As inflation revived, strikes closed the docks at Marseille and
the tire plant at Michelin. Coal was scarce, as output dwindled from
France's old and inefficient mines. The steel mills that had been rebuilt
with Marshall money struggled to keep their tonnage up, while in West
Germany, the Ruhr made more and more. From the right and from the
left, the opponents of the coalition government challenged their credentials to speak for the nation.[1]

A wartime Resistance hero, Colonel Rémy, Catholic and Gaullist,
called for forgiveness for the man so many regarded as a traitor, the
Vichy head of state Marshal Pétain. Meanwhile, the Communist Party
met in honor of Marx and Lenin. In a Paris suburb they gathered on
April 2 for their annual convention. Mostly young people of the Liberation, they pledged to continue the class struggle in the factories and on
the streets and to end the war in Indochina.

Among the speakers was a party member, the physicist Frédéric
Joliot-Curie. He led the French atomic energy commission. At the
convention, he praised Stalin's nuclear achievements, and then he
promised not to help France build an atom bomb. The government fired
Joliot-Curie from his post. All the time, General Charles de Gaulle

stood by, eager to talk to the press and castigate the frailties of the Fourth Republic.

Arms were arriving from America, the weapons authorized by Congress, only to be met with more dissent. NATO might endanger France, said the newspaper Le Monde, by making Western Europe the site of atomic conflict. Others called for France to be neutral. Even President Vincent Auriol feared the consequences if the United States made itself leader of the world.

During a visit to King George VI in London, Auriol was horrified when Churchill said that Britain and America should negotiate with Stalin, but with France excluded from the table. In his diary Auriol observed that perhaps Churchill was growing senile. Around the French president his ministers maneuvered as rivals, united only by their fear that West Germany would rearm. The last socialists had resigned from the cabinet in February, leaving Prime Minister Georges Bidault all the more exposed.

It was said of Bidault that he governed as though he were still what he once was, a journalist writing at the corner of a table in a bistrot. Without consulting his colleagues, Bidault gave a speech in Lyon on April 16 calling for a High Atlantic Council of Peace, in which the French would have an equal voice. The US ambassador David Bruce dismissed this as an empty gesture by a politician whose authority was fragile.

Amid all this sat Robert Schuman at the Quai d'Orsay. In less than a month the foreign minister would return to London for the conference where Dean Acheson expected him to set out a scheme for rapprochement with West Germany. Although Schuman had his mandate from the French Assembly, so far he had failed to find a way to apply it. The Saarland question remained an obstacle. Bidault's words in Lyon embarrassed Schuman, but as yet he had no initiative of his own.

At this gloomy moment, Schuman received the help he needed. It came from Jean Monnet, the master planner. Monnet knew from sources at the Quai about the challenge Acheson had given to Schuman.

While Bidault was in Lyon, Monnet began to draft another plan. He wrote of the need for a federal Europe with Franco-German union at its heart. Churchill supported this concept in principle, and so did Schuman's allies in the French Assembly. Interviewed by an American journalist in March, the West German chancellor Adenauer had said something similar. But so far no progress had been made.

Any project of the kind had to begin with practicalities. Schuman had failed to create a customs union with Italy, Belgium, the Netherlands, and Luxembourg, defeated by French farmers and the labor unions. Monnet's plan was both less and more ambitious. It would be confined to heavy industry, but in that field it would be radical.

The old problem still remained: France's urgent need for coal and coke from the Ruhr, and Germany's requirement for iron ore from Lorraine. Monnet proposed to build a coal and steel common market, sweeping away the tariffs and other barriers that obstructed trade between the two. Coal and steel and iron ore would pass as freely to and fro across the Rhine as they did between Pittsburgh and the Great Lakes. The un-American feature of the plan would be a High Authority to oversee the scheme, curb overproduction, and set up a social fund to provide for laid-off workers.

On April 28—a Friday—the plan went to Schuman. On a Friday night he always took the train home to Lorraine, there to walk the fields and meditate amid his books. On Monday morning an aide met him at the station in Paris. "I have read the plan," said Schuman, "and you can tell Monnet: it will work." The plan might solve so many of his puzzles.

Schuman's concerns about the inequalities and poverty of France would be addressed. The economy would grow more strongly; and if the coal and steel plan made the French more prosperous, it would also render Germany less threatening. A pooling of resources between the two countries would mean that steel made in West Germany would benefit France. The Saarland problem would be eased as well, since its coal mines would fall into the new scheme.

Monnet worked on Auriol and Bidault, while Schuman reached out discreetly to Adenauer. His reply was instant and positive; Adenauer recognized that the plan would return the Germans to the family of nations. The British were left in the dark—something the French embassy in London saw as a mistake—but it could not be avoided. The deep devaluation of sterling in 1949 had left bad blood in Paris, where the government felt that Britain could not be trusted. The French cabinet also knew that Prime Minister Clement Attlee and his Labour colleagues had a scheme of their own to nationalize their steel. Neither Schuman nor Monnet wished the British to quibble at the details of their package, blunting the impact of what was now the Schuman Plan.

The announcement came in Paris on May 9. The Schuman Declaration spoke in American terms about productivity and modernization, higher wages and lower prices. Schuman invited Italy and Benelux to join the plan, and he asked the British too. Passing through the French capital on his way to London, Acheson gave the deal his blessing with enthusiasm. He also had something to offer the French: on May 8 Acheson told Schuman that France could have its military aid to defeat Ho Chi Minh. This could be announced at the same time as the Schuman Plan: America was now involved in Vietnam.

In London the Schuman Plan astonished Ernest Bevin, who feared the erosion of national sovereignty if Britain joined the scheme. His colleagues were divided; but the Labour Party issued a pamphlet rejecting British membership. The Attlee government announced that it would not join talks about the implementation of the plan. Witnessing an Anglo-French divorce, the French ambassador in London blamed Jean Monnet, calling him an autocrat addicted to theory. Churchill and his Conservative Party were left to ponder what to do about European union when next they led Great Britain.

CHAPTER TWELVE

THE ROAD
BACK TO AMERICA

I hadn't had a look at Chicago since my return.
Well, here it was again, westward from this window,
the gray snarled city with the hard black straps
of rails, enormous industry cooking and its vapor
shuddering to the air.

—SAUL BELLOW, The Adventures of Augie March[1]

T he very act of leaving the nation's capital on May 7 seemed
to revive Harry Truman. He loved his country, his train,
and even the downpour that fell as he spoke to farmers in
Nebraska. "I got wet as a drowned rat," the president said when
they reached their next stop, "but I finished the speech." In Idaho
he told jokes about potatoes and the glut thereof. In the sunshine
in Spokane he pinned ribbons on prize hogs and sheep. With him
on the trip were the First Lady and their daughter, Margaret, who
did their duty too. While Margaret flirted with the press corps,
Mrs. Truman played cards with the wife of the state governor of
Washington, who was happily a Democrat.[2]

It was the president's first journey to this side of the country
since he defeated Tom Dewey in 1948. The Republicans complained about the bill that fell upon the Treasury for what they

called a political junket, but Truman had a fine excuse. He had come to the Pacific Northwest to dedicate the Grand Coulee Dam. No better emblem could be found of the age of FDR or of Truman's own philosophy of government.

Since his early years in Missouri politics, when he built roads, hospitals, and a towering courthouse in Kansas City, Truman had believed in public works erected with public money. None could be more ambitious than Grand Coulee. "The biggest thing that man has ever done," in the words of the singer Woody Guthrie, who had worked on its construction, the dam had helped to make the region Roosevelt's greatest arsenal of democracy. Begun as a New Deal project, high up on the Columbia River, in wartime it had fed the power to Boeing's factories at Seattle and the ship-yards at Tacoma and Puget Sound.[3]

Grand Coulee had also played its part in the building of the atom bomb, by providing the electric power to enrich uranium at the Hanford plant downstream. This Truman knew. The occasion called for celebration, and the president—looking tanned and fit—meant to make it as grand as Labor Day.

He called the dam "a work that fires the imagination." Truman was in high spirits, elated not only by the news of the Schuman Plan but also by a victory on Capitol Hill. Congress had at last renewed Marshall aid despite the closest of votes in the Senate—a tie—when Bob Taft tried to slice half a billion dollars from the program. A vote so narrow made the elections in November all the more essential to win. At Grand Coulee and during the rest of his trip, Truman would make the best case he could for the principles that underpinned his plans for a Fair Deal. Again they had to do with the common good, America's resources managed for the benefit of all.[4]

"We still have to fight," he said above the roaring waters of the dam, "those who imagine that every progressive action is another step down that famous last mile to socialism." In Congress a bill was pending, with Truman's backing, to create a western version of Roosevelt's Tennessee Valley Authority. If it had come to pass, a Columbia Valley Administration would have been created, to encompass not only this river but also another, the Snake. There would have been a great dam and reservoir at Hells Canyon, to be overseen by the same new federal agency. Irrigation, flood control, and cheap electric power, all of it democratically controlled: like his predecessor, Truman believed that this was the shape of things to come.[5]

"He's our kind of folks," a local told a reporter as the president left Grand Coulee. The tour was vintage Truman, genial, rapid, and enthusiastic, with the president making forty-nine speeches in the course of his six days on the train. Even the Republican press had to acknowledge that the president had a charming, common touch. Truman covered every item in his social agenda— housing, health care, and the rest—pausing in Butte, Montana, to tell the copper miners that he still meant to do away with the Taft-Hartley Act.

And yet again there was something missing. Had the staff work been as shrewd and well informed as perhaps it might have been? At about this time, Stewart Alsop of the *New York Herald Tribune* paid visits to the chairmen of both parties, Guy Gabrielson of the Republican National Committee and William Boyle from Missouri, his counterpart among the Democrats. Boyle's offices were plush and stylish, while Gabrielson's had a quaint, old-fashioned feel. Alsop found again that curious paradox, that the party of the liberals and labor was so much better supplied with money than the Republican oppressors of the poor. The columnist came away with a sense that while the GOP might need to modernize, the Democrats were smug. Alsop said they suffered from what he called "well-oiled complacency."[6]

Truman called his trip "a report to the people," the phrase that Bob Taft had used in Ohio, but while Taft had toured every district in his state, the Truman journey had been scattershot. Some might even call it self-indulgent. Three of the western states he visited had no Senate races that year. Another three were solidly Republican. Truman gave half of his speeches in a string of mountain states that would muster only fifteen votes between them in the electoral college of 1952.

As the 1950 census showed, California's population had grown by more than 50 percent since 1940. Truman had not visited the state since 1948, and he did not do so this year. Some said this was because he so disliked FDR's son James Roosevelt, a Democrat aiming to run for governor against Earl Warren. If this was Truman's reason for avoiding the state, then it was politically naïve, as California would receive an extra seven seats in Congress at the next apportionment. By neglecting the state, the president might have helped send Richard Nixon to the Senate.

Nor did the DNC pay sufficient heed to the urban voter or those of the suburbs. Coming back through Minnesota, Truman's train skirted around Minneapolis. He did not set foot in the city. And although his speeches on the trip were tailored for each venue, often they dwelled on the past—the Dust Bowl, the Depression, and the golden age of farming before World War I—rather than the pressing issues that concerned the electorate of 1950. Truman addressed himself almost exclusively to farmers and organized labor, as if he did not see that most Americans belonged to neither group. As for the president's dream, the Columbia Valley Administration, it was blocked in Congress and would never happen.

Another question might be asked: How well by now did Truman really know the changing nation for which he cared so deeply? If his ideas had been formed first by Woodrow Wilson, next by Justice Louis Brandeis, and then by the Depression, the New Deal, and World War II, could he adapt to the new scenarios of the 1950s? Television, the automatic Chevrolet, and the growth of California signified a country, depicted in the census and in

Time magazine, that had moved beyond the familiar boundaries he had known for most of his career.

Another sign of change was the rise of Nixon and McCarthy. Despite their different styles, they had one thing in common: they were so much younger than the president. Perhaps the White House and the Democratic National Committee were simply losing touch with the nation as it altered and evolved around them. Even in their heartland they were too attached to old structures and old models that were breaking down. This would be the case in Illinois.

One great city Truman could not ignore. Hog butcher for the world, stacker of wheat and Democratic Party votes, Chicago lay ahead as the final date on his itinerary. Here you could find the fulcrum of America at this moment halfway through the century. Diverse and complicated, Chicago spoke with many different voices. If this was the city of Colonel McCormick of the *Tribune*, it was also the city of Muddy Waters singing the blues and the city of the novelist Saul Bellow, with the architect Mies van der Rohe erecting buildings in the Loop and Milton Friedman teaching economics at the university.

In Chicago and its suburbs you could see a new America coming into being. For many months it had seemed that "consensus" had collapsed or was collapsing, whatever people meant by this elusive word. One thing was certain. If consensus was to be created or renewed, then the job of work had to be accomplished in Chicago. Truman's visit would show precisely why this task lay beyond the powers of the Democratic Party.

CHICAGO WILL BE OURS

Adlai Stevenson, that governor whom Arthur M. Schlesinger Jr. would liken to an acrobat, had sprung into action. As the president was riding through Montana, Stevenson sent state troopers to raid the gambling joints across the river from St. Louis. "Illinois," he said, "must not be a gambling state," as his men smashed furniture, seized evidence, and closed the club where the murder of Charles Binaggio was said to have been planned. The governor also meant to stamp his imprint on Truman's rally in Chicago.[7]

The event was to be the crowning moment of what the organizers called a Jefferson Jubilee, a long weekend of Democratic Party celebrations that would culminate with a speech by the president on Monday, May 15. With confident and optimistic words, Truman would try to silence his critics and ensure the reelection of Senator Scott Lucas. To lend their support, eminences came from across the nation. Eleanor Roosevelt traveled over from Hyde Park, while Boss Edward J. Flynn arrived from the Bronx only to suffer a heart attack in his suite at the Blackstone. That was the hotel in the Loop, dear to party memory, where in 1944 Truman had heard the commanding voice of FDR tell him on the phone that he was going to be his running mate.

Six years on, so much had changed. Stevenson was closely watching Joe McCarthy. He did not think he would ruin Lucas's chances, but he was nervous all the same. To open the senator's campaign, the jubilee would have to be spectacular. This could be guaranteed, given the strength of the party machine in the city; but strength could be a weakness if it carried with it the whiff of graft and payrolls filled with Democrats.

In those days the party in Chicago looked for leadership to Stevenson's ally Lieutenant Colonel Jacob Arvey. From another Loop hotel, the Morrison, Jack Arvey presided over the Democratic machine in Cook County, the home of half the voters in the state. To win and keep their loyalty he had three thousand precinct captains. Arvey also had the power of patronage over more than thirty thousand county and city jobs. The bulk of his machine's electoral support lay in a solid bloc of twenty of Chicago's fifty wards, centered on the Loop and forming a rectangle as large as Brooklyn. The home of first- and second-generation immigrants, it included the Black neighborhoods of the South Side. But around this army of Democrats there lay a ring of suburbs and suburban townships, Cicero, Oak Park, and so many others, that were either Republican already or moving in that direction.[8]

If the experts were correct and machine politics were waning, then Arvey had to watch his step. Like Mayor O'Dwyer in New York, he ran the risk of losing the suburbs; but he also had to keep his voting turnout as high as possible in his urban core. Tales of corruption in Arvey's machine might deter even loyal Democrats from coming to the polls. If they stayed at home, the effect would be felt nationwide, because of Illinois's sheer population and the narrow gap between the two parties in the state. But instead of opting for caution, Arvey chose to practice machine politics at its worst.

Arvey had already picked his candidate to run for county sheriff in November. A disastrous choice, this was Daniel "Tubbo" Gilbert, a Chicago police captain whom the Kefauver Committee would wish to interview. The papers called him "the world's richest cop," because Tubbo Gilbert on his captain's salary had somehow managed to amass a large portfolio of stocks and bonds. Meanwhile, the Chicago Crime Commission had just given a grand jury the results of a long investigation of shakedowns, bribes, and the like in the police department and the municipal courts. If corruption became a theme of the elections, as surely it must, then the Democratic Party might lose Cook County.

Into this snake pit the president descended on the evening of Sunday, May 14. Members of his cabinet were already there, giving a public seminar at the opera house about the benefits of the Fair Deal. Truman spent Monday conferring with his party chiefs, while at the Chicago Stadium the last act of the Jefferson Jubilee was being prepared.

The parade began at 7 p.m., featuring five thousand troops from the National Guard, complete with tanks, followed by Truman's motorcade. In one of the cars behind him rode Elizabeth Taylor, who was beginning to supplant Myrna Loy as the party's brightest light from Hollywood. In the final stretch, after a twenty-one-gun salute, they swept along West Madison Street, the city's Skid Row at the time, past the pawnshops, the stew bums, and the bars, where not long before the French writer Simone de Beauvoir had fallen in love with Nelson Algren.[9]

It was Arvey's show, and also Adlai Stevenson's. Some felt that the rousing speech the governor gave at the stadium that evening was the beginning of his own run for the White House. Onstage Miss Taylor paid a tribute to the president in front of a replica of Jefferson's Monticello; and then Ann Miller, one of the stars of the film *On the Town*, tap-danced a manifesto of her own. A musical pageant unfolded, with actors telling the story of the party's triumphs. Scott Lucas rose to introduce the president, whose speech would be the pinnacle of his cross-country journey.[10]

Truman's address was Jeffersonian too, as he called the Democratic Party "the servant of the people" and pledged to work on everyone's behalf "for equal opportunity and equal justice for all." Like so many postwar statesmen, he issued a plea for national unity, as Generals de Gaulle and Eisenhower had done. Like them, he tried to make himself the holder of the middle ground. Perhaps Truman had read Schlesinger's book on the subject, because he used its language. "We do not share the delusions of the extreme left," said the president. "We do not share the prejudices of the extreme right." The Democratic Party, he proclaimed, was "the party of the mainstream of American life . . . the party of progressive liberalism."[11]

To give these ideas a practical dimension, that spring the administration reached out at last to America's small businesses, the group the Republican Party tried to claim as its own. Ten days before the rally, Truman had sent a special message to Congress. He set out a scheme for tax breaks, federal guarantees for business loans, and new investment companies, backed perhaps by the Federal Reserve, to channel long-term finance toward entrepreneurs. In Chicago he talked about that and about white-collar workers, advancing hand in hand with industry, the farmers, and the labor unions in pursuit of an ever higher standard of living.

Now that the economy was strong, the president had a fine story to tell; but the words in Truman's speech that caused most comment had to do not with unity but with division. He spoke about the enemies of his Fair Deal in Congress, "backward looking Senators and Representatives," and predicted their defeat in November. "I hope," said Truman, "that some of the worst obstructionists will be removed."

This was the line, along with the speech from Adlai Stevenson, that people would remember. Everyone knew whom the president meant: not only Bob Taft in Ohio or other Republicans elsewhere, but also those Democrats who resisted his agenda. But like FDR before him, Truman could not oust them from his party.

Even while his train was still crossing Montana, the president's obstructionists had stabbed him in the back. On Friday, May 12, a Senate filibuster had begun. After months of delay, Scott Lucas was urging his fellow senators to debate that civil rights measure, the FEPC fair employment bill, in its original form rather than the weak version adopted by the House. But the Democratic Party's Southern Caucus, led by Georgia's Dick Russell, meant to kill the bill as they had finished off so many others of the kind. The morning after the Chicago rally, Senator Lucas would have to hurry back to Washington to try to end the southern filibuster with a motion for cloture. Lucas would need sixty-four cross-party votes, and his chances of obtaining them were slim.

They had diminished still further during the Jefferson Jubilee. After Claude Pepper's defeat in Florida, the Truman loyalists in North Carolina had grown anxious about the fate of their candidate Frank Graham. Time and again the liberal Senator Graham had tried to distance himself from the FEPC bill but without success, as his opponents branded him a friend of Communists and an enemy of segregation. Hurrying up and down the state, Graham had given speech after speech, pausing only to return to Capitol Hill for the final Marshall Plan debate. His vote had been crucial to save the program from Taft's attempted cut. And then, on the day the filibuster started, an exhausted Senator Graham collapsed with pneumonia just two weeks before the primary.

Graham's Raleigh friend, the newspaper editor Jonathan Daniels, headed for Chicago. There he betrayed the president whose biography he was about to publish. At the opera house, Daniels spoiled the Fair Deal seminar by rising to his feet to denounce the FEPC bill as something the South could not accept. If this was a gesture designed to save Frank Graham's skin, it was also a gift to the GOP in Congress. As Russell's filibuster ground on, the Republicans jeered at the Democratic Party's internal rift about Black civil rights.[12]

Truman's tour of the West had ended in the shadow of just the kind of internecine strife that he yearned to put behind him. Meanwhile, in Chicago, Jack Arvey's henchman Tubbo Gilbert continued on the party's ticket for the fall, like a bomb primed to detonate beneath Scott Lucas at some fatal hour. It was all so typical of the politics of 1950. The president strove to keep the liberal flag aloft while people and events conspired to pull it down. Consensus remained a project impossible to fulfill.

By twelve votes on May 19, Senator Lucas failed to end the southern filibuster. Only a third of his Democrats in the Senate turned up to support the FEPC bill. Millard Tydings of Maryland failed to show because, he explained, he was examining the State Department loyalty files: a reminder of the way the McCarthy affair had cut across the landscape, pushing other issues to one side. Graham was absent too, confined to his sickbed in Raleigh, unable to prove his credentials either for or against segregation by casting a vote.[13]

In the recriminations that followed the demise of the bill, each party blamed the other, and Lucas blamed the conservative coalition in Congress. The hero of the hour was Arthur Vandenberg of Michigan. Five weeks after surgery he struggled to the chamber to be counted as a Republican supporter of cloture. The senator was greeted by applause in what would be his last appearance at the Capitol. Vandenberg would die from his cancer in April 1951, four days after Ernest Bevin passed away in England.

It seemed to some that everything was falling apart. With so many months still to go until Congress adjourned in October, few expected them to be filled with anything but frustration for the White House. The Tydings hearings ground on, too, bogged down in *Amerasia*, while Senator McCarthy went on talking, attacking Owen Lattimore and Dean Acheson.

In London, the British had reluctantly agreed to allow the FBI to question Klaus Fuchs in his prison cell. Armed with the VENONA decrypts and some leads Fuchs gave them, the bureau traced his contact in America, a Soviet agent named Harry Gold. They arrested Gold in Philadelphia on May 23, while the furor about Louis Budenz and Lattimore was still at its height. McCarthy seized on this as well. As the FBI went after Russian spies, the controversy about his charges became still more intense.

None of this or the other conflicts of the year could be dismissed as merely foam and spray on the surface of America, while beneath the waves the deeper waters were genuinely calm. Instead the feeling grew that something dangerous was occurring. The nation appeared to have polarized in animosity at a time when the Soviet threat seemed to be growing more frightening by the week. Perhaps the time had come to call for reconciliation.

THE FOUR HORSEMEN

Bitterness, distrust, intolerance, and fear: those were the words used by the *Washington Post* to capture the mood of the moment. From the center ground of politics, the American scene appeared to have become a battlefield of destructive forces. Writing from London, where he was covering the Schuman Plan, Joseph Alsop sent an open letter to his country urging it not to pay heed to McCarthy. The *Post* was about to do something similar. This would lead in Congress to the most famous protest of the year against McCarthy, a protest that was also a rebuke to Truman.[14]

At the time, the *Post* had a Briton as its editor. Herbert Elliston, another veteran of the Western Front in World War I, had been at the newspaper's helm since 1940. Ten years on he was horrified by what he saw in his adopted country. Elliston grew alarmed by the damage the strife in Washington was doing to America's reputation abroad.[15]

He and his publisher, Philip Graham, tried to make the *Post* a centrist paper, but they were rewarded with attacks from left and right. Phil Graham and his wife, Katharine—daughter of the paper's owner, Eugene Meyer—were close friends of Schlesinger's. Like him they found that the middle of the road was hard to define and still harder to defend. At first sympathetic to Alger Hiss, which provoked conservative wrath, the *Post* then accepted his conviction and criticized Acheson's words of comfort. This caused a rift with Acheson, whose supporters accused the *Post* of treachery. Meanwhile, Herbert Elliston had also been appalled by the tactics some Democrats were using against McCarthyism. On May 12 Senator Dennis Chavez of New Mexico had taken to the Senate floor to denounce Louis Budenz as an adulterer, a bigamist, an enemy of freedom, and "a congenital conspirator." Chavez accused Budenz of lying under oath to the Tydings Committee. Elliston called all this a descent "to the level of the gutter."

Ten days after Chavez's tirade, the *Washington Post* made a plea for sanity and centrism that resembled Henry Stimson's intervention in March. On the eve of the arrest of Harry Gold, the paper published a long editorial with the headline "The Road Back to America." Phil Graham bought space in the nation's other major papers to reprint the editorial in full. Debated on radio talk shows and made the subject of church sermons, derided by some and praised by others, "The Road Back to America" spoke of "mad-dog McCarthyism" and "a national malaise."[16]

"For weeks," said the *Post*, "the capital has been seized and convulsed by a terror." Everywhere it saw "rising distrust, roaring bitterness, the ranging of Americans against Americans." Elliston traced the roots of the malaise to what he called "a deep and troubled state of the nation's mind. Fear and frustration abound." If the anxieties of the Cold War struggle were the principal cause, the *Post* also laid the blame on politicians out for partisan advantage. Most of all they blamed McCarthy for what they called his "Goebbels technique of the lie followed by the bigger lie."

"The Road Back to America" can be seen today as one of the founding documents of the liberal anti-communism for which Schlesinger would become the most eloquent spokesman. Like Schlesinger—who had his suspicions about Alger Hiss long before he went on trial—the *Post* had no doubt that there were Red subversives in the country. Its case against McCarthy chiefly had to do with the harm he was inflicting on national cohesion: he was sapping morale, sowing confusion, and driving talent out of government. "Witch-hunting," said the *Post*, amounted to "softening and weakening America for Russia."

But while "The Road Back to America" echoed what Acheson was saying in his speeches, it could also be seen as a vote of no-confidence in Truman. "The urgent problem," said the *Post*, "is to find a way back to a basic unity"; but this was precisely what the president thought he was supplying. To restore the nation's harmony, the *Post* wanted Truman to appoint a nonpartisan commission of wise citizens to assess every aspect of national security. The commission, said the *Post*, should examine the Pentagon budget and the need for new weapons, devise a program to defeat "the internal menace of the fifth column," and make recommendations about the economic aid America still had to give its partners abroad. Again, these were subjects the White House was supposed to handle by itself.

In saying what it did, the *Washington Post* voiced the private thoughts of many people in the nation's capital. The line it took also had its parallels with NSC-68. Elliston gathered some support from Stimson and from Democrats in Congress, Hubert Humphrey on the left and Walter George on the right. Then the *Post*'s campaign fizzled out. Truman brushed the editorial aside, saying he did not need a "super-government." Bob Taft and Tom Connally dismissed it too. "The Road Back to America" also had one obvious flaw in its argument. The unifying project it advocated would have to win the backing, like so many calls for consensus at the time, of General Eisenhower. No commission of the kind the newspaper wanted could be complete without him; but Ike still remained politically aloof, publicly neutral but in private a Republican.[17]

Even so, the *Post*'s appeal for concord left its legacy. In these last few weeks before the Korean War, the same perception of America as a nation divided was shared by liberal or moderate Republicans, who were equally alarmed. A group hard to define precisely, they included about a quarter of its senators and more than thirty of its House representatives. Among them was Margaret Chase Smith, a Republican of Maine, the only woman senator and one of only ten women in Congress. At this moment she spoke for her country with a dignity and wisdom that the men of her era all too rarely displayed.

On June 1 on the Senate floor, Smith made her famous speech prefacing what she called a "Declaration of Conscience." The speech and the declaration would come to be remembered as a brave denunciation of McCarthy, which they certainly were. Without naming him directly—the chamber's rules prevented her from doing so—Senator Smith called him "selfish," "reckless," and "irresponsible" and accused him of making the Senate "a rendezvous for vilification." She was not, as has sometimes been said, the first member of Congress to condemn him in this way: that distinction belonged to Scott Lucas and Herbert Lehman. But she was the first *Republican* to do so.

Taking aim at Taft as well as McCarthy, Senator Smith deplored her party's efforts to use what she called "totalitarian techniques" as means to win elections. "I do not wish to see," she said, "the Republican Party ride to political victory on the four horsemen of calumny—fear, ignorance, bigotry, and smear."[18]

Her fifteen-minute speech covered much else as well. Often wrenched out of their context, her words have too frequently been seen as solely a response to McCarthy. In fact, she was almost as severe with Truman and his administration. Senator Smith called them petty, pitiful, bitter, ineffective, and complacent. In her opening lines she referred to the *Post*'s editorial and its call for a nonpartisan commission to strengthen the nation's defenses. She spoke, as Elliston had, of "a national feeling of fear and frustration." Smith mentioned *Amerasia*, Klaus Fuchs, Alger Hiss, and Harry Gold, seeing all of them as proven cases of subversion. But mostly she blamed the nation's state of mind on its politicians: chiefly Truman and the Democratic leadership.

Another plea for centrism and unity, Smith's speech had long been in the making. By 1950 she was fifty-two years old. Her

The Republican senator Margaret Chase Smith of Maine in June 1950, two weeks after making her "Declaration of Conscience" speech on the Senate floor. *Herbert K. White / Associated Press / Shutterstock.*

knowledge was wide and deep. Few could have assessed the state of American politics at the time with such candor and authority.

Elected to the Senate in 1948, but with eight years in the House already behind her, Smith had pledged to be "America's senator-at-large for women." A celebrity in Maine, she counted among her backers in the state most of the labor unions. Elsewhere she often had to suffer the usual patronizing discourse of her era. Her white hair in a bob, her tailored suits, her recipes for blueberry muffins and baked beans: every feminine detail was commented upon. Taking this in her stride, in wartime Smith had made herself an expert on the navy. In 1946 she joined the House Armed Services Committee, and the Pentagon budget became one of her special subjects. Another was old-age pensions, where she wanted to see social security strengthened and expanded. A third was civil rights and a fourth was foreign policy.[19]

An admirer of Churchill, Smith strongly supported NATO and the Marshall Plan. She was close to Arthur Vandenberg but also a friend of Walter Lippmann's. In the fall of 1949, like them she had begun to worry about the collapse of bipartisan consensus and a mood of anger in the nation. Every week Senator Smith wrote a syndicated column. Her views were plain to see and so were the origins of her famous speech. Of course she had to touch on the issues of her state, and she did so by defending Maine's potato farmers against the Brannan Plan. But by the spring Smith was focusing on national security and she was troubled by what she heard.

While Stuart Symington, secretary of the air force, spoke about the nation's loss of air supremacy, Secretary of Defense Louis Johnson said the opposite and then seemed to change his mind. In March Smith began to write about what she called the "defense confusion capers." By May she was still more exasperated. While the Joint Chiefs sounded gloomy, and Senator Millard Tydings forecast war with Russia, the president suggested that the Pentagon could spend even less. "I only wish," wrote Smith, "that the boys would get together and think a little about the American people they are confusing."

She had been unhappy about her party's leadership for months, and not merely because of their support for McCarthy. In February, when the Republican National Committee drafted its manifesto, Smith tried to amend it to make it less negative. Her preference was for what she called the "constructive planning" of federal programs within the limits of a balanced budget. Among other things, Smith wanted the party to commit itself to ending the southern filibuster against civil rights. Her suggestions were either ignored or watered down. Out of all this, and her growing disquiet about McCarthy, her famous speech emerged.

Senator Smith knew McCarthy well, having sat alongside him on the Senate panel that examined General Harry Vaughan and the five percenters. At first impressed by the case McCarthy made at Wheeling, Smith paid close attention to his speeches and noticed how little hard evidence he possessed. She grew worried, and friends began to urge her to speak out.

The day after "The Road Back to America" appeared in the *Post*, a conservative columnist wrote about the piece, echoed its conclusions, and criticized Truman's tour of the West and the Chicago rally. That morning Smith read the column and called Walter Lippmann to tell him she intended to intervene. He encouraged her to do so. To sum everything up, Smith drafted her Declaration of Conscience, had it signed by six other Republicans in the Senate, and read it aloud at the end of her address. "We are Republicans," she said, "but we are Americans first."[20]

Herbert Lehman loved the speech despite Smith's harsh words about his president. Senator Tydings called it "magnificent." Taft ignored the speech and so did Joe McCarthy, with a view to taking his revenge on Smith in due course. An immediate sensation in the press, the speech stole the limelight from "The Road Back to America," which had said much that was similar. For a while it left its mark on the GOP, chiefly on state governors up for reelection. Earl Warren, seeking his third term as governor of California, criticized McCarthy with an eye to the independent voters of the state, while Richard Nixon, running for the Senate, distanced himself—at least at this stage of his campaign—from McCarthy's tactics but not from his message.

In Congress the impact of the speech soon faded. One by one, most of Smith's Republican supporters drifted away, under pressure from conservative colleagues. Lost as well was Margaret Chase Smith's wider critique of the politics of the day. Even so, the issues she had raised did not disappear. Her speech helped to build the case, already strong, for Eisenhower to be her party's next candidate for president. Meanwhile, the quest continued for some form of national consensus, something Truman could not now provide.

If politics is a form of bargaining, then it requires goodwill and negotiation. These faculties were vanishing in the Washington of 1950. In the debates about the Marshall Plan and NATO, Truman and his leaders on Capitol Hill—Scott Lucas, Tom Connally, and Sam Rayburn—had been obliged to make concessions to their critics. The most significant of these was the olive branch they gave to John Foster Dulles. Nevertheless they faced the likely prospect of defeat in crucial votes in the next Congress. The broad and deep agreement that NSC-68 would require if it was to be implemented had little hope of coming to pass. The Fair Deal had even less.

And yet at just this moment when the politics seemed so impossible, another kind of bargaining succeeded. America had the benefit of institutions that lay beyond direct political control. The federal courts, for example: by refusing to find against Lewis and the miners, they had helped bring an end to the coal strike. In June the Supreme Court would also take a great step forward in the field of civil rights. Before that, a bargain was struck in Detroit that showed how much resilience the American system possessed when ideology could be set aside.

Again, it served to illustrate a paradox: American politics descended into strife at a moment when in so many ways the nation had little to fear. The economy showed all the signs of solid growth. Inflation had fallen to 2 percent, and the Fed was lending funds at 1.5. In just nine weeks in March and April more than a million of the unemployed found new jobs. New homes were going up at a speed not seen for decades.

With America now wealthier than it had ever been, a recurring question arose once more: How should the spoils of expansion be divided? Since one in seven of the nation's workers earned their living from the auto industry, the answer that came from Detroit was all the more significant. Charles Wilson of GM knew that this was so. The strike at Chrysler, his competitor, had been long and costly, ninety-nine days in all, and both Chrysler and Ford had been obliged to give the United Auto Workers most of what they wanted. GM was next in line.

For Walter Reuther of the UAW the question was equally pressing. Always a skeptic about Truman, he could see how little likelihood there was of the Fair Deal making progress. Nor could Reuther hope for a better moment at which to make a lasting deal with General Motors.

Peace in Michigan

Flint, Michigan, home of Buick and the spark plug, the wartime builder of engines for Liberator bombers: few towns in America's arc of prosperity were thriving quite as much as this. Flint was GM's largest base of operations. With a little overtime a worker in the car plants could make $4,000 a year, about $900 more than the national average. That spring the overtime was plentiful as Buicks left the factory at a rate that once had seemed unthinkable.

In 1950 the Buick plant at Flint produced, with the same workforce, 40 percent more cars than it had the previous year. Output per worker had doubled since 1946. The cars were better too: the new models of the Super, the Special, and the Roadmaster, with their shark's mouth grilles, their automated transmissions, and the distinctive row of holes, the Buick Ventiports, drilled into the steel of the fenders. Harlow Curtice, Buick's overseer, a man in love with tail fins and trim, had ordained that every Buick should have its Ventiports. They became, like the new transmissions, an emblem of the decade just begun.[21]

As general manager at Flint, Curtice had led the drive to build the bomber engines. After the war he had rebuilt and reequipped the plant with thousands of new machine tools. Flint found itself, even more than Pittsburgh, a town at the leading edge of the country's productivity, applying the innovations developed since 1929. Curtice's reward was to become Charles Wilson's deputy, poised to be his successor as GM's president when Engine Charlie left to head the Pentagon.

Flint was also the greatest stronghold of the UAW. It had been here at the Fisher Body Plants in 1937 that sit-down strikes had forced General Motors to recognize the union and negotiate a contract. Thirteen years on, the combination of Curtice's investment program and the UAW had given Flint its affluence. The 1950 census showed few families with a television, but this was only because the nearest transmitter was far away in Detroit, and so the flickering image of Milton Berle was still too fuzzy to watch. Instead they went bowling.

In 1995 the sociologist Robert Putnam would publish his famous essay "Bowling Alone," making bowling leagues a symbol of social capital, the cohesion that stems from communal games, clubs, and civic good deeds. The citizens of Flint in 1950 played in 160 bowling leagues and spent half a million dollars a year on bowling fees. Of course, Flint had its vices—numbers games and other forms of illegal gambling—but visitors would carry away a picture of just the kind of 1950s town that Putnam would later celebrate: a busy, progressive community, with perhaps its best years still to come.

In this era when America still had no industrial rival, General Motors stood at the peak of its supremacy. That spring the company had two tasks to accomplish. Harlow Curtice had to find a way to build new plants in the West in a hurry to meet the hunger for cars in California. Meanwhile, Engine Charlie had to make his peace with the union. The current contract with the UAW expired at the end of May, and Wilson did not wish General Motors to be another Chrysler.

Reuther and his union had fought Chrysler every step of the way in what the *Detroit Free Press* called "a cruel and useless, exhausting war." His dealings with GM would be very different. While McCarthy raged in Congress, Wilson and Reuther bargained in private and reached common ground. Both men could see how much they had to gain if prosperity could be maintained.[22]

By a fluke of history Reuther had been born in 1907 in the town of Wheeling, where McCarthy gave the speech that began his notoriety. A veteran of the battles of 1937, when Henry Ford's hired ruffians beat him up on camera, Reuther still had his many enemies. In 1948 he survived attempted murder by shotgun by an assailant who was never found; and at the end of 1949 someone tried to dynamite his union's headquarters in Detroit, a case the FBI did little to pursue.[23]

In Michigan Reuther had also had to fight James R. Hoffa of the Teamsters, who tried to bend the Democratic Party in the state in his own direction. But Reuther's enemies did not include Charles Wilson. The two men were professional opponents, able to negotiate at a time when the art of doing so had all but disappeared in Washington. Over eight weeks that spring, Reuther and GM executives met thirty-five times to draft a new contract. At nearly the last minute, Reuther flew to Pittsburgh to confer with his friend Phil Murray of the CIO. The final deal he struck with Wilson on May 23 was instantly seen for the great achievement it was. It would run for five years, providing a pension fund and health insurance as well as extra pay, and it would safeguard the well-being of towns like Flint.

While *Fortune* magazine called the contract "the treaty of Detroit," the city's daily rejoiced at what it saw as a turning point in history. Still counting the cost of the Chrysler dispute, the *Free Press* believed that here at last was closure to many years of strife. The Wilson/Reuther deal, the paper said, was "one of the great milestones in the progress towards not only a united Detroit but also a united America."

In a twenty-first century when labor unions have lost so much of their power and when GM has been through bankruptcy, the national ovations the contract received feel as alien as the life and death of Jimmy Hoffa. Some observers argued that the deal was only possible because Senator Taft had reshaped labor law with the act that bore his name. Most chose to view it as the *Free Press* did, as a victory for an American middle way, avoiding the extremes of left and right. The treaty of Detroit, said the Alsop brothers, "made a monkey out of Karl Marx."[24]

The package was impressive. Walter Reuther reckoned it would give each GM worker an extra $700 a year. Besides an instant raise in basic pay, the contract featured an annual adjustment for inflation; but it also—and this was its most unusual feature—promised an extra 2.5 percent each year to capture the benefits of increased productivity. "We are trying," said Wilson, "to treat our people right," and this meant giving them their share of the gains technology delivered.

At the White House Truman welcomed the deal, but with comments so brief as to suggest that he did not appreciate its full significance. While experts elsewhere debated the obvious questions—Would it become a model for other industries? Would contracts such as this add to inflation? Could GM really go five years without another dispute or a strike?—John Snyder, secretary of the treasury, said nothing. Neither did the Federal Reserve. Congress was mostly silent too.[25]

Coming so soon after the *Washington Post*'s "Road Back to America" editorial, the Wilson/Reuther deal served to underline how little Washington was doing to restore the harmony so many people yearned for. Wilson regarded the treaty of Detroit as a means to end class conflict, but it was also a deal struck without Washington's help: a warning perhaps that if Americans wanted consensus, they would have to create it for themselves. Some might also see it as another sign that Truman was losing the nation's loyalty, as the country forged ahead regardless of the politicians.

Instead of waiting for Truman's health-care plan, the United Auto Workers took what they won from GM: a jointly funded Blue Cross and Blue Shield scheme. The doctors looked on warily, suspecting that the unions wanted to be their masters. In the state of Michigan, the medical profession hated Truman's plan quite as much as their counterparts in Florida loathed Claude Pepper. Their journal contained fiery editorials denouncing socialism and urging physicians to read John T. Flynn's *The Road Ahead*. They studied GM's treaty with the UAW and warned of dire consequences if the union tried to use its buying power to dictate what doctors and hospitals could charge.[26]

Arguments such as these contained the seeds of more conflict to come, years of wrangling about the cost of health care and about how best to deliver it. All of this was new in 1950. For the Democrats, peace between GM and labor might also have its disadvantages. Visiting Detroit and Flint, the journalist Samuel Lubell detected a new mood in the unions, a shift to moderation as they reaped the benefits of struggles in the past and prosperity today. Once they were middle class, with their pay and benefits more secure, would they come loose from the coalition FDR had built? Would they vote Republican instead?[27]

Michigan had been Vandenberg's domain and its other senator was also from the GOP. Even the district to which Flint belonged sent a Republican to Congress. When the votes were counted in November 1950, his majority increased. In 1948, with the help of Reuther and the CIO, the state had elected a liberal Democrat as its governor by a landslide despite fierce opposition from Jimmy Hoffa. But the governor was losing support. Although he won again in 1950, his margin of victory was tiny: another sign of the fading fortunes of the Democratic Party.

In Washington, June saw a deceleration in the pace of politics, but the tone remained as fractious as before, with the Democrats in ever deeper trouble. After the Four Horsemen speech, the Tydings hearings continued to drag on, stuck in the *Amerasia* morass while the focus of politics moved elsewhere, toward the primaries and the civil rights cases pending in the Supreme Court.

In North Carolina at the end of May, Senator Frank Graham won the Democratic primary, but his victory was too narrow. Stricken with his illness and too weak to campaign, and because there were three candidates, he failed to gain an outright majority. Under the election rules of the state his conservative opponent, Willis Smith, could request a runoff. At another time the nuances of Democratic contests in the South might have aroused little interest beyond the region; but after Pepper's defeat in Florida the North Carolina primary became a national talking point. While Willis Smith pondered his next move, the Truman camp looked on with concern but could do nothing to help Graham. In California, meanwhile, everything seemed to be going Richard Nixon's way.

To Missouri Again

So far that year Nixon had been circling around the center ground of politics, but gradually veering to the right. A far more subtle politician than Joe McCarthy, he wove his way between California's many interests. As he toured the state in his run for the Senate he sometimes sounded like Bob Taft, speaking up for liberty against the power of Washington. More often he resembled Margaret Chase Smith. The state's leading issue at the time was the Central Valley Project, a plan to cure a water shortage still more severe than New York's, and here Nixon strove for moderation. He did not want a TVA and federal control, but neither did he want a free-for-all.[28]

Styling himself a "sincere, liberal Republican," Nixon followed Smith's example, speaking up for constructive planning. Like her he called for more spending on defense: the aircraft plants at Oakland and Burbank needed more orders from a bigger air force. He wanted tax cuts too, but also a balanced budget, and somehow Nixon made it all sound plausible. Among his staunchest friends was Kyle Palmer, political editor of the *Los Angeles Times*. Palmer had been fighting for Nixon since January, praising his energy but also his discretion. Nixon, wrote Palmer, was "young enough to be bold and wise enough to be prudent."[29]

Even so, Nixon followed the pattern of the year. His Senate race would come to be remembered for its personal attacks on his Democratic opponent, Helen Gahagan Douglas. The notorious claim that she was a "pink lady," soft on Communists and ultra-liberal, would not come until August. But long before that Nixon's campaign staff had begun to emphasize his credentials as a scourge of the Reds. On May 25, with McCarthy still so much in the news and only two weeks to go until the primary, they ran campaign ads for Nixon pointing out that he had been "the man who broke the Hiss-Chambers espionage case."

Of all the primaries that year, this one revealed most clearly the depth of the trouble overtaking Truman and his party. In California the open primary system allowed registered Republicans and Democrats to vote in each other's contests. Earl Warren, centrist and popular, took more than seven hundred thousand Democratic votes, so that he was certain to return as governor by a huge majority. Far fewer Democrats supported Nixon, but the arithmetic of the primary result still pointed to a solid win for him when the state's independents turned out in November. His campaign, centrist but tilted to the right, had been effective. In reserve he still had the pink lady slogan.[30]

Here, too, the Democratic Party suffered from the problems that dogged it everywhere. When the Democrats had popular policies—public housing, or better old-age pensions—their opponents could borrow and adapt them, as Senator Taft did with his Housing Act. More controversial programs had no prospect of success. Lippmann was correct: five years on from the death of FDR, Truman's party had little left to say that was both new and feasible. The achievements that represented Truman's claims to greatness mostly had to do with foreign policy—the Marshall Plan and NATO above all—but their novelty had evaporated, so that they became a matter for quarreling about details on Capitol Hill.

If Truman could have stopped the clock of history at the end of 1948, his record might have spoken for itself; but this he could not do any more than he could halt the negative campaigning that McCarthy, Ken Wherry, and their allies were pursuing so avidly. And where the Truman Democrats did possess a rallying cry, above all about civil rights, they were unable or unwilling to use it to the full. Soon after their failure to keep the FEPC bill alive, the administration won a victory in this field, but even this could be made to work against them.

On June 5, the day before Nixon won his primary, the Supreme Court gave its verdict on the college segregation cases from Texas and Oklahoma in which the president had shown so little interest. Landmarks in legal history, *Sweatt v. Painter* and *McLaurin v. Oklahoma* went in favor of the NAACP and the Justice

Department. Chief Justice Fred Vinson wrote both decisions, which were unanimous, forcing the two universities involved to give Black students full and equal access.

These decisions did not spell the end of legally segregated education, but they were a first step along the way. Vinson kept his focus narrow, composing brief opinions that steered clear of the fundamentals of the Constitution and the Fourteenth Amendment. He merely stated the obvious: that in these two cases the inequalities had been so blatant that they could not be permitted. In the court's conference room, his Alabama colleague Hugo Black worried that the South would rebel if the justices said the same about elementary and high schools; but Black called segregation "Hitler's creed," and he knew it had to be eradicated. The court was on the way to *Brown v. Board of Education*, the decision it would issue four years later, when eight of the nine justices in 1950 were still among its members.[31]

The South took swift revenge. As news of the *Sweatt* and *McLaurin* decisions spread in North Carolina, a crowd converged on the Raleigh home of Willis Smith and urged him to request his runoff in the primary. Smith did so the next day. In the heat and dust of summer the brief campaign grew all the more unpleasant, with new slurs about Frank Graham printed in handbills saying that he wanted Black and white to mingle in the classroom. In a mill town in the Piedmont on the final afternoon, children jeered at Senator Graham from the sidewalk, chanting "no schools with niggers."[32]

Polling day in North Carolina was Saturday, June 24. Early that morning in New York City, a teenage intruder climbed the fence around Gracie Mansion and found his way into Bill O'Dwyer's bedroom. The mayor, who had far more to fear from the Brooklyn grand jury probing police corruption, dismissed the incident as a prank.

Dean Acheson relaxed on his farm in Maryland, where he liked to do carpentry and jobs in the yard. The Pentagon's leaders, Secretary Louis Johnson and General Omar Bradley, were flying home from Japan, where they had been hearing assurances that South Korea was safe. "You're doing a magnificent job," Johnson had said to General MacArthur as they shook hands on the runway and bid each other farewell. Also in Tokyo was John Foster Dulles, there to talk to Prime Minister Yoshida about the peace treaty they hoped to sign. Dulles had been to Seoul, met with Syngman Rhee, and told his parliament that America stood beside them. Mr. and Mrs. Dulles expected to spend Sunday among the lotus blossoms in the water gardens of Kyoto.[33]

For Truman, the weekend was to be a brief vacation. That afternoon, with the temperature in the nineties and thunderstorms approaching, his plane touched down again in Kansas City. It was the president's first visit since Christmas to his home in Independence. Elsewhere in Missouri, investigators sent by Senator Kefauver's team were looking into the murders of Binaggio and Gargotta; but it seems that this was far from Truman's mind.

His week had brought good news at last from Capitol Hill. Walter George had taken the long-delayed improvements to social security safely through the Senate, adding ten million people to the program and doubling the pensions that the South so sorely needed. Truman and his family spent the evening quietly, with dinner at 6:30 and then small talk on the porch.

At 9:43, Raleigh time, the story broke that in the primary that day Willis Smith had triumphed over Truman's friend Frank Graham. It seems that the president did not hear the news until the next morning. A greater sensation had intervened and swept it to one side. About forty minutes after Graham conceded defeat, the president's telephone rang. Dean Acheson was on the line: war had begun in Korea.

THE 38TH PARALLEL

*T*he monsoon season had already started. Despite the heavy rain expected soon, the final orders had been given. On the night of June 24 along the 38th parallel, North Korean engineers began to clear paths through their minefields, a task that would take six or seven hours to complete. At 4 a.m. the artillery opened fire, and forty minutes later the troops moved forward. Along a front of more than a hundred miles, first it seems at Ongjin in the west, the North Korean army began the invasion of the South.

The sequence of events that followed has been chronicled at length and often. Not until the 1990s, when Russia opened its archives, would Stalin's role be fully known. Even now there remains room for disagreement about Moscow's intentions before and during the Korean War. Still more controversy surrounds each of the many decisions taken by Harry Truman, his cabinet, and his generals in the days and months that lay ahead.

Amid the confusion on June 25, Dean Acheson spoke up for air support for South Korea, but at first it seemed that American ground forces need not be involved. "I don't want to go to war," said the president on the evening of June 26. What he meant by this is not entirely clear— context is everything in matters such as this—but soon the die was cast. South Korea had no tanks, while Kim Il-sung had Russian-built T-34s advancing toward Seoul. The city fell on June 28. The following day, Truman told the press, "We are not at war"; but by the morning of the thirtieth that had changed.

The president authorized General MacArthur to send troops into combat. He did not seek approval from Congress, an omission that Truman could justify but that others would see as a dangerous precedent. With the Soviet delegates still absent, the United Nations had already voted to condemn North Korea's attack as a violation of its charter. It had also called upon its members to support the South. It seems that Truman felt that this was the approval he required.

And so the war was on, whether we call it a civil war, a "police action"—a journalist's phrase that Truman endorsed—or something else again. On July 5 MacArthur's infantry fought its first engagement with Kim's armor. There followed the fighting retreat to the port of Pusan in the far south: more battles, more air strikes, huge numbers of civilians dead. In September MacArthur made his landing at Inchon in the enemy's rear, and Truman approved his plan to cross the parallel and conquer North Korea.

MacArthur reached the Chinese frontier along the Yalu River, and China intervened in the fighting. Another sequence of events began: a second American retreat, talk of using atom bombs, the firing of MacArthur for insubordination, and then in the spring of 1951 the beginning of a stalemate and a war of attrition. It would last until the armistice of 1953 when the frontier between North and South returned to the 38th parallel, where it had been before and where it has been ever since.

Meanwhile, in October 1950 the French had suffered a catastrophe at the hands of General Giap in Indochina. Their attempt to evacuate their post at Cao Bang ended in disaster, the loss of five thousand soldiers dead or captured, and also the loss of Route Coloniale 4 and their base at Lang Son. They grew still more desperate to see America committed to Vietnam.

EPILOGUE

Make war, foolish mortals, ravage the fields and
the towns, violate the temples and the tombs, and
torture the defeated. You will all perish.

—THE GOD POSEIDON, IN JEAN-PAUL SARTRE,
The Trojan Women of Euripides[1]

No one can say precisely how many lives were lost in the Korean War. At least three million people died, more than half of them civilians, killed by bombs, rifles, machine guns, shells, or napalm, in massacres or by disease or hunger. Two million Korean families were broken into pieces or forced into exile. More than a million homes were obliterated or left in ruins. The conflict shattered the economy in both North and South. Neither side could claim a victory, and when the war was over the two men who had been so keen to fight survived as if it had never occurred.

Syngman Rhee—that president whom the State Department so distrusted and disliked—remained securely in place in South Korea, holding on to power in Seoul until 1960. In the North, Kim Il-sung fastened his Stalinist grip still more tightly on his people and bequeathed his regime to his dynasty when he died in 1994.

Meanwhile, during the three years of war, almost thirty-seven thousand Americans in uniform had lost their lives.

It was a conflict some observers had expected. Nearly three years before Kim launched his invasion, the United Nations had sent a mission to Korea led by the Indian diplomat K. P. S. Menon. Reporting back in February 1948, Menon warned that the Soviet and American partition of the country after World War II was almost bound to lead to what he called "a blow up" in the peninsula. It might also cause, in Menon's words, "a vaster cataclysm in Asia and the world."

His warnings went unheeded. By the fall of 1949, Menon was already close to being proved right by the border clashes that occurred at Ongjin. With America's attention diverted elsewhere, to Western Europe, the Taiwan question, and its debate about the H-bomb, Washington failed to appreciate the significance of these incidents along Korea's internal frontier. Whatever we make of the press club speech and its consequences, Dean Acheson also chose to take too broad an overview of the Cold War.

Instead of drafting NSC-68, with its message about the medium and the long term, Acheson and his aides might have tabulated in detail the specific threats that existed along their perimeter in 1950. If they had done so, the risk of war in Korea would have risen sharply up their schedule of priorities, and they might have avoided sending faulty signals to the USSR. Perhaps the State Department should also have admitted that it simply knew far too little about Mao Zedong.

Unable to appraise either Mao or his relationship with Stalin, the United States also failed to pay due attention to the warlike speech by Mao's deputy Liu Shaoqi and the hints from Moscow about armed struggle in Asia. It would be asking too much to expect Acheson or this staff to have prophesied Stalin's decision in January 1950 to support Kim's invasion plan. Even so, what could be known should have pointed to the need for America to show the utmost caution in the region. Instead, while opting to be so wary and noncommittal about Taiwan, the United States stumbled into the devastating crisis in Korea. Immediately after the war began, Truman changed his mind about the island and sent the Seventh Fleet to patrol the Taiwan Strait.

It has been said that the architects of America's stance in the early Cold War world were "wise men," united by liberal values and by faith in democracy, who ensured their nation's global leadership after 1945. This kind of statement can only be made with decades of hindsight and even then it may remain open to question. In the 1980s or 1990s, when the Soviet Union had collapsed and China had emerged from the shadow of Mao, it seemed to make sense to look back and tell a story of wisdom and farsightedness in the corridors of power. Things did not look so clear and simple to those who lived through the hurry and confusion of events.

For Margaret Chase Smith and many others, America in the spring and early summer of 1950 did not seem to be a nation guided by wise leaders. With NATO still unproven, the Pentagon in disarray, and economic miracles yet to begin in Japan and Western Europe, it was too early to award grades and distinctions for lasting achievements in the field of foreign policy. Instead, in the eyes of Smith and others like her in the middle ground, America's stance abroad more closely resembled a process of improvisation, of trial and error, with the cost of the mistakes falling on those millions dead in Asia.

At home the situation did not seem so very different. The horrors and the drama of the war, General MacArthur's dismissal and the politics that followed, have come to occupy the foreground of our picture of that moment in the history of America. Other matters have receded out of view. Least remembered is the mood of agitation and unease that had already overcome the nation in the weeks and months before the Korean War began.

While Joe McCarthy thrived in this atmosphere, he did not create it by himself. It could already be found in the Peekskill riots in September 1949, in the rifts within the Democratic Party in the South, in the fear of corruption and crime in the cities, and in the wild language of the debate about Harry Truman's health-care plan. At a later time, people would talk about a "postwar consensus," but if such a thing existed it was hard to find in 1950, when even the president's own party was divided.

This discord would become all too apparent when the midterm ballots were cast in November of that year. The election campaigns were fought amid a cross fire of competing news reports. In July the Tydings Committee published its findings, exonerating the people smeared by Senator McCarthy, only to be submerged by fresh sensations in Korea and at home. At the end of August, fatally wounded by the Brooklyn scandals, Bill O'Dwyer resigned as New York's mayor. Truman sent him down to Mexico as US ambassador; but he could not save O'Dwyer from humiliation in front of the Kefauver Committee.

On November 1 two Puerto Rican men, demanding independence for the island, attempted to assassinate the president. Any effect this might have had on the elections was drowned out by a bleak message from MacArthur. Twenty-four hours before the votes were cast, the general issued a communiqué warning of Chinese divisions massing to the north of the Yalu. With the war apparently entering a new, alarming phase, and with inflation starting to accelerate, election day brought the Republican revival that Senators Taft and Wherry had tried so hard to engineer.

Senator Millard Tydings lost his bid for reelection in Maryland, with McCarthy doing everything he could to secure his defeat. In Illinois—where the Tubbo Gilbert story exploded beneath Scott Lucas, as it was bound to do—Everett Dirksen swept to victory, taking the Cook County suburbs, while in Chicago the Democratic turnout collapsed. Senator Taft won easily in

Ohio. The governor, a Cleveland Democrat, had helped him along by telling reporters in June that he might vote for the GOP. Richard Nixon was perhaps the biggest winner. California sent him to the Senate at the age of only thirty-seven, and he was bound for what seemed likely to be stardom.

The Republicans took outright control of neither chamber of Congress, but they did enough. By gaining twenty-eight seats in the House and five in the Senate, they solidified the conservative coalition that Truman had been unable to dislodge. Safe at the top of the GOP, Taft became the shaper of his party's message, so that when Dwight Eisenhower won the Republican nomination in 1952 and aspired to be a centrist, he still had to use the language of Bob Taft. The Fair Deal was forgotten as though it had never been. So, too, for a while was that other feature of the scene—the fundamental strength of the economy—whose foundations had been laid in the innovations of the 1930s and then during World War II.

We are so used to thinking of 1945 as a great dividing line in history that other dates fade into obscurity beside it. It may be that the real moment of decisive change occurred much later, in those ten months between Labor Day 1949 and the beginning of the Korean War. Until then, America had been engaged at home and abroad since 1945 in a process of emergency repair and rehabilitation, still clearing up the damage that Hitler and the Great Depression had left behind. Only in 1950 did the 1930s reach their true conclusion, to be superseded by a new and different world.

Mao's victory in China, the birth of NATO and the H-bomb, and Stalin's new aggressiveness in Asia had hardened the Cold War into its enduring shape. Joe McCarthy rose, and so did John Foster Dulles, Adlai Stevenson, and Senators William Knowland and Walter George, to acquire, like Nixon, a new celebrity in the years to come. Truman slipped into decline, and the New Deal era drew to an end. Although NSC-68 never came to fruition in the way Acheson intended, most of what it advocated did materialize in the early years of the new decade.

Some problems were solved, if only partially, or at least the building blocks for solutions were discovered in the Schuman Plan and the Treaty of Detroit. Others—Black and Latino civil rights, and health care for all—were regarded as too difficult to solve or too frightening to face, and postponed. Overseas, the 1950s would fail to bring the peaceful and prosperous world order of which Acheson had dreamed. Instead, the decade would witness what Jawaharlal Nehru had feared: more cycles of suffering, in Algeria, Vietnam, Mao's China, and elsewhere, to be borne by the wretched of the earth.

In the meantime, America enjoyed its new affluence. In the fall of 1949 the economic tide had turned, bringing the commencement of a quarter century of growth far more generous and more sustained than the economists foresaw. Its political rewards would flow first to President Eisenhower, as he persevered with his version of a middle way during his eight years in the White House. "Secular stagnation" would not come to pass, in Ike's new gilded age of *I Love Lucy* and the Buick Special.

ACKNOWLEDGMENTS

This book had its origins in what now feels like a very distant time, the fall of 2018, before Britain's departure from the European Union, before COVID-19, and before Russia's invasion of Ukraine. Since the financial crisis and the Great Recession almost a decade earlier, a mood of febrile anxiety had settled over the nations of the Western alliance. For those inclined to look to history for parallels, the era had come to resemble the 1930s, that earlier period of self-doubt and foreboding.

Everywhere we heard talk of the return of "great power competition," and we saw a new authoritarianism abroad in the world. Old ties of friendship and cooperation appeared to be dissolving. Britain had voted for Brexit, but its political system proved unable to cope with the consequences and descended in 2019 into a chaos of embitterment and indecision. Many observers felt premonitions of a new Cold War, and yet President Donald Trump was threatening to withdraw the United States from NATO. In America it seemed that consensus politics were gone forever. The Republicans and Democrats in Congress could agree on only one thing, their fear or their resentment of the China of Xi Jinping.

I found myself returning to authors from the 1930s, such as André Malraux, John Dos Passos, and W. H. Auden. In his 1937 poem "Spain," written during the Spanish Civil War, Auden had said this:

> *We are left alone with our day, and the time is short, and*
> *History to the defeated*
> *May say Alas but cannot help nor pardon.*

My previous books had delved into the distant past of Britain and America in the seventeenth and eighteenth centuries. By 2018 this sort of preoccupation had begun to feel far less compelling, much as it did for Auden in 1937. My next book, I decided, would explore a far more recent period, ten months in 1949 and 1950 when the world was still struggling with the aftermath of the 1930s and the war to which they led.

With an eye to what was occurring in the Trump era, I would write about another moment of partisan strife in the United States, the one that saw the rise of Joe McCarthy. This was another time of anxiety about China and Russia, but it was also a period of gestation for those institutions, NATO and the European Union, whose foundations now appeared to be in peril.

In 2019 I had the honor to meet one of the dedicatees of this book, the literary agent Mort Janklow. He shared my fascination with the age of Harry Truman. Without Mr. Janklow, whose wisdom was equaled only by his courtesy and his charm, *In the Shadow of Fear* would never have come into existence. His joint dedicatee was another great New Yorker, someone I knew as a loyal and generous friend for more than thirty years: Herb Margulis, for whom the Brooklyn of the 1940s was still a vivid memory.

I owe my deepest debt of gratitude to my wife, Susan Temple, for her love, her wisdom, her stylish imagination, and her unrivaled powers of planning and organization. Sue shared this project from its inception and also my taste for film noir. I am also grateful to my publisher and editor at Basic Books, Lara Heimert and Brian Distelberg; to my translator from Russian, the highly efficient Anastasiya Moroz; and also in New York to Edith, Steve, Isaac, Noah, and Josie Margulis, Sherida Paulsen, Susan and Kenneth Aschheim, Stacy Schiff, and Chip McGrath.

My thanks are due as well to Brandon Proia and Kathy Streckfus for their copyediting, and at Basic Books to Melissa Raymond, Alex Cullina, Kaitlin Carruthers-Busser, Liz Wetzel, Jessica Breen, and Angela Messina; at Janklow and Nesbit, to Melissa Flashman, Mr. Janklow's successor as my agent, and to Judythe Cohen; to Sarah Alex of the Herblock Foundation, Washington, DC; Elizabeth Clemens of the Walter P. Reuther Library, Wayne State University, Detroit, Michigan; Elizabeth Engel and Joan Stack of the Center for Missouri Studies, State Historical Society of Missouri, Columbia; Alice Griffin of the Center for Brooklyn History, Brooklyn Public Library; Melissa Lindberg of the Library of Congress, Washington, DC; and the staffs of the other libraries and collections where I worked on the book, including the Rare Books and Manuscripts Library, Columbia University; the Cambridge University Library; the Library of Congress; the National Archives of Great Britain, Kew, England; and the National Archives of the United States, College Park, Maryland.

The COVID-19 crisis struck when I had not yet completed my research. Unable to remain in America to visit all the archive collections I had hoped to use, I incurred another debt of thanks, to the archivists at the presidential libraries—the Truman Library and the Eisenhower Library—whose digitization projects have helped to make it possible for a book such as this to be written thousands of miles away in the English cathedral city of Lincoln.

ABBREVIATIONS

CNYPS (1949)	Columbia University (Rare Books and Manuscripts), Oral History Collections, *New York Political Studies* (1949)
C.R. (House)	*Congressional Record*, US House of Representatives
C.R. (Senate)	*Congressional Record*, US Senate
FO	Foreign Office (British)
FRUS (1949)	US State Department, Office of the Historian, *Foreign Relations of the United States, 1949*, vols. 1–9 (1974–1978)
FRUS (1950)	US State Department, Office of the Historian, *Foreign Relations of the United States, 1950*, vols. 1–7 (1976–1980)
NSC	National Security Council (United States)
NYHT	*New York Herald Tribune*
NYT	*New York Times*
PPHST (1949)	*Public Papers of the Presidents of the United States, Harry S. Truman, 1949* (Washington, DC, 1964)
PPHST (1950)	*Public Papers of the Presidents of the United States, Harry S. Truman, 1950* (Washington, DC, 1965)
TNA	National Archives (British), Kew, London (UK)

NOTES

Prologue: Monday, September 5, 1949

1. UK Parliamentary Debates (Hansard), September 28, 1949, col. 163.

2. Truman in August and September 1949: Robert H. Ferrell, ed., *Truman in the White House: The Diary of Eben A. Ayers* (Columbia, MO, 1991), 326–328.

3. Truman's September 1 press conference in *PPHST (1949)*, 458. British intelligence: TNA, CAB 159/6, Joint Intelligence Committee weekly situation reports, August–October 1949, especially JIC (49) 78/4, October 7.

4. Truman in the polls: Richard E. Neustadt, *Presidential Power: The Politics of Leadership* (New York, 1960), 95–99, 223–226, and raw data in "The Quarter's Polls," in the 1945–1950 issues of *The Public Opinion Quarterly*.

5. Truman's speaking tour: Robert H. Ferrell, ed., *Off the Record: The Private Papers of Harry S. Truman* (Columbia, MO, 1980), 164–165; and press reports, *Pittsburgh Post-Gazette*, *Pittsburgh Press*, and *Des Moines Register*, September 4–6, 1949.

6. John Gunther, *Inside U.S.A.* (New York, 1947), 615.

7. Productivity: Anglo-American Council on Productivity, *Steel Founding: Report of a Visit to America in 1949* (London, September 1949); and steel and coal statistics from Douglas A. Fisher, *Steel Serves the Nation, 1901–1951: The 50 Year Story of U.S. Steel* (U.S. Steel, 1951), 223–225; US Energy Information Administration, *Annual Energy*

Review 2011 (Washington, DC, 2012), 211; *Times* (London), October 1, 1947, and January 7, 1948; and International Iron and Steel Institute, *Handbook of World Steel Statistics* (Brussels, 1978), Table 1.

8. America's midcentury surge in productivity: Robert J. Gordon, *The Rise and Fall of American Growth: The US Standard of Living Since the Civil War* (Princeton, NJ, 2016), 545–565; Alexander J. Field, "The Most Technologically Progressive Decade of the Century," *American Economic Review* 93, no. 4 (September 2003): 1399–1413; David Weintraub, "Effects of Current and Prospective Technological Developments upon Capital Formation," *American Economic Review* 29, no. 1 (March 1939): 15–32, with figures on R&D on p. 28.

9. Goals of the Marshall Plan: Benn Steil, *The Marshall Plan: Dawn of the Cold War* (New York, 2018), 98–103; Arthur M. Schlesinger Jr., *The Vital Center: The Politics of Freedom* (Boston, 1949), 226–228.

10. Fairless: B. C. Forbes, *America's Fifty Foremost Business Leaders* (New York, 1948), 109–116. Murray: Gunther, *Inside U.S.A.*, 622–623; Robert H. Zieger, *The CIO: 1935–1955* (Chapel Hill, NC, 1995), 54–59, 333–335.

11. Morris L. Cooke and Philip Murray, *Organized Labor and Production* (New York, 1940), ix, 246–247.

12. Robena: Fisher, *Steel Serves the Nation*, 111–113.

13. US Bureau of the Census, *1950 Census of Population*, vol. 2, *Characteristics of the Population* (Washington, DC, 1953), Tables 85 and 92.

14. Truman's Pittsburgh and Des Moines speeches: *PPHST (1949)*, 460–469. Overview of Truman's Fair Deal: Alonzo L. Hamby, "The Vital Center, the Fair Deal, and the Quest for a Liberal Political Economy," *American Historical Review* 77, no. 3 (June 1972): 653–678; Hamby, *A Man of the People: A Life of Harry S. Truman* (New York, 1995), chap. 28.

15. *C.R. (Senate)*, August 16, 1949, 11520–11560.

16. *Philadelphia Inquirer*, September 6, 1949.

17. The five-percenter affair: US Senate, Committee on Expenditures in the Executive Department, *Influence in Government Procurement: Hearings Before the Investigations Subcommittee, August 8th–September 1st, 1949* (Washington, DC, 1949).

18. *St. Louis Post-Dispatch*, July 7, 1949. Criticisms of Truman in his second term: William E. Leuchtenburg, *In the Shadow of FDR: From Harry Truman to Barack Obama* (Ithaca, NY, 2010), 33–37.

19. McCarthy, Vaughan, and Costello: US Senate, Committee on Expenditures in the Executive Department, *Influence in Government Procurement*, 541–596.

20. *NYHT*, August 31, 1949. On the Alsops: Arthur M. Schlesinger Jr., *A Life in the Twentieth Century: Innocent Beginnings, 1917–1950* (Boston, 2000), 378–383.

21. David Holloway, *Stalin and the Bomb: The Soviet Union and Atomic Energy, 1939–1956* (New Haven, CT, 1994), 195–200.

Russia in the Fall

1. Sources: Alexander Werth, *Russia: The Post-War Years* (New York, 1971), xvii and chap. 17; Yoram Gorlizki and Oleg V. Khlevniuk, *Cold Peace: Stalin and the Soviet Ruling Circle, 1945–1953* (New York, 2004), chap. 3; Oleg V. Khlevniuk, *Stalin: New Biography of a Dictator* (New Haven, CT, 2015), 280–286; Elena Zubkova, *Russia After the War: Hopes, Disillusions and Disappointments, 1945–1957* (Armonk, NY, 1998), chaps. 6 and 13; R. W. Davies, *Soviet Economic Development from Lenin to Khrushchev* (Cambridge, 1998), 64–67; Vladislav M. Zubok, *A Failed Empire: The Soviet Union in the Cold War from Stalin to Gorbachev* (Chapel Hill, NC, 2009), 50–61, 78–80; *History of the Communist Party of the Soviet Union—Short Course* (Moscow, 1939), chap. 12; Joseph Stalin, *Economic Problems of Socialism* (Moscow, 1953), chap. 6; *Pravda*, August 8, September 7, 20, 23, and 25, and November 7, 1949.

CHAPTER ONE: THE RELIEF PITCHER

1. James Reston, "Secretary Acheson: A First Year Audit," *NYT*, January 22, 1950. Acheson's personality, appearance, and education: Robert L. Beisner, *Dean Acheson: A Life in the Cold War* (Oxford, 2006), chap. 6.

2. Acheson's parents: wedding notice, *Boston Globe*, June 9, 1892; Bishop Acheson's obituary, *Hartford Courant*, January 29, 1934.

3. Felix Frankfurter, "The Constitutional Opinions of Justice Holmes," *Harvard Law Review* 29, no. 6 (April 1916): 693; also, on legal realism, Frankfurter, "Hours of Labor and Realism in Constitutional Law," *Harvard Law Review* 29, no. 4 (February 1916): 353–373.

4. Acheson's Brandeis years: Dean Acheson, *Morning and Noon: A Memoir* (New York, 1965), chap. 5, quotation p. 88; Alexander M.

Bickel, *The Unpublished Opinions of Mr. Justice Brandeis: The Supreme Court at Work* (Cambridge, MA, 1957), 91–97.

5. Acheson, *Morning and Noon*, 108–109.

6. Acheson, *Morning and Noon*, 146.

7. Yale speech: November 28, 1939, in Acheson, *Morning and Noon*, 267–275.

8. Dean Acheson, *Present at the Creation: My Years in the State Department* (New York, 1969), 286–287.

9. Acheson and Vaughan: Truman Library, oral history interview with Lucius D. Battle, June 23, 1971, 3–4.

10. *NYHT*, June 24, 1949.

11. Bill Davidson, "The Surprising Mr. Jessup," *Collier's* magazine, July 30, 1949.

12. The intricacies of the case of Alger Hiss defy any brief summary. For a basic outline narrative, the best account is still the contemporary book by the British journalist Alistair Cooke, *A Generation on Trial: U.S.A. v. Alger Hiss* (New York, 1950), with references to Jessup on pp. 176 and 302; also, regarding Jessup, *Baltimore Sun*, June 21, 1949.

13. Jessup and the White Paper: Philip C. Jessup, *The Birth of Nations* (New York, 1974), 24–25.

14. *Times* (London), April 17, 1951.

15. The dollar drain: memorandum by Prime Minister Clement Attlee, "The Dollar Situation," July 21, 1949, in TNA, PREM 8/1178, pt. 1. On the British economy and the crisis: J. C. R. Dow, *The Management of the British Economy, 1945–1960* (Cambridge, 1965), 38–46; Sir Alec Cairncross and Barry Eichengreen, *Sterling in Decline: the Devaluations of 1931, 1949 and 1967* (Oxford, 1983), chap. 4. British political situation: Kenneth Harris, *Attlee* (London, 1982), 431–441; Peter Hennessey, *Never Again: Britain, 1945–1951* (London, 1992), 367–376.

16. John O'Donnell, *New York Daily News*, September 6, 1949.

17. Truman's speech: *Philadelphia Inquirer*, August 30, 1949.

18. *New York Daily News* and *Brooklyn Daily Eagle*, September 7–8, 1949.

19. Cripps in Washington: official report to British Cabinet, *The Washington Discussions, 7th–12th September 1949*, TNA, PREM 8/1178, pt. 1. In his account of the talks in Chapter 36 of *Present at the Creation*, Dean Acheson took some literary liberties and misrepresented the sequence of events. The British account is confirmed in Truman

Library's oral history interview with John Snyder, January 15, 1969, 1002–1023.

20. Snyder's comments to Senate Foreign Relations Committee: *Baltimore Sun*, February 16, 1949. Cripps at the Press Club: *St. Louis Post-Dispatch*, September 10, 1949.

21. Kennan's talks with the British: TNA, FO 1093/578, notes dated August 12 and September 19, 1949; Stewart Alsop in *NYHT*, August 16, 1949; and Snyder's oral history interview, 1005–1008.

22. British ministerial brief for the Washington talks, August 29, 1949, in TNA, T 269/3.

23. Strang's policy review: TNA, FO 1093/578, with "British Policy Towards Soviet Communism," July 28, 1949.

24. Strang's Asian tour: William Strang, *Home and Abroad* (London, 1956), 239–250, 313. On the Rimland concept: Sir Frank Roberts, "Ernest Bevin as Foreign Secretary," in *The Foreign Policy of the British Labour Government, 1945–1951*, ed. Ritchie Ovendale (Leicester, UK, 1984), 29–31.

25. Memorandum: "Anglo-American Relations: Present and Future," PUSC (51), August 24, 1949, TNA, FO 1093/578.

26. Bevin quote: Strang, *Home and Abroad*, 287.

27. British view of American leadership: in the August 24, 1949, memorandum, "Anglo-American Relations: Present and Future," 8.

China

1. Sources: Mao Tse-tung, "The Great Union of the Popular Masses," trans. Stuart R. Schram, *China Quarterly*, no. 49 (January–March 1972): 84; *History of the Chinese Communist Party: A Chronology of Events (1919–1991)*, compiled by the Party History Research Centre of the Central Committee of the Communist Party (Beijing, 1991), 209–215; Mao Zedong, *Selected Readings from the Works of Mao Zedong* (Beijing, 1971), 371–386; Dieter Heinzig, *The Soviet Union and Communist China, 1945–1950: The Arduous Road to the Alliance* (New York, 2015), chap. 3; Hua-yu Li, *Mao and the Economic Stabilization of China, 1948–1953* (Lanham, MD, 2006), 26–29, 63–64; Mao Zedong, *The Writings of Mao Zedong, 1949–1976*, vol. 1, *September 1949–December 1955*, ed. Michael Y. M. Kau and John K. Leung (Armonk, NY, 1986), 3–7; Sergey Radchenko and David Wolff, "To the Summit via Proxy Summits: New

Evidence from Soviet and Chinese Archives on Mao's Long March to Moscow," *Cold War International History Project Bulletin*, no. 16 (Fall 2007 / Winter 2008): 105–112; Shen Zhihua, *Mao, Stalin, and the Korean War: Trilateral Communist Relations in the 1950s*, trans. Neil Silver (New York, 2012), chap. 3; George C. Guins, "Russia's Prize in Manchuria," *Russian Review* 6, no. 1 (Autumn 1946): 43–55; details of the Yalta agreement and of the August 1945 Sino-Soviet Treaty: Lyman P. Van Slyke, ed., *The China White Paper* (Stanford, CA, 1967), 113–126; Vladislav M. Zubok, *A Failed Empire: The Soviet Union in the Cold War from Stalin to Gorbachev* (Chapel Hill, NC, 2009), 25–27, 34–36.

CHAPTER TWO: THE GRINDING MACHINE

1. *C.R. (Senate)*, September 19, 1949, col. 13019.

2. *Times* (London) and *Daily Telegraph*, September 29 and 30, 1949; Jacques Dumaine, *Quai D'Orsay* (Paris, 1955), 421–423; Vincent Auriol, *Journal du septennat*, vol. 3, *1949* (Paris, 1977), 324–329.

3. Dean Acheson, *Present at the Creation: My Years in the State Department* (New York, 1969), 266. Senate debate: *C.R. (Senate)*, September 19–22, 1949.

4. Robert Dallek, *Franklin Roosevelt and American Foreign Policy, 1933–1945* (New York, 1995), 419–420; Arthur H. Vandenberg Jr., *The Private Papers of Senator Vandenberg* (New York, 1952), 55–62.

5. Vandenberg, *Private Papers*, 515–516.

6. Truman's budget philosophy: Truman Library, oral history interviews with Edwin H. Nourse, March 7, 1972, 25–26, 89, and Leon H. Keyserling, May 19, 1971, 163–171.

7. Standard of living and real incomes: US Department of Labor, Bulletin No. 1021, *Family Budget of City Worker, October 1950*; Ewan Clague, "Take-Home Pay and Levels of Living," *Annals of the American Academy of Political and Social Science* 283, no. 1 (September 1952): 61–69.

8. Truman's defeats: *C.R. (Senate)*, June 23, 1947, 7538; April 2, 1948, 4026, 4053.

9. Walter George: L. H. Zeigler Jr., "Senator Walter George's 1938 Campaign," *Georgia Historical Quarterly* 43, no. 4 (December 1959): 333–352, quotation from FDR on pp. 341–342; *Atlanta Constitution*, August 5, 1957; Robert S. Allen and William V. Shannon, *The Truman Merry-Go-Round* (New York, 1950), 259–261.

10. *C.R. (Senate)*, September 21, 1949, 13679–13084, quotation p. 13083.

11. Acheson, *Present at the Creation*, 266.

12. Associated Press, August 15, 1946; Tom Connally and Alfred Steinberg, *My Name Is Tom Connally* (New York, 1954), 296–298; William S. White, "Foreign Arms Bill Passes Congress," *NYT*, September 29, 1949.

13. TNA, CAB 158/8, Joint Intelligence Committee, JIC (UK) (49) 80, "Soviet Intentions and Capabilities, 1950," February 6, 1950; Connally's speech, *C.R. (Senate)*, September 19, 1949, 13621.

14. *C.R. (Senate)*, September 20, 1949, 13058.

15. Kerley was a reporter for Hearst's *New York Journal American*.

16. Robert L. Doughton: obituary and tributes, *Raleigh News-Observer*, October 2, 1954.

17. Income tax: Richard Goode, "Federal Finances in 1948," *National Tax Journal* 2, no. 1 (March 1949): 71–87; Randolph E. Paul, *Taxation in the United States* (Boston, 1954), 300–304.

18. Social security and welfare: Sumner H. Slichter, "The Pressing Problem of Old Age Security," *NYT*, October 16, 1949; Sumner H. Slichter, "The High Cost of Low Incomes," *NYT*, March 5, 1950; speech by Walter George, *C.R. (Senate)*, June 13, 1950, 8490–8496; US Department of Commerce, "Changes in Social Security," *Survey of Current Business* (September 1950): 16–17; Edwin E. Witte, "Social Security," in *Saving American Capitalism*, ed. Seymour E. Harris (New York, 1948), chap. 26.

19. Claudia Goldin and Robert A. Margo, "The Great Compression: The Wage Structure in the United States at Mid-Century," *Quarterly Journal of Economics* 107, no. 1 (February 1992), updated in David Autor, Claudia Goldin, and Lawrence F. Katz, "Extending the Race Between Education and Technology" (working paper, National Bureau of Economic Research, no. 26705, January 2020).

20. Folsom: V. O. Key Jr., *Southern Politics in State and Nation* (New York, 1949), 42–44.

21. Truman's budgets: *Budget of US Government: Fiscal Year to June 30th, 1950* (January 3, 1949), M72–M73, A4–A5; *Budget of US Government: Fiscal Year to June 30th, 1951* (January 3, 1950), M5–M13, A4–A6; annual budget analysis by the Federal Reserve, in *Federal Reserve Bulletin*, February 1949, 109–116, and February 1950, 131–140.

22. Nourse and the Pittsburgh speech: Edwin G. Nourse, "Why I Had to Step Aside," *Collier's*, February 18, 1950, 56.

23. NSC 52 (July 5, 1949), NSC 52/1 (July 8, 1949), and NSC 52/3 (September 29, 1949), in *FRUS (1949)*, vol. 1, 349–353, 385–399.

24. Author's analysis based on US Congress, *Statistics of the Presidential and Congressional Election*, November 2, 1948 (Washington, DC, March 1, 1949).

25. *C.R. (House)*, August 18, 1949, 11807; William S. White, "Bipartisan Foreign Policy Runs into Trouble," *NYT*, August 21, 1949.

26. Alfred Toombs, "The Most Difficult Door to Open in Washington," *Collier's Weekly*, January 24, 1953; McMahon obituary, *Hartford Courant*, July 29, 1952; Allen and Shannon, *Truman Merry-Go-Round*, 279–280; Richard G. Hewlett and Francis Duncan, *A History of the United States Atomic Energy Commission*, vol. 2, *1947–1952, Atomic Shield* (Washington, DC, 1972), 179–181, 367–368.

27. *C.R. (Senate)*, September 22, 1949, 13140–13142.

28. Hewlett and Duncan, *History of the United States Atomic Energy Commission*, 371–372; William Liscum Borden, *There Will Be No Time: A Revolution in Strategy* (New York, 1946); Henry W. Harris, "How World War III Will Be Fought," *Boston Sunday Globe*, December 15, 1946.

29. *C.R. (Senate)*, September 22, 1949, 13163.

The French Coalition

1. Sources: Vincent Auriol, *Journal du septennat*, vol. 3, *1949* (Paris, 1977), 345–351; Georgette Elguy, *Histoire de la Ive République: La république des illusions, 1945–1951* (Paris, 1993), 64–65, 373–399, and pt. 2, chap. 6; *L'année politique, 1950* (Paris, 1951), 281–286; Pierre Brocheux and Daniel Hémery, *Indochine: La colonisation ambigué, 1858–1954* (Paris, 2001), 164–175, 335–338; D. Domergue-Cloarec, "La mission et le Rapport Revers," *Guerres mondiales et conflits contemporains* 148 (October 1987): 103–111; Dean Acheson and David Bruce, exchange of telegrams, December 1949, in *FRUS (1949)*, vol. 7, pt. 1, 101–110; François Roth, *Robert Schuman: De Lorrain des frontières au père de l'Europe* (Paris, 2008), 370–371; Acheson, Bevin, Schuman meeting, September 15, 1949, in *FRUS (1949)*, vol. 3, 599–602; Michel Bodin, *Dictionnaire de la Guerre d'Indochine, 1945–1954* (Paris, 2004), 228–229; Daniel Varga, "Léon Pignon, l'homme clè de la solution Bao-Dai et de

l'implication des États-Unis dans la Guerre d'Indochine," *Outre-Mers* 96, no. 364–365 (2009): 300–303.

CHAPTER THREE: AN AUTUMN OF DISCONTENT

1. Testimony of General Eisenhower, October 20, 1949, US House of Representatives, Committee on Armed Services, *The National Defense Program—Unification and Strategy: Hearings, October 6th–21st, 1949* (Washington, DC, 1949), 566.

2. Truman Library, oral history interview with David L. Cole, September 20, 1972, 26, 59.

3. The Keynesian economist Alvin Hansen originated the phrase "secular stagnation" in a paper in 1934. By the early 1940s he and other economists had developed the concept into a powerful theory to account for the Great Depression as the result of a structural excess of savings over investment resulting from factors including inequalities of income and wealth. In the late 1940s economists remained anxious about the possible return of Depression-era conditions. They revived the secular stagnation hypothesis to explain why this might occur. See, for example, Hansen, "Needed: A Cycle Policy," in *Saving American Capitalism*, ed. Seymour Harris (New York, 1948), 218–225.

4. Neil W. Chamberlain and Jane Metzger Schilling, *The Impact of Strikes: Their Social and Economic Cost* (New York, 1954), chap. 9.

5. Hoffman as a "vigorous moderate": Doris Fleeson in the *St. Louis Post-Dispatch*, September 7, 1949; Nelson M. Lichtenstein, "Labor in the Truman Era: Origins of the 'Private Welfare State,'" in *The Truman Presidency*, ed. Michael J. Lacy (New York, 1989), 134–136.

6. Stevenson in 1949: John Bartlow Martin, *Adlai Stevenson of Illinois* (Garden City, NY, 1976), 389–397, 411–414, 418–421.

7. Arthur M. Schlesinger Jr., *The Vital Center: The Politics of Freedom* (Boston, 1949), 153–156.

8. Lippmann on Schlesinger: *NYHT*, October 9, 1949. "Neanderthals" and "libido": Schlesinger, *Vital Center*, 29–30.

9. *NYHT* forum: reports, *NYHT* and *NYT*, October 25–27, 1949, and Martin, *Stevenson of Illinois*, 429–431.

10. Arthur M. Schlesinger Jr., *A Life in the 20th Century: Innocent Beginnings, 1900–1950* (Boston, 2000), 408; *Journals, 1952–2000* (New York, 2007), 10.

11. Eisenhower's visitors: Louis Galambos, ed., *The Papers of Dwight David Eisenhower*, vol. 10, *February 1948–November 1949* (Baltimore, 1984), 677–679 (Dewey), 755–757 (Luce). Nehru on Luce: Sylvia Jukes Morris, *Rage for Fame: The Ascent of Clare Boothe Luce* (New York, 1997), 457. Eisenhower on "the middle of the road": July 7, 1949, in Galambos, *Papers of Dwight David Eisenhower*, 10:678.

12. Eisenhower's speeches: *NYT*, June 2, September 6, and October 25, 1949. Friendship with Hoffman: William B. Pickett, *Eisenhower Decides to Run: Presidential Politics and Cold War Strategy* (Chicago, 2000), 87–89.

13. De Gaulle at Bordeaux, September 25, 1949: Charles de Gaulle, *Discours et messages: Dans l'attente, Fevrier 1946–Avril 1958* (Paris, 1970), 306–307.

14. Leland Olds: *Baltimore Evening Sun*, October 3, 1949. The role of Lyndon Johnson as Edwin Johnson's ally against Olds is brilliantly described in *Master of the Senate* (New York, 2002), the third volume of Robert A. Caro's biography of LBJ.

15. Model T Ford: Jack Alexander, "Stormy New Boss of the Pentagon," *Saturday Evening Post*, July 30, 1949. Johnson's role in 1948: Keith D. McFarland and David L. Roll, *Louis Johnson and the Arming of America: The Roosevelt and Truman Years* (Bloomington, IN, 2005), 133–142.

16. Military waste: Warner R. Schilling, Paul Y. Hammond, and Glenn H. Snyder, *Strategy, Politics and Defense Budgets* (New York, 1962), 110–114. "Get them done quickly": *NYT*, April 13, 1949. Base closures: *NYT*, August 24, 1949.

17. "We are Americans:" *NYT*, April 3, 1949. Presidential ambitions: Truman Library, oral history interview with Marx Leva, June 12, 1970. Johnson and Milton Berle: Alexander, "Stormy New Boss." See also Joseph Alsop, *The Reporter's Trade* (New York, 1958), 14–15.

18. "Off Tackle" and the B-36: Kenneth W. Condit, *History of the Joint Chiefs of Staff: The Joint Chiefs of Staff and National Policy*, vol. 2, *1947–1949* (Washington, DC, 1996), 159–163; Steven L. Rearden, *History of the Office of the Secretary of Defense*, vol. 1, *The Formative Years, 1947–1950* (Washington, DC, 1984), 410–417.

19. Radford testimony: October 7, 1949, US House of Representatives, Committee on Armed Services, *National Defense Program*, 39–52, quotation p. 51.

20. Eisenhower testimony, October 20, 1949, US House of Representatives, Committee on Armed Services, *National Defense Program*, 562–566.

21. Louis Johnson testimony, October 21, 1949, US House of Representatives, Committee on Armed Services, *National Defense Program*, 610, 628.

22. *Washington Post*, November 18, 1949.

Northeast Asia

1. Sources: Associated Press reports of comments by Syngman Rhee, September 30 and October 31, 1949; Wada Haruki, *The Korean War: An International History*, updated ed. (Lanham, MD, 2018), 30–41; Bruce Cumings, *The Origins of the Korean War*, vol. 2, *The Roaring of the Cataract, 1947–1950* (Princeton, NJ, 1990), 227–229, 385–387; NSC 48/2, "Position of the United States with Respect to Korea," *FRUS (1950)*, vol. 7, pt. 2, 969–978; Bruce Cumings, *Korea's Place in the Sun* (New York, 2005), 167–177; Louise Young, *Japan's Wartime Empire: Manchuria in the Culture of Wartime Imperialism* (Berkeley, CA, 1998), 22–40, 241–259; Richard B. Finn, *Winners in Peace: MacArthur, Yoshida and Postwar Japan* (Berkeley, CA, 1992), 221–231; Chalmers Johnson, *Conspiracy at Matsukawa* (Berkeley, CA, 1972), 65–75; A. B. Torkunov, *Zagadochnaya voina: Koreiskii konflikt, 1950–1953* (Moscow, 2000), 12–13, 24, 38–51.

CHAPTER FOUR: ASPHALT JUNGLES

1. Robert S. Allen, ed., *Our Sovereign State* (New York, 1949), 78.

2. *PPHST (1949)*, 377, Truman's press conference of July 14.

3. Wallace S. Sayre and Herbert Kaufman, *Governing New York City: Politics in the Metropolis* (New York, 1960), 690.

4. Edward J. Flynn, *You're the Boss: My Story of a Life in Practical Politics* (New York, 1947), x, 225.

5. *CNYPS (1949)*, interview with Judge Julius Isaacs, October 31, 1949.

6. Paul Robeson and Peekskill: Philip S. Foner, ed., *Paul Robeson Speaks: Writings, Speeches and Interviews, 1918–1974* (London, 1978), 197–200, 230–232, 543–545; Paul Robeson Jr., *The Undiscovered Paul Robeson: Quest for Freedom, 1939–1976* (Hoboken, NJ, 2010), 171–184.

7. Housing: New York Housing Authority, *Housing, 1946–July 1949: A Report to Mayor William O'Dwyer* (New York, 1949), 5–10; schools: "153 New Schools Proposed to Meet Grave City Crisis," *NYT*, February 15, 1949; water: "City Faces Acute Water Shortage," *NYT*, October 15, 1949; poverty: Bureau of the Census, *1950 Census of Population*, vol. 2, *Characteristics of the Population* (Washington, DC, 1953), pt. 1, Tables 85 and 92; pt. 32 (New York), Table 43. Manhattan's median household income was $2,347 compared with a five-borough New York average of $3,073, with Memphis at $2,248 and New Orleans at $2,330.

8. Columbia University (Rare Books and Manuscripts), Oral History Collections, *Reminiscences of William J. O'Dwyer*, interview, March 14, 1961, 453–469; O'Dwyer and Moses: Robert Caro, *The Power Broker: Robert Moses and the Fall of New York* (New York, 1974), 755–779.

9. *CNYPS (1949)*, interview with George S. Combs, November 2, 1949, 53.

10. Daniel Soyer, "'Support the Fair Deal in the Nation; Abolish the Raw Deal in the City': The Liberal Party in 1949," *New York History* 93, no. 2 (Spring 2012): 147–181.

11. *NYT*, November 25, 1964. Costello's reputation and activities in New York: Herbert Asbury, "America's Number One Mystery Man," *Collier's*, April 12 and 19, 1947; Estes Kefauver, *The Kefauver Committee Report on Organized Crime* (New York, 1951), 92–105, with O'Dwyer testimony on pp. 105–125.

12. *CNYPS (1949)*, interview with Newbold Morris, October 31, 1949, 27–28.

13. Michael L. Kurtz, "deLesseps S. Morrison: Political Reformer," *Louisiana History* 17, no. 1 (Winter 1976): 29–34; *New York Daily News*, September 14, 1949; William Howard Moore, *The Kefauver Committee and the Politics of Crime, 1950–1952* (Columbia, MO, 1974), 39–44.

14. Allen, *Our Sovereign State*, 79; *New York Daily News*, October 25, 1949; *Brooklyn Eagle*, November 4, 1949.

15. Columbia University, Rare Books and Manuscripts, MS #0605 (Box 36), diary of Frank S. Hogan, October 7, 1949.

16. FRBCs: Flynn, *You're the Boss*, 123–124.

17. Allan Nevins, *Herbert H. Lehman and His Era* (New York, 1963), 174, 396–397.

18. Duane Tananbaum, *Herbert H. Lehman: A Political Biography* (Albany, NY, 2016), 298–299.

19. *CNYPS (1949)*, interview with Hiram Gans, November 8, 1949, 138–141; Philip A. Grant Jr., "Catholic Congressmen, Cardinal Spellman, Eleanor Roosevelt and the 1949–50 Federal Aid to Education Controversy," *Records of the American Catholic Historical Society of Philadelphia* 90 (March–December 1979): 3–11.

20. *CNYPS (1949)*, interview with George S. Combs, November 2, 1949, 50–51.

21. Mayor Kelly, graft, and integration: Roger Biles, "Edward J. Kelly: New Deal Machine Builder," in *The Mayors: The Chicago Political Tradition*, ed. Paul M. Green and Melvin G. Holli (Carbondale, IL, 2005), 117–118, 123–124.

22. Townsend Hoopes, *The Devil and John Foster Dulles* (Boston, 1973), 53.

23. John Foster Dulles, *War or Peace* (New York, 1950), 8, 16.

24. John Foster Dulles, "Statement on Candidacy," *NYT*, September 8, 1949.

25. Tananbaum, *Herbert H. Lehman*, 310–311.

26. *NYT*, October 25, 1949.

27. Edward T. Folliard, "Smooth Tygoons Succeed Mobsters of 1920s," *Miami Herald*, November 28, 1949.

28. *Brooklyn Eagle*, December 11, 1949.

29. Poll taken October 19, 1949: Mildred Strunk, "The Quarter's Polls," *Public Opinion Quarterly* 14, no. 1 (Spring 1950): 184.

30. Michael Bowen, *The Roots of Modern Conservatism: Dewey, Taft and the Battle for the Soul of the Republican Party* (Chapel Hill, NC, 2011), 86–87.

31. *Madison Capital Times*, November 12, 1949.

Mao in Moscow—1

1. Sources: Dieter Heinzig, *The Soviet Union and Communist China, 1945–1950: The Arduous Road to the Alliance* (New York, 2015), 263–290; Isabella M. Weber, *How China Escaped Shock Therapy: The Market Reform Debate* (New York, 2021), 75–84; I. V. Kovalev, "Report, Kovalev to Stalin," December 24, 1949, trans. Sergey Radchenko, Wilson Center Digital Archive, https://digitalarchive.wilsoncenter.org/document/113441; Alexander V. Pantsov and Steven I. Levine, *Mao: The Real Story* (New York, 2012), 369–370; I. V. Kovalev and S. N. Goncharov, "Stalin's Dialogue with Mao Zedong," trans. Craig Seibert, *Journal of Northeast*

Asian Studies 10 (1991): 71–73; Associated Press, "Gifts, Adulation Pile Up," *NYT*, December 21, 1949; Harrison E. Salisbury, "Malenkov Eulogy of Stalin Stresses Chances of Peace," *NYT*, December 22, 1949; Maya Plisetskaya, *I, Maya Plisetskaya* (New Haven, CT, 2001), 116–117; "British Intentions in China," *Times* (London), November 13, 1949; Shen Zhihua, *Mao, Stalin, and the Korean War: Trilateral Communist Relations in the 1950s*, trans. Neil Silver (New York, 2012), 93–95.

CHAPTER FIVE: FROM CINCINNATI TO TAIWAN

1. Quoted in the *Dayton Journal Herald*, December 31, 1949.

2. Quoted in Robert Dallek, *Franklin Roosevelt and American Foreign Policy, 1932–1945* (New York, 1995), 336.

3. Michael J. Green, *By More Than Providence: Grand Strategy and American Power in the Asia Pacific Since 1783* (New York, 2017), 102–108, 131–136, 268–274; Melvyn P. Leffler, *A Preponderance of Power: National Security, the Truman Administration, and the Cold War* (Stanford, CA, 1992), 81–94, 246–260; Tyler Dennett, *Americans in Eastern Asia* (New York, 1922), chaps. 32, 33.

4. James T. Patterson, *Mr. Republican: A Biography of Robert A. Taft* (Boston, 1972), 424–425.

5. Dick Cull Jr., "Taft Is Concerned About Apathy of Ohio Citizens," *Dayton Daily News*, December 12, 1949.

6. Alfred Steinberg, *Sam Rayburn: A Biography* (New York, 1975), 255; Allen Drury, *A Senate Journal, 1943–1945* (New York, 1963), 10–11; John Gunther, *Inside U.S.A.* (New York, 1947), 435; Arthur M. Schlesinger Jr., "Mine Eyes Have Seen the Glory: Robert A. Taft," *Collier's*, February 22, 1947, 13.

7. Patterson, *Mr. Republican*, 294–295.

8. Robert Accinelli, *Crisis and Commitment: United States Policy Towards Taiwan, 1950–1955* (Chapel Hill, NC, 1996), 3–10; Nancy Bernkopf Tucker, *Taiwan, Hong Kong, and the United States: Uncertain Friendships* (New York, 1994), 24–30; *FRUS (1949)*, vol. 9, *The Far East: China*, text of NSC 37/8, October 6, 1949, 392–397, and meeting with Chiang, 405–407.

9. *FRUS (1949)*, vol. 9, 415–431; Keith D. McFarland and David L. Roll, *Louis Johnson and the Arming of America: The Roosevelt and Truman Years* (Bloomington, IN, 2005), chap. 15.

10. Robert Ross Smith, *The War in the Pacific: Triumph in the Philippines*, Center of Military History, US Army (Washington, DC, 1993), 4–14.

11. Truman Library, Dean G. Acheson Papers, Memorandum of Conversation with Sen. Smith, November 30, 1949; US Senate, Armed Services and Foreign Relations Committees, *Hearings on the Military Situation in the Far East* (MacArthur Hearings) (Washington, DC, 1951), pt. 5, 3315–3326; *Baltimore Sun*, December 2, 1949. On Alexander Smith: obituary, *NYT*, October 28, 1966.

12. Associated Press, December 7, 1949.

13. S. R. Ashton, Gillian Bennett, and Keith Hamilton, *Documents on British Policy Overseas*, series 1, vol. 8, *Britain and China, 1945–1950* (Abingdon, UK, 2002), Documents 105 and 110, memoranda by Ernest Bevin on the recognition of the People's Republic of China, October 24 and December 12, 1949.

14. *San Francisco Examiner*, December 8 and 26, 1949; *Los Angeles Times*, December 11, 13, and 15, 1949.

15. Associated Press report of Knowland's comment, December 7, 1949; Philip C. Jessup, *The Birth of Nations* (New York, 1974), 26–30; US Senate, Foreign Relations Committee, *Nomination of Philip C. Jessup: Hearings* (Washington, DC, 1951), 810–814, and Jessup's testimony regarding the China Round-Table, 602–611, 911–921.

16. Owen Lattimore, *The Situation in Asia* (Boston, 1949), 49, 68–69, 89–90, 148–149, 218–219. See also Stassen quoted in Jessup Hearings, 713–716. On the China Round-Table: Robert L. Beisner, *Dean Acheson: A Life in the Cold War* (New York, 2006), 192–193.

17. *FRUS (1949)*, vol. 7, *The Far East and Australasia*, pt. 2, 1209–1214; Truman Library, Dean G. Acheson Papers, memorandum of conversation with the president, November 7, 1949.

18. Tsarist policy in Asia: B. A. Romanov, *Russia in Manchuria, 1892–1906* (Leningrad, 1928; English trans., Ann Arbor, MI, 1952), 5–27; Dietrich Geyer, *Russian Imperialism: The Interaction of Domestic and Foreign Policy, 1860–1914* (Leamington Spa, UK, 1987), chap. 9.

19. Stalin and China in the 1920s and 1930s: speech on August 1, 1927, in Joseph Stalin, *Marxism and the National and Colonial Question* (London, 1936), 232–253; Alexander V. Pantsov and Steven I. Levine, *Mao: The Real Story* (New York, 2012), 234–237, 269–270, 354–356.

20. Truman Library, Dean G. Acheson Papers, memorandum of meeting with Tracy Voorhees regarding Japanese Peace Treaty, December 15, 1949.

21. NSC 48/1: US House of Representatives, Armed Services Committee, *United States–Vietnam Relations, 1945–1967 (The Pentagon Papers)*, bk. 8, 225–264; John Lewis Gaddis, *George F. Kennan: An American Life* (New York, 2011), 362–365.

22. See the June 1949 speech by Lord Wavell, former viceroy of India, quoted in Olaf Caroe, *Wells of Power: The Oilfields of South-Western Asia* (London, 1951), 81–103.

23. Kennan and "war-making complexes": John Lewis Gaddis, *Strategies of Containment* (New York, 2005), 29–30, 39–40.

24. MacArthur Hearings, pt. 4, 2576–2579, Louis Johnson's testimony.

25. James Reston, "Vandenberg Asks Sharp Cut in 1950 Foreign Aid Budget," *NYT*, December 22, 1949.

26. *FRUS (1949)*, vol. 9, 451–460.

27. MacArthur Hearings, pt. 3, 1667–1669, Acheson's testimony; Truman Library, note from Louis Johnson to Truman, December 15, 1949, enclosing Formosa memorandum from Secretary Voorhees.

28. *FRUS (1949)*, vol. 9, 460.

29. Drew Pearson's syndicated column Washington Merry-Go-Round, *Washington Post*, December 22 and 24, 1949.

30. *FRUS (1949)*, vol. 9, 463–467.

31. NSC 48/2: *FRUS (1949)*, vol. 7, 1215–1220.

32. Steve Early: James A. Farley, *Jim Farley's Story: The Roosevelt Years* (New York, 1948), 28, 42. Early entered FDR's inner circle as early as 1920 and served as White House press secretary in all four of FDR's administrations. For a flavor of the man, see the Associated Press report of his death, *Baltimore Sun*, August 12, 1951.

33. The conflicting reports from Washington (for example, in the *Times* [London], December 30, 1949) led three British newspapers— the *Times*, *Daily Telegraph*, and the *Manchester Guardian*—to publish strongly worded editorials opposing any American attempt to defend Taiwan, in the false belief that on December 29 Truman had decided to do so.

34. *Dayton Journal Herald*, December 31, 1949. On Hoover and Senator Knowland, *Oakland Tribune*, January 3, 1950.

35. *PPHST (1950)*, 11–12; US State Department, *Bulletin*, January 16, 1950, 79–80; Truman Library, Dean G. Acheson Papers, memoranda of January 5, 1950, conversations with Truman and with Senators Knowland and Smith.

36. Arthur H. Vandenberg Jr., ed., *The Private Papers of Senator Vandenberg* (Boston, 1952), 537–538.

37. Vandenberg, *Private Papers*, 539; Taft's comments in the Senate, *C.R. (Senate)*, January 11, 1950, 298–299.

38. *PPHST (1950)*, 107–109.

39. George F. Kennan, *The Kennan Diaries*, ed. Frank Costigliola (New York, 2014), 240–241; David S. McLellan, *Dean Acheson: The State Department Years* (New York, 1976), 209; Dean Acheson, *Present at the Creation: My Years in the State Department* (New York, 1969), 354–358. The text as officially released is in US State Department, *Bulletin*, January 23, 1950, 111–118, but the most comprehensive reports were from the *Baltimore Sun* and *New York Times* of January 13 and the Associated Press. Among the many scholarly analyses of the speech and its significance, see John Lewis Gaddis, *We Now Know: Rethinking Cold War History* (New York, 1997), 72–73; J. I. Matray, "Dean Acheson's National Press Club Speech Reexamined," *Journal of Conflict Studies* 22, no. 1 (2002): 28–55.

40. On Acheson's loss of his listening posts in China, see US State Department, *Bulletin*, December 12, 1949, 908; December 26, 1949, 955; and January 23, 1950, 119–123.

41. Korean aid: US State Department, *Bulletin*, June 19, 1949, 781–787; *C.R. (House)*, January 19, 1950, 631–632.

Mao in Moscow—2

1. Sources: Dieter Heinzig, *The Soviet Union and Communist China, 1945–1950: The Arduous Road to the Alliance* (New York, 2015), 289–295; Oleg V. Khlevniuk, *Stalin: New Biography of a Dictator* (New Haven, CT, 2015), 290–292; Liu Shaoqi, speech of November 16, 1949, *Pravda*, January 4, 1950, and conference background in Milton Sacks, "The Strategy of Communism in Southeast Asia," *Pacific Affairs* 23, no. 3 (September 1950): 231–235; Robert A. Scalapino, *The Japanese Communist Movement, 1920–1966* (Berkeley, CA, 1967), 50–61, 79–81; Jen Min Jih Pao, "The Path to Liberation of the Japanese People," *Pravda*, January 21, 1950; Wada Haruki, *The Korean War: An International History*, updated ed. (Lanham, MD, 2018), 46–48; Marcelle Size Knaack, *Encyclopedia of USAF Aircraft and Missile Systems*, vol. 2, *Post–World War II Bombers, 1945–1973* (Washington, DC, 1988), 24–29, 489–490, 494.

Chapter Six: Motorama, Coal, and the Hydrogen Bomb

1. US House of Representatives, Judiciary Committee, *Hearings of the Subcommittee on Monopoly Power, Part 4A, Steel, April 17th–May 11th, 1950* (Washington, DC, 1950), 467, 471.

2. US Department of Commerce, "National Income and Product in the First Quarter of 1950," *Survey of Current Business* (May 1950): 4–7.

3. Motorama: Horace Sutton, *Confessions of a Grand Hotel: The Waldorf-Astoria* (New York, 1953), 141, 148–149, 169; *Detroit Free Press*, January 18 and 19, 1950; *Boston Globe*, January 19, 1950; *Arthur Godfrey Presents the General Motors Motor Show*, CBS Television, January 25, 1950.

4. Charles E. Wilson: B. C. Forbes, ed., *America's Fifty Foremost Business Leaders* (New York, 1948), 439–449; US Senate, Armed Services Committee, *Hearings on Nominee Designates, January 15th–16th* (Washington, DC, 1953), 26.

5. Alfred P. Sloan Jr.: *NYT*, June 22, 1944; David Farber, *Sloan Rules: Arthur P. Sloan and the Triumph of General Motors* (Chicago, 2002), 235–237. Car sales and the auto industry after 1945: John B. Rae, *The American Automobile: A Brief History* (Chicago, 1965), chap. 10.

6. GM's postwar expansion: General Motors, *37th Annual Report to Shareholders, Year Ended December 31st, 1945*, 11–15; Alfred P. Sloan Jr., *My Years with General Motors* (New York, 1964), 206–209.

7. Sloan, *My Years with General Motors*, 226–230; General Motors, "Chevrolet 1950 Engineering Features: Passenger Cars," 53–58.

8. US Department of Commerce, "Capital Investments and Sales Expectations in 1950," *Survey of Current Business* (April 1950): 6–10.

9. Elwyn T. Bonnell, "Public and Private Debt in 1948," *Survey of Current Business* (October 1949): 6–10; US Bureau of the Census, *Historical Statistics of the United States: Colonial Times to 1970* (Washington, DC, 1975), pt. 1, Table F 1-5.

10. Postwar coal mining: US Bureau of Labor Statistics, "The Changing Status of Bituminous Coal Miners, 1937–1946," *Monthly Labor Review* 63, no. 2 (August 1946): 165–170; Peter Navarro, "Union Bargaining Power in the Coal Industry, 1945–1981," *Industrial and Labor Relations Review* 36, no. 2 (January 1983): 218–220.

11. US Department of the Interior, *A Medical Survey of the Bituminous Coal Industry: Report of the Coal Mines Administration* (Washington,

DC, 1947), 75–80, and *Supplement: The Coal Miner and His Family*, 2–3. Centralia mine disaster: Melvyn Dubofsky and Warren Van Tine, *John L. Lewis: A Biography* (New York, 1977), 470–471.

12. US Department of Labor, Bureau of Labor Statistics, *Analysis of Work Stoppages During 1949* (Washington, DC, 1950), 22–24; Dubofsky and Van Tine, *John L. Lewis*, 483–487.

13. *Pittsburgh Press*, January 15 and 16, 1950.

14. George M. Humphrey and Pittsburgh Consolidation: interview with the company's president, George H. Love, *Pittsburgh Press*, February 5, 1950; Pittsburgh Consolidation Coal Company, *1945 Annual Report to Shareholders*, 1–4, and *1949 Annual Report*, 3–8.

15. *C.R. (Senate)*, February 2, 1950, 1338.

16. Ken Young and Warner R. Schilling, *Super Bomb: Organizational Conflict and the Development of the Hydrogen Bomb* (Ithaca, NY, 2019), 14, 56, 63–65; Mildred Strunk, "The Quarter's Polls," *Public Opinion Quarterly* 14, no. 2 (Summer 1950): 372–373.

17. Richard G. Hewlett and Francis Duncan, *A History of the US Atomic Energy Commission*, vol. 2, *1947–1952: Atomic Shield* (Washington, DC, 1972), 408.

18. Young and Schilling, *Super Bomb*, 16–17 and chap. 2.

19. Alsop columns on the Super Bomb: *Washington Post* and *NYHT*, January 2, 4, 6, and 18, 1950. Leaks to the press: Young and Schilling, *Super Bomb*, 55–56.

20. Strauss's connections: Lewis L. Strauss, *Men and Decisions* (New York, 1962), 11, 84–85, 332, 335–336; US Senate, Interstate and Foreign Commerce Committee, *Hearings: Nomination of Lewis L. Strauss* (Washington, DC, 1959), 4–10.

21. Hewlett and Duncan, *History of the US Atomic Energy Commission*, 380–388.

22. Hewlett and Duncan, *History of the US Atomic Energy Commission*, 389–391.

23. David Alan Rosenberg, "American Atomic Strategy and the Hydrogen Bomb Decision," *Journal of American History* 66, no. 1 (June 1979): 69–83.

24. Keith D. McFarland and David L. Roll, *Louis Johnson and the Arming of America: The Roosevelt and Truman Years* (Bloomington, IN, 2005), 218–220. Robert F. LeBaron: obituary, *Princeton Alumni Weekly* 84 (1983): 52; National Research Council, Washington, DC, *Directory of Industrial Research Laboratories* (1946), entry for Virginia Smelting

Company; and on his wife, Peggy Bancroft LeBaron, Denver Public Library, Denver, Caroline Bancroft Papers, biographical note.

25. George Kennan, "International Control of Atomic Energy," January 20, 1950, in *FRUS (1950)*, vol. 1, *National Security*, 22–44; John Lewis Gaddis, *George Kennan: An American Life* (New York, 2011), 377–381.

26. Paul H. Nitze, *From Hiroshima to Glasnost: At the Center of Decision: A Memoir of Five Perilous Decades* (New York, 1989), 91; Young and Schilling, *Super Bomb*, 63–64. The Joint Chiefs' recommendation: *FRUS (1950)*, vol. 1, 503–511.

27. Gordon Newell and Admiral Allan E. Smith, *Mighty Mo: A Biography of the Last Battleship* (New York, 1969), 78–79, 92–96; *St. Louis Post-Dispatch*, January 19, 1950; *NYT*, February 2, 1950.

28. *PPHST (1950)*, January 19 press conference, 119; Robert S. Allen and William V. Shannon, *The Truman Merry-Go-Round* (New York, 1950), 58–61.

29. Clifford's memorandum (drafted by the lawyer James T. Rowe but submitted under Clifford's name), November 19, 1947, in Truman Library, Clifford Papers (Political File), 20–21; Charles L. Fontenay, *Estes Kefauver: A Biography* (Knoxville, TN, 1980), 164–165; Charles W. Van Devander, *The Big Bosses* (New York, 1944), 167–178.

30. Dean Acheson, *Present at the Creation: My Years in the State Department* (New York, 1969), 354.

31. Joseph Alsop, "Why We Lost China 1: The Feud Between Stilwell and Chiang," *Saturday Evening Post*, January 7, 1950.

32. *C.R. (House)*, January 19, 1950, 655–657, with Lattimore mentioned on p. 651; Walter Lippmann's *NYHT* column, "The Korean Scuttle and What to Expect," January 24, 1950.

The German Question

1. Sources: Vincent Auriol, *Journal du septennat*, vol. 3, *1949* (Paris, 1977), 361–362, 455–463; Pierre Gerbet, *Le relèvement, 1944–1949* (Paris, 1991), 302–307; Raymond Poidevin, *Robert Schuman: Homme d'état, 1886–1963* (Paris, 1986), 231–234, 213–218; *Débats parlementaires, Assemblée Nationale, session de 1949* (Paris, 1949), debate of November 24, 1949, "Politique à l'Égard de l'Allemagne," speech by Schuman, 6350–6351; François Roth, *Robert Schuman: De Lorrain des frontières au père de l'Europe* (Paris, 2008), 91–93, 328–329, 376–378;

Pierre Mendès-France, "Le problème de l'industrie sidérurgique," in Mendès-France, *Oeuvres complètes*, vol. 2 (Paris, 1985), 595–601; Françoise Berger, *La France, l'Allemagne et acier, 1932–1952: De la stratégie des cartels à l'élaboration de la CECA* (Paris, 2009), chaps. 7–9; Konrad Adenauer, *Memoirs, 1945–1953* (London, 1966), 232–238; Jacques Dumaine, *Quai D'Orsay* (Paris, 1955), 451–460.

CHAPTER SEVEN: LOYALTY AND SCHISM

1. Joseph W. Martin Jr., as told to Robert J. Donovan, *My First Fifty Years in Politics* (New York, 1960), 197–198. Martin was Speaker of the House of Representatives in 1947–1949 and 1953–1955.

2. *Baltimore Sun*, March 16, 1931.

3. Alistair Cooke, *A Generation on Trial* (London, 1950), 337–338; Tony Hiss, *The View from Alger's Window: A Son's Memoir* (New York, 1999), 76–80; press reports, January 25–26, 1950, *New York Daily News* and *Baltimore Sun*.

4. Samuel Lubell's "realignment election" concept, outlined in his most famous book *The Future of American Politics*, rev. ed. (New York, 1955), has its critics, but the book remains an indispensable micro- and macro-analysis of changing opinion at the time. Equally useful are his *Saturday Evening Post* articles about Truman's 1948 election victory and Taft's Ohio campaign of 1950, January 22, 1949, and February 10, 1951. For criticisms of Lubell, see Alexander P. Lamis, Everett C. Ladd, William Schneider, Philip Meyer, and John K. White, "Symposium on the Work of Samuel Lubell," *Political Science and Politics* 23, no. 2 (June 1990): 184–191. On Key, see Chapter 10 below. Other pioneering work came from the University of Michigan's Survey Research Center in a book about Eisenhower's 1952 victory: Angus Campbell, Gerald Gurin, and Warren E. Miller, with a foreword by Key, *The Voter Decides* (Evanston, IL, 1954). Polling ca. 1950: Jill Lepore, *These Truths: A History of the United States* (New York, 2018), 542–546.

5. In November 1948, in the ten states with the largest number of electoral college seats, the Republican candidate Thomas Dewey won only 46.5 percent of the popular vote, compared with Eisenhower's 54.9 percent in 1952, representing a swing to the GOP of 8.4 percentage points. In the same ten states, the midterm congressional elections in 1950 already showed a swing to the Republicans since 1948 of 4.4 percentage points, with especially large gains in Texas, Massachusetts, New

York, California, and Missouri. While some of this might have merely been due to the usual midterm effect of losses for the incumbent party, the data also show an underlying hemorrhage of support for the Democrats in the industrial heartland. Suffering a nine-point collapse in 1950 in their vote in Chicago and its suburbs, that year they also lost five seats in the House of Representatives in Illinois, five in Indiana, and four in Ohio. Some of the biggest swings to the GOP were in steel-making cities and towns. In the twenty-seven congressional districts with steel mills in Illinois, Pennsylvania, and Ohio, the GOP saw its share of the vote increase from 43 percent in 1948 to just under 50 percent in November 1950. These results are consistent with Samuel Lubell's contemporary analyses of an underlying trend against the Democrats that preceded the impact of the Korean War.

6. McCarthy's death: Thomas Reeves, *The Life and Times of Joe McCarthy* (Briarcliff Manor, NY, 1982), 669–675.

7. Robert S. Allen and William V. Shannon, *The Truman Merry-Go-Round* (New York, 1950), 291; *C.R. (Senate)*, January 25, 1950, 895.

8. Jack Alexander, "The Senate's Remarkable Upstart," *Saturday Evening Post*, August 9, 1947, 52.

9. *Saturday Evening Post*, August 9, 1947, 16; David S. Oshinsky, *A Conspiracy So Immense: The World of Joe McCarthy* (New York, 1983), 12–14.

10. 1939 campaign: "McCarthy Elected Judge," *Appleton Post-Crescent*, April 5, 1939.

11. McCarthy's war record: Reeves, *Life and Times of Joe McCarthy*, 45–54. 1946 campaign: *Appleton Post-Crescent*, May 13, 1946, story by John Wyngaard, who became McCarthy's leading backer in the Wisconsin press.

12. Wisconsin politics: John Gunther, *Inside U.S.A.* (New York, 1947), 320–325; Leon D. Epstein, "A Two-Party Wisconsin," *Journal of Politics* 18, no. 3 (August 1956): 440–453; McCarthy on Stassen: *Appleton Post-Crescent*, December 18, 1946.

13. Drew Pearson on McCarthy: *Washington Post*, August 1, 1947.

14. *C.R. (Senate)*, July 26, 1949, 10160–10175.

15. Election results in State of Wisconsin, *The Wisconsin Blue Book 1948* (Madison, WI, 1948), 675; State of Wisconsin, *The Wisconsin Blue Book 1954* (Madison, WI, 1954), 757; US Department of Agriculture, *Farm Costs and Returns, 1951 with Comparisons* (Washington, DC, 1952), Figure 3, Table 2, and p. 14.

16. Richard Nowinson, ed., *Who's Who in United States Politics and American Political Almanac* (Chicago, 1950), 931–932; Aldric Revell, "State Republicans to Have $200,000 in 1950 Campaign Chest, Coleman Says," *Madison Capital Times,* January 12, 1950. On Allis-Chalmers: Nelson Lichtenstein, *The Most Dangerous Man in Detroit* (Urbana, IL, 1995), 258–259.

17. Drew Pearson, *Drew Pearson Diaries, 1949–1959*, ed. Tyler Abell (London, 1974), 68, 74; John Pollard, *The Papacy in the Age of Totalitarianism, 1914–1958* (Oxford, 2014), 373–376.

18. Gunther, *Inside U.S.A.*, 359.

19. Bazy Miller and the *Times-Herald*: *Chicago Tribune*, July 21 and August 2, 1949; William J. Conway, *Bazy Miller, Once a Cub Reporter, to Be a Major Publisher at 28*, Associated Press, September 6, 1949; Truman Library, oral history interview with Willard A. Edwards, September 17, 1988, 31–32.

20. *C.R. (Senate)*, October 19, 1949, Appendix AA6625-6627 and AA 6631–6632. The *Amerasia* affair is fully described in Harvey Klehr and Ronald Radosh, *The Amerasia Spy Case: Prelude to McCarthyism* (Chapel Hill, NC, 1996), with its significance summarized on pp. 216–219.

21. *Racine (WI) Journal-Times*, December 7, 1949.

22. Text of the Republican manifesto: *NYT*, February 7, 1950. Coleman's key role: Michael Bowen, *The Roots of Modern Conservatism: Dewey, Taft and the Battle for the Soul of the Republican Party* (Chapel Hill, NC, 2011), 87–91.

23. Dean Acheson, *Present at the Creation: My Years in the State Department* (New York, 1969), 359–361; *Baltimore Sun,* January 26, 1950.

24. *PPHST (1950),* January 27, 1950, 133.

25. Jeffrey J. Littlejohn and Charles H. Ford, "Truman and Civil Rights," in *A Companion to Harry S. Truman*, ed. Daniel S. Margolies (Malden, MA, 2012), 292–299.

26. Glenn T. Eskew, "'Bombingham': Black Protest in Postwar Birmingham, Alabama," *The Historian* 59, no. 2 (Winter 1997): 378–382. Chicago: Ta-Nehisi Coates, *We Were Eight Years in Power: An American Tragedy* (New York, 2017), 189–191. Groveland Four: US Supreme Court, *Shepherd v. Florida*, 341 U.S. 1950 (April 9, 1951); *NYT,* July 19 and 27, 1949.

27. The Mobilization: Denton L. Watson, *Lion in the Lobby: Clarence J. Mitchell Jr.'s Struggle for the Passage of Civil Rights Laws* (Lanham,

MD, 2002), 176–178; Carol Anderson, *Eyes Off the Prize: The United Nations and the African American Struggle for Human Rights, 1944–1955* (New York, 2003), 167–169; Charles V. Hamilton, *Adam Clayton Powell Jr.* (New York, 1991), 189–193; *Pittsburgh Courier*, January 21, 1950. All Souls Church and its British pastor: William O. Douglas, ed., *The Mind and Faith of A. Powell Davies* (New York, 1957), 11–13, 21–22.

28. 1950 arrests in Washington, DC: Clarence Mitchell Jr., *The Papers of Clarence Mitchell Jr.*, vol. 3, *1946–1950*, ed. Denton Watson (Athens, GA, 2010), 158.

29. B. R. Brazeal, "The Present Status and Programs of Fair Employment Practices Commissions: Federal, State and Municipal," *Journal of Negro Education* 20, no. 3 (Summer 1951): 378–383.

30. *PPHST (1950)*, 115.

31. Alfred Steinberg, *Sam Rayburn: A Biography* (New York, 1975), 250–251.

32. *C.R. (House)*, January 20, 1950, 719–720; Mitchell, *Papers*, 151.

33. *Baltimore Sun*, January 18, 1950; *C.R. (House)*, January 23, 1950, 773–774.

34. Mildred S. Strunk, "The Quarter's Polls," *Public Opinion Quarterly* 14, no. 3 (Autumn 1950): 606.

35. William S. White, "Portrait of a 'Fundamentalist': Kenneth Wherry of Nebraska," *NYT*, January 15, 1950; Tom Connally and Alfred Steinberg, *My Name Is Tom Connally* (New York, 1954), 310–311; Allen and Shannon, *Truman Merry-Go-Round*, 248–251.

Stalin and Korea

1. Sources: Yoram Gorlizki and Oleg V. Khlevniuk, *Cold Peace: Stalin and the Soviet Ruling Circle, 1945–1953* (New York, 2004), 89–93; Bolshoi photograph: *NYT*, January 24, 1950; Dieter Heinzig, *The Soviet Union and Communist China, 1945–1950: The Arduous Road to the Alliance* (New York, 2015), 295–307, 337–343; Wada Haruki, *The Korean War: An International History*, updated ed. (Lanham, MD, 2018), 51–54; A. B. Torkunov, *Zagadochnaya voina: Koreiskii konflikt, 1950–1953* (Moscow, 2000), 55–56; Kathryn J. Weathersby, "New Russian Documents on the Korean War," *Cold War International History Project Bulletin*, no. 6–7 (Winter 1995–1996): 25–27, 30–31; Odd Arne Westad, *The Cold War: A World History* (New York, 2019), 166–167; speech by Congressman John M. Vorys of Ohio, *C.R. (House)*, January 19, 1950, 634. To see

the depleted strength of the US Army, Stalin needed only to obtain a translation of the *Annual Report of the Secretary of Defense* (Washington, DC, December 31, 1949), 138–146.

CHAPTER EIGHT: THE NINTH BOURBON

1. Arthur Krock, "An Interview with Truman," *NYT*, February 15, 1950.

2. Sir Harold Scott, *Scotland Yard* (London, 1954), 57–65.

3. Uncovering of Fuchs: Frank Close, *Trinity: The Treachery and Pursuit of the Most Dangerous Spy in History* (London, 2019), chaps. 13–19, with his arrest on 306–310.

4. H. G. Nicholas, *The British General Election of 1950* (London, 1951), 75–76.

5. Nicholas, *British General Election*, 101–104, and on the Communist Party, 42–43, 137–138, 325–327.

6. McMahon and Hoover: *C.R. (Senate)*, February 2, 1950, 1338–1344; *Baltimore Sun*, February 4, 5, 7, and 8, 1950.

7. J. Edgar Hoover, Fuchs, and VENONA: Close, *Trinity*, 213–214, 353–354.

8. *Baltimore Sun* and Associated Press, February 7, 1950; Drew Pearson, Washington Merry-Go-Round, *Washington Post*, February 11, 1950.

9. *Pittsburgh Post-Gazette*, February 7, 1950; *United States v. United Mineworkers of America*, 190 F.2d 865, April 12, 1951.

10. Arthur Krock, *Memoirs: Sixty Years on the Firing Line* (New York, 1968), 269–270; Truman Library, *Daily Appointments of Harry S. Truman*, February 6, 1950; *NYT*, February 15, 1950, and April 22, 1958; Robert S. Allen and William V. Shannon, *The Truman Merry-Go-Round* (New York, 1950), 37.

11. Thomas Reeves, *The Life and Times of Joe McCarthy* (Briarcliff Manor, NY, 1982), 222–226.

12. Text of the Wheeling speech: US Congress, Senate Committee on Foreign Relations, *State Department Employee Loyalty Investigation* (*Tydings Hearings*) (Washington, DC, 1950), pt. 2–3, 1756–1767.

13. Edwin R. Bayley, *Joe McCarthy and the Press* (Madison, WI, 1981), 18–19.

14. McCarthy's cross-country journey: Associated Press reports, February 11–12, 1950; Reeves, *Life and Times of Joe McCarthy*,

227–229; US State Department, *Bulletin*, February 27, 1950, 327–328, statement by John Peurifoy, February 13, 1950.

15. Cabell Phillips, "Broader Loyalty Tests Proposed for US Jobs," *NYT*, February 19, 1950.

16. Malone: obituary, *Reno Gazette-Journal*, May 19, 1961. McCarthy in Reno: *Reno Gazette-Journal*, January 7 and February 13, 1950.

17. Reeves, *Life and Times of Joe McCarthy*, 230–231.

18. Alfred Steinberg, *Sam Rayburn: A Biography* (New York, 1975), 250–251; Sean J. Savage, *Truman and the Democratic Party* (Lexington, KY, 1997), 146–147.

19. *PPHST (1950)*, 159.

20. Armory dinner: *Democratic Digest*, February 1950 and March–April 1950; Hagley Museum and Library, Wilmington, Delaware, Raymond Loewy's scrapbook, in Raymond Loewy Archive, 2251-II.B, vol. 22; *Baltimore Sun*, February 17, 1950; Earl Richert, "Harry's $100 Feed Shades Belshazzar," *Pittsburgh Press*, February 17, 1950; *Life*, March 13, 1950.

21. Truman's speech: *PPHST (1950)*, 164–169.

22. Background to the Kerr bill: "Federal Price Control of Natural Gas Sold to Interstate Pipelines," *Yale Law Journal* 59, no. 6 (December 1950), 1468–1470, 1486–1489. Debates: *C.R. (House)*, March 31, 1950, 4558–4568; *Baltimore Sun*, March 30, 1950.

23. Truman's veto, April 15: *PPHST (1950)*, 257–258; *Baltimore Sun*, April 16, 1950.

24. Clarence Mitchell Jr., *The Papers of Clarence Mitchell Jr.*, vol. 3, *1946–1950*, ed. Denton Watson (Athens, GA, 2010), cclxxx–cclxxxi.

25. *Pittsburgh Courier*, February 25, 1950.

26. Gary M. Lavergne, *Before Brown: Hemon Marion Sweatt, Thurgood Marshall, and the Long Road to Justice* (Austin, TX, 2010), 5–7, 224–225, 240–245; John P. Frank, "The Supreme Court in 1949–50," *University of Chicago Law Review* 18, no. 1 (Autumn 1950): 33–37.

27. Steinberg, *Sam Rayburn*, 250–251; Savage, *Truman and the Democratic Party*, 146–147.

Nehru, Bengal, and Pakistan

1. Sources: Jawaharlal Nehru, *The Discovery of India* (Kolkata, 1946), 474–487, quotation p. 475; Nehru, *Selected Works of Jawaharlal Nehru*,

2nd ser., vol. 14 (New Delhi, 1992), letter to chief ministers, February 16, 1950, 404, and also 54–62, 84–87, 115–121, 133–138; Judith M. Brown, *Nehru: A Political Life* (New Haven, CT, 2003), 193–195; Sardar Patel, *Sardar Patel's Correspondence, 1945–50*, vol. 10, ed. Durga Das (Ahmedabad, 1974), lxxvi–lxxxi, 1–23; Shivshankar Menon, *India and Asian Geopolitics: The Past, Present* (Washington, DC, 2021), 52–56; Nirupama Rao, *The Fractured Himalaya: India, Tibet, China, 1949–1962* (Gurugram, Haryana, India, 2021), 62–79.

CHAPTER NINE: THE COMING STRUGGLE

1. James Burnham, *The Coming Defeat of Communism* (New York, 1950), 282.

2. William F. Buckley Jr., *God and Man at Yale*, 50th anniversary ed. (Washington, DC, 2002), 118; *Hartford Courant* and *NYT*, February 23, 1950.

3. Buckley, *God and Man at Yale*, lxv, 12–16, 92, 109, 177.

4. Buckley, *God and Man at Yale*, lxvi, 123–125.

5. Buckley, *God and Man at Yale*, 116–121, and the text of his undelivered speech in Appendix F, 207–211.

6. Richard Crossman, ed., *The God That Failed* (New York, 1949), 6.

7. A. Rossi, *A Communist Party in Action: An Account of the Organization and Operations in France*, trans. Willmoore Kendall (New Haven, CT, 1949), v–vii, xxii–xxiv.

8. William F. Buckley Jr., *Miles Gone By: A Literary Autobiography* (Washington, DC, 2004), 285–287, 289–290; John Chamberlain, ed., *The National Review Reader* (New York, 1957), xi–xii, 144–150; Jeffrey Hart, *The Making of the American Conservative Mind: National Review and Its Times* (Wilmington, DE, 2005), 5–8; James Reston, "A Chart for Taming the Russians," *NYT*, February 19, 1950.

9. Burnham, *The Coming Defeat*, 111–112.

10. Burnham, *The Coming Defeat*, 33, 249–250, 270.

11. John Foster Dulles, *War or Peace* (New York, 1950), 175.

12. Dulles, *War or Peace*, 167.

13. Monte M. Poen, *Harry S. Truman Versus the Medical Lobby* (Columbia, MO, 1979), chaps. 2 and 6.

14. Robert A. Taft, *The Papers of Robert A. Taft*, vol. 4, ed. Clarence E. Wunderlin Jr. (Kent, OH, 2006), 42 (February 19, 1949).

15. Truman's message: *PPHST (1949)*, April 22, 226–230. Insurance coverage: Oscar R. Ewing, *The Nation's Health, a Ten-Year Program* (Washington, DC, September 1948), 80–85; Margaret C. Klem, "Voluntary Medical Care Insurance," *Annals of the American Academy of Political and Social Science* 273 (January 1951): 99–101. Also Truman Library, oral history interview with Oscar R. Ewing, May 2, 1969, 173–179, 192–197.

16. *Chicago Tribune*, December 7, 1949.

17. Editorial, "The Second Session of the 81st Congress," *Journal of the American Medical Association* 142, no. 2 (January 14, 1950): 110–111; *Chicago Tribune*, October 22 and 23, 1944, and review of *The Road Ahead*, October 16, 1949, by Walter Trohan; John T. Flynn, *The Road Ahead: America's Creeping Revolution* (New York, 1949), 137.

18. Flynn, *Road Ahead*, 126. Distribution of *The Road Ahead*: *NYT*, December 9, 1949; US Congress, House Select Committee on Lobbying Activities, *Lobbying, Direct and Indirect: Hearings, June–August 1950* (Washington, DC, 1950), pt. 4, 25–28, 466–467, and pt. 5, 10–11, 16–18, 48–50. Flynn's popularity with doctors: *Journal of the Michigan State Medical Society* 49, no. 3 (March 1950): 343–345; 49, no. 6 (June 1950): 694; 49, no. 12 (December 1950): 1382–1388.

19. *C.R. (Senate)*, February 20, 1950, 1952–1981.

20. Scott Lucas: obituary, *NYT*, February 23, 1968; John Bartlow Martin, *Adlai Stevenson of Illinois* (Garden City, NY, 1976), 210; Robert S. Allen and William V. Shannon, *The Truman Merry-Go-Round* (New York, 1950), 232–234; Edward L. Schapsmeier and Frederick Schapsmeier, "Scott W. Lucas of Havana: His Rise and Fall as Senate Majority Leader," *Journal of the Illinois State Historical Society* 70, no. 4 (November 1977): 309–310.

21. *C.R. (House)*, July 15, 1937, 7184.

22. The Lee List: printed in US Congress, Senate Committee on Foreign Relations, *State Department Employee Loyalty Investigation (Tydings Hearings)* (Washington, DC, 1950), pt. 2 (Appendix), 1770–1813, with tables on 1814–1817 summarizing the outcome of each of the 108 cases.

23. John F. Day, "Majority Leader Lucas Stacks Up Pretty Well with Alban Barkley," *Louisville Courier-Journal*, July 10, 1949.

24. *NYT*, February 21, 1950; *Tydings Hearings*, pt. 2 (Appendix), 1806.

25. Allan Nevins, *Herbert H. Lehman and His Era* (New York, 1963), 335–336; Duane Tananbaum, *Herbert H. Lehman: A Political Biography* (Albany, NY, 2016), 328–329.

26. Truman Library, oral history interviews with Dr John R. Steelman, February 28, 1996, 101–102, and February 29, 1996, 132–133.

27. *PPHST (1950)*, 190; *C.R. (Senate)*, March 3, 1950, 2730–2732, with comments by Senator Taft.

28. *Pittsburgh Post-Gazette*, March 6, 1950; Melvyn Dubofsky and Warren Van Tine, *John L. Lewis: A Biography* (New York, 1977), 489–490.

29. Arthur Krock, "Coal Case Provides Some Political Fuel," *NYT*, March 5, 1950.

30. US Department of Labor, Bureau of Labor Statistics, *Wage Chronology: Bituminous Coal Mines, 1933–1966* (Washington, DC, 1965), 1–6, 13–15. Trend in strikes after 1950: Bureau of Labor Statistics, *Brief History of the American Labor Movement* (Washington, DC, 1976), 62–64; and annual statistics of disputes and stoppages in Bureau of Labor Statistics, *Monthly Labor Review*, 1950–1965. See also Nelson Lichtenstein, "Labor in the Truman Era: Origins of the 'Private Welfare State,'" in *The Truman Presidency*, ed. Michael J. Lacey (Cambridge, 1989), 148–155.

31. Dubofsky and Van Tine, *John L. Lewis*, 492–493.

China and Vietnam

1. Oleg V. Khlevniuk, *Stalin: New Biography of a Dictator* (New Haven, CT, 2015), 292–293; Yang Kuisong, "Reconsidering the Campaign to Suppress Counter-Revolutionaries," *China Quarterly*, no. 193 (March 2008): 103–106; Mao Zedong, "Soliciting Suggestions on the Question of Strategy for Dealing with Rich Peasants," March 12, 1950, in Mao Zedong, *The Writings of Mao Zedong, 1949–1976*, vol. 1, *September 1949–December 1955*, ed. Michael Y. M. Kau and John K. Leung (Armonk, NY, 1986), 67–69; *FRUS (1950)*, vol. 6, 716–722; William J. Duiker, *Ho Chi Minh* (New York, 2000), 425–427; Michel Bodin, *Dictionnaire de la Guerre d'Indochine, 1945–1954* (Paris, 2004), 51–52; A. B. Torkunov, *Zagadochnaya voina: Koreiskii konflikt, 1950–1953* (Moscow, 2000), 57–59; Wada Haruki, *The Korean War: An International History*, updated ed. (Lanham, MD, 2018), 54–57, 67–68.

CHAPTER TEN: IN DEEPEST PERIL

1. Walter Lippmann, "Defeatism in Washington," *NYHT* and *Boston Globe*, March 14, 1950, and also his columns of February 28 and March 16, 1950.

2. Louis Johnson's speech at University of Virginia, Charlottesville, February 2, 1950; *Baltimore Sun*, February 3, 1950.

3. The four principal Alsop columns attacking Johnson ran in the *New York Herald Tribune* (and were nationally syndicated) between February 14 and 22, 1950. See Joseph and Stewart Alsop, *The Reporter's Trade* (New York, 1958), 73–74, 142–144; Joseph Alsop's memoirs, *I've Seen the Best of It* (New York, 1992), 303–304. Pentagon background: Walter S. Poole, *History of the Joint Chiefs of Staff*, vol. 4, *The Joint Chiefs and National Policy, 1950–1952* (Washington, DC, 1998), 3–13.

4. Truman Library, Acheson Papers, memoranda and conversations file, March 13, 1950, copy of letter from Harriman to Truman.

5. Truman Library, Acheson Papers, memoranda and conversations file, March 21, 1950, conversation with Christian Herter.

6. "Total Diplomacy": Acheson's Advertising Council meeting, February 16, 1950, and his speeches in San Francisco (March 15) and at Berkeley (March 16): US State Department, *Bulletin*, March 20 (427–430), and March 27 (467–478); Dean Acheson, *Present at the Creation: My Years in the State Department* (New York, 1969), 379–381.

7. On the scholarship on NSC-68, see Ken Young, "Revisiting NSC-68," *Journal of Cold War Studies* 15, no. 1 (Winter 2013): 3–33. Two indispensable contributions are Samuel F. Wells Jr., "Sounding the Tocsin: NSC-68 and the Soviet Threat," *International Security* 4, no. 2 (Fall 1979): 116–158, and the rejoinder by John Lewis Gaddis and Paul Nitze, "NSC-68 and the Soviet Threat Reconsidered," *International Security* 4, no. 4 (Spring 1980): 164–176.

8. Text of NSC-68, April 7, 1950: *FRUS (1950)*, vol. 1, 234–292, prefaced by Truman's response of April 12, quotation p. 285.

9. *FRUS (1950)*, 238, 261.

10. Truman Library, oral history interviews with Paul H. Nitze, August 5 and 6, 1975, 241–243; Acheson, *Present at the Creation*, 373–374.

11. *FRUS (1950)*, 196–200. On Lovett: Roger R. Trask and Alfred Goldberg, *The Department of Defense, 1947–1997: Organization and Leaders* (Washington, DC, 1997), 67–68.

12. Charles E. Wilson at the Pentagon: Trask and Goldberg, *Department of Defense*, 69–72.

13. US Senate Committee on Appropriations, *Department of Defense Appropriations for 1951: Hearings* (Washington, DC, 1950), 693–695 (March 29, 1950), Eisenhower testimony.

14. Millard E. Tydings, *The Machine Gunners of the Blue and Gray Division* (Aberdeen, MD, 1919), 34–38; *C.R. (Senate)*, November 7, 1941, 8634; Allen Drury, *A Senate Journal, 1943–45* (New York, 1972), 19.

15. *Tydings Hearings*, pt. 1, March 8, 1950, 28; Thomas Reeves, *The Life and Times of Joe McCarthy* (Briarcliff Manor, NY, 1982), 252.

16. *Tydings Hearings*, pt. 1, March 8, 1950, 32; Eleanor Roosevelt, "My Day," *St. Louis Post-Dispatch*, March 11, 1950.

17. *Tydings Hearings*, pt. 1, March 14, 1950, 178, 204–207.

18. *Tydings Hearings*, pt. 1, March 9, 1950, 68.

19. *Tydings Hearings*, pt. 1, March 20, 1950, 217–225, 271.

20. *NYT*, March 27, 1950.

21. Drew Pearson, *Drew Pearson Diaries, 1949–1950*, ed. Tyler Abell (London, 1974), 113–116.

22. *Baltimore Sun*, March 23, 1950; James T. Patterson, *Mr. Republican* (Boston, 1972), 446.

23. Warren Ashby, *Frank Porter Graham: A Southern Liberal* (Winston-Salem, NC, 1980), chap. 9, 142–143; Woodrow Price, "Senate Race Deals in Bitter Personalities," *Raleigh News-Observer*, May 21, 1950; FBI Report CE 116-1489, November 1, 1947, and memo from Victor P. Keay, FBI inspector, November 13, 1947, Federal Bureau of Investigation, Washington, DC.

24. Julian M. Pleasants, "A Question of Loyalty: Frank Porter Graham and the Atomic Energy Commission," *North Carolina Historical Review* 69, no. 4 (October 1992): 427.

25. V. O. Key Jr., *Southern Politics in State and Nation* (New York, 1949), 212–215; Robert E. Williams, "Kerr Scott Disperses Old Political Machine," *Raleigh News-Observer*, July 4, 1948; Truman Library, oral history interview with Jonathan Daniels, October 4, 1963, 185–187.

26. John T. Flynn, *The Road Ahead: America's Creeping Revolution* (New York, 1949), 79.

27. *Raleigh News-Observer*, March 23, 1950; Frank P. Graham, farewell statement to US Senate, *C.R. (Senate)*, September 22, 1950, 15471–15472.

28. Chatham County Committee for Willis Smith, advertisement, *Raleigh News-Observer*, May 19, 1950.

29. Arthur H. Vandenberg Jr., *The Private Papers of Senator Vandenberg* (New York, 1952), 556–563; Walter Lippmann, *NYHT*, March 30, 1950.

30. *FRUS (1950)*, vol. 5, 125–130; *C.R. (House)*, March 29, 1950, 4344–4348; *NYT*, March 24, 1950; *Baltimore Sun*, March 30, 1950.

31. *Times* (London), March 29, 1950.

32. *C.R. (Senate)*, March 30, 1950, 4379–4380; David L. Oshinsky, *A Conspiracy So Immense: The World of Joe McCarthy* (New York, 1983), 144–147.

33. *PPHST (1950)*, 232–237; *Baltimore Sun* and *NYT*, March 31, 1950.

Sakhalin Island

1. Wada Haruki, *The Korean War: An International History*, updated ed. (Lanham, MD, 2018), 57–58; A. B. Torkunov, *Zagadochnaya voina: Koreiskii konflikt, 1950–1953* (Moscow, 2000), 57–59; Mariya Seleva, "Civil Administration on South Sakhalin and the Kurile Islands, 1945–1948: The Memoirs of Dmitrii N. Kriukov," *Monumenta Nipponica* 56, no. 1 (Spring 2001): 39–43, 70–73; *FRUS (1950)*, vol. 6, 68–70, and vol. 7, 35–44, 48–52.

CHAPTER ELEVEN: CALIBAN UNLEASHED

1. Arthur Krock, "Old and New Problems Await Truman's Return," *NYT*, April 9, 1950.

2. Ernest Hemingway, *Across the River and into the Trees* (London, 1950), 107, 170, 190.

3. Adlai Stevenson, *The Papers of Adlai E. Stevenson*, vol. 3, *Governor of Illinois, 1949–1953*, ed. Walter Johnson (Boston, 1973), 270–272; Morris Ploscowe and Edwin J. Lukas, "Legalized Gambling in New York?," *Annals of the American Academy of Political and Social Science*, vol. 269, *Gambling*, no. 1 (May 1950): 35–38; *Brooklyn Daily Eagle*, April 6 and 10, 1950.

4. *Brooklyn Eagle*, April 6 and 10, 1950; *NYT*, April 11, 1950.

5. Senator Estes Kefauver, *The Kefauver Committee Report on Organized Crime* (New York, 1951), 18–24, 162; *Life*, April 17, 1950, 41–45; *Kansas City Star*, April 6–7, 1950.

6. *C.R. (Senate)*, April 12, 1950, 5079–5080.

7. Patrick K. Hughes, Noel W. Barker, Gail A. Crawford, and Jerome H. Jaffe, "The Natural History of a Heroin Epidemic," *American Journal of Public Health* 62, no. 7 (July 1972): 995–999.

8. Jack Lait and Lee Mortimer, *Chicago Confidential* (New York, 1950), 184, 204; Charles L. Fontenay, *Estes Kefauver: A Biography* (Knoxville, TN, 1980), chap. 9; "Crime Group Assails Graft," *Chicago Tribune*, May 9, 1950; Mike Royko, *Boss: Richard J. Daley of Chicago* (New York, 1971), 53–54.

9. Samuel K. Gove, ed. *Illinois Votes, 1900–1958: A Compilation of Illinois Voting Statistics* (Urbana-Champaign, IL, 1959), 149–155.

10. US Department of Agriculture, Economic Research Service, *History of Agricultural Price-Support and Adjustment Programs, 1933–1984* (November 1984), 12–20; Allen J. Matusow, *Farm Policies and Politics in the Truman Years* (Cambridge, MA, 1967), 125–132; Virgil W. Dean, "The Farm Policy Debate of 1949–1950: Plains State Reaction to the Brannan Plan," *Great Plains Quarterly* 13, no. 1 (Winter 1993): 33–46; Jay Wale, "The Battling Author of the Brannan Plan," *NYT*, August 28, 1949.

11. John Gunther, *Inside USA* (New York, 1947), 796; V. O. Key Jr., *Southern Politics in State and Nation* (New York, 1949), 332–333, 340.

12. Roger K. Newman, *Hugo Black: A Biography* (New York, 1994), 131–134, 221–222; Monte M. Poen, *Harry S. Truman Versus the Medical Lobby* (Columbia, MO, 1979), 155–156, 165–167; *Birmingham News*, April 21, 1950.

13. William Warren Rogers, Robert David Ward, Leah Rawls Atkins, and Wayne Flynn, *Alabama: The History of a Deep South State* (Tuscaloosa, 1994), 535–537; Fred Taylor, "Hill, Abernethy Trade Salvoes in Demo Conflict," *Birmingham News*, April 13, 1950; campaign ad for Lawrence McNeil, *Tuskegee News*, April 6, 1950; speech by McNeil, *Talladagee Daily Home*, April 6, 1950.

14. Stewart Alsop, *NYHT* and Associated Press, April 15, 1950.

15. *Baltimore Sun*, April 1–2, 1950; *NYT*, April 4, 1950.

16. *C.R. (Senate)*, March 31, 1950, 4513–4515; *Cincinnati Inquirer*, April 1, 1950.

17. *Tydings Hearings*, pt. 1, April 6, 1950, 417–442 (Lattimore's statement), and FBI reference, 484; *Baltimore Sun* and *NYT*, April 7, 1950.

18. Drew Pearson, *Drew Pearson Diaries, 1949–1959*, ed. Tyler Abell (London, 1974), 149.

19. "Knowland Assails Lattimore Stand," *Baltimore Sun*, April 6, 1950; *FRUS (1950)*, vol. 6, 343–349, 366–367. Dulles on bipartisan foreign policy: US State Department, *Bulletin*, May 8, 1950, 721; Melvyn P. Leffler, *A Preponderance of Power: National Security, the Truman Administration, and the Cold War* (Stanford, CA, 1992), 353–355.

20. Louis Budenz, *Men Without Faces* (New York, 1950), ix–xii, 260–267; *Tydings Hearings*, pt. 1, April 20, 1950, 487–493; *Baltimore Sun*, April 21, 1950.

21. US Senate, Foreign Relations Committee, *Reviews of the World Situation, 1949–1950: Hearings* (Washington, DC, 1950), 292 (May 1, 1950); testimony from Acheson, Jessup, and W. Walton Butterworth on the situation in Asia, 248–284 (March 29, 1950); "Disintegration," 270, 287.

22. Acheson's May 1 testimony, 292.

23. Acheson's May 1 testimony, 287–288; Curt Cardwell, "NSC-68 and the National Security State," in *A Companion to Harry S. Truman*, ed. Daniel S. Margolies (Malden, MA, 2012), 147–150.

24. Acheson's Caliban speech: US State Department, *Bulletin*, May 1, 1950, 673–677, and May 8, 1950, 711–716.

25. US Senate, Appropriations Committee, *Department of Defense Appropriations for 1951: Hearings* (Washington, DC, 1950), April 26, 1950, 845–851.

26. George Gallup, *The Gallup Poll: Public Opinion, 1935–1971*, vol. 2 (New York, 1972), 911–912; *Public Opinion Quarterly* (Autumn 1950): 604–607, polls taken April 5–May 10, 1950, and Gallup's commentary in the press, May 10, 1950, syndicated nationally.

27. Florida primary: *Miami Herald*, May 4, 1950; James C. Clark, *Red Pepper and Gorgeous George: Claude Pepper's Epic Defeat in the 1950 Democratic Primary* (Gainesville, FL, 2011), chap. 10; Samuel Lubell, *The Future of American Politics* (New York, 1955), 115–118.

28. Marquis Childs, "Florida, Alabama Primaries Important on National Scene," *Pittsburgh Post-Gazette*, April 26, 1950.

29. Full text of Smathers's speech: *Miami Daily News*, January 13, 1950.

30. Key, *Southern Politics*, 83–87.

31. *C.R. (Senate)*, May 3, 1950, 6246–6263.

The Schuman Plan

1. Sources: *L'année politique, 1950* (Paris, 1951), 71–76, 78–79, 90–92, 359–361; Vincent Auriol, *Mon septennat, 1947–1954* (Paris, 1970), 257–262; *FRUS (1950)*, vol. 3, 54–55, 796–799, 816–812; Konrad Adenauer, *Memoirs, 1945–1953* (London, 1966), 244–248; Pierre Billotte, *Le passé au future* (Paris, 1979), 50; Pierre Gerbet, "La genèse du plan Schuman: Des origines à la déclaration du 9 mai 1950," *Revue Française de science politique* 6, no. 3 (1956): 538–547; Jean Monnet, *Memoirs* (London, 1978), 277–287, 295–299; Robert Schuman, *Pour L'Europe* (Geneva, 2000), 118–130; William I. Hitchcock, "France, the Western Alliance, and the Origins of the Schuman Plan, 1948–1950," *Diplomatic History* 21, no. 4 (Fall 1997): 624–630; François Roth, *Robert Schuman: De Lorrain des frontières au père de l'Europe* (Paris, 2008), 382–397; *FRUS (1950)*, vol. 3, 1007–1013; René Massigli, *Une comédie des erreurs: Souvenirs et refléxions sur une étape de la construction européene* (Paris, 1978), 192–200, 203–205, 230; *Times* (London), June 28, 1950, report of Churchill's House of Commons speech, June 27.

CHAPTER TWELVE: THE ROAD BACK TO AMERICA

1. Saul Bellow, *The Adventures of Augie March* (New York, 1995 [1953]), 489.

2. Truman's tour: *PPHST (1950)*, May 8–14, 296–408, quotation p. 303; *Spokane Chronicle*, May 11, 1950.

3. US Department of the Interior, *The Columbia: America's Greatest Power Stream* (film), 1948; John Gunther, *Inside USA* (New York, 1947), chap. 8; Gerald H. Robinson, "The Columbia Valley Administration Bill," *Western Political Quarterly* 3, no. 4 (December 1950): 607–614.

4. *PPHST (1950)*, 369–374, May 11, 1950.

5. Mark Harvey, "The Environmental History of the Truman Years, 1945–53," in *A Companion to Harry S. Truman*, ed. Daniel S. Margolies (Malden, MA, 2012), 276–279.

6. Stewart Alsop, "Boyle and Gabrielson Are a Case in Point," *NYHT*, April 28, 1950.

7. *St. Louis Post-Dispatch*, May 14, 1950.

8. Adam Cohen and Elizabeth Taylor, *American Pharaoh: Mayor Richard J. Daley: His Battle for Chicago and the Nation* (New York, 2000),

40–45; John Bartlow Martin, *Adlai Stevenson of Illinois* (Garden City, NY, 1976), 281–293; David K. Fremon, *Chicago Politics Ward by Ward* (Bloomington, IN, 1988), 83–87, 129–134; State of Illinois, *Illinois Blue Book (1949–1950)* (Springfield, IL, 1950), 63; ward maps of election results, *Chicago Tribune*, November 9, 1950.

9. Press reports in *Baltimore Sun*, *Chicago Tribune*, and *St. Louis Post-Dispatch*, May 14–16, 1950.

10. Martin, *Stevenson of Illinois*, 446–448.

11. *PPHST (1950)*, 409–414; and Truman's May 5 special message to Congress on small businesses, 288–294.

12. "Democrats Discuss FEPC; Daniels Surprise Speaker," *Raleigh News-Observer*, May 15, 1950; *C.R. (Senate)*, May 16, 1950, 7005–7008.

13. Clarence Mitchell Jr., *The Papers of Clarence Mitchell Jr.*, vol. 3, *1946–1950*, ed. Denton Watson (Athens, GA, 2010), cclxxxi; *NYT*, May 20, 1950.

14. Joseph Alsop's letter and comments by Herbert Lehman: *C.R. (Senate)*, May 8, 1950, 6596–6597.

15. James Russell Wiggins, "Notes on Herbert Elliston," May 6, 1982, Wiggins Collection, Maine State Library, Augusta; Elliston obituary, *NYT*, January 23, 1957; Katharine Graham, *Personal History* (New York, 1997), 192–200.

16. Chavez's speech, *C.R. (Senate)*, May 12, 1950, 6969–6975; *Washington Post*, May 22 and 23, 1950.

17. Speech by Hubert Humphrey, *C.R. (Senate)*, May 22, 1950, 7404–7406.

18. The Four Horsemen speech: *C.R. (Senate)*, June 1, 1950, 7894–7895; Smith's elaboration in a speech of June 15, 1951, "Courage to Speak Out," *Social Science* 27, no. 1 (January 1952): 8–11.

19. Margaret Chase Smith, speech on January 3, 1949, *Bangor Daily News*, January 4, 1950; her syndicated column, *Dayton Journal Herald*, February 13, March 27, and May 23, 1950; William B. Pickett, *Eisenhower Decides to Run: Presidential Politics and Cold War Strategy* (Chicago, 2000), 52–53.

20. Margaret Chase Smith, *Declaration of Conscience* (New York, 1972), 7–11. The conservative writer was David Lawrence. His syndicated column on May 23 quoted from the *Post* editorial and then described the "nationwide distrust" to be found in an America "sick and

tired of politics—the machine variety that is tied up with gangster-ism. . . . [T]he country is also sick and tired of political junkets that are brazenly called non-political. It is sick and tired also of the way innocent people are smeared while whitewashes of guilty persons are permitted." Senator Smith drew upon Lawrence in writing her speech.

21. GM, Buick Motor Division, *Buick Magazine*, September 1949, 8–9, and January 1950, 3–7; Ed Cray, *Chrome Colossus: General Motors and Its Times* (New York, 1950), 277–280, 345; Leo Donovan, "Hard-Working Flint Has Struck It Rich," *Detroit Free Press*, February 12, 1950.

22. Editorial, *Detroit Free Press*, May 25, 1950.

23. Nelson Lichtenstein, *Walter Reuther: The Most Dangerous Man in Detroit* (Urbana, IL, 1997), 271–281; Alfred P. Sloan Jr., *My Years with General Motors* (New York, 1964), 397–402; *Detroit Free Press*, May 24 and 25, 1950.

24. Joseph and Stewart Alsop, "Biggest Boom in History May Not Turn to Bust," *Boston Globe*, June 24, 1950.

25. *PPHST (1950)*, 441, May 25, 1950, press conference; 462, speech on June 6.

26. *Journal of the Michigan State Medical Society* 49, no. 10 (October 1950): 1208–1209, 1212.

27. Samuel Lubell, *The Future of American Politics* (New York, 1955), 190–193; "How Taft Did It," *Saturday Evening Post*, February 10, 1951.

28. "Nixon Stresses Nation's Defense," *Oakland Tribune*, April 13, 1950; "Nixon Slaps at Federal Spending in Stump Tour," *Bakersfield Californian*, April 14, 1950; Roger Morris, *Richard Milhous Nixon: The Rise of an American Politician* (New York, 1990), 548–565.

29. Kyle Palmer's eulogy of Nixon: "Come One, Come All . . . ," *Los Angeles Times*, February 19, 1950; and his columns on December 18, 1949, and March 19, April 9, May 14, and May 28, 1950.

30. Burton R. Brazil, "The 1950 Elections in California," *Western Political Quarterly* 4, no. 1 (March 1951): 68–71.

31. *Sweatt* and *McLaurin* decisions: 339 U.S. 629 (1950) and 339 U.S. 637 (1950); Roger K. Newman, *Hugo Black: A Biography* (New York, 1997), 428–431.

32. Warren Ashby, *Frank Porter Graham: A Southern Liberal* (Winston-Salem, NC, 1980), 264–265, 269–270.

33. Associated Press, June 23, 1950; US State Department, *Bulletin*, July 3, 1950, 12–13; Dulles speech in Seoul, June 19; Townsend Hoopes, *The Devil and John Foster Dulles* (Boston, 1973), 96–97.

EPILOGUE

1. Author's translation of Euripides, *Les Troyennes: Adaptation française de Jean-Paul Sartre* (Paris, 1965), 78.

INDEX

NICK BUNKER won the 2015 George Washington Book Prize with *An Empire on the Edge*, a finalist for the Pulitzer Prize for History. His other books include *Making Haste from Babylon*, which was long-listed for the UK's Samuel Johnson Prize, and *Young Benjamin Franklin*. A graduate of King's College, Cambridge, and Columbia University, Bunker was a journalist at the *Financial Times* and then an investment banker, principally for the Hongkong and Shanghai Banking Corporation, before settling in Lincolnshire, UK, where he now lives. For many years he was a board member and then the chair of the Freud Museum, London.